Physical Control, Transformation and Damage in the First World War

Physical Control, Transformation and Damage in the First World War

War Bodies

Simon Harold Walker

BLOOMSBURY ACADEMIC
LONDON • NEW YORK • OXFORD • NEW DELHI • SYDNEY

BLOOMSBURY ACADEMIC
Bloomsbury Publishing Plc
50 Bedford Square, London, WC1B 3DP, UK
1385 Broadway, New York, NY 10018, USA
29 Earlsfort Terrace, Dublin 2, Ireland

BLOOMSBURY, BLOOMSBURY ACADEMIC and the Diana logo are trademarks of
Bloomsbury Publishing Plc

First published in Great Britain 2021
This paperback edition published in 2022

Copyright © Simon Harold Walker, 2021

Simon Harold Walker has asserted his right under the Copyright, Designs and
Patents Act, 1988, to be identified as Author of this work.

For legal purposes the Acknowledgements on p. xii constitute an extension
of this copyright page.

Cover design by Tjaša Krivec
Cover image: Illustration by William Smithson Broadhead (1888–1960) drawn whilst serving
in the King Edward's Horse (The King's Overseas Dominions Regiment) in
England and France (© William Smithson/Picture Sheffield)

All rights reserved. No part of this publication may be reproduced or
transmitted in any form or by any means, electronic or mechanical, including
photocopying, recording, or any information storage or retrieval system,
without prior permission in writing from the publishers.

Bloomsbury Publishing Plc does not have any control over, or responsibility for, any
third-party websites referred to or in this book. All internet addresses given in this
book were correct at the time of going to press. The author and publisher regret any
inconvenience caused if addresses have changed or sites have ceased to exist,
but can accept no responsibility for any such changes.

Every effort has been made to trace copyright holders and to obtain their permissions for
the use of copyright material. The publisher apologizes for any errors or omissions and
would be grateful if notified of any corrections that should be incorporated in
future reprints or editions of this book.

A catalogue record for this book is available from the British Library.

Library of Congress Cataloging-in-Publication Data
Names: Walker, Simon Harold, author.
Title: Physical control, transformation and damage in the First World War : war bodies /
Simon Harold Walker. Other titles: War bodies
Description: London ; New York : Bloomsbury Academic, 2020. |
Includes bibliographical references and index.
Identifiers: LCCN 2020031005 (print) | LCCN 2020031006 (ebook) | ISBN 9781350123281 (hardback) |
ISBN 9781350229327 (paperback) | ISBN 9781350123298 (ebook) | ISBN 9781350123304 (epub)
Subjects: LCSH: Great Britain. Army–History–World War, 1914–1918. | Soldiers–Physiology–
Great Britain–History–20th century. | Great Britain. Army–Physical training–History–20th
century. | Combat–Physiological aspects. | Physical education and training, Military–Great
Britain–History–20th century.
Classification: LCC D546.A2 W35 2020 (print) | LCC D546.A2 (ebook) |
DDC 940.4/1241–dc23
LC record available at https://lccn.loc.gov/2020031005
LC ebook record available at https://lccn.loc.gov/2020031006

ISBN: HB: 978-1-3501-2328-1
PB: 978-1-3502-2932-7
ePDF: 978-1-3501-2329-8
eBook: 978-1-3501-2330-4

Typeset by Newgen KnowledgeWorks Pvt. Ltd., Chennai, India

To find out more about our authors and books visit www.bloomsbury.com
and sign up for our newsletters.

For my sons, Oliver and Isaac:
You are my heroes.

Contents

List of figures	ix
Preface	xi
Acknowledgements	xii
List of abbreviations	xiii

Introduction: 'A different existence' — 1
- War bodies: Locating the male British body within the First World War — 2
- The Victorian and Edwardian military body in public perception — 4
- Suitable bodies for service: 1900–14 — 6
- Choosing men and masculinity — 8
- Care and causality: Taking care of men — 11
- Theory in practice — 14
- Sources and evidence — 17
- Chapters — 20

1 A fine body of men: Recruitment and enlisting for war 1914–18 — 23
- No guts, no glory — 24
- Clothes maketh the man — 27
- A body of statistics — 32
- No body wanted — 38
- Conclusion — 43

2 Forging bodies: Training and creating soldiers — 45
- Everybody at once — 46
- Dressed to kill — 48
- Food and feeding — 52
- Improving civilian bodies — 57
- Playing the game — 61
- A pound of flesh — 69
- Conclusion: Different men equal different tactics — 73

3 Lives on the line: Active service — 77
- A clean bill of health — 78
- The greater good — 85

	Comfort food (and drink)	90
	Morale over morals	98
	Conclusion	107
4	Bodies under fire: The front line	109
	Feeding under fire	110
	On guard	113
	Fighting bodies	115
	Keeping the men in line – on the line	125
	Broken bodies	128
	Conclusion	137
5	Soldiers no more: Death, debilitation and demobilization	139
	Dead bodies	140
	Recovering living bodies	148
	Revelling bodies	158
	Trials and tribulations	162
	Conclusion	170

Conclusion: Bodies of war	173
Notes	185
Bibliography	215
Index	235

Figures

1. Private Broadhead and his surprise bedfellow, sketch by William Broadhead — xiv
2. Are you in this? Recruitment poster 1915 — 25
3. Vacancies exist in all branches of His Majesty's army recruitment poster — 31
4. Specimens of men in each of the Four Grades, report by the Ministry of National Service 1920 — 34
5. William Broadhead, sketches in undated letter to his parents during training in 1916 — 64–5
6. William Broadhead, sketches in undated letter to his parents during training in 1916 — 66–8
7. British Army Field Service Manual, 1914 — 94
8. Sketch by William Broadhead, letter dated 11 April 1915 — 116
9. Sketch by William Broadhead, letter undated — 117
10. Two stretcher-bearers removing a wounded man under fire. Wash painting 1916 — 150
11. A scene in the trenches showing stretcher-bearers wearing gas masks as they carry in a man who has been gassed — 151
12. The manufacture of artificial limbs for the Princess Louise Scottish Hospital for limbless sailors and soldiers — 167

Preface

This book examines the processes by which British male civilians became soldiers during the First World War. It contributes to the historiography on the British experience of the war by placing the human body at the centre of the analysis and considering the impact of bodies under the control and care of the British army. It expands upon the sociological literature of 'the body' by establishing how these theoretical concepts are evident within the empirical research. Through an analysis of official records and publications, it explores how the state sought to transform the male civilian body for military purposes. A significant aspect of this research stems from the personal experiences of the men who served by painstaking consideration of their letters, diaries and oral testimonies.

This research illustrates that the body was a core concern for the British military as well as being central in perceptions of physical worth within British society during the First World War. Between 1914 and 1918 British men's bodies were assessed, categorized, improved, damaged, recovered, repaired and destroyed. From enlistment to the end of service, soldier's bodies were repurposed for the pursuit of victory as the British military and the government focused on constructing, conditioning and controlling the bodies of regular, territorial, volunteer and conscript soldiers. In a letter to his mother, Lieutenant Godfrey classified the war as a 'different existence altogether' and indeed it was for many men whose bodies became fitter, healthier and more skilled, while paradoxically also allowing them to resist military control, be wounded, harm their own bodies and die. This work, therefore, explores the male military body within the chaos of the First World War, not simply as a faceless man in uniform but as an individual whose 'war body' was a site of conflict focused upon the struggle for agency, indoctrination and military action.

Acknowledgements

This book would not have been possible without the kind generosity of my PhD funding from the Economic and Social Research Council. I also gratefully acknowledge the support of Bloomsbury Publishing and my editors Laura and Rhodri for putting up with my inability to reply to emails. Thanks also go to Dr Emma Newlands and Professor Matt Smith for their constant support, with special thanks to Dr Emily Mayhew, Professor Joanna Bourke and Dr Clare Makepeace whose work and support have been inspirational in the creation of this book. I also owe much to my reviewers whose thoughtful guidance and kind words gave me the courage to finish. Thanks also go to the staff at the Imperial War Museum, The National Archives, The Scottish National Archives, the St Andrews Special Collections, Sheffield City Archives and Local Studies Library and, the Wellcome Trust Library. Special thanks also go to staff at the King's Own Scottish Borders Regimental Museum, Mr Adam Culling at the Royal Army Physical Training Corps Museum, Major Charley Whitely at the 101 (Northumbrian) Regiment RA Museum and Paul Evans at the Royal Artillery Museum. Much of the original research omitted from my thesis has returned within *War Bodies* with the hope you will appreciate the findings presented. I must thank my dear friends Rachel Hewitt, Rowena Hutton, Elena Romero Passerin, Jack Nyhan, Louise Bell and Jasmine Wood, who reviewed various versions of this book and were always kind, supportive and inspiring. Additionally, thanks to my family: Fiona, Neil, Dulcie, Harold, Lyn, my sons Oliver and Isaac, and Pond, my constant puppy writing companion. You all shared the impossible task of keeping me going; this is as much your book as mine. Thanks also to Simon and John for keeping me sane during the painful task of editing; those heists helped more than you know. I am also so grateful to my amazing fiancée Emily. You were my sounding board and greatest critic, as ruthless with a red pen (and Mario Kart) as you are generous with your heart. Finally, while I did not have the chance to personally know the men whose experiences form the basis of this book, they have become an important part of my life. I could never fully understand what you saw, felt and did, but for a brief time I was honoured to shadow you over the top. To Lieutenant Godfrey, Private Purvis, Second Lieutenant W. Lindsay and so many others, I say thank you for the chance to retell your stories; I hope I got them right.

Abbreviations

AMAB	Army Medical Advisory Board
AMS	Army Medical Service
ASC	Army Service Corps
ATA	Army Temperance Association
AWOL	Absent Without Leave
BMJ	British Medical Journal
BEF	British Expeditionary Force
CB	Confined to Barracks
CO	Conscientious Objector
CO	Commanding Officer
DCM	District Court-Martial
GOC	General Commanding Officer
IMS	Indian Medical Service
IWM	Imperial War Museum
JRAMC	Journal of Royal Army Medical Corps
MO	Medical Officer
MOH	Medical Officers of Health
NCO	Non-Commissioned Officer
POW	Prisoner of War
RAMC	Royal Army Medical Corps
RFC	Royal Flying Corps
TNA	The National Archives

Figure 1 Private Broadhead and his surprise bedfellow, sketch by William Broadhead. Sheffield Archives. Private Papers of W. Broadhead.

Introduction: 'A different existence'

In 1917, 19-year-old Lieutenant Godfrey wrote to his mother and claimed, 'The war is an extraordinary life altogether: one feels as if one had got right out of the ordinary world one knows, and been pitched into a different existence altogether.'[1] Godfrey's experience of the First World War was not unique, the experiences that he described in his private papers are echoed repeatedly in the accounts of thousands of men who experienced similar trials and tribulations as they served their country between 1914 and 1918. Godfrey's words succinctly encapsulated the reality of serving during the First World War as men's bodies were recruited, assessed, categorized, adapted, improved, organized, wounded, praised and rejected over the course of the war between 1914 and 1918. It is this association between the First World War and the British soldier's body that this book considers while questioning who held control over the transforming bodies as these men became, not always entirely willingly, soldiers.

Having joined up in 1915, Godfrey was eventually dispatched to the Western front to take charge of a labour company bound for Mt Kemmel. His letters home and diary entries invoke images of the adventures typical of a British soldier during the First World War. Within these pages he described marching, basic training, sleeping in shared and single officer billets and being disgusted with frequently insanitary conditions such as when he passed through 'the filthiest port I have ever seen'.[2] As an officer Godfrey's experiences were often more varied than that of his rank and fellow brethren. He recounted 'shepherding a mob of [drunk] miners' onto their ship for France', eating fine meals and drinking 'occasional champagne' as he and his fellow officer chums found fun and sport in their postings abroad. His experiences in the war were certainly not all fun and games. Later, Godfrey described how the thundering of field guns made his body tremble, 'the occasional 60-pdr really shook you', and explained that during the most intense battles the bodies of the dead remained where they fell as 'it was pointless to get more people killed burying corpses'.[3] As time wore on, Godfrey wrote in his diary how the constant pressure of war and particularly the regular gas attacks were affecting him. 'I am in a funk most of the time; but we are only mortal, and everyone admits the same at first. I don't think I show the fact more than anyone else, which is the main point.'[4] Godfrey endured combat and injury several times, and was finally wounded off the frontline to be returned home to recover in England after a severe gassing.[5] Once his body had healed he returned to the frontline and saw the rest of war out in Belgium until being demobilized in January 1919 while suffering with the Spanish influenza.[6] Godfrey's account continually reiterated the importance the individual body played in the creation and implementation of the

British soldier during the course of the First World War. As Godfrey himself stated, the physical experience of the war was like a completely different world. Men found their bodies transformed and changed while also losing control over them as they were harnessed and dispatched for combat. By the end of the war, no individual man's body returned in the same condition in which it had left. Damaged, transformed or destroyed, the scars of the First World War bore deep physically and psychologically after long periods of service and hardship that placed the British male body at the centre of the conflict.

War bodies: Locating the male British body within the First World War

It is the focus of this book to explore the creation and translation of these scars by viewing the First World War from the perspective of the British bodies that fought within it. The body and the physical experience of the war was a unifying factor of the First World War that affected all associated with it. Unquestionably, no matter what occurred to an individual during this period, it is certain that the impact of the first all-encompassing global war was felt through, demonstrated upon and often changed their bodies. This book expands on this assertion by considering the First World War from the perspective of the British male militarized body as a vehicle to understand the experience of transformation, conditioning, destruction and rehabilitation for the British men who served. New soldiers like Godfrey found themselves clothed, directed, abused and controlled as they adapted to military service. From the food they ate, the haircut they wore, to the places that they served and the way that they relaxed, the British Army remained a constant controlling presence. Persistent attention was paid to soldier's bodies by the army from enlistment to demobilization as men were tailored for service. Men's behaviours were continually controlled by the threat of negative consequence being enacted upon their bodies. This book builds upon the existing historiography and social theory to explore the extent to which the militarized body was central to the experiences of men in the first decades of the twentieth century and how this focus impacted on men's self-reflected identity as they served. It also investigates how soldier's bodies became sites for conflict as men's agency clashed with the agenda and control of the British Army. During enlistment, the army, the British government and the public colluded to project a physical and masculine ideal that many men appropriated for presentation and validation in exchange for a uniform and service number. Within training and active service, conflict was not limited to antagonist armies but occurred between individual soldiers and their military leaders as men endured significant physical transformations as well as extensive restrictions. With each curtailing of liberty, the British Army often faced a breach in conformity elsewhere as soldiers conspired to find ways to damage, often inadvertently, the bodies that their military trainers and commanding officers had so intrusively sought to improve. Furthermore, combat and the conditions unique to the First World War proved particularly destructive upon the army's designs on the body as mud, disease and wounds incapacitated men and removed them from the fray. As a result, this meant in contrast that the men became a burden on the institution that had tailored them so carefully for battle.

Central to the theme of this book is the argument that the First World War heralded a new level of scrutiny, control, categorization, cultural consideration and state-level interference of the British male body. This is evident in the ways that men's bodies were continually assessed, reviewed and directed as part of the process of selection, improvement and regulated military life. Yet, this does not mean that there was blanket acceptance over the loss of physical autonomy that accompanied indoctrination and military service. Godfrey's assertion that the war was a 'different existence altogether' was just as true for the British Army as it was for soldiers who served within it.[7] Not only did the British military face the largest conflict in its recent memory but it was also required to meet the enemy with a combination of volunteer, conscript, territorial and regular soldiers. With each group of men came unique physical idiosyncrasies, priorities and demands which the British Army attempted to overcome through training, indoctrination, patriotism and control. The New Armies presented significant issues for maintaining discipline as new 'soldiers' often complained and protested vociferously about the army's inability, or apparent reluctance, to meet their physical needs, despite the promises to the contrary often made during recruitment. This was behaviour that was less likely to be witnessed in the professional soldiers who preceded them, although said men were also not without their ability to challenge the British military. Particularly as these regulars had significantly more practice historically. Faced with a fighting force constructed from all aspects of British society, the First World War raised new questions for the British Army on how to best prepare and control men's bodies as it was forced to adapt to the range of new soldiers under its command. To further complicate the issue, 1914–18 also brought new tactics, weaponry and challenges. Never the best at adapting quickly historically, the British Army had to become increasingly adept at incorporating these changes into the indoctrination and leadership of their soldiers to best direct, control and protect men's bodies at the front and behind the lines.

To explore the physical experiences of the First World War is to attempt to consider some of the most personal aspects of an individual's thoughts, actions and motivations. When engaging with the history of conflict often it is best to interpret the world that was from the words of those who experienced it first-hand. Godfrey's view of the world is clearly conveyed through the remains of his letters that were sent home as he served. His narrative as a dialogue between writer and reader presents a unique perspective of the war, personalized by Godfrey's own history and coloured by his individual experience. Alone, Godfrey can only recount an infinitesimally small aspect of the war; yet it is his voice, combined with many other voices retained through testimonies, diaries and oral history recordings, that provides the multilayered analysis that resonates throughout this book. Together these glimpses of the past allow this book to engage with the lived experiences of the men who witnessed first-hand the calamity of the First World War and crucially described their experiences through recollections of their physical hardships and transformations. For validity, official records, newspaper articles, images and parliamentary debates provide context for these personalized, and therefore likely heavily biased, accounts. Yet, authenticity is also affirmed through repetition of events and experiences as often within testimonies men recount similar accounts of physical encounters. This is also not the first academic work to consider the body as a framework for analysis of historical conflict. It follows in the wake of several seminal investigations that will be discussed further in this chapter. However, originality stems from the detailed examination of the lived experience of the men who served and the engagement of social theories of masculinity, agency and physical control that reiterate the role of the male body at the centre of British society during the militaristic and industrialized war period at the beginning of the twentieth century and the impact of industrialized war on British society.[8] The First World War was very much a physical conflict with a revolving cycle of preparation, stagnation and destruction of the male militarized body. It is therefore the focus of this book to explore this cycle and its impact on the British male body between 1914 and 1918.

The Victorian and Edwardian military body in public perception

In order to successfully consider the male body within the context of the First World War, it is first important to recognize that the relationship between the assessment and transformation of the body and the British military long predated 1914. The complicated relationship between the British public, the state and the military in the nineteenth century cannot be understated in terms of importance to the perceptions of the male military body within the coming war. As a prophetic social norm for the inequity that was to follow during the First World War, in the nineteenth century men of the higher classes typically enjoyed a level of respect for their military service and societal admiration long before such accolades were paid to the rankers under their command. Despite the abolishment of purchasing under the Caldwell reforms, officer service remained the purview of the gentry. Those who accepted military roles often did so as an aid to social standing, for the aesthetic of the uniform or the glamour of military command and power.[9] According to Cunningham, class determined every minutia of the service experience in the nineteenth century as 'soldiering was traditionally an aristocratic calling and a lower-class way of life'.[10] Still, in nineteenth-century Britain, soldiers and the military had maintained a tumultuous relationship with the general public which ranged from disgust and mistrust through to admiration and pride. This relationship often centred on perceptions of the men's bodies, particularly in relation to their appearance and behaviour while including aspects of class imperceptibly within the considerations of physical prowess and masculinity.

At the beginning of the nineteenth century, British soldiers were more commonly considered to be licentious, drunken reprobates. This view was seemingly shared by civilians and military leaders alike, as the Duke of Wellington once famously described the rank and file as the 'scum of the earth'.[11] This distrust and negative image of the armed forces was made worse in the early nineteenth century after the British Army violently subdued civilians during the Peterloo 'massacre' of 1819 and the Kennington

Common Chartist rally in 1848.[12] According to John Keegan these views were also influenced by the discrepancies in class within Britain, and that by 1914 the country still remained the polarized nation for the classes it had been seventy years earlier.[13] For the lower classes motivation for enlistment regularly lay in escapism over patriotism prior to 1914. Spiers argues that before the First World War military service stood as indicator of an individual's inability to progress successfully in society. The military was often the final option for the lowest class of men where the alternatives when work was not possible were death through poverty, the workhouse or prison.[14] Both Bourne and Miller separately reiterate this lack of choice for the lowest classes but also consider that life within the rank and file could be just as bad as living on the poverty line, particularly physically in terms of sustenance, comfort and life expectancy.[15] This disparaging view of servicemen came to a head around the same time in 1877 that a heartbroken mother wrote to her newly enlisted son, 'I would rather bury you than see you in a Red Coat.'[16] Barnard argues that prior to the outbreak of the Boer War, upon which military personnel became heroes, voluntary soldiers were believed to have been socially deficient in some way. She quotes Frank Richards, a war veteran and author of *Old-Soldier Sahib*, who claimed, 'It was commonly believed ... that any young man who entered the Army did so either because he was too lazy to work or because he had got a girl in the family way. Hardly anybody had a good word for a soldier.'[17]

The rank-and-file soldier resided within a climate of ever-increasing control throughout the nineteenth century and beyond the First World War. This is reminiscent of Foucauldian notions of lost agency within institutions such as the military or prisons. Poor food and nutrition, insanitary conditions and institutional control were often part of the daily existence for most of the rank and file.[18] These controlling factors on the individual were also to be found outside of the military as they were increasingly incorporated into factories and workplaces in the nineteenth and early twentieth centuries.

By 1914 much of this attitude had changed while focus on the physical body of the soldier had exponentially increased as militarized masculine fitness dominated within British culture. Graham Dawson explains that by the start of the First World War the British military had significantly risen in cultural popularity as historical and fictional figures such as Gordon and 'Tommy Aitkens' attained hero status accompanied by growing perceptions of physical fitness in relation to military training and combat.[19] This heroic visage for the British soldier, John Peck argues, owed much to the celebration of victory following the Crimean War (1853–6) and the Indian Mutiny (1857).[20] This ties into shift of the British military diverting its attention from domestic troubles to reinforcing colonial control. As is alluded to by John MacKenzie, gone were the aggressors against British society, replaced by the stalwart protectors of the British Empire.[21] This public relation transition was aided, Anne Summers explains, by the growing Victorian obsession with the governing of Empire. This internalizing of militaristic ideals, she continues, would ultimately contribute to the mass voluntary move to recruitment for the war that occurred after 1914 driven by notions of 'patriotic soldiering'.[22] Summer's argument is also backed up by Michael Brown, who reiterates that esteem of the military improved as a reflection of the changing political landscape within Victorian Britain. As a beacon of the adventurous masculine heroic figure, such depictions helped to make military service a much more desirable career.[23]

By the turn of the twentieth century, the popularity of the military in Britain had led to an adoption of military rhetoric and practice within society. Paramilitary groups such as Baden Powell's Scout movement which advocated enhanced fitness and military physical prowess were significantly growing in popularity. Military training regimes and drilling had also become a regular aspect of many boys' lives in private schools at the end of the nineteenth century.[24] Paul Deslandes considers the increasing obsession with militarized healthy bodies within his exploration of students at Cambridge and Oxford in the nineteenth and twentieth centuries. He argues that militaristic masculinity was intrinsically linked to the experience of young men actualizing at university prior to the war.[25] Deslandes uses the example of the boat race to draw similarities between terminology, training and perceptions of self that existed within the militarized indoctrination into student life at Oxbridge. He notes that students used pseudo-military terms and compared the race using terms similar to considerations of soldiers in battle.[26] Additionally, he claims that the rivalries between the two colleges developed the same cultural tone as was usually associated with what Dawson explains was the perception of the soldier hero.[27] Andrew Warwick makes a similar argument and discusses how studies and physical ability were intrinsically linked at Cambridge in the Victorian period. He notes how students were expected to maintain a peak level of fitness, by using their recreational time to hone their bodies through exercise and regularly contribute to sports and games.[28] Additionally, Warwick notes the ethos of endurance that students were expected to maintain resiliencethroughout. This obsession with physicality and fortitude would continue throughout the First World War as men's bodies were continually assessed for effectiveness and suitability for service.

Suitable bodies for service: 1900–14

At the heart of this book is the underlying argument that the First World War was very much experienced through the physical bodies of those within it. Within this perspective resides the means of recruitment and training that make the First World War unique in British history. Between 1914 and 1918 a vast array of men entered the armed forces, differing in class, background, education, region and religion as well as method of enlistment – be they a conscript or a volunteer, a territorial or a regular, rank and file or officer. Differences even existed in the way that they served, such as if they were infantry or artillery, combatant or non-combatant, support or frontline. It is within these significant differences that this book seeks to uncover the individual experiences of the men as their bodies interacted, were conditioned and directed during the First World War.

The militarized obsession with civilian physical prowess in Britain in the twentieth century predated the First World War by over a decade. Reform had very much been the watchword of the military since the end of the Boer War in 1902 after so many hopeful British enlistees had been declined entrance on a range of health and physical deficiencies. In 1899, for every 1,000 enlisted men for the Boer War, 330 were rejected as unfit. In 1900, 280 out of every 1,000 men were rejected for military service.[29] This prompted the British government to quickly re-evaluate the state of physical fitness and health within British society. In search for a solution to the deteriorated health, particularly evident in the lowest classes, Searle argues that state turned to the military to provide a 'solution to a problem which had such grave military implications'.[30] This began an increase in state-directed intervention into wider public health under the objective of increasing physical effectiveness and contribution to society at the turn of the twentieth century. One of the immediate victims to this robust platform of health improvement was alcohol. Assisted by several long-standing campaigns for temperance Duncan maintains that the British public were increasingly encouraged towards physical improvement through a 'perversion of social Darwinism'.[31]

Diet also received much attention for much the same reason. Zweiniger-Bargielowska argues that in the early twentieth century the British had been forced to 'take stock of the health and physique of (its) manhood', leading to a range of improvements in relation to diet and nutrition.[32] Drawing comparisons to the large numbers of rejected men for the Boer War campaign between 1899 and 1902, she notes that lower-working-class men were particularly unsuitable for military service on grounds of ill health through malnourishment. As the First World War began, much was still misunderstood about the importance of nutrition in relation to health. Searle argues that Benjamin Seebohm Rowntree's attempts at the turn of the century to determine the requirements for calories, proteins and fats for an effective healthy body were hampered by this lack of knowledge.[33] Lynda Bryder also highlights this increasing state involvement, noting that medical officers in Britain prior to the war had instituted nutritional programs in schools as an aid to improving health. The impact of the 1913 Educational Act was that by 1918 one in every three children received a meal every day at school.[34] According to Richard Titmuss, this focus on nutritional improvement for children also contained a wartime focus on preparation for the 'next generation of recruits', particularly as the population in Britain was also beginning to decline.[35]

Despite the increasing attempts by the British state to improve the bodies of its citizens, by the outbreak of war in 1914, there was a significant discrepancy between the number of men willing to serve and the number of men that the British military considered physically suitable for service. In Chapter 1 the opening stages of physical assessment and military categorization upon civilian bodies during enlistment will be explored from the perspective of the men who experienced their bodies subjected to the process. This process of inclusion or exclusion proved to be significantly more complicated than perhaps hoped by the British military. David Silbey explains that despite the programmes which focused on improving national efficiency after 1901, many working-class volunteers still failed to meet the requirements for military service in 1914.[36] From the first moment that a British military official ordered a man to disrobe, his body began a continual series of questioning, classifications and measurement against standards that rose and fell according to the need for men on the front lines. The significance of this first stage of many men's experience of the armed forces in relation to individual acclimation and actualization within wartime British society cannot be understated. In *Civilians into Soldiers*, Newlands explains how during the Second World War this visual and written indication of effectiveness could ostracize or glorify men as their value was determined by a military-trained medical officer.[37] During the First World War, this process of validation was not as complicated as what would follow two decades later. Yet, this did not make the first physical inspection any less formative for most men who served in the First World War, as their worth was decided on the appearance and capabilities of their bodies for the rest of the world to see.

Choosing men and masculinity

Interwoven with the cultural conception of the physical soldier in Britain in the years preceding and during the First World War is the impact of idealized masculinity which became synonymous with soldiering between 1914 and 1918. The scientific and popular focus on physical fitness that had arisen as part of the cultural obsession with militaristic heroics in Britain was underscored by lasting interpretations of masculinity.[38] Within her examination of the link between men's bodies and masculinity during the First World War, Bourke argues that men who were accepted for service often experienced a sense of social belonging and camaraderie.[39] Bourke explains that the men's new uniforms were an important aspect of the transitionary process from civilian to soldier as they enhanced men's physicality by allowing them to present the masculinized soldier ideal.[40] Paris agrees that the wearing of a uniform served as a demonstration of masculinity but concludes that the adorning of the body in military clothing carried a message of patriotic collusion with state and irrefutable proof of physical prowess.[41] This link between the presentation of the desirable body and military epitomizes the imagined socially constructed ideal of the 'proper man' within the context of the First World War that would be used to shame those who could not or would not don the uniform.

Nicoletta Gullace continues the argument by explaining that the act of wearing a uniform was regarded by many as an overt symbol of masculinity.[42] Gullace's seminal book *The Blood of Our Sons* takes pains to demonstrate how men's citizenship became threated as women were enlisted by the British state to sacrifice their brothers, fathers, husbands and lovers for the war effort. This war on masculinity waged by women, but directed by the British government, Gullace argues, was merciless as masculinity was welded to military service with the unenlisted civilian branded 'a coward beneath contempt'.[43] Added to this association was the issue of sexual viability enhanced by the projection of idealized masculinity. In her consideration of 'khaki fever' in Britain during the war, Angela Woollacott dispels the myth of sexual histrionics apparently brought on by a flash of khaki, while reiterating that a worn uniform communicated an individual's conformity to the state in a way that surpassed any other blatant demonstration of patriotism and bravery during this period.[44]

Unlike any other British military conflict that came before 1914, British soldiers during the First World War were separated into four distinct groups, regulars, territorials (reservists), volunteers and conscripts.[45] These groups would contextually draw judgements within British society about the levels of heroic masculinity and physical prowess ostensibly associated by the means by which a man gained his military uniform. Despite the emphasis on the bravery and patriotism of the volunteers, the use of volunteer men in times of war was by no means a new phenomenon within British society. From 1905, under the direction of the new war minister Richard Burton Haldane and the director of military training Major-General Douglas Haig, the British military underwent a period of significant improvement across the board, ranging from distribution of command and organization of the regiments to training and physical preparation of men's bodies.[46] Mallinson argues that much of this process focused on how to 'echelon the regulars and the auxiliaries at home', as opposed to a focus on how to organize and utilize them in the most effective way.[47] The ultimate result of these changes was the distribution of new service manuals which directed men's bodies in a variety of new ways including new tactical directions and mobilization instructions.

By the time that Lord Kitchener assumed the mantle of secretary of war on the 5 August 1914 the vastly improved British Expeditionary Force (BEF) had already been committed to service in France. A product of a decade of training and improvement, Brigadier Sir James Edmonds considered the BEF in 1914 to be 'incomparably the best trained, best organised and best equipped British Army which ever went forth to war'.[48] Still, as highly trained and skilled as the BEF were considered to be, what they held in fortitude they lacked in numbers. In 1914, Britain only had around 150,000 regular soldiers with which to field for battle and many of those were dispersed around the world as guardians of the British Empire. Recruitment had also been a continual concern as despite the widespread reforms and the increasing popularity of the military, during the interwar period of 1902–14 the regular army had consistently failed to achieve its annual target of thirty thousand recruits.[49]

Support was also not to come from the newly reformed territorial forces that were theoretically supposed to fill this breech. Beckett argues in *Britain's Part Time Soldiers* that the new secretary of state for war was extremely distrustful of 'amateur' soldiers.[50] Dismissing their masculinity and physical readiness for fighting, Kitchener overtly referred to them as a 'town's clerk army' rather than actual 'soldiers' who enjoyed unprecedented levels of independence and autonomy.[51] This relaxation of physical control and direction meant that the territorials, at least according to Kitchener, were unsuitable for front-line combat. Kitchener's solution instead was to raise a whole new army of volunteers as had been the traditional practice. Despite having been training and preparing their bodies for the moment they were needed; Kitchener dismissed the territorials from his plans in 1914. These part-time soldiers were dispersed into several regiments around the world in order to free up regulars from colonial outposts or to shore up gaps at the front until his army of volunteer men were physically prepared enough for battle.[52] In an excellent demonstration of irony, the mantra of 'those who cannot, teach' is applicable, as much of the responsibility for training initially fell to territorial men. This state of affairs would continue until war pressures ironed out this prejudice and increasingly territorial trainers were replaced by returning men from the front line. By 1918, the segregation imposed by Kitchener had eroded completely. Serving in the same capacity as their fellow regulars, volunteers and conscripts, territorial men ultimately saw as much action as the rest with their bodies serving in uniformity and solidarity as a combined force with the aim of victory on the battlefields.

In terms of sheer numbers, most of the British men who served during the First World War were either volunteers or conscripts. Coming first between August 1914 and January 1916 were the volunteers encouraged by notions of duty, patriotic fever, recruitment promises, propaganda, societal pressures surrounding worth and masculinity and a sense of adventure augmented by an increasingly militarized culture. Volunteers often receive the most attention within historiography as they were the everymen, physically fit enough to pass the enlistment criteria and inexperienced enough to actively look forward to their 'adventures' abroad. Simkins argues that the Pals Battalions represent the last manifestation of 'late Victorian and Edwardian Liberalism' in that they illustrated a blend of social, political, military and economic factors that were forever changed by the continuation of war and the creation of conscription in 1916.[53] One hundred and forty-five service and seventy reserve battalions were eventually created, which made up 40 per cent of the British Army in the first two years of the war.[54] Motivations for enlistment are wide and will be given due consideration in the first chapter; however, it is important to note that Clive Hughes argues that for some men the war offered 'a brief respite, [and] an exciting and adventurous opportunity'. He is also keen to point out that the conception of the 'rush to colours' may be inaccurate as many men with commitments at home such as family or well-paid jobs did not immediately choose to sign up.[55] Krisztina Robert adds to this argument the role of women in aiding the war office to recruit soldiers, highlighting the link between the women's movements and the military campaign. She argues that 'in the first half of the conflict, they invited the volunteers to lead army recruiting marches hoping that the sight of female soldiers would shame "slackers into enlisting"'.[56] This is an important aspect of the construction of the British military during the war, which includes an extensive focus on the male body to be explored in detail through this book.

Finally, in 1916 conscription was introduced to meet the continually lowering rates of enlistment and to replace the partially successful Derby scheme. Mitchinson argues that this relatively unsuccessful programme implemented by Lord Derby throughout 1915 had sought to stave off full conscription by allowing men aged 18–41 to attest and then wait to be called up.[57] On 27 January 1916, the Military Service Act came into force which allowed the enforced enlistment of every British man aged between 19 and 40. Ilana R. Bet-El has conducted one of the most definitive investigations into the final selection of British soldiers during the Great War in *Conscripts*. She argues that conscripts came from all elements of life just like their regular and volunteer counterparts and that they were by no means a minority with 2,504,183 men being conscripted between January 1916 and the end of the war.[58] These conscripts joined with the 2,466,719 volunteer soldiers to become an essential part of the British Army over the course of the war. Yet, Bet-El argues that conscripts experienced particular hardships as they were enlisted as their entry after 1916 occurred during extreme pressure on the army which resulted in reduced training that was frequently made more difficult by the increasing inclusion of less physically able men to meet staffing shortages.[59]

Within the four armies that served for Britain, there was a significant amount of diversity among the men. They received different training, had different experiences and even wore different uniforms as a result of their entrance into the war effort. However, their end goal remained the same, to undergo the process of transitioning the civilian man into a fighting soldier capable of fighting the enemy and achieving victory. While there were discrepancies in the way that they were treated, all the enlisted men received some aspect of physical assessment, training and experience of service which promoted physical uniformity, compliance and efficiency. This will be considered further within this book's investigation into how men's bodies were improved, indoctrinated and controlled over the course of the war.

Care and causality: Taking care of men

As this book moves with the enlisted men into service and beyond training into conflict, the focus on the body fixates on to the pleasures, irritations, transformations and damages that men's bodies experienced as par the course of military service during the First World War. Within the rigid command structure accentuated by class status in the British Army in this period, Victorian traditions of upper-class officer paternalism spilled over into the First World War despite the unprecedented expansion of serving men. Within his examination of officer–man relations, Gary Sheffield reiterates how often officers took a paternalistic outlook for the rankers under their command.[60] This could consist of asserting and dogmatically pursing policies that kept men from damaging the bodies that the military had trained so hard to create, or extend to the protection of said bodies through forced medical treatments or turning a blind eye to deviant behaviours. In extreme cases this could even include protecting men's bodies from physically debilitating punishment as exhausted sentries would be woken and quietly reprimanded by the NCO or the subaltern in charge rather than endure a court martial and punishment.[61]

This notion of care and the battle for control over the body of the serving British soldier is recurrent within the centre chapters of this book as it follows men progress through training and continued experience in service through interpreted by a myriad of physically oriented events. A pertinent example is the constant obsession with food that seemingly makes up part of every British soldier's account of the conflict. The famous expression often attributed to Napoleon that an army marches on its stomach seems correct as countless memoirs and oral testimonies reflect on the role of 'hard tack' and bully beef as a soldier's primary and often despised daily sustenance.[62] Chapters 2 and 3 of this book take an extended look at the role of food in the sustaining, hardening and satisfying of the male military body in the First World War. The obsession with diet and food throughout the First World War demonstrates that physical sustainability and improvement within and beyond the climate of the war was an important focus for the British government and the military.

Several historians have considered the role of food within the confines of the First World War including Rachel Duffett and Andrew Robertshaw who both have reiterated that how the military scrutinized food provisions and intake minutely for the purpose of keeping the fighting men fit and healthy.[63] Campbell agrees with this and recognizes within *The Army Isn't All Work* how food was essential in conditioning and preparing the training men for the trials they faced on the front lines.[64] Duffett's assessment of food is even more nuanced as she argues that 'food was the site of complex and, it must be said, frequently contradictory, emotional responses: for many soldiers, it represented the best and worst of times'.[65] Clayton backs this point up by noting the importance of food in 'maintaining the fighting man's morale and combat efficiency'.[66] Certainly, food makes up much of the narrative within soldier's letters, testimonies and memoirs. Food also offered an opportunity for control as punishment frequently included the removal of luxury food items or the absence of a meal as a direct punishment to the body of the serving man to re-establish dominance. It is for this reason that considerations of food and provisions reoccur often within the following chapters, as food and drink were used as tools to keep men healthy, complacent and fighting.

As well as being clothed and fed, soldier's bodies within the First World War also needed protection and medical treatment. Even before the First World War there had been increasing state interference on the health of the soldier. This level of interference upon the body also occurred significantly within the public sphere by the end of the nineteenth century through inniatives like the madatory smallpox inoculation introduced in 1853 and the sanitation reforms spearheaded by public medical officer John Simon.[67] At the close of the century, medical science had continued to innovate and had yielded new experimental inoculations for cholera and typhoid. These latter inoculations were never introduced to the British public fully, and mandatory inoculation was abolished in 1907 after half a century of protest for the infringement of civil liberty. However, the early twentieth century still represented a turning point in the continued invasion into the body by the state with the overarching desire to make one and all better.[68] Mark Harrison reiterates this intention within the perspective of colonialism as he explored the British colonial government's attempts to improve public health through state-institutionalized mechanisms in the latter nineteenth and twentieth centuries. He explains how these programmes, punctuated by drug regulations, vaccination efforts and sanitation improvements, stand as examples of British colonial dominance as well as a core component of the civilizing mission.[69]

In Chapters 3 and 4, the relationship between the soldier's body and medical care is considered extensively as a platform to debate the power struggles between man and war machine. For context it is important to recognize that the British military long had a history of trialling enhanced medical practices on soldiers in the name of physical progress. During the last Boer War British troops acted as guanine pigs for new vaccines for typhoid and cholera between 1899 and 1902. Despite the repeal of compulsory vaccination in 1907, 97% of the British armed forces were fully inoculated against typhoid several times, ostensibly with their informed consent.[70] This was unsurprising as within British society concerns over individual autonomy of the body had clashed for decades with the British government's attempts to improve public health and had part of the basis for the repeal for mandatory inoculation. Not all improvements were related to inoculation. Changes to sanitation and hygiene were successful responses to the curtailing of epidemics in the late nineteith and early twentieth centuries. Yet, this enhanced focus on the care of the militarized body was not without calamity. Despite a significant period of improvement and an overhaul of the Royal Army Medical Corps (RAMC) between its introduction in 1897 and 1914, the outbreak of the First

World War did much to weaken initially the ability of the British military to respond successfully to disease prevention on the front line. Harrison notes that while 'the army on the western front certainly gave a great deal more thought to the organisation of sanitary work than in any previous campaign ... in practice, military hygiene often left much to be desired'.[71] Harrison argues how the early stages of the campaign saw the RAMC hampered by a lack of equipment, something that alarmed the British public, and a loss of manpower as forces were stretched more thinly as the war developed.[72] However, as is argued by Meyer in *An Equal Burden*, as the First World War developed the RAMC developed with it and became an efficient force for dealing with the sick and wounded. So much so, that Meyer concludes eruditely that the members of the RAMC stolidly bore the brunt of an unimaginable war and contributed to the revolution of medical care that followed both within and outside of the military.[73]

Chapters 4 and 5 follow the British soldier away from the front lines, sometimes permanently. While these sections consider the complicated process of ownership and repair of the British military body as a result of military service, for context it is important to note the long-standing argument associated with First World War military medicine, namely its impact on civilian medicine as a result of desperate innovation. Bourke is openly critical about a link between military and civilian medicine as she argues that many of the improvements made were specifically conflict-orientated and rarely found applications within civilian life. Innovative methods of dealing with mass causalities affected by poison gas or being hit by a shell were significantly less useful in civilian medicine. The same can be said for battlefield medical training as, with the exception of a significant accident, triage and split-second decisions of life and death were not required outside of a war zone.[74] Bourke does concede that the expansion of orthopaedics and enhanced understanding of fractures was useful in aiding disabled soldiers and civilians.[75] Still, she argues that the impact of military medicine on civilian medical advances, and therefore civilian health, must not be exaggerated because much of the improvement should be credited to the work of the Ministry of Health which was created in 1919.[76]

In opposition, Joan Lane's examination of health and medicine argues that 'the unprecedented demands placed on the medical services in the 1914–18 brought great advances in therapies and equipment, some of relevance later in civilian practice'.[77] Roger Cooter's debate over war's impact on medicine has very much been on the vanguard of this discussion within the historiography.[78] Uniting medical advances and military conflict, Cooter consistently asks if war is good for medicine and/or if the reverse is also true. Within his examination of the First World War, Cooter demonstrates that the rigours of war both at home and abroad encouraged scientific and medical exploration to produce a range of new responses towards ill health and disability. Focusing on orthopaedics, Cooter argues that war stimulated immense growth into the field, which proved beneficial for both soldiers and those disabled by combat as well as those injured by munitions work.[79] Pickstone also regards the evolution of war medicine positively and argues that 'the lessons taught by the war to young surgeons and their superiors facilitated the development of specialists in civilian medicine'.[80] Pickstone focuses on Manchester hospitals and considers at length the improvements in surgery and orthopaedics that assisted the rising number of crippled soldiers. He argues that this focus developed beyond the war. Hospitals such as Grangethorpe in Manchester became research centres. These went on to be funded by the Royal College of Surgeons and the Medical Research Council, formed in 1919.[81] Simpson and David add to this argument by reiterating the impact of Harold Gillies and Henry Newland innovation in reconstructive surgery, necessitated by the wounds sustained by war that became the basis of an entirely new field of medicine.[82]

The question of military medical prowess has been expertly investigated by scholars who have shown the intricacies of medical care and disease prevention during the First World War. However, within the context of the individual soldier bodily experience, the lasting impact of medical innovation is less relevant than the way that such innovations were first enacted on his body and how this shaped his experience of the First World War. In Chapter 5, within the examination over the final stages of the British military body such questions will arise alongside considerations of respect, perception and treatment of the soldier's body by the individual, the state and other serving men.

Ultimately, the history of the First World War soldier has been told and told again; yet, within each narrative there is new evidence, theory or analysis to better gauge and understand the experiences of those who endured the unendurable. It is within this framework that this book sits by utilizing the body as a lens by which to comprehend the pressures, powers and motivators enacted upon the British serviceman during the First World War.

Theory in practice

To best analyse and comprehend the multitude of evidence, anecdotes, official reports and extensive historiography it is essential to employ a rigid analytical framework. When considering the place of the body within society it would be unwise to overlook the theories of French philosopher Michel Foucault as he remains one of the most authoritarian voices upon the body as a site of power and control. Using the seventeenth- and eighteenth-century French soldier as an example Foucault considered the entry of the body into a 'machinery of power', which deconstructed and constructed it in line with the demands of those in power. Defining this as a 'political anatomy' Foucault explained that the body developed as a docile vessel that was manipulated and directed by the individual, institution or state that held dominance over it through discipline.[83] He claimed that 'the classical age discovered the body as an object and target of power. It is easy enough to find signs of the attention then paid to the body – to the body that is manipulated, shaped, trained, which obeys, responds, become skilful and increases its forces.'[84] Essentially, according to Foucault the body within increasingly modern society was a blank slate which dominant powers could imprint upon and mould for their purpose against the agency and will of the individual.

Yet, Foucault has come under criticism for presenting a restrictive view of the individual body within society. Shilling discounts this narrow argument of the body as docile by arguing that Foucault's malleable and unstable body view makes little room for considerations of resistance to dominance and control. He writes, 'Even when Foucault makes the occasional reference to the body putting up resistance to power and dominant discourses, he cannot say what it is about the body that resists.'[85] For Shilling, the body is overtly absent from the Foucauldian analysis of power. Obsessed with the domination of the institution over the mind, the Foucauldian blank slate body is left on the fringes of the argument. By missing out the body from the constructive framework, it becomes difficult to recognize it as 'material component of social action'.[86] As opposition Shilling offers Turner's 'phenomenology of embodiment' as a counterpoint to Foucault, arguing that internalization of normative values was a symbiotic process of internal and external change that does not overlook the role of the individual and their agency within a transformative process.[87]

It is within these arguments on the construction of the body that this book considers the tailoring of the First World War soldier's body in Britain. As it considers how men were prepared, directed, treated and respected this book will examine the place of the body within a myriad of controlling factors that sought to direct and influence the body of serving men. The focus of the military, the state and culture as well as input from medical institutions will be considered to show how men's bodies were prepared for conflict. This consideration will also include a focus on the quality of men and fluctuations in standardized requirements, physical and behavioural modification through training, the impact of technological and medical improvements and the treatment of men's bodies when they were unsuitable for conflict. As Foucault makes clear, when a body in society is ascribed a purpose by the state it is invariably adapted to best fulfil said purpose. During the First World War, men's bodies were indeed transformed and honed for the purpose of military service at the state's behest, yet this conversion was not without complications. Certainly, men's bodies were changed according to state need, but in many cases this transition occurred as the aims of the man and the military were in unison. As the following chapters will explore, as the aims for the usage of the body by the military and the man diverged, a power struggle ensued which invariably meant that no matter the outcome, the body would ultimately suffer the consequences.

Caught up within this examination of autonomy and power over the body is the issue of class. Within their extensive treaties on the individual within society both Marx and Weber recognized the disparity in the way that men were treated physically.[88] Both argued that class in the nineteenth and early twentieth centuries designated health, occupation and opportunity that several impacted upon the body. Class defined for most, if not all, exactly how they lived, how they were perceived and how they interacted. Very much tied to class is the concept of rationalism as British society progressed into a period of modernity as an increasing obsession developed over the control and improvement of the body in service of the state for societal improvement and capitalist profit.[89] Returning to the argument by Searle that 'National Efficiency' became the mantra for the early twentieth century in Britain, it should also be noted that it was at this junction that Charles Bedaux incorporated 'scientific management' into Britain.[90]

Adding to this focus on physical efficiency was the work of Frederick Taylor who had coined the term 'scientific management' in the United States within his *The Principles of Scientific Management* in 1911.[91] Taylor focused on solving the problematic relationship between management and labourer by viewing the worker as an 'object of knowledge and an asset for management'.⁹² In breaking down key components of a task into a series of actions that could be measured, assessed and importantly controlled, Tailor introduced a measurement of efficiency that would have lasting effects on both the worker and the soldier in the coming decades. Miller and Rose argue that this deconstruction of tasks in basic repetitive steps occurred during the incorporation of scientific rhetoric focused on improving effectiveness through management within industry.⁹³ Rabinbach offers a similar view and claims that the climate of war would further lead to significant reform within the workplace under focuses on efficiency.⁹⁴ Kries agrees and explains that by the end of the war, organizations such as the Health of Munitions Workers Committee (HMWC) sought to further improve effectiveness, having learned by experience during the war the extent to which the body could endure, by surpassing Taylor to make 'scientific management more scientific'.⁹⁵ The HMWC reported that improvements for fatigue, working hours and health requirements could dramatically speed up production. This lead to the reduction of working hours, the introduction of breaks and holidays and rudimentary health and safety.⁹⁶ Arthur McIvor and Vicky Long consider these improvements in detail and conclude that this evolving period of development significantly benefited worker's health as well as being advantageous for productivity.⁹⁷ While these arguments of rationalism are more widely relevant to the evolution of the British manufacturing industry and wider culture post war, the arguments of physical capability and obsession with quantifying each action in order to ascertain the most effective method of physical interaction were very much key concepts within the training and service experience of British men in the First World War.

Finally, the work of Bourdieu also arises within this consideration of the body within the confines of political, social and cultural control. Bourdieu's theory of how individuals internalize their perception of the world and their position within it through 'habitus' indicates the role of stature and social interaction in the construction of the self. Within his consideration of the importance of food as a signifier of social status, Bourdieu presents the assessment of the physical body as a primary site for the perception of worth, status, usefulness and wealth.⁹⁸ According to Bourdieu, the body constantly communicates non-verbally to others significant amounts of information which allows perceptions to be made about it and the individual who inhabits it. Ervin Goffman explores this discourse between bodies within his examination of the 'body idiom', a mutually understood non-verbal form of communication.⁹⁹ He writes, 'Although an individual can stop talking, he cannot stop communicating through body idiom; he can either say the right thing or the wrong thing. He cannot say nothing.'¹⁰⁰ Goffman argues that communication and interaction are ceaseless between beings; therefore, the body is constantly being used to expose, comprehend and internalize attitudes, emotions and desires, through the means of social interaction.

Within the context of the First World War, multifaceted bodily communication was utilized to classify, assess and direct men's bodies for combat. Body idiom also provided different opportunities for different types of men whose non-verbal communication potentially indicated class status, education, work experience, physical capability or health. Bonding between men within the military was also dependant on their shared experiences, which would be reinforced through perceptions of the physical self as men

Introduction 17

looked for kindred spirits often from similar class, regions or working backgrounds. In many ways body idiom provided the format for reducing the difference between the wide range of men, transforming them from individuals into uniform soldiers. It is within these interactions that this book will consider the role of the body in the experiences of men within the British Army during the First World War.

Sources and evidence

It is important to recognize the boundaries and limitations of this book. There are hundreds of thousands of individual accounts of the First World War, significantly more than a single study can consider. While this book draws from a wide array of source materials comprising of official documentation, contextual publications, oral testimonies and, significantly, private paper accounts covering diaries, letters and memoirs, it is recognized that each account presents complications for validity and analysis. It is for this very reason that this array of sources was chosen so to allow for a broad investigation into the impact of the First World War on soldier's bodies, with an emphasis on their individual perception and experience, and a commitment to validity and accuracy.

Official documentation makes up much of the groundwork for the discussion of soldier's experiences. Between 1914 and 1918 a significant amount of propaganda literature was created by and in support of the Parliamentary Recruiting Committee (PRC).[101] These documents, when used in tandem with soldier's accounts and the military enlistment forms, illustrate the perceptions held of soldiers and their bodies by the public, the military and the British government during the period of recruitment and enlistment. Official forms and documents recur in every chapter of this book. Several military training manuals have been examined to determine how the soldier's body was improved during training and active service and to outline the changing standards the military enforced upon men's bodies. Service manuals and battalion records illuminate the dangers and pressures upon the body under active service while medical records and the articles printed in the Journal of the Royal Army Medical Corp (JRAMC) offer insight into the medical advances, hazards and impacts of service upon men's body. Finally, documents such as those prepared by the war graves commission and the demobilization forms used as men left military service shine light on the care of the body at the end of military service and explain how soldier's bodies were monetized and broken down literally to the 'sum' of their parts.

These documents have not always been presented in chronological order, nor has every single document been included in the analysis. Instead, the documents presented have been chosen as they aid the understanding of the environment in which the body was controlled, crafted and curtailed. Newlands uses the work of Turner and Waitzkin to explain that reviewing the contextual medical gaze in the Second World War illustrates how judgments arose on physicality through scientific knowledge.[102] This is just as true for the First World War as official documents allowed for a categorization process, either formal or informal, to be applied to men's bodies. These documents illustrate the physical ideals that were purported at the time and demonstrate how bodies were assessed for service. Still, when using them as a historical source care must be taken not to overstate their effectiveness when interpreting their motivation and reception.

While official documents provide the bedrock of the examination, the true 'body' of the evidence is drawn from the voice of the soldier himself. Oral testimonies make up a significant part of the examination. These interviews, the majority of which were created and stored by the Imperial War Museum (IWM) over the last century, usually take on the form of a guided narrative. These structured conversations invite the listener to engage with the experiences of the subject as they often relive their experiences on tape. While this book was not involved in the process of creating the recording and therefore is not at risk of influencing the evidence provided, the information should still not be taken at face value. Peter Hart argues for both the value and the limits of oral history, particularly when utilized for an examination of former soldiers. Hart explains how oral history provides the opportunity to correct misconceptions and provide a unique bottom-up perspective of an event. Veterans are more likely to recount the 'gorier' details of their experiences long after the event as opposed to writing about it in letters which could alarm family members. Hart also argues that this form of evidence should not be considered 'testimony' as each fact must be checked as opposed to simply accepted. He writes, 'As a source of evidence, interviews are by no means perfect and the veterans are not saints.'[103] While investigating, it important to be aware of bias, as well as issues with memory or the altering of recollections for a variety of reasons.

These are the pitfalls of engaging with oral history; yet, this does not diminish how important and fascinating these sources are. While dates may occasionally be wrong and events tempered by encroaching experiences, often the perception of the event, either then or at time of the recording, provide crucial evidence for soldier's perceptions over their experiences and the impacts on their bodies during the course of the First World War. To balance the pitfalls of oral history this book has also investigated extensively memoirs, diaries, and letters of soldiers from the First World War. Memoirs both published and unpublished are an invaluable source of soldier's experiences. Often these sources have been collected from diaries or notes taken over the course of the war. Many of the memoirs begin by explaining that the motivation for being written is to honour those that the author served with or to explain to future generations what happened between 1914 and 1918. On many occasions, the writing of these sources can be interpreted as cathartic, particularly the unpublished or posthumously published. This is not to state that the extensive number of published memoirs that have been in circulation from the start of the war onwards are completely sanitized or censored. Often accounts of death, living conditions, disease, sex, alcohol and misdemeanour are less visible in some of the earlier publicly published narratives.

Bourke's *Dismembering the Male* remains one of the best examples of drawing together written accounts, along with oral history testimony, to uncover a level of detailed barbarity which enhances the understanding of the impacts of war upon the body.[104] It is from Bourke's example that *War Bodies* approaches its analysis of the primary source material. Stephen Morillo also offers advice by stating that written and pictorial serviceman's sources are particular important as they offer perspectives and bias that are more difficult to find in other sources.[105] The flipping of the drawback of the written account illustrates how conscious recognition of inherent bias allows for an enhanced analysis of the primary source, allowing the reader to draw conclusions from individual perception as well as base facts. However, Morillo also explains that it is imperative to evaluate the validity of the source by cross-comparative analysis.[106] Anthony Brundage agrees and argues that scepticism must be applied when using letters and diaries, especially if these testimonies have been made public or published.[107] He continues that it is essential to recognize the authors' 'motives, ignorance, or capacity for self-deception'.[108]

Another issue is the lack of literacy within the period. Richard van Emden recognizes in *Tommy's Ark* that 'literacy rates among pre-war soldiers were poor, much as they were among the civilian population that volunteered or were conscripted'.[109] Within this book there are testimonies from both officers and rankers. As proof of van Emden's point often officer's testimonies can be more eloquent with significantly less grammatical mistakes.[110] However, this does not demean the importance of the wide array of recollections by rankers as many still wrote home, kept diaries and created testimonies after the war that have then been incorporated into this book.

Reiterating the point of Morillo above, one of the best ways to ascertain validity when using such accounts is to collect as much appropriate evidence as possible. One of the best demonstrations of it is to be found in *Wounded* by Emily Mayhew who explains that her extensive research allowed her to 'assemble a history of the central experience that was repeated hundreds of thousands of times up and down the Western Front'.[111] Mayhew explains how this was only possible by the bringing of 'all these [men and women's] voices together'.[112] This is very much the same process undertaken in this book as sources such as testimonies, diaries and letters are challenged by comparison to each other to locate the body within the experiences of men over the course of the First World War. Together, this combination of official, oral, personal and published testimony provides a vivid image of the experiences of the First World War British soldier.

These sources can then be directed to consider the primary themes of this book. In terms of power, the dichotomy between what was and what was hoped to be is clear between the memoirs of soldiers and officers when set against the official documentation of the period. As Foucault indicates that control was directed downwards from those in charge, the accounts of men, both written and spoken, illustrate how control could and was subverted from the ground up. As this book continues to explore the relationship between the war and men's bodies it is from these sources that most of the analysis is formed. Drew Leder argues that individuals do not particularly acknowledge their bodies unless they are in a state of dysfunction.[113] However, this book clearly accentuates that this is not the case, as men continually use their bodies as a framework from which to describe their lives in conflict. Yet again it is Joanna Bourke which this book turns to for validation and guidance as she highlights that perceptions of the body are not as simple, particularly during times of discomfort and pain, where there is a divergence, often in war, between wound and perception of pain.[114] Within the sources used within this book, the body is not simply brought forward because it is suffering or even dysfunction but also because it has changed or an event has happened to it – be that a reflection on increased fitness, the undergoing of a sexual act or the implementation of a medical procedure such as inoculation.

This book seeks to use these sources not to explore battles or events but to analyse how soldiers have reconstructed their physical experiences of war. This book will question how men prepared their bodies for enlistment and how it felt to be successful or rejected. It asks how men felt about preparing their bodies for battle only to find that the training ground and the battlefield bore little resemblance to each other. What were men's responses to constantly watching their bodies change, especially as this was frequently outside of their own control? How did men view their bodies in combat as they both entered and left the fray and what was their opinion of those ultimately responsible for their bodies after the dust settled? These are just some of the questions that this book seeks to answer through its analysis of the sources. Still this book recognizes that it cannot incorporate the experience of every single British soldier in the First World War. There is no blanket all-encapsulating analysis throughout the following chapters. Instead, what makes this research unique is it builds on the seminal work that preceded it and the focus upon the body as being central to men's experiences and the British military's needs during the First World War. This research seeks to uncover the considerations of men who found their bodies in a state of flux, transition and extensively controlled. Indeed, themes such as masculinity, medical improvement, physical disability and soldier's experiences have all been considered expertly previously. It is the goal of this book to contribute to the current historiography by bringing the body to the forefront of the discussion on the creation, crafting and controlling of soldiers during the First World War. This analysis will, therefore, focus on the individual agency of physicality, combined with a predominately bottom-up approach, to enable the research within these chapters to provoke new interest into the activities and actions of the British men whose conceptions of their time within the First World War were shaped by the experiences of their bodies.

Chapters

As this book is focused on the lived experience of British soldiers and their bodies over the course of the First World War it is logical that the chapter structure is presented in a semi-chronological format. Over the course of five chapters, examination will be given to the enlistment, training, active service, combat experiences and the end of service. At the heart of these chapters lay the personal testimonies and official records that placed the body at the centre of the soldier experience between 1914 and 1918.

Chapter 1 considers to what extent the condition of the body was a crucial factor in the earliest stages of a soldier's career. Regardless of the condition of enlisting, for example, if the men were regulars, territorials, volunteers or conscripts, this chapter demonstrates how the body as an object was singled out in recruitment propaganda and practice and held in contrast to a physical ideal which both men and the military aspired to achieve. Zweiniger-Bargielowska has argued that by the occasion of the war in 1914 British society was already taking stock of its population's health.[115] Jay Winter supports this argument and contends that the war presented the chance to increase this focus through regulated inspection as part of the enlistment process.[116] At the centre of this discussions lies the recruit and his body and it is this aspect that Chapter 1 examines as it charts the experiences of those who were weighed, measured, wanted and found wanting during the First World War.

Chapter 2 continues the investigation into the preparation of the body for war, while also reflecting on what possibly could be considered the most controlled aspect of a British soldier's existence. Rachel Woodward explains that soldier's bodies were produced in training, yet this book argues how this distinction is not nuanced enough to cover the transformation process between 1914 and 1918.[117] As this chapter will illustrate, men's bodies were certainly made fitter, better and stronger through a regime of drill, practice and games. Their bodies in training also served as a site upon which to enact military domination. Internalizing indoctrination through clothing, diet and discipline was just as important for training soldiers during the war as was meeting the physical challenges of training. Yet, as their bodies and behaviours were brought in line with the requirements of the army, new challenges over control developed as many of the men in training were unlike any who had joined the army in recent memory. Many of whom refused to entirely submit their bodies to military regulation. Most men left training fitter and somewhat prepared for battle, but the process of getting them to that standard was not clear-cut as conflict over the body defined many men's experience during their early days in uniform.

The release from training into active service provides the focus for Chapter 3. This chapter discusses the range of experiences that awaited the soldiers and their bodies as they embarked around the world to take up their duties. Mark Harrison has discussed at length the issues of disease and poor sanitation, despite the improvements having been made within British military during the prelude to the First World War.[118] As men arrived in their new living conditions a plethora of new experiences greeted their bodies and impacted upon the army's ability to control them. New technology such as inoculation offered protection from sickness but raised questions of individual agency. Exposure to alcohol and opportunities for sex offered new challenges for the army and new opportunities for men to damage their own bodies as they sought to please themselves. Chapter 3 examines, through the experiences of soldiers, how their bodies were continually at odds with their environment. Indeed, they were controlled by assigned living conditions, diets, clothes and military discipline. Yet, soldiers also increasingly regained the autonomy to have impact and input upon their own bodies, particularly through ways in which to disable them.

Chapter 4 brings the examination to the fighting front as here the fighting body and its experiences are considered. The occasion of combat resulted in a myriad of physiological responses from the men which the British Army was forced to attempt to control. To counter fear, the army distributed alcohol, pity was curtailed through masculine rhetoric and compliance controlled by discipline. This chapter examines how men were encouraged over the lines and the consequences of taking that action. Here men displayed their physical vulnerabilities as they became physically and psychologically wounded. Bourke has discussed the emasculation of fear and wounds showing how bravery and masculinity were often linked in an aid to keep men fighting and even lessen the burden of medical demands.[119] Not all could simply 'soldier on' as this chapter continues to investigate how men and the military were forced to adapt to the trauma soldier's bodies received as a cycle of control, encouragement and recovery developed around the act of combat. For some avoidance of combat or escape meant finding an alternative. In this chapter deliberate destruction to the body will also be examined as some soldiers tested to what extent they were willing to sacrifice parts of their body and even their lives to escape the reality they lived in.

Chapter 5 ends the analysis by considering how men left the battlefield, be that via being demobilized with a pay packet, wounded on a stretcher or buried in a grave. For the dead attention will be given to those men who failed to escape army control as they were buried in their uniforms, with no control over how or where they were interred. Dying evidently removed men from combat but not from service as their bodies often became tools for the living, weapons for the enemy through the spread of disease and their impact on morale and a reminder of the potential fate of each serving man in uniform. Next the wounded enter the analysis as their removal from the battlefield could often mean relative safety and comfort for their bodies but not necessarily escape from authoritarian control as command shifted from commanding officers to military staff. Wounded soldiers also could find their physical identity challenged as they exchanged their uniforms for 'hospital blues' and their damaged bodies kept hidden from public view. Men even sought to retake control over their bodies by allowing them to deteriorate to prevent being returned to the front line. Finally, consideration turns to the reverse of the entrance processes that began in 1914. With the end of the war came an enhanced desperation for many to reclaim their civilian lives that so clashed their soldier status. For some men, the announcement of the armistice was justification enough for them to begin to more openly reject the army's control over their bodies and lives as they demanded to be brought home, often complaining bitterly about the unorganized chaos that hampered demobilization efforts. As the military and the soldier battled over the process of returning him home, men and their bodies were once again reduced to a series of physical attributes and skills as they were assessed to determine their financial cost to the military and the government.

Ultimately, this investigation owes much to the wealth of research that has preceded it. Drawing from the scholarship of sublime theorists, historians and researchers, *War Bodies* seeks to expand understanding of the militarized male body within the First World War, with an emphasis on control and indoctrination.[120] This book will ultimately illustrate how the body was central to the process of turning civilians into soldiers and explore how control over men's bodies was uneven and incomplete. Many men enlisted, wore a uniform and fought on the front line, but that did not mean that they thoughtlessly followed orders. Between 1914 and 1918 the average British Tommy was much more likely to be a volunteer or conscript than a regular or territorial. The army quickly realized that it could not control and direct these men in the same way that it had its traditional forces in the previous century. Even if they were professional soldiers, the First World War was unlike anything any of them had faced before. This was a 'different existence altogether' and it was one that was intensely felt through the bodies of the men who served.

1

A fine body of men: Recruitment and enlisting for war 1914–18

The First World War American recruitment marching song 'A Fine Body of Men' by J. B. Ingle cheerily combined physicality and heroism, ending acerbically with 'Let's put in to vigour and vim, Make sure work of this German Spew'.[1] In Britain, the fine bodies of British men were under substantial scrutiny, medically, politically and socially as over six million British men were accepted into military service as regular, territorial, volunteer and conscripted soldiers between 1914 and 1918.[2] Of all the military conflicts that Britain was involved in, the First World War was unique in that the majority of those who fought served as volunteers rather than professional soldiers or conscripts. At the centre of this zeal for battle lay a combination of targeted recruitment campaigns; societal pressures which forced men to reassess their value, purpose and place within Britain; and an intricate assessment system designed to overtly identify and clarify the 'best' men for the job. Throughout the various enlistment phases of the First World War fixation remained on the body. Examinations of men's bodies meant rejection or acceptance for service. Emulation of the militarized physical ideal impacted on fashion, physicality and social desirability. Between 1914 and 1918 men found themselves constantly challenged to think about their bodies in new ways, including, but not limited to, the practical corporal factors that may have made life in the armed forces seem attractive. Recruitment and assessment practices were also remarkably fluid as the war progressed. In 1918, assessed bodies were viewed, weighed and touched much as they had been in 1914, yet the categories and criteria required for entry had significantly shifted in references to acceptability for service. Hidden within the changing acceptable standards lay a continual contest between subversion and flexibility, as both recruits and assessors attempted to play the system for their own benefit. Enlistment was a complicated and often actualizing experience for many in Britain during the war; therefore, this chapter will examine the propaganda, recruitment process and societal responses to enlistment and service, within the framework of the body, to illustrate how physicality and suitability ultimately came to define an entire generation in the early twentieth century.

No guts, no glory

The 'rush to colours' in Britain in the early stages of the war in 1914 was unprecedented. During the Last South African War (1899–1902), the British government had amassed four hundred thousand regular, irregulars and militia men.[3] Within eight weeks following the declaration of war in August, British volunteers surpassed this number and kept climbing.[4] By the end of 1915, a total of 2,466,719 men had voluntarily enlisted in the army.[5] After volunteer numbers began to dramatically dwindle throughout 1915, conscription was introduced in the following year to shore up the gap, though it was never as successful as that first surge of enthusiasm for service. In the final year of the war, only around five hundred thousand men enlisted.[6] By comparison, in September 1914 alone, 462,901 men, the highest number of recruits for a single month, joined up.[7] After the declaration of war in 1914, regular and territorial men were immediately dispatched. Four of the six standing British Army divisions marched to meet enemy forces in Belgium and Northern France.[8] Since the beginning of the twentieth century, the British Army had been undergoing a significant period of improvement and adjustment. Under the direction of Lord Haldane, these reforms meant that the British Expeditionary Force was most equipped and organized of any former British unit; yet in comparison to the enemy they faced the British military was still vastly undermanned.[9] Stepping into the breech was Secretary of War Earl Kitchener who managed the most successful public military recruitment campaign in history, first through volunteering before finally introducing conscription. The enacting of the Military Service Act on 27 January 1916 and its successor, the Second Military Service Act, on 25 May 1916 no longer left the decision to enlist to the privacy and agency of the eligible man. Over the course of the year, stipulations continued to relax, as the need for men on the front lines demanded further flexibility. In May eligibility was extended to married men. From August only men who were not physically able or were working in exempt industries, aged under 18 or were over 41 were considered unsuitable for service.[10]

Physical suitability was the key criteria from the opening stages of the war. This was not a new phenomenon as theorists of masculinity recognize that 'manhood' was a long-standing socialized idealization.[11] Dawson explains how over the course of the nineteenth century masculinity and militarism became linked within a form of heroic masculinity to be emulated.[12] By the outbreak of the First World War, 'manhood' had become intrinsically linked within British culture with notions of duty, and physical presentation. Physical size and muscular presentation were particular identifiers of masculinity.[13] By the outbreak of the war, this notion of physically demonstratable masculinity was further cemented by the role of the assessment criteria for military and the onslaught of recruitment and propaganda posters which frequently questioned physicality, masculinity and capability to encourage men to enlist. The role in these visual demonstrations of physical idealism and self-critique must not be understated, as they played a crucial role in the soon to occur rush to the recruitment office after the outbreak of war on 4 August 1914. Yet, recruitment initially began slowly with the occurrence of the 'Pals Battalion' being the first successful initiative to encourage so many men to enter military service. The 'Pals Battalions' were made up of communities of colleagues, teammates, students and neighbours, who sharing a commonality

Figure 2 Are you in this? Recruitment poster 1915. Library of Congress (hereby cited as LoC), LC-USZC4-621, 'Are You in This?' Recruitment poster by Baden Powell, published by the Parliamentary Recruiting Committee, printed by Johnson, Riddle and Co., Parliamentary Recruiting Committee Poster No. 112 (1915).

had enlisted together on mass, often retaining elements of their unique method of entry through 'Pal's Battalion regiments', which by designation clarified the men's associated heritage. Simkins makes it clear that the 'Pal's Battalion's' were far from a new development as historically Volunteer battalions were a common means of recruitment; indeed, he argues, the Territorial and Volunteer forces owed much to this tradition.[14] The innovation came from allowing the forces to celebrate more visibly their shared heritage, and that they were being raised for offensive action abroad rather than domestic security. Successful as this form of motivation was, it was the work of the Parliamentary Recruiting Committee (PRC) which did the most to galvanize enthusiasm for service and the war.[15] Formed on 31 August, the PRC recruited a network of local political organizations to act on the behalf of the War Office and encourage men to enlist. This innovative approach resulted in a mass recruitment drive supplemented by the production of 54 million posters and 5.8 million leaflets and pamphlets.[16]

A famous example this campaign is the 'Are you in this?' poster created by Scout movement founder Baden Powell in 1915 (see Figure 2). At first glance, the physicality associated with professional soldiering is apparent within the poster. The physically fit and square-jawed soldier and sailor, aided by the brave Boy Scout, immediately draw the eye as they face the enemy steadfast and centre stage. In support of them, the robust hammer-wielding industrial worker and dutiful women workers focus on their tasks with keen determination. All these figures show their bodies caught in moments of activity and convey purpose and dedication to the task in hand. Set aside is the clear abnormality, a diminished man who looks from the sidelines having not contributed himself. This man stands as physical contrast to the other heroic male figures. Dressed unsuitably for war-related activities, he is slope-shouldered and cross-legged. He also lacks the square chin of the other males, and has his hands hidden from view in his pockets. Whereas the hands of everyone else are occupied, empty-handed observer clearly has no purpose. The message of the poster, that the outsider is clearly less of a man, is self-evident, supported by the unsubtle demand underlining the image challenging men to defend their role within the war. The message is transparent: 'Join up and clarify your masculinity or refuse and reveal yourself as less than a man.'

Posters such as this were often very effective. Albrinck recounts the story of a clerk who felt pressured, by the visual depiction of the heroic men in the posters, to improve his physique before seeking enlistment in order to ensure he measured up to the ideal.[17] The importance of the military uniform as factor in encouraging enlistment must not be understated. This is particularly evident as a form of visual appeal that was central to thousands of posters and pamphlets that aimed to pressure men into military service during the First World War, such as the 1915 'To the Young Women of London' poster.[18] The 1915 'Thank God I Too Was a Man' was the epitome of this recruitment tactic. Targeting men through women, this poster recruited lovers, wives and sweethearts to strengthen men's resolve to enlist. Focusing on the physical demonstration of both service and affection, the poster belittled un-enlisted men by determining that the measure of a man was visible by 'wearing khaki'. The poster boldly pronounces that without a uniform acting as a literal badge of honour declaring masculinity through service to king and country, a man is not 'worthy' of a woman's attention or affection. This interplay on heterosexual relationships and early twentieth-century gender politics is as ingenious as it is insidious. The questioning of a man's virility and viability for a relationship is made doubly profound by the recruitment of women to internalize and repeat the message. The end of the poster even suggests that a lack of commitment to the country could translate to a loss of interest in a partner, conveying the unsubtle message: 'If he does not love you enough to wear the uniform, he probably does not love you!' Desperate times may indeed call for desperate measures; still this approach was extremely incongruous as a method to enlist the male body during the First World War.[19]

Propaganda focused on physicality was particularly common and effective. Historians such as Michael Brown, Graham Dawson, R. J. Q. Adams and Philipp Poirer have individually shown how men were treated differently in and out of uniform throughout the First World War, with the latterly attired for service frequently receiving a much more welcome and pleasant response than their civilian dressed counterparts.[20] As a consequence, some men enlisted with the primary purpose of shedding their socially unpopular civilian dress. Lieutenant Palmer, who served throughout the war in the RAMC, wrote as much within his memoir:

> As far as men were concerned, the great idea was to get into uniform so that they could be classified as having enlisted to fight for their King and country; the more men clothed in Kharki [sic] the more noticeable became those who had enlisted. Enlistment too meant popularity and pride and a certain amount of favour with the ladies and older people. Indeed, those not in uniform were despised by those who wore the Kings uniform, and the populace generally.[21]

Palmer went on to explain how the homogeneousness of khaki in Britain shifted public perceptions of men, as civilians became heroes by covering their bodies with a military uniform and associated apparel. He explained, 'The wearing of Kharki [sic] made all men look more or less the same and the populace opened their doors to one and all who wore Kharki [sic]; their rank mattered not one bit, all were heroes and treated as much.'[22] For Palmer, as it was for millions of others, the first powerful step away from civilian life was the embracing of the military uniform and the all-important visual demonstration of pride and service to the world. For the state and the British military, appearance was a vital weapon in the recruitment arsenal which was exploited at any opportunity. Throughout the war the masculinized idea of the serviceman's body was continually depicted and promoted in posters and pamphlets, as well as personified by home front-serving personnel and the recently recruited whose mere presence provided an advertisement for the splendour of military service to the rest of British society.

Clothes maketh the man

Attitudes of awe and a yearning to emulate the uniformed men were common, especially in the earliest stages of the war. This is particularly visible in the diary of

Private Buffey whose awe of the recruiting sergeant ultimately overruled his intended career direction as he enlisted.

> [The sergeant was a] picture of what he represented, the ramrod straightness of his back, the immaculate tunic with its colourful medal ribbons plus the red and white and blue rosette sported in his hat, all tended us to look upon him as someone above the ordinary, which indeed he was ... Gradually he talked us into following his sage advice especially after he told us that our local regiment was just our cup of tea. It's a regiment bursting with honours, not just campaign honours but these won at sport, boxing, swimming, running, soccer, the lot. All won by local lads like yourselves, lads whom you might know, lads will love to show you townies the ropes.[23]

Resplendent in his medal and uniform, the recruiting sergeant in Buffey's memoir encapsulates the valorized image of the Edwardian soldier. His appearance communicated the glamour and potential of the militarized body, while his calculated speech delineated the corporal rewards stemming from donning the uniform in the form of sporting victories and sexual adventures.

> Yes, chaps you plump for the York and Lancaster regiment and ill warrant you will not rue your decision, for it is as I say a regiment you will be proud and happy to serve in. your shoulder badge, just a plain Y and it will be a puzzle to the girls until you tell them it stands for Young and Loving. His spiel sounded so good and his manner so friendly we couldn't do any other than heed to his prompting, so we forsook the cavalry for the infantry.[24]

Buffey's persuasive sergeant's allusion to increased sexual attention draws attention to another long-standing myth from the First World War, the fawning and apparent promiscuity of women encouraged by men in uniform labelled anecdotally as 'Khaki Fever'.[25] While the voracity of 'Khaki Fever' is somewhat questionable Acton maintains that the belief that a uniform would enhance a man's chances of gaining sexual attention remained an important, if not solely impacting, factor in encouraging men to enlist.[26] As a concept 'Khaki Fever' has more recently drawn heavy criticism by historians who have challenged the lack of acknowledgement of women's agency in their own sexual practice. Cree argues that this apparent rise in women's libido and daring was in fact part of a long-standing programme of moral regulation that stretched back into the nineteenth century. Citing the work of Foucault and Cox, Cree asserts that the policing of working-class women and girls from both classes by middle-class women illustrates a countermovement to the efforts taken for women's emancipation and equality in the preceding decades.[27] This raises questions about the reality of a sudden lust for uniformed men over the creation of a moral panic utilized as a form of social control. However, this does not diminish the possibility of belief or deliberate allusion to enhanced attractiveness as part of recruitment campaigns and encouragement for enlistment.

Be it for sex, adventure or patriotism, many men were visibly excited to be dressed as a soldier. Private Bickerton quite unnecessarily changed immediately into his uniform upon receipt, disregarding the fact he would not be called up for two more days and that his uniform in his words was 'a rather badly fitting suit of khaki' complete with a 'hat which was much too large'.[28] This was a common attitude of excitement and pride in physical appearance that existed beyond the boundaries of the First World War. In the first years of the twentieth century, the rise of militarism and respect for the armed service meant that soldiers could take pride in their uniforms and role within society. Private Silver was also just as keen to show off his new uniform to his family immediately, despite having enlisted before the outbreak of war and national patriotism in 1914.[29] Pleased as punch as he was with his traditional scarlet tunic, Silver was significantly less happy when he had to trade his beloved scarlet uniform in for the much safer, but significantly less striking, khaki uniform just a few months later.[30] Clothing the body in a British military uniform communicated strong messages of compliance, service, and allegiance. Reiterating this Meyer quotes Gullace when arguing that the dressing of the body in a uniform conformed to the 'social power of the narrative of victimhood' and that the residing cultural expectation in Britain during the course of the war remained that men must be in uniform; to lack this fundamental symbol of overt masculinity and duty was to take a visible stand against the rise of war support and patriotism.[31] For many men like Private Brady, the lack of uniform meant a stain on their character and dedication. This fear could extend to the manner under which a man entered the forces. Conscripts could often be considered as lesser men, in that they had been unwilling to step forward voluntarily. Brady's desperation and concern for being thought anything less than heroic is obvious within his memoirs.

> I didn't want to wait until they came and got me; I didn't want to be a conscript – a pressed man – I wanted to go under my own volition – a volunteer – like the regular who had fought and won many British battles on foreign fields – and made the Empire what it was. Most of us were like that – blindly eager to get into uniform come hell or high water.[32]

In contrast to Brady, there were also men who firmly resisted the uniform and the message it conveyed. Against these conscientious objectors the military uniform became a tool to force actualization into military service as they forced into attire they swore to resist. These men, regardless of if they submitted voluntarily or were arrested for ignoring their call-up, were reviewed by the British Army in local barracks. In a parody of the willing recruit, conscientious objectors underwent medical assessment, classified under their suitability for service, and were given equipment and a uniform with instructions to put them on.[33] This mimicry of the official recruitment process resulted in many obstinate conscientious objectors refusing to wear the uniform as a reiteration of their non-military status. This created a complex battle between individuals and the British military as their resistance to join the military countered against the militaries' typical methods for forced acquiesce. Faced with such resistance, often conscientious objectors were forced into uniform to enable them to undergo the process of punishment and court martial. This farcical scene was played out often as the British military attempted to militarize men by proxy through the wearing of military clothing. Fred Murfin recalled in his memoirs how the experience was surreal and, in some cases, almost comedic. 'The officer said: "now my lads, we want you to put khaki on." We all refused, I think, and we each had a soldier to undress and dress us. … One man came in later very flustered. [shouting] "they have got the uniform on but they haven't got the man!"'[34] Murfin recounted calming the man down by repeating that they were prisoners not soldiers, while returning to joke with the man dressing him about the smell of his feet. Again, the importance of the uniform is clear as its adoption clarified socially subordination to the armed forces. Quakers also regarded the rejection of the uniform as a statement of disinclination to allow the military to claim their bodies.[35] G. Ewan was a devout Quaker who recalled how a young sergeant bluntly told him in no uncertain terms that he would end up in uniform. 'He then told me I should be forcibly stripped and put in uniform if I objected to putting it on otherwise. I simply implied that I should speak on those points of interest with his superior officer.'[36] Ever polite, Ewan went to explain how he had strenuously maintained a dissociation between himself and the refused uniform despite having the regiment cap placed unceremoniously onto his head.

> Last, a place to collect khaki suit and cap. Would I try it on? 'No! thank you'. A few more charming words, then a laugh … then it was stuck, none too lightly, on my head … then the kit bags were brought in, and instructions as to how to pack these was the next move. The young men who went with me packed the bag as shown. 'Aren't you going to pack yours?' 'No! I am not all interested in government property, and I will leave you to your own devices.'[37]

The uniform played a critical role in many men's experience of enlistment. The act of gaining the uniform was a mark of pride, reiterated by the social response to wearing it in public. Dressing the body in uniform significantly changed the messages and meanings of that body and denoted, particularly in the early stages of the war, valour, masculinity and patriotism. For those like Ewan and Murfin those messages and meanings were precisely the reason to reject it. Their resistance of the military dress was not simply a reticence to wear a uniform but a symbolic rejection of the state's attempt to militarize their bodies. Idiosyncratically, those without a uniform found their social status diminished, rejects of a society that predominately judged their bodies, and therefore their character, immediately by the clothes that adorned it.

In the seminal *Telling Tales about Men* Lois Bibbings explored in detail the antagonistic relationship between the uniformed and non-uniformed. Within her analysis of how conscientious objectors were despised and mistreated within British society during the war, she notes how the need to distance one's self from those considered by many as the epitome of cowardice resulted in the adoption of pseudo-military dress for both women and children. Bibbings explained, 'Women and children seemed to feel the need to wear a uniform or some visible signification of their support for and involvement in the conflict, even if they could only approximate the look.'[38] The association between clothing and physicality is startlingly clear within the guise of public perception during the First World War. As popularity for the military reached fever pitch, encouraged by the climate of war from 1914, the importance of

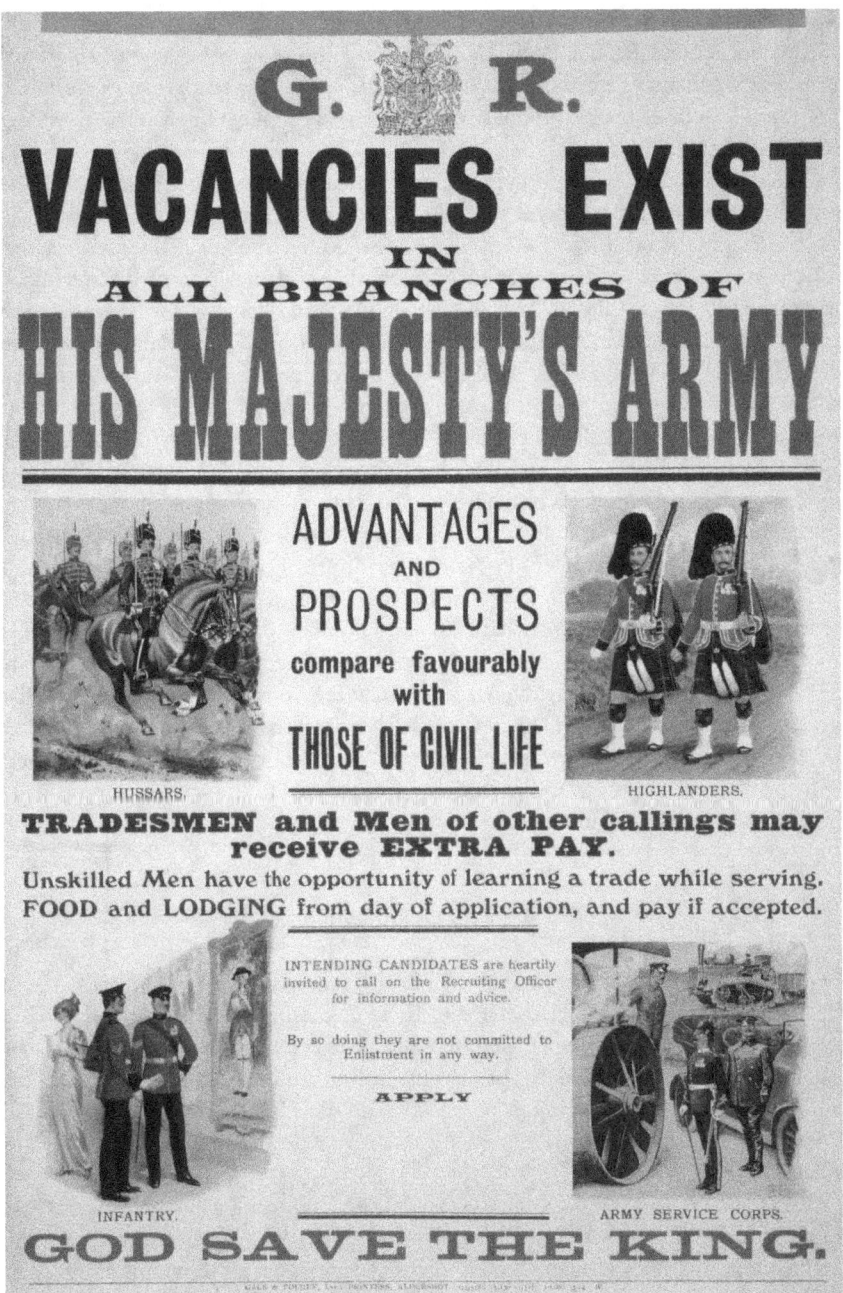

Figure 3 Vacancies exist in all branches of His Majesty's army recruitment poster. LoC, LC-USZC4-11973, E. Ibbetson and J. McNeill, 'Vacancies Exist in All Branches of His Majesty's Army', Recruiting poster for British Army Ernest Ibbetson and John McNeill (Aldershot: Gale & Polden, 1914–18).

being clothed in a way that reflected support for the nation and a dedication to duty should not be understated. Evidently in this period, the body became a beacon for advertising personal allegiance and patriotism. This was preference that was certainly not limited to men, but for whom it potentially had the most impact in influencing their behaviours.

The needs of the body also implored some men to enlist in the First World War for altogether more pragmatic purposes, such as accommodation, sustenance, education and opportunity. The 'Vacancies Exist' poster combined all these attractive aspects of service within a single advert alongside a glamorizing of the splendour of military finery (see Figure 3). The offer of 'food' and 'lodging' even precedes the promise of remuneration. Several great military figures, and Ernest Hemmingway, are credited with proclaiming that 'an army marches on its stomach'.[39] At the beginning of the twentieth century the British Army was no exception with the average soldier consuming over 4,000 calories per day.[40] For many these would have certainly been 'advantages' compared with 'civil life'. Jay Winter and Ina Zweiniger-Bargielowska have explained how the diets of the lowest classes were especially poor at the turn of the century.[41] Too many mouths to feed and precarious employment prospects could prompt familiar encouragement for enlistment. In the face of social deprivation and unrest the Irish republican and socialist leader James Connolly lamented in 1914 that 'hunger and fear of hunger have driven thousands of our class into the British Army'.[42] Service could mean emoving the burden of an empty stomach to feed while also bringing the opportunity of a wage chit into the household, not to mention the potential for better 'grub' for the new soldier.[43] With this in mind it is unsurprising that recruitment sergeants were heard to promise 'meat every day' as part of their enlistment speeches, much to the chagrin of opponents of the war who argued that hunger was forcing men into the army.[44]

A body of statistics

One of the fundamental experiences of all British recruits in the First World War was the process of official physical assessment. These medicalized examinations placed the body at the centre within the decision to enlist or reject. For many this was their first experience to the rigours and regulations of their future military career; for some it was a devastatingly disempowering experience where their entire worth was condensed to an array of statistics and measurements that would determine their future value to society.

The structure of these assessments was typically uniform. First, men would report to a recruitment sergeant doubly tasked with hooking the curious and coxing the enthusiastic to a branch of the armed forces. As gatekeeper, the recruiting sergeant could immediately end a hopeful's career based on age or visible physical stature. Beyond the critical eye and gaudy promises of the sergeant, recruits then endured the evaluation and subsequent categorization of their bodies in line with their apparent suitability for service. To allow for such a laborious and complicated analysis to be completed quickly and efficiently, from 1914 men were sorted into five categories:

A. Fit for general service
B. Fit for service overseas
C. Fit for home service only
D. Unfit but likely to become fit within six months
E. Unfit and unlikely to become fit within six months[45]

In 1917 this system was streamlined again, replaced with a 1–4 grading protocol.

1. Grade 1 covered all the men deemed fit from the former category A.
2. Grade 2 contained the men who had belonged to B1 and C1 which had been classified as fit because they could walk 6 miles with ease.
3. Grade 3 covered the men unsuited for combat in the former category C.
4. Grade 4 covered those entirely unfit.[46]

This visual clarification of the ideal physique presented after the war reiterates the prevailing message of a link between physical superiority and worth within early-twentieth-century British society. Height, weight and muscular development were all quantified in terms of viability for service. Joanna Bourke also presents these images and facts within *Dismembering the Male* while explaining that the new categories were not designed to single out the disabled or diseased but to rather clarify suitability for service.[47] She reiterates how the categorization systems were used effectively to create a recognizable schism within British society that was wholly focused on the bodies of the male population. She notes that while the wounded and scarred could still be utilized to demonstrate the bravery and heroics of the serving man, 'it was the bodies of those who remained at home that symbolised all that was degenerate in the male physique'.[48] Within the image of the four kinds of men, the message is resoundingly clear of what was considered acceptable and unacceptable – of what could be clarified as worth and worthlessness (see Figure 4). These images depict a process of normalization that would have profound impacts in Western society for the rest of the century.

These markers lay at the centre of the assessment process; however, it fell to the assessor, often a military official but sometimes a doctor, to recognize them in practice as he took each man through a routine physical examination prior to entrance into service. Each recruit underwent eye and chest exams, while their body was checked for deformities including lost limbs, fallen arches of the feet and missing teeth. Pivotal to this process was the measurements recorded for age, weight, chest expansion and height.[49] These four aspects formed the cornerstone of the process of acceptance or rejection. At the beginning of the war, enlistees were required to be over 18, with a minimum height of 5 feet 3 inches and a chest measurement of at least 34 inches.[50] In 1845 enlistees had to be 5 feet 6 inches. By 1900, as damming evidence of the decline in the health of the lowest classes, 565 per 1,000 men were shorter than 5 feet 6 inches. To attempt to meet recruitment targets in 1872, 1883, 1897 and finally 1901, the height requirement fell from 5 feet 5 inches, to 5 feet 3 inches, to 5 feet 2 inches before a flat 5 feet in 1901 to solve the recruitment crisis made evident by the Last South African War.[51] During the first year of the First World War the height requirements would also fluctuate, again determined by the increasing need for more soldiers on the front line.

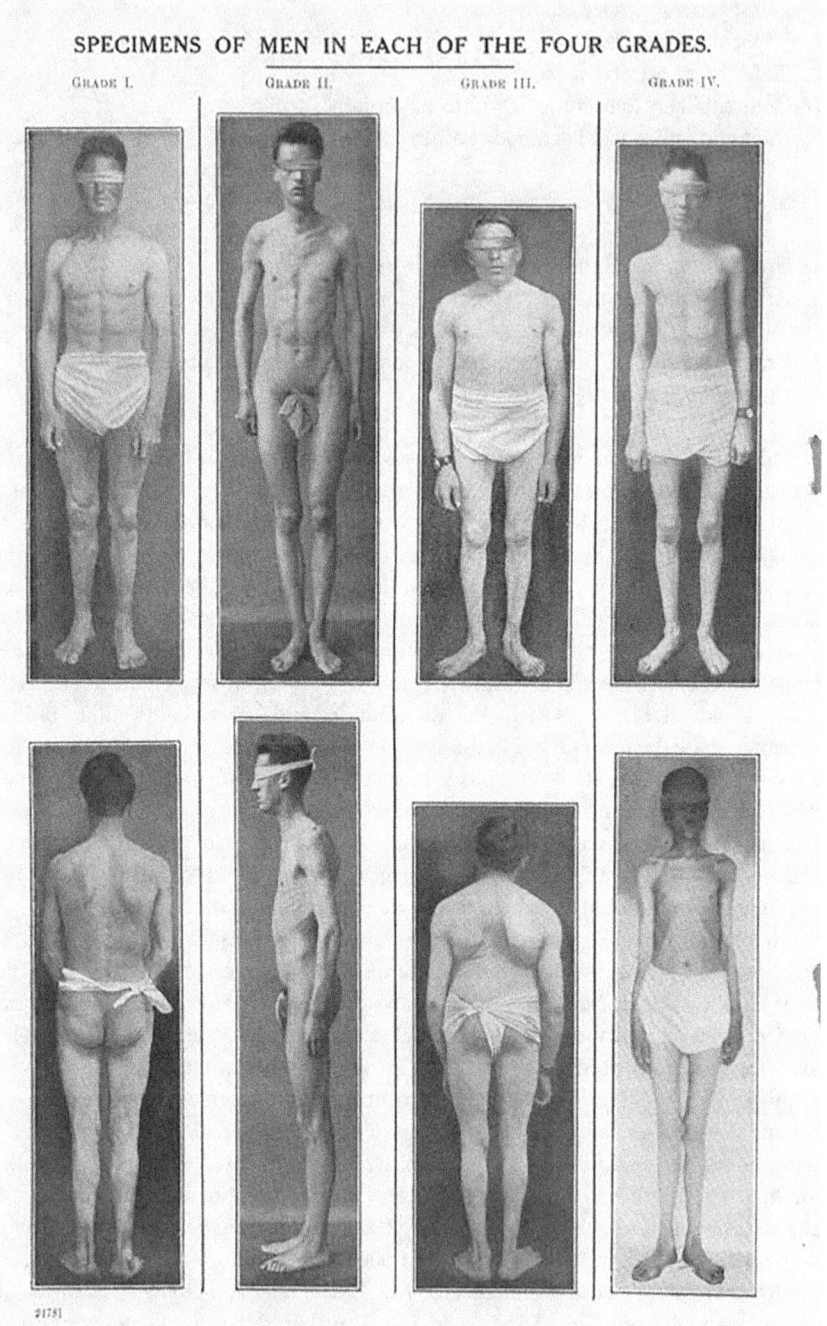

Figure 4 'Specimens of Men in Each of the Four Grades, Report by the Ministry of National Service 1920', Wellcome Library London (1920). Wellcome Collection.

At 5 feet 4 inches with a chest expansion of 34 inches and no deformities, 19-year-old Arthur James Walkden was the ideal recruit when he enlisted with the Corps of Hussars of the Line in Birmingham on 14 August 1914.[52] Walkden's enlistment form contains the signature of both the medical and recruiting officers, along with the confirmation of a commanding officer. Examination of the form clarifies the extent to which men's bodies were scrutinized prior to service and illustrates how many officials were involved in the continual evaluation process of men's height, weight and deformities. Evident on the form are sections for the recording of the man's age, height, weight, chest measurements, heart rate and visual acuity. Men rapidly became the sum of their parts as function overtook temperament. At no point within the initial process was any form of intelligence test undertaken within British recruitment in the First World War. Warfare demanded fighters rather than thinkers, with cunning and obedience to be drilled in during basic training. Both the enlistment form and medical history attestment form solely concentrated on physical aspects to ensure that the body being considered for service would be capable of the physical trials ahead. Medical forms demanded even more invasive examinations as the completion of the form required closer inspections of the body to certify vaccination scars, discover any physical evidence of disease and measure muscular physical development and pulse rate.

The assessment experience was one that linger in the memories of the men who experienced it. It was a formative event in many men's lives and the ramifications of the assessment would socially define that man for the rest of his life. Within Lieutenant George Cotton's account of his enlistment in London in 1914, he described the process of being assessed in detail and noted how the process made him feel inconsequential.

> The first stage consisted in giving information as to my age and many other personal concerns and a note of the corps we should like to join. The Sergeant who was in charge of this work, having heard we were clerks, strongly recommended the army pay corps where he said with that assurance which always accompanies there [sic] stripes, we should not only have every opportunity of covering ourselves with glory (and ink) but would also in all probability be sent overseas within a few days of enlistment. The ordeal of medical examination now had to be faced. In the early days of the War, when the number of recruits was large, the medical test was severe and only thoroughly fit men were accepted. ... I was ordered to enter a cubicle which was made to fit three men on each side and told to take off every article of clothing and be ready to leave as soon as my name was called. The knowledge that all had to go through the same ceremony helped to lessen the shock.[53]

Cotton's experience was typical of many men who sought to enlist over the course of the First World War. His identification of the experience as an 'ordeal' and his self-reassurance that all endured it are indicative of how distasteful he found it. Though clearly uncomfortable having his body exposed, objectified and classified, he recounted how the heroic rhetoric was again repeated to him as he signed on the dotted line. For many men, this first-stage humiliation was part of the process to progress on to the more exciting aspects of soldiering. Cotton's description of the assessment as significant impediment to 'glory' emulated the feelings of many recruits who dreaded the entry process. Worse for Cotton was the inhumanity of the physical examination. Stripped and put on parade, Cotton was mortified to find his body put on show, and having been 'weighed, measured, thumped, probed, questioned, and generally treated like an animated piece of butcher's meat'. Cotton was also disgusted to be crawled around nude on the floor, leading him to question his dedication to gaining entrance to service. Unsurprisingly Cotton claimed that his 'enthusiasm was on the wane'.[54] The official guidelines for enlistment regulations demanded that men should be able to walk the length of the floor. Medical officers were even instructed to have men 'hop across the room on the right foot. Back again on the left foot. (The hops should be short and upon the toes.)'[55] Cotton's crawling is unusual and it is possible that he exaggerated for the narrative to indicate just how humiliated and powerless he felt, or perhaps a distortion of the memory again brought about by his reaction to the ordeal. Regardless, it is obvious that he felt that the whole process had been dehumanizing and humiliating.

Cotton was successful in his attempt to enlist but his friend was not. This recollection reflects the other side of the ordeal, where men walked away from assessment dehumanized and demoralized. 'Jack' eventually made it into the service, but not because his body improved to meet the criteria set, but because the need for men forced the British government to lower standards at enlistment. In the early days of the conflict the flood of recruits meant that the British Army could afford to have a selective criterion for physical proficiency. Winter has argued that entrance into the military in the early stages of the war was particularly easy, given that the assessors were paid 'one shilling' for each successful man; he claims that 'they passed everyone in sight'.[56] Accounts such as Cotton's clarify that this statement is not true. Ian Beckett explains that rejection for men continued throughout the war, even against pressures to lower the requirements further in 1918. Together with Bowman and Connelly, Beckett asserted that 'rejection rates naturally reflected pre-war deprivation', adding further evidence to the fallaciousness of Winter's comment of a universal entry attitude. Beckett, Bowman and Connelly continue by reasserting that the body played a crucial role in the recruitment of men during the war, stating that 'there was also an application of a suspect criteria as to what constituted fitness: physical ability was too readily equated with stature'.[57] As the war progressed entry requirements would continue to be exceptionally fluid. In relation to these fluctuations David Silbey argues that assessment process that men underwent was neither as regulated nor as fixed as was commonly assumed as men and the military continued to reassess and negotiate the terms of their enlistment.[58] In fact as the war continued it became more apparent that the acceptable requirements for soldiers to be able to succeed past the process of enlistment were extremely malleable and dependant on a combination of individual determination, assessor leniency and the need for manpower at the front.

Private Walkden became caught within the tide of this transition as his initial acceptance in October 1914 was overturned a month later based on his height. Deemed worthy one month, only to be reclassified as inadequate weeks later would have been a devastating blow for many. This came about as part of the British government's attempt to stem the tide of volunteers which had initially overwhelmed the British Armed Forces in August and September 1914. As the height requirement for enlisted men was raised in December from 5 feet 3 inches to 5 feet 6 inches, disappointment, disillusion and dissent arose. William Anderson, Member of Parliament for Sheffield Attercliffe, was among those who voiced opposition as late as 1916 to the change while clarifying the impact such measures could have on an individual.

> R. Hope, of Exeter, who attested under the group system in November last, was medically examined both at Taunton and Bristol, and passed as fit for service and placed in Group 6; whether he is aware that this man when his group was called up made all arrangements to leave civil life and gave up his employment as a shop manager; that on presenting himself he was again examined, informed that he was fit for Home service only, given 2s 9d., and sent away by the military authorities, who told him to hold himself in readiness to be called up in a week or a month or six months.[59]

Anderson's claims indicated how much men took on good faith, as the man had placed himself, his family and, by proxy, his body in a difficult situation for the purpose of serving a state that suddenly no longer wanted him. In response, the undersecretary of state, Harold Tennant, clarified that all men were welcome to volunteer for assessment prior to call-up, and that in doing so the men's record would be admissible in the future should the regulations change again. He remained politically vague about the acquiescence of the former assessment, stating, 'If upon such examination the man is rejected as unfit for service, he is not called up. If he is passed as fit for service he will be again examined when he is called up, but the former certificate will be attached to his papers.'[60] Arthur Marwick has argued that these fluctuations were particularly damaging to the enthusiasm and patriotism of the lowest classes.[61] By again branding the same class of men who had failed for enlistment in 1901 as unfit and unworthy of fighting for their country the working class was quickly alienated in the closing weeks of 1914. The repercussion of rejection of men's bodies was that enlistment figures would never again attain the level of enthusiasm and volume of the first months of the war.

The rejection of those under 5 feet 6 inches in late 1914 had another lasting impact, as it allowed an entire new battalion to develop that actively 'celebrated' the physical inadequacies that had kept many men out of the armed forces. In 1914, permission was gained by MP Alfred Birkenhead to raise a special 'Bantam' battalion after a 5-foot 2-inch Durham miner had threated to 'thrash' anyone in the room in a fight to prove his suitability after he was declined for service on the basis of his height.[62] This battalion publicly asserted that 'a man is as a good soldier and as plucky a fighter at 5ft. 2in., as at 5 ft. 6ins'.[63] Situated somewhere between an innovative solution to the growing resentment and a figure of ridicule, the Bantam battalions directly challenged the notion of physical supremacy for combat. Despite being a short-term sensation in the media, the Bantams were a disaster in the field. The physical capacity of the Bantam men was severely overestimated, and through the requirements of the war, the battalion was disbanded to shore up fissures in other regiments. This inadvertently reinforced the need for a physical standard for service as the bodily disadvantaged men struggled outside of their own units to keep up with their counterparts and quickly became an active tactical drawback during combat.[64]

No body wanted

Be they accepted, encouraged, overlooked, conscripted or forced, most of the men presented so far were deemed worthy of service and, by proxy, of respect in British society. For the others who left by the same door they entered, the assessment process was often more than an ordeal to be endured; it was immutable gateway which cast them back out, unwanted and unworthy to be judged by the war-enthused British society. Failure to match up to the military's ideal body type was for the men keen to enter the war a particularly dispiriting experience. Private Brady recalled being told: 'Too small: said the MO. "You'd never be able to carry full marching order lad." '[65] In failing to become what he considered was a 'proper soldier' and 'devastated [and] humiliated' Brady recalled his homeward journey was a 'gloomy, painful experience'.[66] Having tried to enlist as a typical regular, the future Private Brady refused to consider the Bantam Regiment as an alternative.[67] His dismissal of these men mirrored his own rejection for lack of physical stature. His anger and shame at his body's failure is evident within his testimony.

This fear of failing to meet the ideal physical standards even resulted in some men trying to modify or enhance their bodies ahead of the enlistment examination. Echoing the worries of many men in this period, Private Shaw recalled his anxieties and his plan to gain entry in late 1914, noting in his memoirs, 'I had misgivings that I could not pass the physical test of (I think) 35 inches' chest measured ... I purchased a "chest expander" and "dumb bells" and in convenient times slipped up to my bedroom for exercises, especially deep breathing.'[68] Faced by the realization that his body would be the cause of his rejection, Shaw took significant efforts, that he kept secret from his family, to modify his body in order to meet the military criteria. Shaw belongs to a set of dedicated men whose determination to serve their country caused them to attempt to dramatically alter their physique. In modern society, the idea of conditioning the body before enlistment is logical, if not even essential.

Yet, at the turn of the century recreational exercise was not as prevalent with preference deferring to ensuring there was food to eat and hard labour to be carried out by the lower classes. This is perhaps why Shaw keeps his efforts hidden from his loved ones as he prepares himself for examination. However, this is not to say that there was not a culture of fitness growing within Britain in this time. Ina Zweiniger-Bargielowska explains that as a result of the disastrous Boer War recruitment effort at the turn of the twentieth century individual fitness and physical capability had increasingly become cemented within the mindset of the British public.[69] This was augmented by the growing popularity for militarism within British culture within which, Dawson argues, the military hero took on a 'plurality of forms' that promoted physical ideals.[70] Alongside a range of scholastic and youth-orientated movements designed to promote and improve physical health there was a deliberate link made at the highest policy level to link physical fitness to patriotism. Zweiniger-Bargielowska continues that a rise in sport and volunteerism for para-military organizations combines what Hugh Cunningham identifies as 'patriotic recreation' and a deliberate attempt by British policymakers to 'endeavour to enthuse men about their bodies, inspiring them to acquire health, strength, and fitness carried at least an implicit, if not explicit, military purpose'.[71] Therefore, it is possible that Shaw was embarrassed by his inability to reflect the socialized physical expectations of the period, hence his determination to improve his body in secret. Despite his best efforts, Shaw was rejected twice for his chest size and weight until finally being accepted into the 25th Royal Fusiliers as a Frontiers Man on 13 March 1915, weighing 8 stone.[72]

Age was another decisive factor in the enlistment process, and a common reason for refusal. At the beginning of the First World War recruits for the British Army had to be between 19 and 35, the latter being an increase of five years from the standard regulations in peacetime. In *Boy Soldiers*, van Emden argues that the patriotic excitement encouraged many young men to risk prosecution and lie about their age to gain entry into the military.[73] Boys as young as 12 attempted to enlist, with around 250,000 under 18-year-old recruits estimated to have served between 1914 and 1918.[74] Not all were successful and the repercussions for attempting it were varied. Under the age of 18, the future Private Mullis faced the wrath of a shrewd sergeant who quickly rejected Mullis's youthful appearance as he tried to enlist at the local territorial battalion, the 20th London Regiment, on Blackheath.

> Entering nervously, I found myself in a large room where were dozens of men in various states of nudity awaiting their medical examination. I was approached by a large red-faced man in uniform. 'what do you want?' he demanded. Timidly I said that I had come to join up. 'get out' he roared. 'we don't want boys of 12 in here.' My first attempt to join the army thus ended ignominiously. I was just one month past my 18th birthday.[75]

Mullis had just turned 18, and this would be the first of several unsuccessful attempts to enlist before finally being accepted as part of the Derby scheme in 1915. This belittling of the eager recruit is not an uncommon event as would-be soldiers found their masculinity questioned and ridiculed as they attempted to enlist. Private Brady lamented in his private papers that 'it was quite obvious we were not being viewed by outsiders as we saw ourselves' after being loudly humiliated by another recruitment sergeant who took exception to his youthful visage and yelled, 'Why don't you two lads bugger off home and tell your mother to change your nappies?'[76] Evidently, Brady and the sergeant held very different views over the presentation of Brady's body. Determined to enlist Brady clearly considered himself a potential soldier, capable and worthy of service. However, the sergeant perceived him, through immediate consideration of his physical body, as a child, too young and inexperienced and completely physically unsuitable for war. Brady's humiliation illustrates the common questioning of an individual's masculinity through the gaze of his physical suitability. Faced by the loud brash sergeant, neither Brady nor his friend contested their banishment, instead turning tail and leaving. This submissive behaviour reinforces the physically influenced summation made by the sergeant and explains the contrast in the underlying perception that was commonly held of soldiers being 'men' and rejects as 'boys'.

However, these barriers were by no means absolute as many men were successful at skirting the regulations once they understood how to beat the system. Belfast-born David Starrett recalled being declined at first glance for being underage as he attempted to join the Ulster Volunteer Force in August 1914, but used his inside knowledge to try again, this time, successfully.

> Down I went with the boys, to stand outside all day long. At long last it came my turn to go in, and I got short shrift. 'Well boy, what is your age?' 'sixteen years, sir', 'underage, son: next please.' I could hardly believe I was turned down, but I tried again some days later, with the same fate. Determined to get into the army by hook or by crook I hung round that recruiting office all hours. On the 11th of September, I spotted a change of staff within, so had another go. I was expecting to hear 'get out son, and come back later', 'when the new officer looked me up and down, but instead he says: 'name?' 'David Starrett, sir' 'age?' 'Nineteen years, Sir.' My! I had the face of brass. And it worked. He reached me a paper. 'doctor' he said, and away I went to the other room. 'Take your clothes off, boy' said the doctor. When I was stripped, he caught hold of me in the way old soldiers know. 'cough' he says. I coughed like the shipyard knock of siren. 'enough' he said, 'orderly, pass this man A.I.' So, inside an hour I was a soldier and got a railway voucher and orders to proceed to Donard [sic] Camp.[77]

The filtering process was not always identical from officer to officer, nor was it infallible. The standard enlistment form reiterates this idiosyncrasy as it asked for 'apparent age' rather than 'age'. Within this simple phrase lay significant fluidity for granting leniency at the discretion of recruiting staff. While new recruits were officially mandated to provide printed evidence of their age, accounts such as Starrett's demonstrate that such aspects could be overlooked as recruiting officials judged men on their appearance rather than official paperwork. This subversion of the rules could work both ways, allowing some underage men entrance, while denying others cursed/blessed with a youthful appearance and without formal proof of their eligibility. Silbey argues that the process of medical assessment was extensively flexible as officials and the potential recruits cooperated and collaborated to assist men in obtaining the result they desired.[78] Private Calverley was another eager underage recruit who successfully flaunted the rules to negotiate his entrance into the army. He confessed in his memoirs: 'I got away with my height measurement by cheating a little and the question of my birth certificate arose. I told the officer it had been lost, and though I do not think that he believed me he appeared to do so outwardly, and I was accepted.'[79]

Although old enough, Private Styles encountered a different issue as his physique gave the medical assessor cause to dither over his suitability. His success at enlistment was only achieved through a combination of a relaxed attitude to his ineligibility and the impatience of another officer for his lunch: 'another doctor came in and he wanted his lunch and he asked, "what was the trouble?" When the first doctor said "20 & 20", of course, I didn't understand, he said "oh he'll do" so my papers were signed A.1. Sometime later I had trouble when examined.'[80] This sentiment of 'he'll do' was not uncommon, as the need for men was ever prevalent, and the combination of reward for accepting men and the eagerness of many who enlisted in the opening stages of war combined with what Jay Winter regarded as a laissez-faire approach.[81] Private Butler passed the medical in 1915 despite being half an inch short of the height requirement. The Regimental Quarter Master who had assessed him seemed to part reassured himself and part Butler as he declared, 'You're young, probably you'll grow the other half inch. Anyway, we'll take you on.'[82] The consequences of these deliberate decisions were not always lost on the men who made them. Private Mullis's break into the military came with a reassuring comment from his assessor that he would either die or physically improve as a result of his experiences in the army: 'The two officials sought to appease their consciences as they devised a scheme to pass me: anyway, I was measured and medically examined, the doctor reluctantly passing me with the encouraging remark that "it will either kill you or make a man out of you."'[83] This necessity to salve the conscience was not uncommon according to Bourke as throughout the First World War the National Service Medical Boards frequently passed unfit men through assessment with the assurance that training would improve their deficiencies.[84] Men's bodies during enlistment were therefore not only viewed in their current state but also assessed for their potential to improve, their bodies being regarded as malleable sites from which the British Army could synthesize effective soldiers. Promises of eventual improvement were commonplace, such as that made to Private Buffey, who was advised by his medical officer that the arduous training would improve his body and that a 'few weeks of gym and square drill we would become perfect gladiators'.[85] In reality, criticism of the War Office and Army Council arose in 1915 as men passed as grade A at enlistment were subsequently being discharged from training due to physical unsuitability.[86] An internal war memo from September 1915 claimed that 245,457 men were discharged after enlistment having failed to adapt to the physical hardship of training. Silbey explains that haphazard medical assessments during the early stages of the war received the blame for these unsuitable recruits, with 60 per cent of them being redirected to undertake critical war industries.[87] This led to a tightening of physical assessment protocols and continual questions over the practice of mass enlistment and assessment. A glaring issue within the process was the reward system which provided financial renumeration to recruiting staff for the number of men cleared into service. At the outbreak of the war both the sergeant and the civilian medical officer received a 'capitation fee' of two shillings and sixpence for each man who cleared the recruitment process. After complaints and concerns arose surrounding the clearance of unsuitable men for personal profit this financial reward system steadily decreased. By 1916 recruiting staff were paid only one shilling for a successful applicant and, as an extra measure of correct assessment, medical officers were restricted to assessing only forty men a day.[88]

Despite the seemingly vast opportunities for deception, negotiation and sheer luck, many men still failed to enter the army as a result of their identifiable physical insufficiencies. Lieutenant Palmer was one such man, so desperate to enlist that it was only after twenty-seven attempts that he was finally accepted into the RAMC.

> Each time I had tried to enlist and I stood on the scales prior to going before the doctor for medical examination; the soldier or civilian weighing me, took a look as I stood on the scales and invariably said that I was a fine-looking chap and the army need men of my physique; it was all very set to me but after this had happened several times it got a bit boring because I guessed what the doctor would do with me. I am some six feet in height and then weighed about 12, ½ stones and I had a chest expansion of thirty-four inches. I was a fair athlete and had played many games with success and I consequently took a poor view of being rejected each time I tried to enlist; I certainly did not look the part of an unfit man and so I worked on the principle of if at first you don't succeed, try, try and try again.[89]

Physically, Palmer failed to meet the requirements of the assessment. On paper, his height, weight and chest all met requirement but beneath the exterior Palmer suffered from a hernia and poor eyesight. Palmer and his assessors yet again perceived the applicant's body very differently. At first glance the officials tended to agree with Palmer's belief that his body was fit for service. It was only through further investigation that these opinions deviated as the assessors located the physical flaws that precluded him from service. R. McKay was also rejected but, in his case, it was his lack of teeth that counted against him as he attempted to enlist at the Brunswick street Dublin recruiting office, intending to join the Royal Inniskilling Fusiliers: 'After a cursory glance into my mouth, he told me I wouldn't do as I had bad teeth. As a matter of fact, I had no bad teeth as all these had been removed before I entered college.'[90] Andrew Robertshaw explains that the state of a man's teeth had been a primary focus of military recruitment since the introduction of the 1890 General Regulations. Strong teeth were essential because a large part of a soldier's emergency rations contained the practically inedible hard tack, which men with poor teeth would be unable to eat.[91] Kochhar clarifies this by demonstrating that the British Army also had offered little provision for dentistry, at least up until the First World War. This has been a significant aspect of the monumental disregard of so many men during the Last South African War as five thousand men had been rejected for enlistment as a result of having poor dental health.[92] During the First World War, however, the needs of the war effort overrode concerns over physical suitability. Again, the regulations proved flexible and in 1915, the allowances were made for men if the cost to improve the man's teeth came to no more than £3.[93] On 26 August 1916 teeth and exclusion for service was raised as an issue in parliament by the Member of Parliament for Wednesbury; yet his concerns were dismissed as he was reassured by the Secretary for War that very few men had been refused for poor teeth and that any such men who were refused were so on the basis of malnutrition, indicating a greater physical deficiency, as opposed to the strength of their teeth alone.[94]

Attempts to circumvent the issue of physicality-related rejection increasingly occurred throughout the First World War, as men's bodies were deemed simultaneously more valuable in terms of presence on the battlefield, and less valuable according to the state of health in which they were permitted to enter service. Between 1914 and 1918 physical standards for military service in Britain were continually under scrutiny and review and ultimately subject to flux and requirement. In 1914, unsatisfactory teeth were enough to deny a man enlistment, and by 1916, this fault in the body of the recruit was to be corrected or ignored, rather than provide a reason for rejection. Lieutenant Creek was one such man whose teeth had marked him as borderline at enlistment. He was allowed entry under the condition that he immediately receive corrective dental work, a reiteration of the claims of the Secretary of War in Parliament.[95] Creek recounted in his memoirs that while officially he was dispatched for treatment, he instead was directed to his training camp before promptly being sent to the front not too long after, his dental issues forgotten.[96] Evidently, the enlistment process bore less significance once the new soldier had been turned over to the care of his trainers and commanding officers.

Despite all the negotiation, deception and nervous moments, for the most part these experiences remained the exception rather than rule as many men easily passed their enlistment assessment as suitably fit and advanced on to their new military career. Private Williams, of the 7th East Yorkshire Regiment, barely mentions his enlistment experience in his oral history interview saying only that 'all four of us passed' before moving on to describe in detail to discuss the more relevant experiences in training'.[97] Private Warsop also expressed no difficulties as he joined the 'Robin Hoods' (7th Reserve Battalion). Apparently for Warsop entry was easy, yet again a focus, or indeed lack of focus, on the body proved to be advantage. He exclaimed in his memoirs that assessment was particularly lax due to the sheer desperation for men on the front line, 'I went to enlist on march 15th, my twentieth birthday and they passed as fit anyone who could walk up to the office.'[98] For some the enlistment was certainly a titanic traumatic struggle where their bodies and value to society was surmised as the enlistee held their breath. However, for men such as Warsop and Williams, it was a straightforward affair and inconsequential footnote in their larger recollection of their time in service.

Conclusion

> I was called first as I went in I met a dejected or rather a rejected chap coming out and believe it or not, he had tears in his eyes as he passed me and he furtively whispered to me, saying 'Gosh! He's keen, he's failed me. Says I have got fallen arches.' Perhaps in later circumstances, his poor feet were a godsend to him and kept him out of the wr [sic].[99]

As the above tale from the account of Private Buffey reiterates, enlistment was a complicated, ever-changing and, in some cases, almost cartoonish experience for many men during the First World War. This was a chaotic process within which the body remained at the centre of a decision-making process which would have severe ramifications. In the early stages of the First World War the body was central to the strategies by the government and military authorities to encourage enlistment. The promise of food and lodging was an attractive one to many who, at this time, lived without the comforts of regular food, a varied diet and a decent bed. Yet, recruitment strategies were even more complex than that as visual and written propaganda directly linked the ideal of British manhood to the undertaking of uniformed service. To pass the examination and to enter the armed forces was a private and public confirmation of an enlistee's masculinity. As a result, failure to be accepted could be devastating, as the rejection transcended a simple inability to join up but communicated to the rest of society a defect in the individual's body, causing their masculinity patriotism to come under question. Rejection also risked association with those who were seeking to avoid service or who were conscientious objectors, yet again social pariahs ostracized by an exceptionally militarized society. The normalization of these messages is apparent within the evidence presented as wider society were keen to, or were actively encouraged to, endorse these assessments. The instances where women doled out white feathers stand at the extreme end of the ways in which society policed those not in uniform, but it does clarify and justify the rationale behind the complex reasons men rushed to enlist. It also explains the remarkable persistence of many who remained determined to do so despite repeated rejections, and the decisions of those who adjusted and enhanced their bodies in advance of the medical examinations.

Of course, this chapter has also shown that between 1914 and 1918 the precise nature of the ideal military body changed. The rush to serve in 1914 meant that the authorities could set high standards and insist upon them in those they admitted to the ranks. But as the demand for troops continued, alterations were made to the height, age and physical ability requirements for enlistment so that those initially considered 'unfit' could suddenly find themselves meeting the ideal despite very little effort on their part. If the ideal British body was in fact a concept that the authorities shifted and redefined as the conflict went on it was often also unstable because of the room for negotiation and collusion in the enlistment process itself. The 'he'll do' outcome of the medical examination quoted in this chapter points to the incredible amount of room within the assessments for local decisions and where strict requirements could be ignored or manipulated. Many men found out that the ideal British military body over the course of the First World War was a malleable concept and used it to their advantage. For those who were successful at navigating the enlistment process this was the point where their body first fell under the control of the British Army.

2

Forging bodies: Training and creating soldiers

Beyond the first hurdle of assessment, the enlistees, volunteers and conscripts fell under their first official military command as they entered basic training. Initially the eager volunteers formed the basis of the five hundred new active and reserve battalion branded as the New Armies in late 1914 where the men underwent a stringent training period in preparation for their experiences abroad.[1] This physically gruelling programme included army staples such as drill, parade and basic combat. After three months of physical improvement, the trainees then progressed to the development of specialist skills ranging from training as bombardiers, machine gunners and scouts to learning the expertise of sappers, engineers and drivers.[2] Throughout the experience their bodies were constantly challenged, changed and conditioned for the conflict awaiting for them abroad. With the pressures of the war mounting and the need for men becoming more urgent it was not only the entry requirements that proved flexible. The introduction of conscription in 1916 was accompanied with a streamlining of the training process. This shortened version proved to be erratic as, governed by the turn of the war, some men were trained and dispatched within three months, while others remained for in camp for over five. Stating that all men received the same level of training would be untrue. Without doubt the late arrivals from 1916 onwards, while more aware of what they would be facing, were certainly less prepared when they took the field than their predecessors had been two years previous. Nevertheless, all men experienced similar aspects of training with the purpose of transforming their bodies for purpose of combat and military direction.[3] It is this focus on physical improvement that is the basis of this chapter as it follows the experiences of the training men as their bodies were conditioned and transformed for the purpose of service. Training was designed to prepare and improve men's bodies for service, while also indoctrinating and conditioning their minds for military obedience and active combat. Unquestionably, the body was the primary focus within the British Army's strategy of transforming civilians into soldiers. This chapter therefore examines the ramifications of this strategy by exploring the experiences of men who both loved and loathed their tenure under the command of training officers.

Everybody at once

While the methods and ways of conditioning the male body for combat between 1914 and 1918 were multifaceted, at the basic level the primary programme remained the same throughout the war. The *Special & Supplementary Tables for Physical Training* pamphlet, which was distributed and widely used as part of basic training by the British Army in 1916, clearly outlined the physically transformative and psychological conditioning objectives of the new soldier's introductory training. It began by clarifying that 'Physical Training should be regarded as the foundation of all training', before espousing the apparent benefits of training upon the male body.

1. Strengthening of the body = Power to overcome obstacles and perform arduous duties.
2. Improvement and maintenance of health = Endurance of hardships and privations.
3. Quickening of the brain = More rapid assimilation of instruction in other training, orders readily understood and rapidly executed.
4. Increase of power of mental concentration = The foundation of good shooting.[4]

This was the basis of all training regimes that training men underwent after the British declaration of war in August 1914. However, it is fair to say that the training arm of the British military began with something of a false start as it immediately floundered, inundated with eager enlistees determined to join the fight. Almost immediately the previous training process collapsed as barracks and training facilities proved unable to accommodate the onslaught. Simkins explains how the British military struggled to adapt to the sudden onslaught of enlistees having only recruited an average 29,626 recruits into the British Army annually between 1908 and 1914.[5] From the start of war in July to the end of September 1914, over 761,000 men had joined up. Completely overwhelmed, the British military soon attracted widespread criticism as men were forced to live in tents, overcrowded barracks and even commute from home or private accommodations. Immediately, the private physical luxuries of civilian life were lost for many men as their living environments were replaced by functional communal billets often accompanied by a loss of privacy, security and comfort. Within his diary, Private Milner recounted how comfort and individual privacy were low priorities in the face of the task of being battle ready as quickly as possible in 1914. He explained, 'There was no official concern for creature comforts – the only thing that seemed to matter was to maintain a man in health and strength and train him to be proficient with a number of weapons.'[6] Private Parks came to the same conclusion several years later, as he sardonically described his morning routine in a letter to his daughters in 1917.

> The trumpet call awakes us in the morning at 6 o clock ... when you open your eyes you see some very funny sights – right opposite me this morning the first thing I noticed was a big ugly dirt & stained pair of feet projecting from a very small bed. Most of our men are very tall & when they pull their dirty blanket round their shoulders, they expose their feet. ... then you will see another man

sitting up in bed half scratching his head & some of them scratching their --- well never mind what.⁷

Within both accounts, it is noticeable that the men describe their initial experiences from a particularly physical perspective. Training was an exceptionally physical experience, where much was done to, on or drawn from the body of the enlistee. Exposure, forced intimacy, itchiness and overcrowding feature in countless recollections from the First World War, often together with complaints of fellows with questionable hygiene and personal physical discomfort. These complaints about the men's bodies' first experiences within military service would become recurrent laments throughout the war as for many their living situations continued to decline.

Another complaint was about the uniform-sized beds and blankets with humorous comments about bare appendages and exposed feet again common within soldier's narratives. These illustrate the integral experiences of uniformity, as the identical amenities were designed and assigned without consideration of the individual physical idiosyncrasies of the men they were meant for. Unquestionably, the British military were not able to tailor the equipment and conditions to the unique needs of all the men, nor was there any intention to do so. One of the primary aspects of the initial training was to establish cohesion with the men around them. British military training reinforced uniformity in both a psychological and physical sense, starting with acclimatization to the close proximity of other within the uncomfortable living quarters that many found miserable.

Unfortunately, scratched genitals, uniform-sized beds and dirty feet were the least of Lieutenant Minnitt's concerns during his first night in the barracks in February 1916.

> The first night in the overcrowded barracks was horrible. Huge 12-gallon buckets were placed at intervals down the centre of the building, and drunks were coming in at all hours of the night. Fellows who wanted to use the latrines were constantly falling over sleeping figures, the lights all being out, and the language and the resulting mess was enough to put any decent fellow against the army forever.⁸

Minnitt was alarmed not only by the loss of control of body in regards to his new cramped communal living but also at the lack of control by other men over their own bodies as they incapacitated themselves with alcohol, or failed to adopt the level of decorum that Minnitt expected of his fellow recruits. Still, Minnitt, Milner and Parks were more fortunate than many as some recruits did not even have a bed. Private Rickett complained in his diary that he spent his early training days sleeping on a hard floor. He wrote, 'I went into billets, if you could call them as much. It was in a hotel in some empty rooms where we had to sleep on the floor with only to [*sic*] blankets to sleep on.'⁹ The jury remains out on which would have been more comfortable, an overcrowded barrack room with a lacklustre straw mattress or a patch of floor in a shared hotel room; still neither experience was obviously in keeping with the expectations of the new recruits. Private Jones and his friend were not even issued with a bed as they were instructed to sleep outside until the billeting situation had been resolved.¹⁰ Yet again, negotiation and subversion provided a solution against the military instructions as the men bonded with the guard officers and were offered to bunk down in their barracks using a floor mattress until they could be transferred to another regiment.

One of the promises that the posters, propaganda and recruiting sergeants had gushed about was the opportunity for decent lodgings. Once through the gate, for many men the truth of their military existence, devoid of such comforts, became a disheartening reality. Yet, billeting experiences varied considerably and it was not doom and gloom for all new recruits. In the very early days of the war some men were assigned accommodation outside of the training camps either at home or given an allowance to find alternative lodgings. Those who found themselves with this dilemma could at least balance their disappointment at the introductory stages of military life with significantly nicer lodgings. As a recruit into the Army Pay Corps (APC) in October 1914 Private G. Cotton had a much more comfortable experience as he was put up in a hotel complete with board.[11]

Not all were quite as lucky as Cotton; nevertheless, some new recruits embraced the squalor of their temporary surrounds as another formative aspect in the readying of their bodies for war. Lieutenant North's poetic description of his discomfort provides evidence for this viewpoint as he drew strength from his forced intimacy with other men: 'In spite of the rough nature of our beds, we let our spirits soar above our discomforts.'[12] Similar to the obtaining of the uniform, for many the simple novelty of bedding down in an official military installation represented a badge of honour and process of self-actualization central to their training. Private Herbert Smith's relocation into a regimental barracks clarified as much for him as he claimed that he was ever growing closer to becoming a soldier and wrote proudly, 'Here we were in barrack-rooms and I can tell you we felt quite proud of ourselves being able to sleep in better surroundings.'[13] Yet, these accounts are often overshadowed by the frustration of the many men forced to sleep on the ground or in overcrowded bunkrooms. The official introduction into actual military life was for many new recruits a sobering and somewhat disappointing experience. As the war progressed and the stream of recruits entering service steadily matched the British militaries' ability to cater for them, much of these temporary measures were rendered redundant; however, this is not to argue that for the duration of the war training men did not receive a shock as the comforts of their civilian lives were stripped away as part of the training process.

The realities of military existence proved to be removal from their homes and comforts to be dispatched to new destinations where sleeping, dressing, washing and eating were suddenly, and often shockingly, communal. As these men first entered the uniformity of military life, they each paradoxically experienced it from inimitable perspective. While some balked at the forced intimacy and initial discomfort, others were thrilled by the sense of shared camaraderie and the formative element of habitual physical uniformity that would remain a staple of their career in the military.

Dressed to kill

As noted, one of the most fundamental aspects of formalized military training is the internalization of uniformity. Tynan argues that '[the standardization of] practices like washing and grooming presented bodies under control'.[14] This was a particularly effective way of instilling total obedience to military discipline, as every hair on the soldier's body fell under the control of British military. The lengths to which this would be enforced were extensive and included physical inspections, rebukes by commanding officers and even forced hygiene activities that could be regarded as unnecessary. Richard van Emden clarifies this overarching form of physical control within the army by quoting a humorous account of one man who was forced into shaving his pristinely smooth chin: 'One morning, I was asked by the sergeant when I shaved last. This was rather embarrassing as I had to tell him I had not started to shave yet. I only had soft hair on my face, but I got the order to "get a shave". Hence my first attempt with a cut-throat razor.'[15] The experience of the fifteen-year volunteer reiterates the ways in which the military hierarchy attempted to assume total control of the newly militarized bodies, not to mention a restatement of the leniency that was practiced within the entrance assessments considered in Chapter 1.

Regardless of the necessity for a shave, tradition and rules combined under Command No. 1,695 of the official regulations which demanded that the 'the hair of the head will be kept short. The chin and the under-lip will be shaved, but not the upper lip.'[16] Like many seemingly odd and absurd aspects of military life the undertaking of the task was not particularly practical for the trainee but it was formative as it reaffirmed the loss of individual agency while also acclimatizing men to undertake bodily acts publicly within an alien shared living space. For Private McKay, communal shaving was a source of amusement and fascination. To his astonishment, his bunkmate shaved unashamedly in public, without a mirror and while wandering around.[17] Impressed despite the absurdity of his current living situation, McKay's recollection of the conditions during his training reiterates how quickly men were forced to adapt from their private bodily habits to communal spectacles.

The demand for physical uniformity also extended to hairstyles.[18] In contrast to his excitement to enlist, Private Buffey suffered the loss of hair as a trauma comparable to the battles he would later endure.

> The inevitable hair cut was our next ordeal, but it was going to be no ordeal to me. An old seat had put me wise and told me that if I didn't want a prison cut I was to drop the Napy twopence [sic]. Gosh, what a shock I got when I viewed the hairdresser's handiwork through the mirror. I was nearly bald. I could understand how Samson felt after Delilah had shorn him.[19]

Even an effective way of removing physical differences, the cropping of the hair proved to be final straw for several men as they acclimatized to military service. Private Copson was incensed that the army now had complete control over his physical appearance after he was conscripted in 1917. He bitterly referred to his new hairstyle as a 'prison crop' – something he considered to be a marker of his lost physical autonomy.[20]

However, it is difficult to argue with success. Once shorn and shaved, the physical distinctive traits that had singled out men from one another began to dissipate. Yet, Buffey's attempt to retain his physical presentation by subverting the will of the military and bribing the barber implies that the loss of individuality and agency was not given up gracefully. Moreover, Buffey apparently got the tip from an experienced soldier implying a tradition of bucking authority that transcended the New Armies. Tynan argues that 'grooming habits could draw attention to the body as a focus on management and control'.[21] However, this shared conspiracy of subterfuge reiterates that control was not absolute and that resistance remained, inherent in the experience of soldiers new and old. Evidently, even after years of indoctrinated service and conditioning it was clear that the individual could still retain aspects of autonomy in spite of the efforts of the British military.

Within training, the presentation of the body as a militarized asset was essential. Accompanying the adoption of a unified sanitary regimen was the military uniform, which many had already received before entering their training accommodation. As was the case with the newly enlisted men desperate to get into khaki, Tynan argues that many men only felt like soldiers once they were in uniform and that the clothing of the body appropriately was essential in the establishment of the masculine identity of the soldier.[22] In 1914, having entered at officer level, the newly enlisted Second Lieutenant Carter of the Kitchener Army 7th Hull battalion was dismayed as the state of the men on parade with him was far from the idealized specimens of soldiers he had evidently expected:

> Twenty-four hours after enlisting, I was on parade with other recruits, all in civilian clothes, wearing an armband and carrying a rifle. In those days, everyone wore a hat of some kind. Some had caps, some trilbies, and some bowlers. Some wore macs and everyone was wearing a collar and tie. Our instructor was a restored regular sergeant and if he shouted 'Form fours' once he shouted it and all the other elementary movements a thousand times.[23]

Carter was immediately disenchanted by the reality of his service, though things soon improved as in November Carter's training platoon were finally supplied with uniforms, weapons and greatcoats. Carter's elation at being issued with his official uniform is obvious, as he made the distinction between civilian and military life: 'We were real soldiers and all class distinctions were gone forever.'[24] For men like Carter, acting like a soldier was not enough. Only once the men found their bodies appropriately clothed, and often held the rifle in their hands, did the transformation solidify in their self-perception.

Unfortunately, for such men, Carter was one of many whose early career as a soldier was without a uniform, namely because the British Army was so totally unprepared to equip so many new recruits. To meet the demand initially, spare uniform was taken from regulars for new recruits. Regular soldier Keller recalled in his memoirs having much of his kit taken despite having paid for it out of his own pocket.[25] This demonstrates that the overarching priority to field more men as quickly as possible overtook precautions to ensure the existing men were fully equipped. This 'robbing Peter, to pay Paul' approach also indicates the lack of consideration for individuality between the recruits as the clothes they acquired and reissued were never tailored for the new recipient. For the British Army, the pressures of the war meant often that 'one size fits all' as comfort and practicality gave way to uniformity and a mass production line of combat-ready men.

While presentation of the body in uniform was for many an actualizing experience, for many as part of their transition into the role of a soldier, their physical experience of wearing their uniform was just as formative. Rather than dressing the part, the physical discomfort of the untailored woollen khaki was not the spectacular transformation that many expected. In his memoirs Private Milner grumbled, 'A very awkward squad we must have looked in our new and ill-fitting uniform.'[26] Some men's physical discomfort went beyond itches and chaffing. Early into the war Private Clark recalled how his new uncomfortable footwear actually damaged his body as he trained with the Hampshire regiment: 'We went up to Winchester first and had our hair cut off and got these great big boots that, after wearing light shoes, your feet used to get right sore when you were on marches.'[27] Paradoxically, the clothing that had been provided to enable men to fight and serve initially damaged their bodies as part of the 'toughening up' process of early-stage indoctrination. Private Barraclough found his new uniform immediately problematic and developed an immediate and intense dislike for his 'dreadful puttees'.[28] Barraclough was certainly not alone; Private Buffey in 1915 also found his uniform confusing, mystified by the sheer amount of clothing he was expected to wear and carry. He wrote in his memoirs, 'We were truly flabbergasted by the amount of kit we drew. There was so much that I, who only had but one suit in civy [sic] street, thought I shall never get around to wearing it all but eventually I did.'[29] Regardless of his confusion, Buffey at least illustrated that some of the recruitment patter claimed by recruiting sergeants around the country was true. The armed forces certainly seemed to provide men like Buffey greater access to clothing than they had previously. Still, the men above may have considered themselves lucky, as not that all men received a khaki uniform when they first enlisted.

Instead, as a result of the mass enlistment a temporary blue alternative, dubbed the 'Kitchener Blue', was introduced to clothe the large numbers of volunteers who enlisted in 1914. Prior to the war khaki dye had been imported from Germany; with tensions being significantly less than cordial in 1914, an alternative was sought, in a much more obtainable blue until the British could synthesize their own khaki dye.[30] This meant that in September 1914, Private Donald Murray, who enlisted into the 8th Battalion King's Own Yorkshire Light Infant, like many men began his training in the widely disliked Kitchener blues which were a far cry from the promises of the enthusiastic recruitment sergeants.

You have never seen Kitchener's uniforms; you should have seen it. It was blue serge, with blue borne [sic] buttons down the front, for all the world like a convict and we were all on parade in our rags one day and the colonel was on his horse in front and he says, 'fall out all the men with bad clothes' and I thought 'I'm stopping where I am because I want to see what it looks like', so a lot of them fell out and when they came back and we just rolled about laughing. They looked for all the world like a lot of convicts rolling out to do their day's stint you know. However, eventually we had to have one of these uniforms, but to make them all look a little better, they issued us all with brass buttons, we could sew them on ourselves, soldier's buttons you know and a little pink cap with one side with little buttons on and that started our training.[31]

Comparing his new uniform to that of a convict twice, Murray reiterated within his memoir just how important it was for many men during the early stages of training to regard themselves as soldiers. This was a combined physical and psychological experience within which the uniform played a key part in helping men actualize into the role through the presentation of their bodies. Private Johnston also detested the 'hated blue convict-style' uniform having joined in September 1914 and later complained bitterly about the lack of equipment available. He lamented, 'The Battalion presented a rather motley appearance on parade. Apart from the uniforms, there were only 200 or so rifles between us, the rest having pieces of wood shaped like rifles for drill purposes.'[32] Ill-equipped, lacking key amenities and dressed in cast-offs or a hurried dye job, it is unsurprising that the first physical experiences of military life for many men came as a disappointment. Peter Simkins explains that dislike for the uniform led to its comparison to that of a postman and that some regiments such as 19th Manchesters (4th City Battalion) were subject to taunts as a result of their appearance.[33] This resentment did not go unnoticed, as the disquiet was obviously perceptible for the British military as they distributed of shiny brass buttons for the training men to attach to their uniforms, in an attempt to instil pride in their attire. While these buttons held no tactical value, the act of sewing on a button implied ownership of the garment while also ostensibly confirming the respect the British military held for the New Army men as soldiers.

The association between Kitchener blues and an image of a prisoner rather than patriotic hero indicates just how important uniform often was to the men who had enlisted. Many had been sold on the idea of khaki as the colour of the national hero, and to find themselves clothed in a way that made them look more like criminals and convicts caused much initial resentment. It is important to note of course that not all trainees were as critical. Private Smith claimed that his blue uniform made him 'feel like a soldier' and Private Whitehouse adored his new attire, explaining, 'It was essential to be fully dressed in full blue uniform, complete with gloves and whip wearing spurs before leaving barracks. I was very proud of my uniform in those early days.'[34] Their enthusiasm to be re-clothed in martial dress, regardless of the colour, was shared by many, as although the wrong colour the uniform was still a badge of status and responsibility. Regardless of the love or loathing for the new uniforms, it is indisputable that physical appearance and bodily experiences in the earliest days of training were particularly formative for both the training men and military authorities.

Food and feeding

Another staple of the recruitment speeches was the promise of a good meal. Food had been a key aspect of a soldier's life for centuries. Recognition of the role food played in enabling men to fight and conduct their duties led to an overhaul of the British military diet at the turn of the twentieth century. Rachel Duffett, Anthony Clayton and Andrew Robertshaw have separately discussed the focus of food and diet within the military as attempts were continually made to keep the men fit and healthy.[35] Duffett argues that 'food was the site of complex and, it must be said, frequently contradictory, emotional responses: for many soldiers, it represented the best and worst of times'.³⁶ Certainly, food makes up much of the narrative within soldier's letters, testimonies and memoirs. Yet, there is still much to consider regarding the impact of food on the body as it was controlled under military rule. After the disastrous recruitment campaign in South Africa between 1899 and 1902 where the health of the nation had been laid bare for all to see by the high enlistment rejection rate, there was a significant focus on the diet of soldiers, and indeed the British population as a whole. This was also encouraged by the growing focus upon the links between physical health and nutrition as part of the rapid medicalization of the late nineteenth century. As Haldane had instigated his reforms to overhaul the British Army, much was also done to improve the daily life and physical health of the common soldier, including a change to diet and food.³⁷

In 1909 the Committee on Physiological Effects of Food, Training, and Clothing on the Soldier published its third extensive report on the role of food within the military in the Journal of the Royal Army Medical Corps (JRAMC).³⁸ Within this twelve-page analysis it was argued that that food was 'absolutely necessary for the maintenance of health and vigour, and for the supply of energy during the performance of muscular work'.³⁹ Focusing heavily on the amount of calories men required to endure the physical constraints of soldiering, the report surmised that weak undernourished men were ineffectual soldiers.⁴⁰ Somewhat revolutionary for the time, the report demanded that a diet varied and rich in energy-providing foods such as fresh meat and vegetables was essential. Tinned food, a staple of the mobilized soldier's diet, was criticized for having a low nutritional but high fat content.⁴¹ Tinned food also had a propensity to spoil or become contaminated as a result of the canning process which further endangered the effective military body during service. Alfred Keogh, twice director general of the Army Medical Services, described the work of the committee at the time as being crucial in the creation of the healthy and strong soldier.⁴² These measures all combined to provide the fighting man at the beginning of the First World War a substantial and nutrition-laden focused diet, designed above all else to ensure his physical efficacy and ability on the front line.

At the peak of this dietary ideal in 1914 soldiers were recommended to ingest 4,200 calories per day.⁴³ This included 1 lb 4 oz of meat and 1 lb 4 oz of bread, 3 oz of sugar, 4 oz of bacon, 3 oz of cheese and 8 oz. of vegetables.⁴⁴ As the war progressed, these requirements became increasingly difficult to fulfil. Within the 1915 *British Army Manual for Military Cooking and Dietary* sample menus for soldiers advised significantly less proportions than were outlined at the start of the war. Within the seventeen daily menus for cooks to prepare for one hundred men at a time the amount of meat allocated per man ranged from 1 lb 4 oz to 0.6 oz.⁴⁵ All but two of the menus fell short of the regulated amount of meat. Often, Bacon was substituted for the lack of other meat; however, with the average per man being less than two pieces of bacon, these menus still fell significantly under the prescribed amount. Opposingly, sugar remained consistent at around 0.9 lb per man per menu, as did bread, which was noted simply as 'as required' and present in every menu.⁴⁶ As shortages escalated and underlying grumbling increased as meat allocations further fell, it fell to Captain Basil Williams to publicly defend the reduction of rations. In 1917, Williams publicly released a comprehensive report that clarified that the initial allowance of certain food stuffs, especially meat, was considered excessive and harmful to the bodies of serving soldiers and had therefore led to a revision of allowances.[47] Williams explained that as a result of these requirements, 'the meat ration was reduced, and instruction handbooks for the systematic handling of the soldier's ration were issued to all units of the new armies, which had the effect of improving the soldier's diet as well as reducing its cost'.[48] While this may have improved the bodies of the men in service, it certainly did not improve their morale or make Williams any friends across the battlefields and training grounds.

Food quantities were not the only underlying issue as almost from the very start of the war; complaints echoed across the training camps about the quality of the sustenance the men were presented with. Lieutenant Bernard Minnitt's rude awakening to the difference between his civilian and military life came not because of his accommodation but at the horror that met him in the mess hall in 1914.

> A few words about that tea, never to be forgotten. The tea was served in a huge hall, on long grease covered tables, seating some twelve men on benches each side of the table. Having been issued with a plate, cutlery, and a large, blue-striped basin, we watched some rather scruffy looking old soldiers (nicknamed 'Old Sweats') come in carrying lard boxes, unwashed, full of inch-thick slices of bread. Going to the head of each table, a grimy hand clutched a handful of bread, which was slung down the table with the remark, 'Help yourselves, boys.' This was followed by other men carrying a box each of butter, in balls as big as a cricket ball. These were <u>rolled</u> down the table, and a request made to pass your basins up for the tea. The basins were dipped into the tea and were then passed down the table, dripping tea on route. This so disgusted us, most of whom were used to clean tablecloths, etc. at their homes, that a general complaint ensued. One lad, whose father was an M.P. in Nottingham, was the means by which we got the 'Old Sweats' shifted, after which we took turns to serve, scrub the tables, and clean the place.[49]

Minnitt's experience remained permanently etched into his memory. Interestingly, the dichotomy that Minnitt and his trainee colleagues faced between their old and new roles brought about a clash resulting in the men employ uncharacteristic levels of agency and influence for the typical soldier to change their environment for the better.

Yet, most of the men who 'enjoyed' such meals were not officers and lacked the power, opportunity and financial means to improve their menus. Unlike Minnitt, Charles George Templer was a successful businessman who entered in 1916 as a private into the 13th Battalion Gloucestershire Regiment. His fondness for sport and physical activity did little to compensate for his disappointment over the food on offer and as he trained at Malvern camp he gave voice to the rumour that the 'cooks were flogging the best meat to local tradesmen'.[50] Templer's disgust for the cuisine was shared by many within the training camp, and the not uncommon divide between the infantry men and the support services ultimately led to a campwide disturbance in protest.[51] Evidently within training there was often a discrepancy between what the soldier's body was supposed to be fed and the reality of the quantity and quality on offer. Private Lenfestey managed to complain about both within his diary as he lamented the rough starts to his training days. 'During the winter months at dawn, we did physical training first having a hot cup of tea & biscuit ... We were shivering before falling in but after cantering round a few jerks we were so warm ... Then we had an appetising breakfast followed by gun drill & lectures.'[52] Lenfestey's grumblings were not unusual. For many men training typically began at first light and comprised of a gruelling regime of physical exercise with only a hot drink and biscuit to sustain them.[53] There is no immediately apparent information within the military training manuals of the period of exactly why men were forced to exercise before breakfast. James Campbell has pointed out that throughout history soldiers had to travel long distances with limited nourishment and a significant bout of exercise after a night-time fast could effectively simulate these conditions.[54] This explanation fits the parameters of Lenfestey's misery. Of course, being forced to get up and immediately start to follow commands was also a powerful form of indoctrination and therefore instant preparation for combat on the front lines. A potentially cynical view may be that that this occurred simply because the officers in charge had the option to do it. Not necessarily cruelty for cruelties sake, although the above accounts may agree with that reductionist assessment, but an opportunity for fortitude development through physical misery that would prepare the men's bodies for the arduous tasks ahead. At least Lenfestey was able to enjoy an appetizing breakfast; perhaps the strenuous exercise on an empty stomach did much to stimulate his palate, though this seems an overly extreme way to diminish criticism of the food on offer.

Not all men adapted as well as Lenfestey or found themselves willing or able to accept the repetitive paltry diet on offer. Faced with meagre food some men turned to defiance to improve their situation. One of the most extreme cases of this resistance was the suicide of a young soldier in 1916. Discussions in the House of Commons concluded that this rare act was a consequence of the harsh conditions and poor food the man had endured within training.[55] Suicide, particularly because of food, was extreme and unusual but it illustrates how important it was to the serving men that their bodily needs be appropriately satisfied. This may explain why in response to the inquiry the Secretary of State refused to commit himself to an official response and therefore acknowledge a lasting deficiency in the fair offered to the British ranker. The satisfying of the bodies' needs was certainly a significant motivator for resistance throughout the First World War. Discontentment caused by the food on offer was common and could result in extreme behaviour. Private Stanley Roberts's damming review of the food, during training within his diary, identified a growing level of defiance.

> Rations have been very poor. The bread mouldy and scarce. Tea, soup, and coffee cannot be distinguished from each other excepting by the time of the day. The cooks have never cooked before and it almost appears as though they will never cook again. Their sole efforts seem to be concentrated on spoiling whatever rations come within their sphere of operations. Some of the troops are able to purchase food at nearby restaurants, but others are too poor to do so, and have either to live on the swill that is thrown to them or starve. Many prefer the latter course, but obviously, this state of affairs cannot go on indefinitely, so there is grumbling and muttering of threats.[56]

Roberts's complaints are remarkably like that of Lieutenant Minnitt; however, in Roberts's case, appealing to a family connection and managing improvements was not an option. Duffett has argued that responses to the standards of the food varied according to class, as those from better-off backgrounds were used to a higher-quality diet in their civilian lives and were therefore more likely to complain.[57] These men, many of whom entered the military in more superior roles and had access to money and connections, could at least take steps to improve their experience. Roberts did not belong to such a class. His father had died while he was young, and Roberts had supported his mother by working multiple jobs until enlisting in 1914 to serve.[58] Yet, this did not mean that his ostensibly lesser-defined palate meant that he would accept the measly food on offer. Instead, as would become a staple for many new recruits, alternatives were sought to meet the needs of the unsatisfied bodies through complaints and bargaining.

The men in Private Grindley's company went one step further in their protest of the meagre fair on offer in 1915. Like Lenfestey, Grindley and his comrades were also awoken at first light for hot drink and a bout of exercise. Early into their military career, Grindley and his mates decided that the way their bodies were being treated was unacceptable. In retaliation, the men refused to put their bodies at the disposal of the military by refusing to undergo the morning exertion, resulting in a haranguing and crucially the loss of their lunch for the day.[59] Seemingly the punishment befits the crime. Lack of food had prompted refusal to follow orders; therefore, the forsaking of lunch served as the consequence of disobedience. The restriction of food was a common military disciplinary device, not restricted to training. This inflicting of punishment upon the body of the soldier through the removal of physical pleasures and comforts continued throughout their service. As will be considered in latter chapters, it was particularly typical for men's bodies to pay for the repercussions of their choices.

At the extreme end of the scale, resistance could be even more confrontational than simply slipping away from the rear of a run. The limited food on offer encouraged half of a newly recruited civilian company to show their disgust by marching in protest to the officer's quarters in 1915. Lieutenant St Leger recalled that a munity broke out during training over the quantity and quality of the food on offer. He notes that 'the food was quite good and there were no more big complaints after the protesting men were rebuked for marching around the compound'.[60] Relatively unusual, mutiny stands as an ultimate act of defiance. Prophetic in his earlier notes in his diary, Private Roberts had rightly predicted an upcoming battle between the men and the officers over the state of the food.

> Mutiny is declared. The majority of the men have not been in the army a month. Morning Parade comes, and no one turns out. Everybody stands firm … One result of the mutiny is apparent within twenty-four hours. The food improves, and we are no longer desired to eat mouldy bread.[61]

In both cases, the food improves. This unusual dynamic between the wants of the soldier to satisfy their bodily needs and the actions of the military hierarchy illustrates the pressures of the First World War. In both cases punishments were doled out in official recognition of wrongdoing and reiteration of consequences of non-compliance. Yet, without overtly acknowledging that they had done so, the military authorities often addressed dietary complaints subtlety by making small improvements. This acquiescence illustrates the occasional fragility of the relationship between the military and the men under its care, as overarching authority was forced to compromise in the face of the need to convert rapidly as many civilian men into soldiers as possible.

Food evidently had a crucial role to play in the preparation, indoctrination, encouragement and control over the training soldiers and their bodies during the First World War. The body was centre within many soldier's resistance as their diet failed to meet the expectations pledged at enlistment. The body was also at the root of the army's response which made a deliberate show of restoring order while quietly responding to the challenge by enhancing the experience of the bodies of those men. Significantly, the troops had demonstrated that they were not powerless victims at the mercy of their officers but were willing exercise agency to improve their experience if their physical needs were not met.

Improving civilian bodies

Unquestionably, the primary purpose of military training during the First World War was to turn civilian men into effective soldiers. While much of the process was focused on physical indoctrination and adoption of the identity of the compliant British soldier, most of the concentration remained on the intensive preparation of the body for the extreme rigours of service. Within the military soldiers' bodies were rested, fed, clothed and groomed differently than in civilian life. Men immediately found their bodies seized and forced to stand, move and shape themselves in entirely unfamiliar manners. Between 1914 and 1918 training was diverse and changed in intensity, focus and duration as a result of where it took place, the desperation for men on the front lines and the role that the training men would undertake.[62]

Typically basic training for all men focused on the three core elements: drilling (marching in unison), parading (similar, but associated with military demonstrations or inspections) and physical improvement (exercises and games that were designed to develop strategic and combative skills as well as to strengthen the body).[63] This was designed to ensure that the individual met the physical requirements of soldiering while reiterating and indoctrinating submission to military control. After joining up in August 1914, Private Drage outlined in his diary the immediate physical strain and discomfort of his new role as a soldier placed upon his body as he endured a gruelling physical training schedule.

> Aug 16th, received clothes and equipment and had cot in barrack room to sleep on. I stayed in barracks until the following Wednesday in the meantime we had a parade at 6 am, 11.15 and 2.15 pm each day and we also did two route marches of 8 miles each day with full kit on, it was terribly hot. We were finally approached by the Colonel in command those that were approached were taken to Redam hill camp about 1 mile from the depot, we had to sleep under canvas there. On the

Saturday we had a route march of about 14 miles. On Sunday, we all had to attend church parade in the morning.[64]

Like all newly uniformed men, Drage immediately lost the ability to choose what he did with his body. Now under military direction, Drage's body was drilled, paraded and marched through a succession of endless exercises designed to improve his suitability for combat; opportunities for Drage to decide his pursuits were considerably limited in comparison to his existence as a civilian.

Above all else, drill remained the staple of military training throughout the First World War. Drill was, and still is, a series of movements in unison with other men in the platoon directed by an NCO or officer. This basic act of physical improvement and compliance was synonymous with serving within the military. Within his published war memoirs Private Lycette reiterates this symbiotic relationship as the activity was accompanied by lectures on army service. He wrote, 'We were formed into platoons and handed over to NCOs who lectured us, telling us "We are in the army now". We were taught to move in formations and all kinds of drill.'[65] Winter adds evidence to this by quoting the memoirs of a Private Noakes who described his experience in similar terms. 'We sloped, ordered, presented, trailed, reversed, piled arms and did everything possible with them except fire them,' wrote Noakes, 'with rifles we marched, counter-marched, wheeled right and left, inclined and formed squads and about turned until we were streaming in sweat and weak in the knees with exhaustion.'[66] This was a common complaint as men's bodies were set to repeat motions ceaselessly to commit the act to muscle memory.

The challenges to the body of this new physical regime featured recurrently in the accounts of the soldiers whose complaints were also often accompanied by recognition that their bodies had changed and improved. In his memoirs, Private Barraclough recalled how his training caused both physical and behavioural changes. He proclaimed, 'What with physical jerks, route marches, bayonet practice, firing, bombing, and drilling, I became much harder both in body and soul and further, I learned to swear with the worst of them.'[67] Private Milner wrote much the same in his own memoirs, as he recalled how essential training was in the transformation into their new military selves. He complemented his experience by writing, 'The cumulative effect of these conditions and training was to tighten, coarsen and harden us. We were being transferred from Civilians into Fighting Men, and in the infantry this new toughness was, we were to learn, necessary for survival.'[68] After he joined in late 1914, Private Williams endured an intensive training program which he also felt had dramatically improved his overall health. In his account of the war he wrote, 'Easter came in 1915, I was in wonderful health. I was never so well in my life, I'd overcome various little defects, colds and such.'[69] Training was constant and often brutal as men's bodies were pushed to the extreme to increase their readiness for combat. Despite the unpleasantness of the experience, the above sentiments are to be found frequently within the accounts of many training men who seemingly regarded the experience as necessary despite the pain and discomfort. This resignation and determination in some cases even belied gratitude as men's bodies became more attuned and capable.

The positive impact of training significantly also encouraged men to realize their previously unconsidered physical capabilities. Private Whitehouse presented in his account of training a common response to the training experience. He recalled that at the time he and his comrades resented the arduous physical training but were not blind to the physical benefits it was providing in equipping their bodies for the trials to follow.

> After about eight weeks at Widley, we were transferred to Fort Purbrook, a similar establishment about a mile to the East. Here we were under another lot of instructors and our training was stepped up becoming somewhat harder and we became more skilled in every way. Every day we had what appeared to be a relentless repetition of all conceivable types of training so that we could almost do it in our sleep, we had to be perfect. I could throw a rifle about and go through musketry drill without thinking about it, it was irksome at times but later I realised how essential it all was. I felt as fit as a fiddle. We were out on the downs before breakfast running all over the place and slept like logs from lights out to 'reveille'.[70]

Without question, Whitehouse regarded the transformation of his body as being the primary purpose of his extensive training. He notes also the importance of compliance and developing instinctive abilities which not only enhanced his physical abilities but also made him fell 'more skilled in every way'. Others similarly took great pride in their new physical skills. As an enlisted private, training in the 1st Battalion King Edward's Horses, 2nd Lieutenant F. B. Wade wrote home explaining how his training became not only easier but also enjoyable. Wade depicts a scene of gallantry and heroism in the mental image of his endeavours.

> I'm getting along famously now with all the details of my training. At the firing-range I am doing well in the practices and hope tomorrow when we commence the actual course to become either a marksman or a first-class shot. In the riding-school, I am in the first 'ride' and fast becoming accustomed to jumping hurdles ad ditches with my sword drawn. Today we made a charge with drawn swords: it was very thrilling especially when we actually received the order and galloped off shouting at the tops of our voices.[71]

Wade's letter conjures for the reader images of the masculine military heroes Dawson argues were the mainstay of the Victorian masculine precedent within the preceding Victorian era.[72] These were the idealized model men who endured hardships for the good as others. Examples include Dr James Thomson, a military surgeon in 1853 whose care of 750 wounded and sick men alone for five days before succumbing to a fatal bout of cholera, hasten on by his exhaustion, less than a fortnight later.[73] Another is the heroic tale of martyred Major-General Charles George Gordon in defence of Khartoum in 1885, standing firm and brave against all odds, shares similar imagery.[74] Increasingly over several decades such men had captured the adulation and affection of the public – providing for the hopeful, the uniformed and the British society at large, the military role model of gallantry and physical prowess to aspire towards.

Unfortunately, not all men could achieve the physical prowess necessary to emulate their masculine heroes. Despite having made it passed the enlistment assessment, the training programmes frequently separated out those whose physicality failed to meet expectations. As noted in the first chapter, Silbey illustrates that a minor scandal erupted as it became clear that many men were being dismissed from training in 1915, as a result of overly zealous, or morally questionable, assessors.[75] In a letter to his daughters in 1916, Private Parks recalled his continual inability to correctly follow directions.

> Parade again & then marched up & down sideways backwards and all ways until you get so messed that you do not know which is your 'front' or whether you belong to the front rank or the rear rank. & [sic] that is a dreadful crime in the army because they call you all sorts of very nasty names & then make you run over so far as a penalty.[76]

Far from the gallant deeds of men like Gordon, Parks struggled with the basic aspects of military training and received physical punishment as a reward for his inability. Similarly, Private Niblett recounted in a letter to his mother the shame he felt as his body failed to adapt to his training.

> I myself have fallen off with sheer fright at the Sergeant Major's voice on one occasion when with sword in hand and arm locked, we would charge a supposed enemy. They were large sacks filled with sand swinging on a rope with a black disc in the middle representing the heart of a man. Somehow my spurs touched the side of my mount and he inclined away from the target. I heard galloping hooves and coming up behind me on a white charger the Sergeant Major, shouting 'What are you trying to do, tickle that man to death?'[77]

For men such as Parks and Niblett physical failure was a very unpleasant and public affair as they were ridiculed for their ineptness. Public humiliation was of course useful as it would teach others not to follow their poor example; yet, the failure of a man to meet the task set to him through a physical deficiency could indicate his inferiority to those around him or be internalized.

Within Niblett's private papers he laments and questions his ability to fight in response to his failings in training.[78] Private James Porter Murray recounted within an oral history interview how physical appearance could inspire negative reactions from other training men. Murray explained that while bullying was not something that he saw often, it did happen, and typically towards those considered to be 'soft'.[79] However, in many cases what would be considered in modern parlance as 'banter' perhaps overrode clearly defined notions of bullying for the training men. Private Albert Hurst, a middle-class enlistee who joined the 17th Battalion Manchester Regiment in 1915, recalled that as the only teetotaller in a barrack full of northern miners he received a great deal of 'kidding' from the frequently drunk men.[80] Hurst is however keen to clarify that this was 'kidding' not bullying, having already mentioned being bullied in private school as a child.[81] While, it is possible that this is indeed true, and Hurst was happy to engage with some barrack room mockery, the point that his emasculating trait, ergo his refusal of alcohol, allowed for derision against his character reiterates the relevance between physical ability and conformity that was so very important during the First World War for many men during and beyond their training.

For those who remained physically incapable training was often intensified to ensure the positive transformation of their bodies. One of the most illustrative examples of this during the First World War was the reconditioning of left-handed men. As an experienced training NCO within the British Army, Sergeant Davidson argued that the complete retraining of a man against a lifetime of habitual behaviour was practically impossible but necessary due to the construction of British fighting technology. According to Davidson, 'The worst man to try and train was a left-handed man, he couldn't use the rifle with his right hand. I just had to try and get him to use his right hand. He was the worst man to train.'[82] Impractical for the left-handed, the British soldier's uniform kept small arms such as swords, pistols or batons on the left of the Sam Brown belt designed to be retrieved by the dominant right hand in a swift sweeping movement.[83] The design of the primary British soldiers' rifle, the Small Magazine Lee Enfield Mk III, meant it could only be fired with the right hand as the bolt for reloading was situated on the right side. All the firing training was designed to make the process of aiming, firing and reloading as efficient as possible. This meant that men carried the rifle on the left shoulder as it was easier to bring the rifle quickly into a firing position.[84]

In *Unwanted Warriors*, Clarke explains that left-handed men were significantly less effective in the field than their right-handed colleagues as left-handed firing significantly reduced the soldiers' rate of fire and accuracy.[85] In 1914 the British Army deliberately trained men to rapidly and accurately discharge their rifle at an optimum rate of fifteen bullets a minute. As a result, left-handedness was an unwelcome complication that trainers were forced to eliminate as 'recruits were to adapt to the weapon, not the weapon to the recruits'.[86] Rather than diverting from the norm in civilian life, in its desire to recondition the left-handed the military replicated similar medical practices that had been growing in popularity towards the end of the twentieth century. In British society of the early twentieth century, right-handedness was the social norm. Chris McManus argues that forcing of left-handed children to switch writing hands was a symptom of an increasing focus on social Darwinism and the topic of eugenics which regarded the left-handed as physically inept and physically inferior.[87] In both spheres of existence, the left-handed were considered ill-equipped to handle the physical pressures required of them and were therefore systematically retrained and repurposed to contribute to society.

Playing the game

Marching, shooting and running in unison was not the only way that men were conditioned for service during the First World War. The rigours of drill, marches and parade certainly provided the basis for the early stages of transformation from civilian to soldier. The role of games and sport was also significantly influential. The

1916 British Army instruction pamphlet *Games for Use with Physical Training Tables and Training in Bombing, 1916* opened by remarking on the importance of games such as 'bomb ball', rugby and 'maze' within soldier's training, stating, 'The essence of the following games is that they should be conducted with the utmost amount of energy and the rigid observance of all details connected with them.'[88] While games and sport were never allowed to take priority over other forms of training and as such were often limited to around ten minutes of effort. The physical and mental skills that they developed proved to be invaluable for the conditioning and creation of fighting men.

Games and sports provided an esprit de corps and a sense of camaraderie. They also significantly encouraged the development of tactical cooperation and strategic teamwork skills which could then in turn be effectively employed in a battle situation. David French argues that team sports were particularly useful in the training of soldiers as the practice accustomed men to accept physical risk as a sacrifice for achieving their objective.[89] In their excellent analysis of the link between sport and the British military, Mason and Riedi respond that sport was not regarded in this period as particularly good training for combat as the usefulness of dodging and strafing against a barrage of shells and machine gun fire was limited.[90] They do recognize that beyond the practical implications the mythos of sport was directly entwined with the rise of militarism and masculinity towards the end of the Victorian period. They are clear to state that as result of the public school focus upon sport in the latter nineteenth century, 'a sportsman [was] already half a soldier' and that it was widely believed at the time that 'the best sportsman [was frequently] the best soldier'.[91] This masculinized association between skill and sport illustrates the role that sport played in the life of an active soldier. The 1918 pamphlet issued by the army titled *Hints on Assault, Physical and Recreational Training* made this case plainly as it instructed that while games were not to replace official training measures, they were an important addition.

> There is a tendency to replace entirely or almost entirely the Trained Soldiers Table by Games. This should not be done ... Games are an invaluable tonic and have a stimulating effect; especially after some of the monotonous forms of training. Instructors should preach everywhere that games should be taken for VERY SHORT periods when troops have become stagnant.[92]

The extent to which games such as football, cricket and rugby were played differed according to the regiment and its location.

Sport could also be influenced by class as officers tended towards equestrian sports such as polo and hunting, while the rank and file was more likely to play football.[93] The vocabulary around the description of sport often linked enthusiasts to demonstrations of militaristically desired attributes. An image within the 1914 December edition of the *Illustrated War News* depicting two officers proudly showing off their prize hunt illustrated this combination of prowess and military skill as it was accompanied by the caption: 'The British officer, who is once more showing what a magnificent sportsman and fighter he is in the field, is not altogether neglecting sport as he knows it at home while he is at the front.'[94] Sport unified men through a shared vocabulary and passion that transcended training and while the physical effort not only kept men fit it also taught them strategy and helped unit cohesion.

For the trainees the number of sports and games on offer were varied. They included official sports such as football, rugby, boxing and cricket and numerous games such as 'jumping the bag', 'maze' and 'bomb ball'. Many of these games focused on improving physical strength, fitness and hand-eye coordination. Jumping the bag focused on agility and anticipation as it consisted of leaping over a bag on a rope that was swung from the centre of a circle. Maze was concerned with problem-solving while simultaneously encouraging men to act on command and turn as a chaser pursued a runner around a man-made maze. Bomb ball, a combination of rugby and football, is perhaps the best known and taught quick reflexes, dexterity and strategy for bombers.[95] One of the most popular sports, rather unsurprisingly as a popular British pastime, was football. So much so that each camp quickly assembled a team as there was no shortage of men capable of organizing a football programme.[96] Private Snailham recalled in his memoirs that his role within the football team meant he enjoyed a comparatively easier life because he was physically talented enough to represent the regiment. 'I could hold me own because I was in the football team and the Colonel was a sport … the team must be fit to play other regiments, I got away with things because we had to be able to play.'[97] For Private Lycette, his prowess on the field quickly overtook his primary purpose in attending military training as his talent for sport after he enlisted in 1914 meant that he became a celebrity for the men around him, even receiving special treatment and dispensations to ensure that he could win accolades for his regiment. He explained, 'I used to keep up my training in athletics, running and walking and I was very fit. The Battalion held a sports meeting on the college grounds. I had entered in eight events, and was successful in five, so I became popular as an athlete in the Battalion.'[98]

Sport was also a popular form of entertainment and recreation. In his letters home Private Parks recounted an evening in 1917 of fierce boxing between the drummer boys for which most of the men turned out to watch as the General awarded the winner a trophy.[99] Away from the home training camps, sport was no less popular. As Private Fox trained in Lucknow, he noted in his diary how the participation and watching of sport was incredibly popular. Like Parks, Fox had the opportunity to attend several exhilarating boxing matches during his training in India.[100]

Sport certainly allowed men to relax and combined competition and recreation as a perfect way to improve men's bodily fitness and coordination. However, heated sporting enthusiasm could also run against the training that the men were undertaking to ready their bodies for war, as the practice could also damage the body, rendering them unable to perform their duties as a soldier. Additionally, while sport may have been enjoyable, it was often just as deteriorating upon men's bodies as their constant training. Some recalled sport as being just as physically gruelling as training, if not even more so. Writing home to his parents during his training William Broadhead, a talented artist and future journalist, depicted the physical toll sport could take over the course of several sketches in his letters home to his parents. Over five drawings he showed rapid physical deterioration as his body suffered the exhaustion of a soldier's rugby match (see Figures 5 and 6).

Figure 5 William Broadhead, sketches in undated letter to his parents during training in 1916. Sheffield Archives, L.D. 1980/54/1 and 980/54/2, and L.D. 1980/54/3, 1980/54/4 and 980/54/5. Private Papers of W. Broadhead.

Figure 5 (*continued*)

Figure 6 William Broadhead, sketches in undated letter to his parents during training in 1916. Sheffield Archives, L.D. 1980/54/3, 1980/54/4 and 980/54/5. Private Papers of W. Broadhead.

Figure 6 (*continued*)

Figure 6 *(continued)*

Albeit somewhat satirically presented, the overall impact of sport on Broadhead's body is unmistakable in his drawings, besides which he described how tired he felt.[101] Closer examination of the images can detect a visible wilting of his body as his muscular physique crumples into a puddle of sweat, soon accompanied by a buckling of the knees, failing of the back and a physical injury to the head. Private Fox was also a prolific sports player and once was hospitalized for almost a week.[102] However, the event does not seem to have been too traumatic, as the only reference he makes in his diary is his entry and exit from hospital, with a slight description of his injury. Treating injury as part of the course of military training and body improvement would also explain the popularity of boxing where men would ferociously fight during three-minute-long rounds with the singular aim of damaging the opposing man's body until submission. Not only useful for developing physical strength and fighting ability, boxing was also used to settle scores between ranks. Private Cordy explained how a fellow soldier resolved a grudge with an overbearing sergeant in the ring, illustrating how sport could be used as a disciplinary tool or avenue to challenge authority without insubordination.

> The sergeant came across with a pair of boxing gloves and three [sic] them at Ted, hitting him in the face. Ted lost his temper and went for him, but an instructor grasped him – 'the ring is the place for that'. Ted cooled down, a referee was chosen, and the bout started. Ted made rings round the sergeant, and in the second round, he wanted to call the bout off. Ted was not having it and gave him a real hammering before the referee could stop him. About a fortnight later the instructor persuaded Ted to enter the depot competitions. This he did and took the championship at his weight.[103]

In the case of Ted, not only did boxing allow him to settle a score with an official that would have gained him a severe punishment under any other circumstance, it also increased his standing within the regiment by exemplifying the ability of his body through the bringing of competitive success.

Unquestionably, sport was an important part of the soldier's experience in training throughout the First World War as it improved physical conditioning and promised enhanced coordination in individuals and in platoons and regiments. Often sport was also an important source of fun and recreation. Regardless of the motivation behind it, the use of sport was also directly related to body regime of the military which sought to physically produce soldiers from civilians.

A pound of flesh

Without a doubt the primary purpose of training was to improve and positively condition the body for combat. Compliance and indoctrination were also essential elements of an effective soldier. Here again the body of the enlisted was at the centre of the militaries program to encourage obedience and conformity; yet for the purposes of this area of indoctrination, it was not improvement but punishment and discomfort which were the primary tools in use. Prior to the First World War control over soldiers was maintained through harsh and visible physical punishments which inspired obedience and fear. These methods would not be as easily applied during the First World War as the military was constructed of a mix of regular, territorial, volunteer and conscript men. David Englander argues that discipline during the First World War could emulate the methods of the previous century due to the believe that the new civilian soldiers, used to enjoying certain civil liberties, would baulk more openly to such forms of coercion.[104] This assertion, reinforced by a number of reforms towards the end of the nineteen century which had included the forbidding of sentencing lashes for disobedient men, meant that discipline within the First World War had to walk the fine line between being sufficiently punitive and being still palatable. Rather than corporal punishment, which had historically meant a brutal public whipping, military punishments between 1914 and 1918 tended to discomfort the body through fatigue, withholding of privileges or temporary incarceration. As a deserter, Private Calvert would likely have been whipped, if not summarily executed, in the nineteenth century for his crime. In 1915 his body still took the brunt of his disobedience, but his punishment had the positive impact of improving his fitness rather than disabling his body.

> The C.B. [Confined to Barracks] punishment included going on parade after the usual daily parades, carrying a full kit in the webbing pack and marching around the Barrack square for one hour. Sometimes if the drill sergeant was vindictive, he ordered all kit carried to be laid out for his inspection and shortage was duly noted by the Corporal who paced the march. For every article of kit short, the punishment was one extra drill … This to me was all part of becoming a soldier so accepted without a grumble.[105]

Calvert's crime had been deserting his first regiment and joining another to try and get to the front faster. An obscure situation to judge, as Calvert's AWOL actions were carried out with the intention to serve his country at the front as quick as possible. As this was a desire in alignment with that of the British military it is hardly surprising that the punishment for his actions was no worse than being confined to barracks (CB), additional PT and temporary suspension of privileges.[106]

Calvert was not the only man to experience increased duties and drill as punishment for a misdemeanour. Late into the war in 1918, while training with his new Middlesex Regiment at the Kitchener Barracks, Private Arthur Smith's body paid the price of his tardy return from leave after he was assigned a regime of 'punishment drill'.[107] Private Bill Smedley in 1917 received a particularly vigorous bout of 'punishment drill' after falling foul of a zealous NCO who claimed he inadequately managed to respond to orders while he trained in Cork, Ireland.[108] British Trooper and regular soldier James Goodson, who had enlisted in 1902, explained that 'pack drill' consisted of wearing a full pack during full drill practice and was a regular punishment for men who stepped out of line. 'In fact I've done some, oh yes I done 7 days' pack drill for being absent over leave, I lost a stripe, I lost a stripe and I did 7 days' pack drill for overstaying my leave, I accepted it, I accepted it, all my life I accepted punishment if I had done wrong.'[109]

Not all punishment was so officially implemented. Private Lycette recalled that his punishment for failing to meet standards was a public haranguing and a somewhat ludicrous threat rather than actual physical discomfort.

> 'I could bloody well eat you, now you listen to me: do you know Mrs Grocott, soldier?' I said 'No', 'well', he said 'you will bloody soon know her, son. Now listen to me for a few moments. When I call your name in future, I want you to spring to attention immediately double up to me, click your heels and say, "sir". Now go back to your tent and wait until you are called.'[110]

Later Lycette performed the act perfectly, and was warmly rewarded by his CO who congratulated him with the words: 'Splendid, I want to make a soldier of you.'[111] Evidently, a mild threat of physical punishment and a good public telling-off was enough to ensure that next time Lycette was in the same situation, his body responded appropriately. For some men, the punishment they received was more rough and ready. Private Goodson recalled an instance where an altercation with his NCO as a punishment for not conforming on command effectively enough nearly led to a behind-the-barrack-room brawl.

> The cry is from the instructors, 'brace your knees, brace your knees'. Well you brace your knees as well as you can, but you find that you can't do it like they want it done. So one of young assistants, a cocky fella, comes along and whilst I'm doing it just kicks me behind the knee and I go down. I get up and I'm going to bash him … The gym bloke comes after me and says, 'that's enough of that' and I said, 'well that man kicked me behind the knee'. He says, 'if you fancy your chance, you come over here tonight you'll be accommodated'. It was dropped that way. The NCO was in the wrong for kicking me, he would have been in trouble if I had a go at him, he started it … though in that moment, I could have hit him you know.[112]

A quick burst of physical pain was not an uncommon motivator employed by training officers to encourage men to fall inline during training. Neither was the practice of sorting out differences through physical confrontation. Goodson's account illustrates that punishment could be informal and often violent. At the most extreme end of the spectrum of physical punishments was Field Punishment No. 1, which involved being strapped to a gun wheel on public display for an hour at a time. Field Punishment No. 1 was rare in training but not entirely uncommon.

One of the most well-known examples occurred at the 'Bull Ring' training camp at Étaples, which John Fairley and William Allison explain in *The Monocled Mutineer* had the British soldiers 'crucified' daily.[113] On 8 August 1916 during a debate in parliament, Mr Morrell, the MP for Burnley, raised inhuman aspect of field punishment to Mr Forster, Secretary of State for War. Morrell asked Forster if he was aware of the case of Army Driver Graham whose minor speeding infraction had earned him ninety days' field punishment which included being strapped to a gun wheel for twice daily for an hour as well as suspension of pay. In response Mr Forster clarified his lack of control over the use of field punishment as a punitive measure, but promised to reverse the charges brought against Graham and ensure that his wife received monetary allowances as normal.[114] Despite the reduction, the use of Field Punishment No. 1 still seems disproportional. Within the 1914 reprinted *Kings Regulations and Orders for the Army Service Manual*, the guidelines for Field Punishment No. 1 stated that the punishment must not extend beyond twenty-eight days.[115] Paragraph 496a, which focused upon offenses including the misuse of 'mechanically propelled vehicles', stated that punishment should 'be limited to the equivalent of a fortnight's pay. Any such recovery will form part of the disciplinary action taken in such cases.'[116] At no point is speeding directly referenced, but the paragraph does state that punishment would be levied for the damage caused by negligence or carelessness.[117] Unless Graham had killed or injured someone, which seems unlikely as there is no mention of this, the punishment would have been justifiably more severe. In the light of the crime, the use of field punishment for sixty days seems excessive.

Certainly, we do not have all the facts surrounding the case of Driver Graham and perhaps his punishment was a cumulative response from a series of misdemeanours, or a more serious crime. Regardless, the punishment of Driver Graham illustrates how men could be severely punished for a range of offenses, their body becoming forfeit as a result of their devious action. Towards the end of 1916 field punishment continued to be debated in parliament without any sign of compromise or resolution. Mr Morrell again attacked the use and apparently popularity of the disciplinary method, claiming from an unnamed source that employment of the method was even more prevalent in 1916 than it had been pre-war; after speaking in parliament about the draconian aspect of the treatment of men who had given up their liberty to fight in defence of the nation, he concluded, 'This is a hard and degrading punishment, and it breaks the spirit of any man. Therefore, it ought not to be inflicted except for the gravest offences.'[118]

This ongoing debate throughout the war counters Englander's argument that the spectacle of severe and humiliating physical punishment was considered inappropriate and counterproductive for volunteers and conscripts.[119] Field punishment even developed as an early moral panic after public outcry erupted in 1916 following reports that the methods had been used on imprisoned conscientious objectors.[120] In 1923, long after the end of the war, Field Punishment No. 1 was officially banned by the War Office.[121] Still, it was not until the end of the 1920s that field punishment was officially abolished by the Labour government along with a number of other penalties such as execution for cowardice.[122]

Not only was field punishment controversial, its employment could also be counterproductive. Private Templer recalled unrest during his training at the Horfield Barracks in Bristol after a fellow trainee was splayed out in the sun as punishment for drunken misbehaviour. Far from encouraging compliance, the result of such public humiliation at the Horfield Barracks was complete rebellion and insubordination.

> The spark that set it off was the arrest of one of the most popular men in 'C' company who, with others, got drunk and very tough. He was put into the guard compound and the next morning taken before the C.O. who ordered him to be confined to no. 1 field punishment, which was to be tied to the wheel of a limber in the guard compound for a number of hours each day. The weather was very

hot at the time and his pals got angry and demanded his release or they would go and take him out ... the 'C' Company men surrounded the area, pulled up the railing, untied the prisoner and in spite of an officer, marched him round the camp yelling.[123]

In some ways, this event at least encouraged the comradery that would sustain many soldiers during the arduous years to follow. This however was certainly not the intention of the officers who first sentenced the man to his fate. Yet again, the body lies at the centre of his story, as the recruits had resisted military discipline through unruly behaviour by getting, in Templer's words, 'drunk and very tough'. One of the men was singled out as to make an example and his body subjected to a public punishment that was considered by the rest of the men as overly harsh and degrading. In defiance of their instructing officers the disgruntled men freed his body and then publicly paraded him around. Such was their anger and commitment to their cause that even the rumours that another regiment was being prepared to come in to quash their brief rebellion could not dissuade them from their protest.

This short-lived uprising over physical treatment was not an isolated event. A regiment made up almost entirely of volunteer working-class Welsh miners in 1915 twice refused to fall out and partake in training.[124] Their grievance concerned the recent assault of a soldier by a particularly disliked instructor and the sentencing of another man to Field Punishment No. 1 for protesting vociferously against the perceived injustice. Angry at the behaviour of the commanding officers, the rest of the regiment withdrew their labour resulting in a stalemate between the military and their training men. Desperate for a resolution, but determined to not lose face, the military authorities decided it was wise to transfer the instructor out of the camp.[125] This allowed the army to maintain the appearance of control while simultaneously appeasing the rebellious trainees. Clearly, the New Army recruits could be controlled through punishment; yet, the nature of their enlistment could also make traditional military discipline harder to maintain as physically punitive action could actively incite resistance. Such punishment and resistance were certainly at the extreme end of the typical soldiering experiences, as verbal admonishment, physical discomfort and public humiliation were much more routinely employed to break down a recruit's pride than as an encouragement for him comply.[126]

Conclusion: Different men equal different tactics

Drill Sergeant Robert Davidson of the 2/4th Gordon Highlanders explained that all men were relatively unique when it came to military training, and as such there could be no definitive length of time for turning men into soldiers.[127] He proclaimed in an oral history interview: 'Men are different. Some could fall into it and the drill quite quickly, some took a long time.'[128] Still, the focus of the training was to remove the individuality from the man and render his body in sync with the needs of the military and the movements and behaviours of his fellow soldier. To achieve this, the body had to remain central to this process of transformation and conditioning. The British military determined that to create the effective soldier it was essentially to change the way in which men groomed, clothed, fed, rested, deployed and viewed their own bodies. The uniform was the first step as reclothing civilians began almost immediately upon recruitment. Many men looked forward to this transformation because, as the previous chapter has argued, the uniform had deliberately been associated with prestige and glamour. But the reality often sat at odds with the rhetoric as many early recruits found themselves disappointingly in blue uniforms rather than khaki as the military failed to source enough materials of the latter colour. The spell of the 'shiny' glamourous uniform was also often soon broken as men found their new clothing and kit awkward to use, devoid of any personal tailoring and, often not particularly, uncomfortable to wear.

The sheen of military duty was also tarnished by the instigation of rigorous control over the habits, actions and physical presentation of men's bodies. French philosopher Michel Foucault argued that punishment and discipline are essential tools in the transition from civilian to soldier.[129] During the First World War it is clear that men were punished when they opposed military control, or their bodies failed them in training. This punishment focused almost exclusively on the body and could be brutal, but for the most part smaller transgressions earned the non-conformist extra drill or public humiliation through shouted threats and insults, often directed at the man's body. Above all, training was designed to ready men for combat physically and psychologically. Therefore, punishment that ultimately physically inhibited the ability of soldiers to fight was counterproductive. The end goal for the British Army was to prepare and release as many men as possible out to the front line. Therefore, it is understandable that even serious cases of resistance on the part of soldiers could be met with compromise rather than retribution. Still the rigours of military life and the physical controls that accompanied it was a jarring transition, very different to their pre-enlistment conceptions, for many as they transformed into combat-ready soldiers.

The gap between the preconceived fiction of soldiering and the reality was just as visible throughout various aspects of training. The promise of enjoyable and diverse food which had been a key element of some recruitment campaigns proved to be less appetizing and bountiful as advertised. Certainly, efforts were made by the military authorities to ensure that dietary rations were enough to produce fitter and healthier fighting bodies. This focus lay in statistical analysis of calories to be consumed by each soldier and made recommendations that were simply not possible in the face of the Total War that Britain had entered. Much to the chagrin of men and their bodies, the quality and quantity of food varied, particularly as the war carried on and provisions became more difficult to source.[130] Complaints of hunger and disgust at the quality of the food invariably led to demonstrations of resistance either through direct protest or by circumventing the militaries control over the men's stomachs and bodies by sourcing additional nourishment elsewhere. This discontent was also impacted by the fatigue generated as men's bodies were increasingly put through excruciatingly intense training programmes. With the need for men on the front lines ever present, recruit's bodies were under constant pressure to improve their fitness and skills quickly so as to join the war effort. From the moment they awoke men found themselves obligated to run, parade, drill and march in order to become fitter and more physical adapted to combat. Before long they were expected to learn new skills such as the shooting of weapons, throwing of bombs and operating equipment and machines – all the time by repeating basic exercises designed to make these techniques second nature to be completed without thinking.

Training was remembered and recorded vividly by many recruits, particularly in physical terms. From the outside, one could be almost forgiven for viewing the process of training as a controlled assembly line where the soft civilian enters and the hard combat-ready soldier leaves. In reality, training was incredibly complicated and ironically personal for an experience designed to create varying degrees of uniformed automatons. Whether it was learning to shave for the first time, attaching brass buttons to a Kitchener uniform to make it more impressive, eating 'swill' or enduring a run before breakfast, men experienced training extensively from the perspective of their individual bodies. They watched as their bodies transformed beneath them, became indoctrinated and directed for the singular purpose of combat and lost aspects of their own individuality, as 'one' became 'many'. Yet, not all autonomy was lost as men resisted and satisfied their own desires at the expense of military discipline. Soldiers they may have become, but as they departed for war, their bodies retooled for military use, aspects of their individuality, wants and desires developing in their civilian lives accompanied them to the front lines.

3

Lives on the line: Active service

I have not had a wash or a shave for over a week. How pleasant it feels to be clean again. When washed I am carried into the operating theatre and the second operation is performed. I am so comfortable in bed, a real bed, with white sheets, and a pillow nice and white. At last, this is heaven, glorious heaven. They gave me chicken broth to drink and chicken to eat.[1]

Private Roberts (1917)

After being seriously wounded in his arm at the Third Battle of Ypres in 1917, Private Roberts chose not to document the agony of his wound or the terror he experienced in battle but celebrated the sudden comfort, cleanliness and food he had gained access to while convalescing. Roberts subsequently told his attending doctor, 'I have never felt more comfortable in my life. I have no pain and I am so cosy.'[2] Roberts's response to hospitalization goes far to illustrate the harsh living conditions experienced by those in the midst of active service, in that his joy for simple comforts overrode any discussion of his physical injury. Active service was a multifaceted experience during the First World War. In contrast to common misconceptions of trench warfare, the majority of serving men spent only part of their time on the front lines. Recovery, rest, relocation and restocking of equipment primarily took place behind the lines, as men prepared themselves for the tasks ahead or experienced a reprieve from the enemy's sights. Many found life behind the lines an opportunity to experience comforts not found either in training or at the front line. Non-combative active service also allowed for further training and provided access to canteens and recreational activities. This was an existence still keenly felt through the body of the soldier as everything from the beds they slept to the food they ate brought with it physical experiences that would remain vivid in the diaries and memoirs of the soldiers for decades to come.

During the First World War millions of British men travelled to the Western front as thousands more dispersed around the globe to campaigns in the Middle East, Africa and Mesopotamia.[3] When not engaged in direct combat, men sustained supply lines in camps, billets or support trenches.[4] Still the men had to remain alert and ready to spring into action or engage in support duties such as rebuilding trenches, carrying out fatigues (menial tasks) or burial duties. These roles were acting in support to organizations such as the Army Service Corps (ASC) or the Royal Army Medical

Corps (RAMC) or undergoing training. Even during periods of rest and recreation, men's bodies remained in focus as recuperation enabled successful returns to the front, while men also found ways to damage their bodies – much to the irritation and concern of the British military. With a focus on hygiene and health, food and drink, and dangerous hedonistic behaviours, it is possible to see how the treatment of men's bodies by the military, each other and themselves was a crucial aspect of non-combative active service life. During the First World War men's bodies constantly needed to adapt to their surroundings as they learned to live in unsanitary conditions, were medically assessed and treated to prevent disease, fed and watered and even sought out ways to relax. Even without an enemy to oppose, men could endanger themselves or find their bodies punished for misdemeanours.

A clean bill of health

Soldiers living at the front typically spent eight days serving in the front line with a further four in a reserve trench before being pulled back for four days of recuperation. This was designed to keep fit fighting men on the front line and to help sustain morale by allowing recovery time and even the chance to take leave to return home.[5] The frequency and duration of time behind the lines frequently changed according to battle location and intensity of the war. A typical rotation would consist of a three-day period in the front line to a base camp to get cleaned and washed followed by a few days of reduced duties with time for recreational activities. Next, the men would be rotated to serve in the further back reserve trenches which, while still being open to attack from aerial bombardment and shelling, were significantly less dangerous than the front-line trenches.[6] For Trooper Hollis, who served with the Bedfordshire Yeomanry on Western Front, his rotation in the intensely fought over Hohenzollern Redoubt trenches in 1915 was 'four days in reserve, four days in support and four days in the frontline.'[7] Private Swales of the 7th Battalion York and Lancaster Regiment served for only forty-eight hours at the Somme in June 1916 before gratefully being relieved from combat duty.[8] However, Sergeant Ward demonstrated that a man's stint at the front could be significantly longer by remarking on their ability to endure extended service. He explained that 'in 1916, after the Somme battles we used to do 16 days on the frontline and 8 behind resting. After 16 days, they were covered in mud.'[9] In reality, the length of service and respite could dramatically change dependant on the circumstances. As a result, in 1916 the Canadian Expeditionary Force division, the 60th Canadian Overseas Battalion, endured over eighteen days on the front line before relief while serving at the Eble trench at the Somme.[10]

While periods of relief and front-line service were determined by the state of the war, all men eventually would be withdrawn from the front to allow them to recuperate. As a ramification of the pre-war reforms and mindful of fielding a largely civilian fighting force, through the First World War, the British military made a concerted effort to preserve and replenish the physical health of its combatants. A significant element of this focus was hygiene. Within his private papers, Private Phillipson retained a copy of the 1914 *Notes for Lectures to Recruits of the Brigade of Guards* from which he had learned much about soldiering. Philipson had joined the 5th (Reserve) Battalion Grenadier Guards in early 1916, being too young to join the regular battalion. By October 1917 he was fighting with the 1st Battalion Grenadier Guards on the Western Front where he remained until being wounded out close to the end of the war. As an eager recruit Philipson had taken to heart many of the lessons, he was taught during his induction including instructions on correct military appearance, how to gage distances and measure wind resistance for the purpose of accuracy and a basic semaphore.[11] One of the most important lessons he learned, along with every other trainee, and as was clearly outlined in the lectures given to the men, was the importance of avoiding disease and staying healthy during service. This lesson was printed in the booklet that Phillipson had kept and even underlined in places. These guidelines placed responsibility of the care and health of the soldier's body upon himself. In a seemingly counterproductive move of incongruence, the painstaking removal of individual agency that had made up much of the training process was returned, albeit repurposed to suit the needs of the military. The recognition that only healthy soldiers could fight had driven the initial enlistment process and training regimen the men experienced. Beyond these supervised steps, the personal assessment of a man's own health and strength of self-control and compliance within the military body regime were considered vital. To keep men in line, soldiers were reminded of the immorality of hedonism and self-indulgence in contrast to the importance of duty and honour in the service and protection of their country.

> Health which goes with cleanliness, is most important to a soldier; it is the absolute duty of every soldier to do all in his power to keep himself healthy, for a man, who is not strong and healthy can neither march nor fight, and a soldier is of no use unless he can do both. A man too, who goes to hospital is nuisance to his comrades, who have to do his duty. Men must therefore take great care of their health. For instance, no man needs get ill by loitering about in the cold half dressed, after getting hot or leaving a hot room nor by running out in slippers to the pipe clay sheds or elsewhere during wet weather. Moreover, men must be careful not to drink too much, for excessive drinking will not only get them into trouble but will also injure their health and the same applies to excessive cigarette-smoking, which may ruin a man constitution. Everything possible is done by drill and gymnastics to make soldiers strong, active and healthy, but men can do a lot for themselves by cultivating regular and temperate habits. When a soldier feels ill or when he requires medical treatment of any kind, he will give in his name to the corporal-in-waiting at reveille, in order that he may see the surgeon. If he should be taken ill at any other time he will report himself to the sergeant-in-waiting. He will not treat himself or consult private doctors, as men are very severely punished for concealing disease, that is to say, for not reporting themselves sick to the military surgeon. Men must, however, make it a point of honour not to go sick, unless they are really ill.[12]

Effectively, the military attempted to convince men to police their own bodies as officers reiterated the message that the man's body was not his own and therefore those inhabiting the trained vessel must defend and protect it through self-regulation and obedience, for the sake of the military and their country. Internalization of these values and the importance of self-policing were widespread throughout the serving men across the course of the war. As he served with the 86th infantry brigade Private Hubard was certain that no soldier would report sick unless necessary. In the grand tradition of carrying on regardless, he wrote home in September 1915 to confess that sickness had gripped his entire platoon: 'None of us are feeling exceptionally grand. I have had a touch of dysentery and have almost felt at times that a rest would be very welcome. I, of course, haven't reported sick.'[13] Regardless of how they felt physically, short of hospitalization, demobilization or death, many men simply carried on with their duties. Private Fowler of the 1st (Lowland) Field Ambulance RAMC was one such dedicated recruit who in 1915 wrote in his diary that he simply had no time to be ill, due to six hundred ill patients who demanded his care and so refused to report sick.[14] Fowler's dedication may not have solely been down to military instruction. A week later he revealed that significant understaffing, a barrage of ill patients and fatally horrendous conditions meant his personal health could not take precedence.

When required, the individual needs of the body often came secondary to duty as conditions demanded that men remain at their posts at all costs. This was not without its paradoxes. In order to 'soldier on' men were expected to self-diagnose to determine the severity of their ailments.[15] Bombarded with the rhetoric of the stoic masculine soldier, men could disregard the order to report sickness to their medical officer. This grey area was tacitly acknowledged by the military authorities as a solution was found through self-medication via easy-to-prepare home remedies. In the 1915 *Manual of Military Cooking and Dietary, Mobilisation* several recipes are provided to relieve illness: including chicken broth, jellied calves' hoofs and beef tea. While questionably palatable, each dish was designed to enable ill soldiers to recover quickly on their own or through their comrade's amateur intervention rather than demanding the expertise of a medical officer. The manual listed these instructions under the heading 'when soldiers are required to attend their sick and wounded comrades the following simple recipes are useful.'[16] Delicacies such as onion porridge (which thankfully was not actually porridge), which the manual claimed was 'an excellent remedy for colds', were often employed by the temporarily ill or injured without the need to recourse to medical facilities.[17] Within this murky grey area, men could find themselves being punished for taking responsibility for their own medical treatment. This was very much the case for Private Silver as he made clear in an extended narration within his memoirs.

> I was on listening post duty out in no-man's land in a hole half full of water and I had to stand in that freezing water for two solid hours I dare not move because of giving my position away to the enemy and that's where I got frostbitten. … the first time we came out of the frontline we were relieved at night and by the time we had marched back to our billets we were too tired to do anything and we were up to our neck in mud so the next morning the sick cpl. [*sic*] came around about six am and I reported sick then. Just before we marched off to the MO's quarters the RSM spotted me and he shouted to the Col. 'Where is the man going?' and

the cpl [sic] replied 'sick sir', so the RSM said 'if that man gets medicine and duty report him to me' and so I did get M and D and I had to go back to the CO who asked how I went sick in that condition so I told him that I had no time to clean the mud off my clothes and my feet were more important so he sentenced me to seven days punishment which meant I had to do more dangerous and dirty jobs than the other lads, it include going out into no-man's land putting out barbed wire and cleaning latrines. Then after a rest we went up the line again and through the same procedure and when we came out again I went sick and this time the docter [sic] reported me for going sick in a filthy condition which was not really my own fault because the medicine that I received the first time I went sick was whale [sic] oil which I had to rub on my feet and I was having to wear dirty socks and walking about the muddy trench and no hot water to wash my feet so I got another severn [sic] days field punishment.[18]

Private Silver's experience is atypical; however, the clash between rhetoric and reality for treatment of the body within the confines of the combat environment is particularly visible in his account. Silver lacked the opportunity to improve his rapidly declining physical state; yet, despite his immediate priority post front-line service being to rectify his self-diagnosed and ignored 'frostbite', he was severely reprimanded by his commanding officer (CO) for a lack of self-care which had rendered him physically incapable for duty. Silver's tale of hardship continues within his private papers as he recalled being unable to do right for doing wrong as he continually received conflicting orders and reprimands for the state of his feet which paradoxically worsened after each round of punishment duty. Eventually, bleeding, desperate and unable to stand after receiving punishment duty for over fourteen days followed by having to march back to the barracks with heavily frostbitten feet, Silver's body reached the limit of its endurance. Once carried to a medical officer after a sergeant major steps in to help, Silver is dispatched to a clearing station to finally receive the treatment he should have undertaken in the first place, the irony remaining that his body now was in significantly worse shape than necessary as a result of his mistreatment by his superior officers.[19]

Silver's experience as he was passed from official to officer and back again reiterates the inconsistencies that soldiers could face while attempting to navigate the perplexing and often contradictory regulations and expectations. 'Trench foot' was a particularly difficult physical malady to curtail and treat; due to the extreme living conditions that men found themselves enduring during the war, the various presentations of frostbite and infected limbs became a significant issue for the British Army. Harrison explains that various forms of cold-related damage to the lower extremities brought about by the combination of trench conditions and limited sanitation meant that over seventy-five thousand men were admitted to hospital, many of whom eventually required extended treatment back in England.[20] Responses to dealing with trench foot evolved over the course of the war. In the 1911 RAMC training handbook, a section on 'foot-soreness' advised that 'the ablution of the feet at least once daily should be compulsory for troops in the field'.[21] It also recommended that a salicylic acid of potash was to be mixed with Vaseline or a powder made up of salicylic acid, starch and talc, and applied to washed feet each day. Atenstaedt explains that that by November 1915 the rise of trench foot forced the British Army to demand that all men dried and rubbed their feet and put on dry socks before they entered the front line.[22] From 1916 onwards debate increased both within the military and the medical community, as medical journals such as the *Lancet* published several opposing articles each suggesting the best treatment for chilled feet and frostbite. By the end of the war, treatment ranged from the application of powders just as before the war, a method favoured by the French Army, through to the more common practice of applying whale oil which continued until the end of the conflict and was the preferred method in the British Army.[23]

Despite these ongoing investigations, the reality on the front line often meant that the clinically written advice to be found in manuals and journals was almost impossible to put in practice. The primary enemy to the responsibility of each man to keep his body healthy for combat was the extremely insanitary conditions they lived in. For cases such as Private Silver's, it proved impossible to do both and men could find themselves both incapable and punished while having little to no control over either. A significant element of this responsibility for self-care was the maintaining of grooming and cleanliness that had been imposed in training. The same RAMC Training Manual which had reiterated the personal responsibility of each man for self-diagnosis also outlined the importance of hygiene and prompted men to wash beyond the collars and cuffs of their uniforms.

> The act of washing further improves the skin, opens and cleans its pores and keeps it sweet and healthy. Most persons wash their hands and faces, but often forget parts covered by clothes. Of these, the following should be washed every day when possible: (1) between the legs and buttocks; (2) the armpits; (3) the feet and toes.[24]

The section on personal hygiene which filled nearly two pages also focused upon the importance of washing hands before meals, and the manual argued that even in the worst environments steps must be taken to maintain levels of hygiene by carrying a hairbrush and 'cleaning, shaking and exposing [underclothes] to air and sunshine'.[25] Again reality clashed with medicalized instructions devised far away from actual service. On deployment, caught within a cycle of constant rotation between the front, recuperation and back trench training, the ideals of hygiene as set by the military authorities were difficult to maintain. In his memoirs Private Keller explained that while hygiene was often very important to the men, even pleasurable, it was not always possible.

> There were hot showers which were a treat to a crowd of dirty men, and we were permitted to use them as often as we pleased. Most of the men used them every day following the physical exercises and the route march which lasted from morning roll call until noon and this gave us a chance to get rid of the lice and other vermin that we were being bothered with. We did use them regularly at least once and sometimes twice a day. The French people seeing us going to the showers all the time remarked that the English soldier must be dirty as he is always washing himself. When we were retreating, we had very little time to even wash and when

we wanted to shave, we often had to use our tea to get something hot to soap our beards.[26]

For many the simple act of being clean was not a burden to be endured, but a pleasure to be enjoyed. The practical aspects of showering and clean clothes meant healthier bodies and the removal of lice which had become a constant irritant in the trenches almost immediately. Acknowledging the score of regulations and the punishments meted out for poor hygiene, one could be forgiven for assuming that men often resisted being clean, and that the battle for sanitation was one that was hard fought between the control of the military and the agency of the soldier. Keller's account demonstrates otherwise. The front lines were not just insanitary; it was also the fact that the life of the serving soldier could be so restrictive during the First World War that opportunities for sanitation were extremely limited. After being relieved from the front Keller and his comrades did not need to be forced to remove the grime that demonstrated their extended stay on the front lines; in fact, the showers were a 'gift' to be enjoyed liberally. Something of which many serving men certainly took advantage for the benefit of their bodies and perhaps their sanity.

Shaving was another element of sanitation and control which had been so consciously indoctrinated during training but became particularly difficult away from the relative comfort of the training barracks in Britain. Chapter 2 has already noted how the act of hair removal was utilized by the military as a form of indoctrinated control. In service shaving also had a practical element as the removal of excess hair could restrict the spread of lice. Private Watson, who served with the Northumberland Fusiliers on Western Front between 1916 and 1918, recalled that their bodies became covered in lice and had to buy candles and strip naked in the trenches to burn them off.[27] This was a potentially dangerous pastime as is made clear by poet Private Isaac Rosenberg in his famous trench poem 'Louse Hunting', where he humorously described a man setting his shirt on fire as he attempted to rid his clothes of the perpetual itch and infestation.[28]

Despite the risks and unpleasantness, the reward was worth the effort. This was certainly the case for Watson, for whom personal hygiene was important but very difficult as frequently there was not enough water to go around all the men as they scrambled to the water bucket provided to clean off some of the grime. In desperation, Watson innovated an alternative: 'I used to save tea to wet my face and shave myself. Some days I went a week or more, in those days when you were a young one, the beard didn't grow as fast as it does now.'[29] Watson and Keller both repeat the same story of repurposing their tea to allow them to shave. It is a mark of the importance of shaving for men close to the front lines that some choose to sacrifice the dregs of their often one and only hot nourishing drink of that day to cleanse their bodies. This balancing of internal and external pleasure is understandable within the recollections of Captain Rogerson whose memoirs vividly recalled the bodily pleasure he felt when he finally managed to tackle his unkempt chin, 'what bliss it was to lather up and feel the razor shaving of this unwelcome growth.'[30] For many men, an aspect of cleanliness enabled them to separate themselves from the surroundings and experiences they were continually subjected to. As is made clear from the accounts above, opportunities to be clean could serve as miniature respites interspersed between the extended periods of mud and battle.

However, grooming was not purely associated with hygiene and personal taste but continued the cementing of authoritarian control that had begun for many men during military training. Culturally, throughout the nineteenth century facial hair had a peculiar role within society, both within Britain and around the rest of the world. Withey and Evans explain that after 150 years of clean-shaven chins, in 1850 facial hair returned into societal popularity as a signifier of masculinity.[31] French soldiers in the nineteenth and early twentieth centuries remained mostly unshaven which earned them the nickname *poilu* meaning 'a virile man with a beard'.[32] In Britain, by the turn of the twentieth century moustaches were more common and British soldiers were encouraged to grow them as a demonstration of 'military esprit de corps'.[33] The military moustache folded into the heroic militaristic hero sensibilities of the latter nineteenth century, leading to emulation in the civilian population. This is superbly explained by Oldstone-Moore in *Of Beards and Men* who describes this as an 'embracing [of] the image of the warrior'.[34] Prior to enlistment and during training grooming and cutting of hair was a fundamental aspect of the creation of new soldiers and encouraged conformity. The upkeep of these physical constraints was taken very seriously. So much so that prior to the First World War any woman who attempted to convince her husband to remove his facial hair could be accused of encouraging dereliction of duty.[35] As the war continued, attitudes and regulations towards shaving changed. In 1913 General Nevil Macready voiced the view of many soldiers that the moustache regulation should be repealed, something vehemently opposed publicly by King George in 1915. In his memoirs, Macready recounts how the court martialling of a New Army officer in 1916 on active service drove his efforts for reform.

> In the summer of 1916, a case was brought to my notice of a wretched officer of the New Army who had been court martialled for being clean shaven. In his defence he made the ingenious excuse that by profession he was an actor, and that if he grew a moustache it would spoil his upper lip and militate against his success when he returned to the stage after the war. I thereupon drew the former papers on moustaches from the registry, asked my colleagues on the army council if they had any views on the subject, to which apparently, they were quite indifference, and finally obtained the approval of his Majesty the King.[36]

This somewhat bizarre case illustrated the long-standing implications of service in the military. The soldier in question was already considering his future upon returning from the front and a physical change such as a moustache would apparently mean a blow to his future career. Although this justification seems weak in hindsight, it is interesting that during the same year as the devastating battle of the Somme, significant time and energy were spared to debate long-standing regulations on physical presentation while in service. Evidently, faced with a unique blend of serving men drawn from four separate recruitment methods, bridging class divides and hosting a wide age span, compromise proved to the best course of action. On 8 October 1916, Command No. 1,695 of the King's Regulations which had demanded that soldiers wear a moustache was abolished by General Macready. For the first time in decades, soldiers, regulars, conscripts and New Army men alike regained some control over their facial hair and ostensibly over their appearance while under military control. Perhaps in the case of the military moustache the British authorities knew when it was best to pick their battles.[37]

The greater good

While men were expected to do what they could to remain healthy though self-discipline and hygiene, military authorities also intervened in their bodies in more direct ways seeking to preserve their preparedness for service. Disease prevention was a core aspect of this focus and vaccination against infectious diseases was a central strategy. By the outbreak of war in 1914 the British Army routinely inoculated men for diseases such as smallpox, typhoid and cholera, to mixed results. Towards the end of the war, the relative ease of implementation and rise in military official popularity of vaccination led to trials of a mixture of pneumococci and streptococci to unsuccessfully combat the influenza virus.[38] In 1919, the *Times* reported that by the end of the war nearly 97 per cent of all British servicemen had been protected against typhoid and paratyphoid using the TAB vaccine that had been developed in the middle of the conflict.[39] According to Mark Harrison, typhoid inoculation was a significant tool for British forces in the First World War, having been responsible for a substantial decrease in cases, ranging from 'a peak of 3.1 admissions to hospital per 1,000 troops from all typhoid fevers in 1915, the disease was gradually brought under control so that by 1917 it had fallen to 0.7, and by 1918, to 0.2 per 1,000'.[40] Inoculation was certainly successful as means of combatting typhoid, and its implementation worked particularly well in tandem with a focus on sanitary improvement. These reforms having been instituted as part of the military overhaul in the first decade of the twentieth century resulted in most of the regular soldiers in the British Expeditionary Force (BEF) entering the battlefield in 1914 with unprecedented knowledge and expertise in sanitary procedures.[41]

While effective, vaccination was also contentious as its use was supposedly voluntary but extensive evidence proved the opposite. Reports and recollections from the period suggest that inoculations were regarded by men as another essential aspect of military service, much like succumbing to a haircut or being required to don a uniform. Private Roberts recalled exactly that in his diary, writing, 'We are now paraded for vaccination. All those who have not been vaccinated before have to be vaccinated. This is compulsory, although not mentioned upon enlistment.'[42] Leonard Stagg served as a British nursing orderly with the 2/3rd South Midland Field Ambulance RAMC between 1916 and 1918. He also had believed that the inoculations that he received were a mandatory part of military life, as he recalled only ever hearing about one fellow soldier who declined to be inoculated. He told an interviewer, 'I think they were because he was the only person, I ever heard of who refused it.'[43] Thomas Mitchell-Fox was another who appeared to be under this misconception. After being captured by the enemy in 1918 he and his fellow British captives refused to be inoculated by their captors on the grounds that they already received it. He noted, 'Most of the officers concerned said: "oh we've had it before, we have all had it before, you 'had to'. Have to be vaccinated when you enter the service before you go abroad." '[44] In reality, there was no rule which stated that men had to submit to the anti-typhoid inoculation. Because of the 1907 repeal of mandatory vaccination, the choice was supposedly left to the will of the individual soldier.[45] Yet many men simply failed to recognize the lack of legal obligation to comply. This indoctrinated reluctance to ask questions may be why William Collins of the 3rd and 1st Northamptonshire Regiment also claimed in his oral interview that 'you had to be inoculated'.

Even politicians seemed confused about the voluntary aspect of inoculation during the war. In November 1914 Mr William Brace, the Labour MP for Glamorganshire South, demanded clarification from Mr Tennant, Undersecretary of State for War, that inoculation was not a requirement to be able to serve abroad as was commonly assumed.[46] Tennant's reply to the positive seemed only to confuse matters as many men seemed to regard the process as par the course of service. Certainly, the British military and government valued the protection of anti-typhoid inoculation as they took a dim view of the anti-typhoid inoculation rhetoric being published by the British Union for the Abolition of Vivisection (BUAV).[47] Colonel Leishman, one of the creators of the original vaccine and future director general of the RAMC, angrily accused them of 'doing much harm' as their opposition had resulted in battalions being dispatched filled with uninoculated men. This quarrel was printed in a report of a round-table debate in 1915 where members of the military and medical community clashed over the use of inoculation. As a leading opposer of inoculation surrounded by supporters of the procedure, Dr Snow made his case for the lack of safety in the use of the inoculation vehemently.

> Dr. Snow (London) said that as one of the antis he was glad to have the opportunity of putting before them the views of those who did not agree with the practice of inoculation at all. He gratefully acknowledged the moderate way in which Prof. Sims Woodward put the case before them. The case before them that evening was 'protective inoculation'. Speaking on behalf of a large number of people present, he utterly denied that any inoculation hitherto brought forward was protective against disease. He utterly denied its power of protection, and he would address himself to that point, and to the question of inoculation and its results. On the question of the scientific principle, nothing was more uncertain and halting than the manner in which Prof. Woodhead put it before them. 'It is assumed there are antibodies'; 'we think it may be so', 'perhaps', and so on. There was no note of scientific certainty from beginning to end.[48]

Snow continued his tirade by outlining that repeated occurrences of reported deaths as a result of the vaccine before concluding on the 'evils' of inoculation. 'It was murder to use a thing like inoculation, which was scientifically unsound (it made the men always very ill, and even caused their death in some cases) and to inflict it upon young men going out to fight.'[49] This vociferous dissent could also be located within the ranks as some soldiers resisted and refused to be inoculated. In response, and against the supposed remit of the British Army, some men found themselves being punished for their failure to accept the army's control over their bodies. In January 1915, Lord Tenterden raised in parliament the issue of soldiers being refused promotion and being badly treated for non-compliance.[50]

This was raised again a month later after reports of Colonel Davies-Colley, of the 6th Reserve Manchester Regiment, attempting to forcibly inoculate his men. Six men who refused the treatment were subsequently sent to the doctor under escort, which in turn resulted in the physical restrain and attempted inoculation of one man while four others escaped and sought refuge with the brigade officer.[51] This was not an isolated incident; numerous complaints arose demonstrating that men were punished as a result of not accepting vaccinations. This could include the suspension of privileges, refusal for promotion or leave and even accounts of bullying, where men were labelled 'cowards' in the army, which led to a series of articles printed and questions raised in the House of Commons in reference to coercive treatment of New Army and conscript soldiers. One of which was raised incredulously in January 1915 by Lord Tenterden as he told parliament, 'I have in my hand many letters from soldiers complaining of hard treatment … [because] they have refused to submit to inoculation.'[52] Tenterden continued to vent his frustration on the parliament floor regarding the discrepancies between the rhetoric of the conduct of the British military and the reality of how men were being treated: 'It is perfectly evident that inoculation is made as compulsory as it could possibly be. Men are refused promotion … they have been badly treated in many ways by having their passes stopped and by being made to do disagreeable work. And this simply because they refuse to be inoculated.'[53]

Tenterden's evidence and accusation reiterates how important the maintenance of soldier's physical fitness was during the First World War. His calls for recompense for those who had their bodies abused and violated against their will were also strengthened by the visible and often extremely unpleasant side effects, resulting in many men suffering a short bout of illness after the procedure. A member of the Officer Training Corps (OTC), Jack Briscoe Masefield, recalled that his inoculation made him very ill. 'Well it gave me hell I know that. For about three days you were like nothing on earth and I suppose it worked.'[54] The hell that Masefield described often included swollen limbs, sickness, fever, fatigue and, in extreme cases, death. In 1915, Private Watson wrote to his mother to say that he was pleased that his inoculation seemed not to have taken, something he had interpreted as the result of remaining well while his friends became ill: 'I'm glad to say it did not take … I was very glad because I didn't want to be done again, some of our lads are very bad.'[55] This incomprehension of the medicalized impact of the process was also apparent in the pride some men displayed in their ability to withstand the effects of the vaccine. Walter Clark, who served with the Hampshire Regiment in 1917, recalled how the myth developed that those who were the fittest, and by proxy most masculine, were more immune to the debilitating effects of the inoculation. He claimed, 'Some got over it quicker I suppose they were fitter stronger physically, getting you fit, doing a lot of marching, PT, that was one of the main things.'[56] In reality, while the enhanced physical prowess that had been developed through arduous training may have somewhat improved their physical recovery, their responses were more likely to be attributable to their long-standing physical health and history of overcoming disease, rather than a singular impact of their training program.

Of course, while the side effects made the procedure an often unwelcome part of service, there was concern over the overall safety of the procedure. During his passionate speech in 1914 Dr Snow cited several historic military deaths attributed to vaccination.[57] In November 1916, while concerns over typhoid had against began to arise accompanied by a new virulent strain of typhoid, the Secretary of State again found himself under fire in parliament after the reported death of a soldier caused by inoculation. Private Edward Jobling had reportedly enlisted in 1914 without a single illness within his history; according to the report repeated in parliament, this was to change as 'immediately after vaccination he felt ill, and never regained his former health … Jobling was discharged in August, 1915, as no longer physically fit for war service, and was registered as having served 352 days.'[58] Jobling was one of three reported inoculation deaths that year, each of which was quickly explained away by ancillary medical conditions.[59] Regardless of what had caused these fatalities, this association with sudden debilitation and death did not help allay suspicions over the process; yet, it is important not to overstate this concern for the majority of the serving men.

When considered together, these depictions of vaccination, domination and resistance during the First World War illustrate that while the majority accepted inoculation as part of a wider process of bodily subjection, surrendering control of their bodies to the authorities for the greater good, others opposed it.[60] The doctor stood alongside the barber and the store clerk who issued their uniforms as agents of control asserted over the bodies of civilians as they were transformed into soldiers. Like the issue of shaving, some resisted this chemical intrusion into their body. However, crucially it is clear that the occasion of the war encouraged some officers, and perhaps the British military in its role as authoritative body, to offset the agency of the men under their command in return for increasing the chance to maintaining their physical bodies.

Disease was not the only killer to be wary of behind the lines, as surrounded by weapons, uncertain terrain, crowds of men and instances of intense boredom; accidents are bound to happen. Reid explains that researchers face a significant problem in recognizing those who suffered or were killed through accidents as such cases were often simply recorded as 'other casualties' within the official figures.[61] However, this does not mean that the British military were blind to the ability of men to damage their own bodies. The 1932 published report *Medical Services; Casualties and Medical Statistics of the Great War* stated that 46,309 men had suffered an accident and were returned to duty and a further 506 had died as a result.[62] Additionally, it is important to recognize the potential impact of individual non-reporting of injuries which is a typical action associated with presentations of masculinity.

In 2019, Novak et al. studied a range of American men to ascertain their likelihood to visit a physician for a health complaint. Their research validated a long-standing cultural stereotype in many Western nations, in that many men were exceptionally reluctant to seek medical attention.[63] Novak et al. argue that as a result of socialized masculine orientation influences, men frequently attempted to fix their own minor ailments or ignore them entirely.[64] Applying the same logic to the hyper-masculinized atmosphere and indoctrination that the majority of the fighting men in the First World

War had been subjected to, it is not unreasonable to assume that men would frequently fail to report minor injuries. This is further backed up by the previous discussion in this chapter, illustrating how men would overlook sickness or disease in favour of duty. However, no matter how far the 1932 figure may be from the actual total it demonstrates that the body of the soldier was often in danger even when far away from the enemy.

Vehicles could also be particularly hazardous; NCO Oswald Croft crashed his motorcycle and was injured enough to be sent home after, somewhat ironically, a red cross ambulance pulled out in front of him as he returned on a food run in 1918.[65] Motorcycle dispatcher Private Eustace Booth was another who was no stranger to accidents. His task of riding around the back of the lines at night meant that he regularly encountered unexpected perils in the dark. For Booth, this seemed to just be part of the job, as he recalled: 'Oh I came off my bike many a time, I had fallen off, I was knocked off ... I got bruised, oh yes, oh yes sometimes I did hurt myself quite a bit.'[66] The presence of live ammunition and the requirements to keep weapons ready for use and skills up to scratch also carried all sorts of risks. In the middle of an excited letter home about the end of the war written on 13 November 1918, Lieutenant Erskine noted in his diary that 'I'm not taking risks now and I am not going to fire any more live shells' after a third accident had killed several of his men.[67] He noted in his diary that this was becoming a regular event, 'they have had an accident with 1/4th. A gun burst. The 2/1st officer and three Askari were killed a week ago at firing practice, another officer of the cap corps and ten others were killed accidentally a short time before.' While serving as an orderly with the RAMC in 1917, William Fowler also reiterated that accidents were fairly common as he noted how he had been injured in a bomb accident along with twelve other men, many of whom later died.[68] Private Prew recounted a similar experience as he trained with the Seventh London where a bombing accident, which had killed several men, had left his battalion 'down in the dumps'.[69] Firearms could be just as dangerous. Early into the war Private Hare almost shot himself at point blank range while staring down the barrel of his regimental sergeant major's revolver during cleaning. Hare explained how this event, a momentary lapse of concentration, stayed with him as the most vivid memory of the war. 'Do you know, that upsets me more than all the shellfire and machine guns, to think that I was so near to death and it would have been my own fault.'[70]

Access to weaponry could also mean self-harm. The next chapter considers in detail actions of self-inflicted wounds and suicides. Yet, it must be noted that suicides, like accidents, are particularly difficult to identify. In his diary, Private Reynolds recorded a series of tragic events as several men took their own lives in early November 1915.

> Other incidents of the week were one man cut his throat on Parade ground – effects of home trouble and barrack life. Wounded soldier broke out of hospital – insane crying 'war is over! War's over' Caught with difficulty. Later in week another Recruit Smith of Anstey, cut his throat in entry in town. On Saturday night recruit in Black B went silly, caused a disturbance, overpowered with great difficulty, result of drink on mind affected by separation from home and home comforts. Tonight, rumour of another suicide. No details known so hope it is untrue.[71]

Seemingly desperate to relieve themselves from the strains of military service such as separation from home, life in the barracks and alcohol consumption, these men used their remaining agency over their own to escape the confines they had found themselves within. Clearly, even in the relative safety of the camps behind the front lines, men were wounded and died. Unfortunately for the understanding of those looking back at these events, these cases were by no means as contentiously documented as the wounding and fatalities on the front lines.

Comfort food (and drink)

As should now be overtly apparent from the presiding analysis within this book, food was important. It kept men alive and their bodies capable of fighting. The food on offer ranged from hearty meal to the dreaded iron ration of hard tack and tinned stew; still its purpose in maintaining the men at war remained the same.[72] Food is one of the most reoccurring elements within accounts of the First World War. So many papers, diaries and interviews of men who served in the First World War detail accounts of seeking bodily pleasures to satisfy cravings and to alleviate their strain. Food could provide much-needed respite from the conditions of the front. So much so that when leave was granted it was often devoted to the pursuit of more appetizing dishes. Food was a favourite conversation piece as soldiers guarded, rested and prepared to fight. Accolades for the poor fair offered and pleas for more pleasant nourishment are recurrent in songs, jokes, poems and plays from the period. Additionally, food also played an important emotional role as a link to home through parcels, as the home comfort for their bodies was accompanied by letters of love and news. These parcels also helped to strengthen camaraderie as men shared out their consumable treasures.

The provision of food to the active soldier in the First World War was not an easy feat. Most of the food provided while on active service came from one of the many field kitchens that were established by the military authorities behind the front lines. Maintained and staffed by the ASC, these kitchens would be the origin for nearly all the freshly prepared food that the fighting men would consume. Yet, instead of being treated with gratitude for their role in delivering much-needed sustenance to the front, the ASC frequently endured scathing remarks from their fighting comrades for rarely being directly in the firing line. Stories abounded between soldiers of the nepotism and corruption in food distribution as imagined slights that the infantry would get the worst portions while the service corps dined on the finest cuts spread disquiet from trench to trench.[73] In actuality most of the criticism and distaste, which often was redirected against the men who provided it, was aimed at the food the soldiers received. Widely considered unappetizing and repetitive complaints such as that by Private Peyton below were common:

> We were given the inevitable stew, potatoes in the skins (and dirt), the meat was half raw and very fatty, the vegetables uncooked. Being boys, or most of them were boys of tender ages, the expected thing happened – a huge lump of fat was thrown, hitting someone in the face – result pandemonium started – potatoes, meat etc.

flying all over the place – when in walked the orderly officer. All names were taken, and we were put on half rations for a week's well-deserved punishment. This meant no 'afters' and at that age, I was prepared to eat anything edible, so we were truly punished. Your pay was then eight pence per day. This was gone over the weekend in cakes (I remember them now, hard lumps of royally overcooked flour and little else – but we scoffed them as if they were really delicious) in the canteen.[74]

Evidently poorly prepared and of questionable quality, Peyton and his comrades disgust at the food they had been given manifested in a minor resistance which at least proved highly entertaining, albeit briefly. Interestingly, the resulting punishment suited the crime, as their bodies were deprived of more satisfaction, forcing them to financially compensate for their lost luxuries.

Behind the lines, the supplementing of the military diet through the buying of food from canteens, soldiers' homes or local towns was a common activity. Voluntary organizations such as the YMCA, as well as the ingenuity of Army Chaplains, was particularly instrumental in providing alternatives to the usual menus. The Reverend Creighton, an Anglican Vicar who had volunteered after the outbreak of war, noted the importance of a full stomach for the men's morale and was proud of his busy canteen which supported the overburdened field kitchens. He recorded, 'The men patronise it all the time. It is really extraordinary the part played by the stomach in life. It simply rules the world and affects all our outlook on life. We are paralysed, absorbed, hypnotised by it. The chief topic of conversation is rations with the men, and food and wine with the officers.'[75] He was also unfortunately frustrated that his spiritual role was diminished as the soldiers seemed to prioritize physical comforts over his spiritual teachings despite his assertions to his reluctant flock that 'man shall not live by bread alone'.[76] Perhaps to avoid similar lectures, Private Whitehouse noted how men would spend much of their wages at the soldier's home, another type of canteen, as they attempted to add variety and pleasure to their lacklustre diet. Whitehouse wrote, 'We could augment our rations by buying extras at the soldier's home, such as rice pudding, cakes, buns and biscuits and cups of various drinks. Most of my meagre pay went in this way.'[77] For Private Niblett the opportunity to enhance his dietary fair came with a severe price, as he was forced to choose between better food and entertainment. He noted in his memoirs that most of his wages went on 'egg and chips or crown and anchor', clearly a stark choice between additional nutrition and the entertainment of gambling.[78]

On the front line, improvisation was often key to finding ways to supplement the diet offered to the men. In 1914, the *Illustrated London News* published an image of four soldiers, including a French officer alongside the British men, cooking two plucked birds suspended from a spit constructed by rifles. In the background a fellow soldier can be seen to be prone and on guard as the men prepare their feast.[79] It is unlikely that these men were directly on the front line as the fire would potentially make them a target; yet, the presence of the man on guard implies that still there was an element of danger to be had simply for the purpose of having something different to eat. While such an elaborate set-up was more the exception than the rule, clearly soldiers would often go to extreme lengths to diversify their diet. The other issue is the question of where the birds came from in the first place? While men could purchase food from civilians nearby, this was typically carried out behind the lines and regulated. On the front, taking the initiative to purchase some food could be regarded as going absent without leave which brought severe penalties. There was also the issue of how much money soldiers tended to have as was made clear by Private Niblett. An alternative to buying food was 'requisitioning' it. Duffett notes that during times of shortage the British Army frequently turned a blind eye as men scrounged and stole from land and local areas, not least of all as officers would also occasionally acquire food in this manner.[80] Private Keller recounted how a fellow soldier, a former fisherman, managed to 'bag' them an alternative dinner by stealing chickens from a local farm using a 'a small net on a wire loop and put it on a long pole to get hens out of the hen house which the farmer's wife always kept locked'.[81] According to Keller it is likely that this escapade resulted in the British Army having to reimburse the injured party after she caught the men in the act of the thievery.[82] However, despite clear guidelines which demanded harsh physical punishment for theft, none of the men suffered conviction. Not entirely oblivious to the trials the fighting men faced COs who were often willing to overlook and even cover for the misdeeds of their men, perhaps as further nourishment would likely improve their physical stature, whereas punishment would all but certainly diminish it.

A significantly safer method of supplementing the army diet was parcels from home. These gifts often provided variety and additional nutrition, alongside welcome news from home and a distraction from the men's daily drudgery. On receipt of his parcel, Lieutenant Lindsay replied to thank his mother profusely and remarked that her gifts had allowed him to supplement his lack of nourishment. He wrote, 'I can't say how much the tablets are welcome for our water, and the Horlicks tablets will supply nourishment which bread and jam cannot'.[83] Parcels could also provide alternative types of food where needed. During a particularly bad case of dysentery Private Mann became completely dependent on the food he received from home as the dry biscuits were all he could stomach during the three days he recovered in hospital.[84] Marrying physical and emotional needs, parcels from home also provided severely needed connections with loved ones as well as sating cravings for luxuries unavailable during active service. In parody of a mail order catalogue system, soldiers frequently wrote home with requests for clothes, food, tobacco and even medicine to improve their physical existence at the front. Many became as dependant on this link with home as the rifle they carried. Unfortunately, the receiving of parcels could also be inconsistent as food could arrive spoilt or simply go missing. Lieutenant Colonel Philip George Anstruther complained about this in 1917 in a letter home where he complained that his parcel had been lost for a time and the supplies, he had been sent, had turned inedible.[85] The use of supplementary parcels was not equal across the ranks. Influenced by factors such as rank, class and personal circumstances, parcels were more often for the men from more affluent backgrounds whose family could afford to provide the luxuries denied at the front. Officers had more opportunity to send and receive mail, and the highest ranks would move significantly less often than the lowly private. Parcels may have offered an opportunity for all to improve their experience during service, but this by no means an employable option for all.

For some the lack of parcels was not too much of a concern as not everyone found their meals dirty, uncooked, overcooked or unappetizing. Private Butler remembered in his memoirs that as he served on the western front for most of the war there was decent food on offer for him and his mates: 'There was always stew. The bobagee [sic] very often made a stew of bully beef, McConachie's stew and all that sort of thing and biscuits. They'd boil it all up in a big cauldron and it was good food.'[86] Likewise, volunteer soldier Private Whitehouse, who saw action at Battles of the Marne, the Aisne, the Second Battle of Ypres and the Somme, wrote in his memoirs of the war about his fondness for the food on offer: 'The food was plain but quite good, we had a fairly regular diet having certain items on certain days. It must have been alright because we were all kept very fit and hardy.'[87] A veteran of battles and military meals, and in spite of his protestations earlier in his memoirs, Whitehouse claimed that on the whole he continued to enjoy his military-issued fare until he was demobilized in March 1919. For soldiers like Whitehouse and Butler the quality of the food was not a matter of concern, although still quantity often made men grumble. Men such as these appeared to accept the promises of the recruiting sergeants and found the meals on offer to them palatable. While they may have been satisfied, historians have argued that the plain food, and its monotony, may have had unintentionally negative nutritional consequences. Beckett, Bowman and Connelly argue that the limited variety and lack of focus by the British Army on providing a healthy and varied diet meant numerous cases of 'boils, sore gums and bad teeth' for serving soldiers.[88]

Alcohol was a different issue entirely. Drinking was not only a typical soldier's recreational activity but also something that was an intrinsic part of their military service. Wages often went on beer, wines and spirits despite nearly all men already receiving an officially distributed alcohol beverage as part of their experience of soldiery during the war. Justification for this derived from the belief that alcoholic drinks were therapeutic substances and tonics. In 1907 the *British Pharmacopeia* had published that 'as a circulatory stimulant, the value of alcohol is undoubted; it increases the output of blood from the heart'.[89] Support for the distribution of alcohol is also visible in the official recommendations within the 1914 *British Army Field Service Manual* (see Figure 7). Republished on the eve of war, the manual clarified that ideally 126 pints of rum would be allocated to each battalion per day, to be distributed at the discretion of the general officer commanding (GOC) and with the recommendation of the medical officer.[90]

During the First World War, the distribution of alcohol at the front was designed to enable the men to cope with the trials of service and combat. The giving of rum at dawn was often accompanied by an enthusiastic double-meaning cry of 'Up Spirits'.[91] By the end of 1915, the British military had received over a quarter of million gallons of rum for their forces in France to be distributed twice weekly. The ration per man could also be increased for front-line troops during times of poor weather.[92] Alcohol was believed by many to have restorative and regenerative physical properties. A late comer to the war in early 1918, Private Stapleton recalled how his rum ration was essential as he served with the Royal Inniskilling Fusiliers:

> We had a very hard day, when up came the Major on his horse and said 'every man to get into battle order ready for an advance' I trod over these miles of ground again, no sleep, no rest and the ground sodden, your feet slipped back as fast as

54

D.—FORAGE.

Detail of forage carried in the field with units and in Army Service Corps trains and supply columns for each horse.

How carried.	Corn ration 12 lbs.	Remarks.
On the horse	1 (a)	(a) The day's ration issued the previous evening less any portion consumed.
In A.S.C. trains or } In supply column }	1	
Total	2 (b)	(b) Less any portion consumed of the ration carried on the horse.

Notes.—1. The above scale of forage is applicable to a country where hay is available.
2. Forage for the day of entrainment will be carried as directed in Mobilization Regulations.

E.—SUPPLIES REQUIRED FOR ONE DAY.

The following table, which is inserted for the purpose of easy reference, shows the detail of supplies which would be required by a battalion for one day:—

Detail.			Battalion Head-quarters.	M.G. Section.	One Company.	Battalion.
*Establishment { personnel		...	81	18	227	1,007
{ horses		...	31	5	5	56
Biscuits		lbs.	81	18	227	1,007
Bread (in lieu of biscuits) ...		,,	$101\frac{1}{4}$	$22\frac{1}{2}$	$283\frac{3}{4}$	$1,258\frac{1}{4}$
Bacon		,,	$20\frac{1}{4}$	$4\frac{1}{2}$	$56\frac{3}{4}$	$251\frac{1}{4}$
Cheese		,,	$15\frac{3}{16}$	$3\frac{7}{16}$	$42\frac{3}{16}$	$188\frac{11}{16}$
Groceries:—						
Mustard		,,	$\frac{4}{16}$	$\frac{1}{16}$	$1\frac{2}{16}$	$3\frac{9}{16}$
Tea		,,	$3\frac{3}{16}$	$\frac{1}{2}$	$8\frac{1}{4}$	$39\frac{5}{16}$
Sugar		,,	$15\frac{3}{16}$	$3\frac{5}{16}$	$42\frac{3}{16}$	$188\frac{11}{16}$
Salt		,,	$1\frac{1}{2}$	9 ozs.	$7\frac{3}{16}$	$31\frac{1}{2}$
Pepper		...	2 ozs.	$\frac{1}{2}$ oz.	$\frac{5}{16}$ lb.	$1\frac{3}{4}$ lbs.
Jam		lbs.	21	5	57	252
Meat, { fresh (in lieu of preserved)		,,	$101\frac{1}{4}$	$22\frac{1}{2}$	$283\frac{3}{4}$	$1,258\frac{1}{4}$
{ preserved		,,	81	18	227	1,007
Oats		,,	372	60	60	672
Vegetables—fresh (a)		,,	$40\frac{1}{2}$	9	$113\frac{1}{4}$	$503\frac{1}{4}$
or dried		,,	$10\frac{2}{16}$	$2\frac{1}{4}$	$28\frac{5}{16}$	$125\frac{1}{16}$
or						
Lime juice (b) † ...		pts.	2	$\frac{1}{2}$	$5\frac{1}{4}$	25
Rum (c) †		,,	10	$2\frac{1}{4}$	$28\frac{1}{4}$	126
Tobacco (c) †... ...		,,	$1\frac{7}{16}$ lbs.	5 ozs.	$4\frac{3}{16}$ lbs.	18 lbs.

* Excludes A.S.C. drivers and horses of the train.
(a) To be issued when available, but not to be carried in regimental transport when troops are marching daily.
(b) Lime juice is issued when fresh vegetables are not supplied, or at the discretion of the G.O.C. on recommendation of the medical officer.
(c) Issued at the discretion of the G.O.C. on recommendation of the medical officer.
† Not carried normally in supply columns or A.S.C. trains.

Figure 7 British Army Field Service Manual, 1914. Anon, *British Army Field Service Manual, 1914* (London: HMSO, 1914), p. 54.

you put one forward. There is nothing for it just a drop of rum and it gave us some heart and settled our burden and went forthwith. I for one could not have been one of the party, if I had not had the rum.[93]

Stapleton was certainly not alone in this sentiment; according to Sergeant McKay, it was only his and his comrades access to a surplus of rum that meant they could survive the constant barrage of patients they treated while part of the 109th Field Ambulance at the Somme on 15 August 1916. McKay wrote, '[We have been] working day and night. Fortunately, plenty of rum can be had as there are jars lying about which ration parties throw from them when they get caught in shell fire at night.'[94] This theme of physical enhancement is also evident within the papers of Private Bigwood who served with the 7th Battalion Worcestershire Regiment. He recalled how alcohol had made him almost a super soldier, as it reportedly granted him the physical strength and confidence to single-handedly win the war. 'I drank a good deal of rum and then I went back up on the frontline and they came around with the rum ration and I could have won the war as easy as anything, absolutely. That was the first time I had ever been drunk.'[95] Bigwood's potentially deadly overconfidence aside, not all men were as positive about their rum ration. Before the war, NCO Alfred West with the 1/1st Battalion Monmouthshire Regiment had never partaken in drinking alcohol; still, he felt that the meagre rations of rum allotted to him and his men were too small to have an impact on their bodies and dismissed the notion that a spoonful of rum would warm up the men as they shivered on the front lines.[96]

Like Bigwood, Private Ching also became particularly drunk through the rum ration. Rather than preparing to take on the enemy single-handed, however, the liberal amount of rum his CO had issued to help his platoon build a bridge over a freezing river in Northern France served to render him physically incapable.

> You had a tot of rum when you went in, a tot of rum when you went out … this rum was special SRD, it was rum, not diluted I'm telling you, and this was distributed by the corporal … all that I can remember about that incident, all that I can remember and things that I've been told. Now we were so drunk with rum that I was hung over the side of this big bulk of timber and ten thousand troops had passed over that bridge without them kicking me over the side, this is what I was told, and I can well imagine it because I was brought back off the bridge, I was let on the ground. I must have been asleep by then of this drink you see, and I woke up and sick, being sick with it, and I spewed all over the Sergeant Major.[97]

Not only had Ching's drinking rendered him insensible but he also vomited on his CO. Never a good idea for anyone looking for opportunities to impress and progress. Here elements of agency and autonomy are recognizable as to avoid a situation like Ching; some men abstained from alcohol for fear that it rendered their bodies incapable of effective military service. Cecil Burnell Tubbs recalled that offers of alcohol meant he could barely conduct his duties and as such decided to abstain in future: 'I had to go around four companies by day and all four companies by night and everywhere I went, "Tommy Boy have a drink". So, I had to cut it out, I just had to cut it right out, otherwise, it was impossible.'[98] Others experienced the reverse and found their convictions dissolved in the face of front-line service. British stretcher-bearer Joseph Yarwood had been a strict teetotaller his entire live as a result of his own parent's alcoholism. This changed after he arrived at the front where his first ever alcoholic drink was the rum ration, something he later laughed about during an oral history interview as he continued to imbibe alcohol throughout and after the war as a result of the experience.[99]

Such was the importance of alcohol for serving men that the topic was satirized in the trench newspaper the *Wipers Times*, by a mock advert placed by 'J. Supitup' which offered to turn any applicant to drink. The advert also makes light of the youthfulness of the newest recruits, joking about sobriety before the age of 16 before the author experienced his alcohol epiphany and has since 'never been to bed sober'.

THE DRINK HABIT ACQUIRED IN THREE DAYS

If you know anyone who doesn't drink alcohol regularly, or occasionally, let me send my free book, 'CONFESSIONS OF AN ALCOHOL SLAVE'. It explains something important, i.e: How to quickly become an Expert 'Bona-fide Toper'.

For the first 15 years of my life I was a rabid teetotaller, since the age of 16 I have never been to bed sober. If your trouble is with reference to a friend, please state in your letter whether he is willing to be cured or not. Letters treated in a confidential manner. I can cure anyone.

Address: J. SUPITUP, Havanotha Mansions. Telegrams: RATS.[100]

This complex relationship between soldiers and alcohol was not unique to the twentieth century. The culture of drinking in the military had long been an issue and had increasingly become a matter of public and political concern in the mid-nineteenth century. As a counterweight to these concerns soldier's abstinence associations such as the 1888 Army Temperance Association (ATA) were in the run up to the twentieth century.[101] By 1900, abstaining soldiers were given medals for abstinence as a badge of honour.[102] Nevertheless, alcohol remained a significant part of military life and crucially an important tool for the British Army during the First World War in the form of physical stimulant and fortifier during service.

Alcohol was not only available as prescribed by the military. Much as with food, men often sought to drink beyond their rations. In 1916, Private Perry recognized a link between alcohol and respite as he described resting away from the front line with his battalion at Coulonvillers. He wrote in his diary 'Moved to Coulonvillers. Somewhere we can spend 13 enjoyable days only 13 kilometres from Abbeville, very nice. I go to Abbeville almost every day for beer and canteen stores.'[103] During his time as a 15th Battalion King's Liverpool Regiment NCO Percy Valentine Harris recalled witnessing many men spend their wages on a few drinks, he claimed 'living was cheap however … some men managed to get drunk once a week, but smokers and drinkers, unless they had money from home, had a poor time from Monday to Friday'.[104] A veteran of the Somme, Ypres and Lake Garda, Private Thorley was familiar with the lengths that men would go to in order to secure a drink and recalled in his diary how men were prepared to take considerable risks to secure a little variety in what they consumed. Thorley described how a corporal from the British side had attempted to trade some rum for whisky with the enemy. The man subsequently was arrested and sent off the line to await a court martial as a result of his desperate actions.[105]

As fallible as anyone, some soldiers would drink beyond their tolerance and the resulting effect could be catastrophic. As noted, unused to the drink he imbibed during strenuous miserable duties Private Ching received an unpleasant haranguing and extensive punishment duty for his lack of judgement and self-control after he vomited on his CO following being tied to a recently constructed bridge while an entire battalion marched passed by his insensible body.[106] On Halloween 1915 Lieutenant Stiven wrote home to his parents in Dundee to recount another tale of a lost drunken fellow who had wandered wayward into his barracks. Stiven recounted that the insensible man was subsequently hauled before the men's CO, waking him particularly early on a Sunday. 'I imagine that the result would have been guardroom at least for the poor delinquent. But such was not the case with Dummer, who gave him a wiggings [sic] and let him go unmolested'.[107] The man in question was certainly lucky to be found by such an understanding NCO; in place of a shouted lecture the man could have been executed given that drunkenness was a serious military offence. Within the published memoirs of Private Iriam who joined the war through the Canadian Overseas Expeditionary Service lies the account of a man who was nearly court-martialled for desertion, a crime that could also have earned him the death penalty, after being too drunk to join his regiment on the line. A tale of daring and desperation followed as his friend broke into the jail to rescue him, ultimately through physically damaging the culprit:

> The drunk pretended he wanted to go outside to a latrine or something he and his mate went down the stairs and around the back of the building. Here his mate got hold of a bit of wood hitting the court-martial case a wallop on the arm breaking the arm. He explained that the drunk had fallen when going down the stairs. He was sent down the line to a hospital and in that way escaped court martial.[108]

Faced with a decision between punishment and physical sacrifice, these men ironically subverted the military authorities and the assured physical punishment by sacrificing the drunk man's physical wellness. All too often alcohol served to damage the bodies of the men that the military had taken pains to prepare for war, either directly or indirectly as a consequence of action or misdeed. Private Farrer recounted how a drunken regular stretcher-bearer in 1915 with the 3rd Battalion Green Howards was given strict punishment after, embolden by drink, he decided to unburden himself of the animosity he felt towards the regimental sergeant major and quartermaster. His tirade possibly descended into a violent confrontation the result of which ended in his arrest and subsequent court marital.[109] Having received six months of imprisonment, the man's folly came to its fruition, as upon his eventual return to the front line he immediately received a very severe wound.[110] Tragically for the unfortunate man prior to his incarceration he was due to be released from service having served his thirteen years of service, not an uncommon event for long-serving regulars prior to the introduction of conscription in 1916. For this particularly unlucky soldier the price of intoxication proved to be extremely high and felt extensively through the experiences of his body.

Punishment for drunkenness could be extremely severe and at first glance out of proportion for the crime. While appearing harsh, the reasons for such harsh penalties for lapses in judgement were dramatically illustrated by Private Lancaster who recalled discovering a disaster waiting to happen where a camp full of drunken British soldiers was blissfully unaware of the proximity of the enemy in 1918. 'About 500 of our troops, absolutely paralytic drunk and Jerry couldn't have been far off, in fact, they were entering the other side of the town at that moment.'[111] Keen to protect his men from such folly, 2nd Lieutenant McCracken subjected one of his men to Field Punishment No.1 for three days after being arrested for being drunk and disorderly in 1915. He noted in his diary how the man's punishment was particularly important to disincline any future drunken behaviour from the rest of men: 'So (he) is strung up to a gun wheel for an hour per diem, I think it will be very effective.'[112] For the unluckiest men, and exclusively for the lowest ranks, an overindulgence of alcohol could mean execution, particularly if that consumption of alcohol directly impacted on the soldier's effectiveness on the front line. For this very reason, Private Evans was executed on 6 February 1915 as through his alcohol-induced stupor he had failed to report for duty.[113] Private Knight was also executed after he became drunk and opened fire indiscriminately on his fellow soldiers in the 10th Battalion on 3 November 1915.[114] While the execution of these men were very rare exceptions rather than the rule, and both men were tried for behaviour misconduct not intoxication, the dangerous impact of alcohol on the fighting body is evident.

Alcohol may have been used to blunt the edges of the extended unpleasantness of extended service and hasten men over the top into the fray. However, it also allowed for men to continually damage and endanger the bodies that the British military valued so preciously. This continual battle between the military and the soldier ultimately cost physical capabilities and even caused strategic losses in terms of lost lives and lost men from the front lines. Unmistakably, the impact of alcohol on the physical body of the soldier proved to be as debilitating, if not more so, than it was believed restorative over the course of the First World War.

Morale over morals

Food and alcohol were certainly not the only pursuits that men sought out to comfort their bodies. The pursuit of sex had been a part of soldiering for as long as men wore uniforms to fight other men. Many historians, including the seminal work of Bourke and Cherry, have researched extensively how the pursuit of sex played an active role in soldier's experience of military service during the First World War.[115] Yet, this is typically focused on heterosexuality with very little consideration of those who eschew conventional sexual activity within this period.

Of course, sexual satisfaction could also be sought by servicemen from other men, but this is not always easy to recognize while conducting historical research. Weeks and Porter have argued that homosexuality in the military in the nineteenth and early twentieth century only became visible when it occurred between ranks.[116] Indeed the official records of homosexuality are questionable. According to George Robb, 22 British officers and 270 rankers were court-martialled for homosexuality between 1914 and 1922.[117] A. D. Harvey adds that there was a significant increase in the prosecution of officers for homosexual and indecent acts in the immediate aftermath of the war and further notes that of the seventeen officers tried of homosexuality during the war, ten men were convicted in the twelve months prior to 30 September 1916.[118] He explains that this was associated with the sudden lowering of the entrance rates and requirements during a period of rapid expansion under the Derby scheme and conscription.[119] Interestingly, despite the need for men on the front lines Harvey explains that several men imprisoned for homosexuality were denied the right to join the war effort. This included several former soldiers who had previously served and had been cashiered out as a result of their sexuality.[120]

This was the case for Captain Alfred C. Boyd who had been sentenced to two years' hard labour for eight counts of indecency. In a pleading letter Boyd petitioned for his release on the condition of no leave until his sentence was complete and renouncing his homosexuality with the words: 'I want to show that I am a man, and I am determined to live a straight and manly life in the future.' In refusing his request, both the military and Boyd himself illustrated the disassociation between sexuality, masculinity and usefulness that reigned over the course of the war in British society. His lack of heterosexuality seemingly overruled his physicality in the eyes of the military, a state of mind that Harvey theorizes led to the creation of a 'H.O. Special List' which he notes is not officially recorded anywhere other than on Boyd's index card, and potentially consisted of a list of known homosexuals not to be enlisted for any reason.[121] While the existence of the list is questionable, given the culture surrounding homosexuality and the physical punishments that awaited those uncovered, it is unsurprising that many men including Captain Joseph Randell Ackerley, Wilfred Owen and Siegfried Sassoon worked hard to keep their sexuality a secret for the duration of the war, potentially for fear of retribution or ostracism.[122]

Paul Fussell argues that within the work of men such as Owen, Sassoon and Ross the homosexual love between men was particularly visible in the language and affections demonstrated within the verses.[123] However, accounts of homosexuality are particularly rare within the testimonies and records from the First World War. In a rare mention as part of an oral history testimony, Private Holbrook claimed that homosexuality was not a regular occurrence, at least within his estimation: 'Don't think I knew of it, they were very strict about it I found out afterwards, I didn't know at the time, the sergeant would come in, they wouldn't dare, there wouldn't be any of that sort of thing, none of that sort of thing, very strict.'[124] Holbrook goes on to explain that within his barracks a game was played called the Cork Club which both satirized homosexuality and policed any such activity in his unit. Each member had to retain a cork on their person which they had to show on demand or be fined a penny.[125] Holbrook describes this as fun and useful for establishing a kitty for the barrack and while he is unclear about how the presentation of the cork meant men were not homosexual, he infers that without it you were considered questionable and potentially unprotected from homosexual advances, therefore having left yourself open to deviancy you were financially punished. This 'fun' game reiterates the idea of homosexuality as a crime or immoral act, as the process of humorously punishing those suddenly labelled as homosexual accompanies a socialized reflective response of negativity. This internalization of behavioural norms, the process of which was at the heart of the military indoctrination experience, according to social theorists such as Ervin Goffman, would ensure the validation of culturally acceptable behaviours – in this case the rejection, humiliation and stigmatization of homosexuals.[126]

In Weeks and Porter's *Between the Acts*, there are several rare accounts of homosexual men who served as soldiers in the First World War. Again the narrative is focused on punishment, fear and suspicion. One former soldier, 'Gerald', noted that he 'only met one other homosexual in the army' and that he only ever had sex with one man during his time in uniform as his rise to the rank of sergeant made any further sexual experiences impossible.[127] 'Gerald' was forced not only to deny his own physical and psychological needs, he was also forced to report another man for homosexual behaviour in order to protect himself. He explained, 'There was nothing I could do; I couldn't protect him. I had to look after number one. See, I couldn't let the world know that I was homosexual, not in the army! Otherwise what was going to happen?'[128] Another former soldier called 'Fred' describes a more open environment but where still homosexuality was mocked and treated as abnormal. 'Fred' was billeted midway through the war in Cardiff barracks full of serving soldiers and rumours had abounded that he was a homosexual. Seeking to torment 'Fred' in front of the rest of the men, one night a very drunken soldier openly presented his erect penis to him demanding he pleasure it. In response Fred eyed the member coolly and replied that he would indeed grant his demand, provided that the man allowed Fred to 'shag' him first. Fred recalled, 'His old boy went down just like that. And they all burst out laughing now, making him look like a fool.'[129] This reversal of power served to cause the man to immediately lose his erection much to the raucous laughter of the men around him. This raises the question of boundaries of heterosexuality and homosexuality within the confines of the soldier's experience.

Homosexuality within a military environment is a complicated topic, as situation, opportunity, previous inclination, social pressures and individual perceptions of sexuality all intersect within the consideration. Jane Ward makes the argument that dependent on circumstance, many sexual interactions between men are not regarded as homosexual in nature. In *Not Gay: Sex between Straight White Men* Ward considers the history of male heterosexual discourse over homosexual action within key social groups or situations.[130] On the topic of the military she notes that homosexual-type actions are typical within 'hazing' rituals, like events common to fraternities and sports teams. Nudity, penetration and eating from orifices are common events in such cases, yet Ward explains that these actions are typically exempt from the label of 'homosexual' act.[131] Ward's argument is centred on men within a modern context, as she notes Judith Kegan Gardiner's assertion that the twentieth century witnessed a shift from anally retentive masculinity in the early to mid-century to an 'explosive anality' towards the end and beginning of the twenty-first.[132] Ward also builds on the work of Belkin whose research in American military homosexuality has done much to define the field. Belkin explained in *Bring Me Men*,

> Penetrating and being penetrated have been central to what it means to be a warrior in the U.S. armed forces. And yet … rape and other forms of penetration have implied a range of meanings. In some cases, being penetrated is a marker of weakness, subordination, and lack of control. In others, it is an indication of strength, dominance, and power. In some cases, it signifies infantilization. In others, maturation. It some cases, being penetrated is a precursor to excommunication and signals that one is not qualified to be a member of the warrior community. In others, it marks inclusion, welcoming, and membership. Some military practices construct being penetrated as the ultimate taboo for a warrior. Others construct it as central to what it means to be a real man.[133]

Clearly homosexuality within the environment of the armed forces is more complicated than simply the choosing of a same-sex partner. In *Tommy: The British Soldier* Holmes presents several different accounts of homosexual behaviour within the war which break any attempt at labelling. He notes how many frequently found privacy to mutually masturbate, a theme that continues within the work of Ward on the modern military where such acts are not culturally considered homosexual; and also that often homosexual relationships, if known, were protected by others around them.[134] In the case of 'Fred' and his flaccid comrade, this interaction of a heterosexual forcing sexual gratification from an assumed homosexual again has modern comparisons. The research of Zeeland on the relationship between homosexual and heterosexual sailors included the account of one former American sailor who recalled being used as 'sea pussy' as a result of his known sexual proclivity, to which he would frequently fend off drunken straight sailors who demanded sexual favours.[135] Sociologically, this is regarded as the impact of an 'opportunity structure', a term describing the association of external factors that combine to influence a singular or collective action. Certainly, for some men in the First World War such opportunities for physical pleasure transcended the boundaries of normative sexual behaviour within the period. While 'Fred's' story sits at odds to the experience of those who hid their sexuality like Wilfred Owen, Siegfried Sassoon and Private Holbrook, it reiterates how the male body remained at the centre of sexual gratification and the pursuit for it during service. If this story provides a glimpse of the segregation of 'strange chaps' in the services during the First World War, or is an instance where men who have sex with men managed to organize themselves a safe space and one another's company, then it shows just how far the body and its urges could shape life in the military during this period.

In one of the best investigations into the topic of male sexual activity can be found in Clare Makepeace's article 'Male Heterosexuality and Prostitution during the Great War' within which she explained that until the spring of 1918 brothels in France were open to men of all ranks, although the rankers and the officers could not frequent the same establishment.[136] Aside from the blue and red lamps used to denote different establishments for officers and rankers, respectively, amateur prostitution also swelled dramatically during the war as women traded sexual favours not only for money but also for gifts, evenings of luxury and prestige.[137] Despite the widespread issue of venereal disease (VD), the British Army unofficially turned a blind eye to men's activities with prostitutes. Beliefs ran firm that men's physical need for sex would overpower common sense and morality. Immoral women were still centre of the campaigns to restrict disease spread. Key to this mentality were the interpretations of Royal Commission for Venereal Disease reports, the final of which was debated with gusto in 1916. Quoting from an lengthy article within the *Edinburgh Review* even the British Medical Journal seemed keen to illustrate the danger of immoral women against men's continual struggle to control their physical urges.

> Short of imprisoning every woman who approaches a military camp and absolutely cancelling all military leave, it is impossible to begin to prevent soldiers from running the risk of venereal infection. Nor would even these impossibly drastic measures touch the case of soldiers living in billets. The seriousness of the matter is fully recognized by the military authorities and lectures are given on the horrible character of the risks that a man runs in consorting with immoral women, but the results are disappointing. Therefore, the question raised whether, in the interests of their health, of the health of their wives and their unborn children, and also the military strength of the nation, it is not desirable to give our soldiers the opportunity of guarding themselves against the disease.[138]

The military continued to show leniency in 1916 after the introduction of conscription as the practice of telegraphing a soldier's next of kin to alert them of the contraction of VD was stopped due to concerns for men's morale. This focus on morale rather than morals was not well received by all as the ambiguously supportive but tentatively critical response by the National Council for Combatting Venereal Disease (NCCVD) printed in the British Medical Journal in August 1916 made clear as it publicly lambasted the preventative measures.[139] Makepeace explains that many men feared this telegraph 'more than anything else' due to the personal controversies it could cause at home, much more than docked pay or unpleasant medical treatment. Faced with the exposing of a long-standing issue within the midst of an incomprehensible war, evidently the British military authorities arrived at the view that a less morally stringent approach which appeased the bodies of soldiers was preferable than sexual health or faithfulness to spouses.[140]

For some men, it was less that they needed the physical act of sex, but that sex was perceived as being part of the masculinized experience of being a soldier. Towards the end of his training, as his body reached its peak level of preparation for combat, Private Barraclough was advised to have sex in order to fully reflect his role, 'to be a "real" soldier I was told that I must get syphilis or some such disease and have a spell at Lichfield hospital. I was determined never to become a "real soldier".'[141] Despite Barraclough's previous eagerness to demonstrate his newly earned soldier persona in the rest of his papers this suggestion was deemed too high a price for acceptance. He was unwilling to sacrifice his morals or his physical health for the sake of appearance. NCO George Ashurst also witnessed how sexual activity played a key role in the recreational pursuits of men behind the lines. Ashurst recalled drinking wine in a local brothel while billeted behind the lines at Armentieres in April 1915 and watching a stream of men parade in and out of the bedrooms keen to achieve physical gratification: 'It was absolutely crowded and there were five women in there and it was 5 francs a time. To do, you know, up the stairs and into the bedrooms … On the stairs, leading up to the bedroom, was full, a man on every step, waiting his turn to be with a woman.'[142] Ashurst claims he did not partake; still, his proximity illustrates how normalized the acquisition of sex was within the culture of the military, particularly for the men returning or waiting to go to the front. Within his oral history interview, Ashurst tells the story as an amusing anecdote, unconcerned with being associated with a place of ill repute, as he focuses instead on the hysterical army chaplain who had chosen that evening to save their bodies and souls from the evils of the flesh. The chaplain had stormed in to berate the men, crying loudly, 'Have none of you any mothers, have none of you any sisters?' before storming out again threatening to tell the battalion commanding officer (BCO). The result of the chaplain's righteous outrage was cancelation of leave until the battalion moved on.[143] In this instance, the involvement of the padre meant that willingness to turn a blind eye had reached their limit as the actions of this outraged priest combined with authority of the BCO to impose his sense of order and morality on the bodies of the troops within the battalion.

Responses to the pursuit of physical satisfaction could be varied from battalion to battalion. While some commanders were lenient or ignorant, others rewarded men's sexual impulses with harsh disciplinary measures. Lieutenant Creek was one such man whose body was submitted to particularly harsh punishment after his impulses to meet a local girl overtook his sense of duty.

> It may be wondered why I had gone intentionally to meet Selma as I knew she came from the station through the coppice but in truth, I had no idea I would meet her as it was getting late. This was a very unfortunate incident for me, I heard later that some of the boys had been meeting girls in the wood and the MP had been alerted. I was marched in front of the battery commander the next morning, I had been caught red-handed so to speak and excuses were futile. I do not think that the C.O. would have been so severe if the MP had not pressed the case, but I suppose they were justified and fourteen days' number on field punishment I got. I had never been to the gun park in the evenings so I do not know if I was the first to undergo this torture; that evening I was marched by the sergeant of the guard with two escorts to the gun park, where my wrists were fastened with drag ropes to the rim of a gun wheel. The sergeant looked at his watch and said one hour Creek, I had just enough play in the ropes to enable me to bend my head to clear midges from my face, it was indeed torture, the next evening Bombardier Bridges gave me some lotion he had got from the farrier and told me to smear it over my face, before I was tied, it helped a lot.[144]

As an officer and guilty of a common crime by other serving men, Creek was not simply punished as lesson for his own actions, but just as Lieutenant McCracken had intended during the physical punishment of one his men mentioned earlier, the crucial element here was a public display of physical punishment to dissuade others and curb behaviour. In Creek's case, his desire for physical pleasure earned him the exact opposite as he was publicly crucified and feasted on by insects as mark of warning to others.

Still not all men regarded sex as an all-encompassing need worth breaking rules and risking punishment for. Even though the option presented itself, Private Grainger recalled that the majority of the men in his unit were uninterested with coercing sex out of the women in the army kitchens close to their barracks. He claimed that 'the majority of them were never bothered about sex, I was never bothered about it, I would much rather a game of football then bother about going knocking about with girls, we didn't bother at all'.[145] Grainger admits that it is possible that some of the men did enjoy trysts but is clear that this was more of an exception than the rule. Private Holbrook was another soldier who was not overly interested in sexual adventures. Holbrook was, by his own admission, very young, innocent and naive, when he joined up as a regular before the outbreak of war. His indoctrination into soldiering had not simply been about fitness and killing but also hypermasculinized descriptions of sexual activity. These lewd stories complete with anatomical descriptions and coarse language had the inverse effect of discouraging Holbrook from pursuing tales of his own.[146]

Of course, the pursuit of sexual satisfaction was not limited to soldiers, as was lamented by Marine Reginald Bethell who served on *HMS Amethyst* in South Atlantic from 1916 to 1918. Bethell explained in an oral history that the sexual impulses and subsequent ramifications seemingly condoned by the Navy were in his opinion the result of not enough activity. Bethell identified as a moral man and someone whose personal desires were controlled by self-discipline and hard work.[147] Philippa Levine explains in *Prostitution, Race and Politics* that with the beginning of the First World War, military officials anticipated that rates of VD would increase and that there was some surprise by 1918 that these had not risen to the extent feared.[148] As illustrated in the discussions highlighted previously within the British Medical Journal and the British parliament, the moral issue of sexual behaviour still remained one of the primary methods of protecting men from VD. It was this thought process that had led for calls to restrict prophylactic measures as such as considered to encourage the men to indulge. Private Surfleet of the East Yorkshire Regiment (31st Division) recalled the vivid educational campaigns organized by the army to encourage abstinence.

> There seems a danger that 'our war' may only be remembered as a series of drunken orgies interspersed with a few cases of rape and almost nightly immoral relations with every available French and Belgian female. This sort of picture is far from the truth … At times, it was bloody and terrifying but, as for sex, most of the females were too old or too tired doing a man's job to be interested. There were 'red lamps' (brothels) in some of the bigger towns but they were, comparatively, little used. The propaganda against VD before we went out … and later … was good enough to deter the vast majority of overseas soldiers and those who 'caught a dose' suffered so much in so many ways, their misery killed the urge and discretion usually triumphed. I never saw any girl molested in any way; they were invariably treated with the utmost respect by most of the troops.[149]

While Surfleet may have restrained himself, between 1914 and 1918, 153,531 British and Dominion soldiers were given medical attention for the contraction of syphilis, gonorrhoea and any other form of sexually transmitted disease. During the war discussions increased over who held the fundamental responsibility to protect men from VD. Within the April 1916 British Medical Journal published synopsis of the recent report by the Royal Commission on Venereal Disease; the article reiterated the commission's conclusion that it was within the purview of each soldier's agency to remain disease-free.[150] After January 1917, the levels of leniency previous enjoyed evaporated in light of concerns for the war effort. The incapacitation of fighting men's bodies was a strategic weakness to be avoided at all costs resulting in the forbidding of visiting brothels and a harsh policy of restricting privileges for men who contracted the disease, which could include having leave denied for a year.[151] Post-war societal anger increased against the Defence of the Realm Act 40b, which allowed the incarceration and vilification of women for male infection. In 1918, Mr Lees-Smith led a scathing criticism of the War Ministry and the soldiers under its care for its inability to 'protect these young soldiers from temptation' and failing to keep 'all opportunities for the indulgence of this habit out of their way'.

Yet, as demonstrated previously, many men went to extreme lengths to physically satisfy their bodies. Furthermore, the military were not against turning on their own men and handing out punishment for their perceived lack of judgement. However, many of such disciplinary measures were punishment for men who concealed their illness. Seeking to avoid punishment and pay loss many men sought to conceal their ailment. Others may have chosen to do so as a result of the significantly unpleasant physical experience of treatment. Standard treatment for VD during the First World War was an arsphenamine regime which confined men to hospitals for several weeks. The average stay in hospital lasted between fifty and sixty days as men were subjected to Salvarsan substitutes and mercury treatments that could be very dangerous.[152] While serving within the RAMC Sergeant Alfred West took the care of the men under his command very seriously. He described in his memoirs how the practice of filling the bladder as a douche and forcing the man to attempt to urinate out the infection was explained to him and his men as the best way to protect them from VD.[153] Such treatments were perhaps understandably very unpopular with patients. This was a particularly uncomfortable and painful operation to carry out, so much so that during a series of trials for treatments, RAMC officers Donaldson and Davidson reported that all of their patients rejected irrigation in favour of the more dangerous and damaging chemical treatment.[154]

Chemical treatments involved coercive substances such as arsenic and mercury. As an orderly, James Payne developed a healthy respect for the dangers of these medicines as he assisted doctors with the treatment of VD. His task was to dissolve the arsenic and the mercury for injection into the patient's body. He recalled in an oral history interview that 'it had to be done most carefully because it was deadly of course. Arsenic, if it wasn't utilised properly, it would kill you.'[155] Payne also explained that effectiveness of the horrifically unpleasant treatment was impossible to determine, even for the medical staff.

> Well we wouldn't know, it takes years to know, but the treatment was 21 day's treatment 7, 7, blank, 7, 22 day's treatment with so many days blank in between you see. And then the other mercurial treatment on alternate sides of the buttocks about once a week but not every time … because the doctors had to do that, I would haven't experience to do it, but I learned by doing it, they all injected the needle into the veins, it's simply waiting for it all, er … gravity, the saline in one bottle and the err … sort of arsenic in the other bottle, it had the white clip in the bottom release them both together until they emptied, they got up and walked away then.[156]

Although he had never experienced it himself, Payne claimed that the process wasn't that unpleasant and linked it more to the brief unpleasantness of inoculation.[157] While questionable as to how pleasant the injection of two highly corrosive compounds into body or genitals could be, Payne's comparison also demonstrates a commonality in the military methods of ensuring their soldiers bodies were suited for combat. Even if the initial experience was particularly unpleasant, be it inoculation sickness or the burning of the inside of the urethra, the military was willing to sacrifice the comforts of men's bodies for the potential of being combat-ready in the future.

As unpleasant as it was, not receiving treatment could be even more hazardous for the soldier's body. Private Trafford who served with 1/2nd Battalion Monmouthshire Regiment recalled how he saw several men being treated for VD while he recovered from a leg injury in 1915.

> This particular day, I was stood outside … and I started looking at these fellas, and when I went back inside I said to the nurse, Curly they called me, she said, what were you watching Curly and I says 'I can't understand prisoners of war so near a hospital.' She said 'them are not prisoners of war they are our fellas'. So, I said, 'What's the matter with them' and she said 'they've all got the disease, you know the pox'. Dirty women like, and the barbed wire to keep them in. So, I went back out again to take a good look at them, oh the sights, I wouldn't look at a woman for years. Oh, their noses half rotted and their arms all bandaged up, oh the s … [trails off] some of them with their ears half eaten. It's unbelievable, you wouldn't believe it.[158]

Trafford's chilling description of rotten body parts being kept behind barbed wire like prisoners helps to visualize the dramatic consequences for soldiers who engaged in risky sexual encounters for the purpose of physical gratification combing damage to the body with social ostracization. His recollections of these consequences were more haunting still as he recounted the chilling story of a fellow man's suicide due to the contraction of a VD.

> Anyway, this sergeant had got it, a Welshman he was and we was [sic] going over the top … I know we were going over the top, as usual you know in a trench with 5 or 6 men, this sergeant came to me and he says, you lads, he says I want to get over first, he says you lads hold back whilst I'll get over. He says I don't want to go

back home he says, I've got, you know, he says I don't want to give it the wife, he said. So, long story short we let him go over, and he hadn't gone far and he got it and he was killed you know. If I don't get killed he says, I'll have to do myself in, he says, I've got it bad he says, I haven't reported it, you were supposed to report these things, because, in different places, they'd have a little list of what to do if you'd been with a woman, but I never was with a woman after I saw those in the camp, but he killed himself.[159]

The shame of contracting a VD could be as damaging as the disease itself. Still the stigma of contracting a VD did not always dissuade men from their pursuit of sexual pleasures.[160] Part of this unwillingness to self-protect issued from the chaos of life in combat as a temporary culture developed where the pendulum of some soldiers' rationalities oscillated between men seeking hedonistic pleasure before certain death and the lasting ramifications of a brief moment of pleasure.[161] Evidently, treatments were as embarrassing and socially ostracizing as they could be unpleasant. Not to mention haphazardly made available. Torn between a punitive unpleasant treatment and a morally abhorrent debilitating illness, it is possible to recognize why the sergeant ultimately decided that destruction of his body was a better alternative than the ramifications of admitting his illness.

Conclusion

The British military authorities sought to maintain the control over the bodies of servicemen that they so carefully developed during training. Punishments were meted out to those who became ill and failed to report it, who managed to get themselves drunk or who transgressed rules on sexual activity. But this control was complex in practice. In the first place it often relied on self-discipline rather than on punishment. Troops were warned of the dangers of VD and informed of best practice in maintaining health and hygiene, and many complied and conformed. But military efforts over control of men's bodies while on active service but away from the front also seem to have been limited and partial. Troops were plied with alcohol to encourage them to take on tough duties or to prepare them for combat. A 'blind eye' could be turned to sexual activity when rules were broken. Men found themselves responsible for self-diagnosis and reporting illness as the limits of medical surveillance were reached. It was as if many in the ranks of the military authorities felt that preparing the bodies of men for effective participation in the war meant allowing indulgence and pleasure as much as imposing control and discipline over them. Whether indulgence and pleasure were licensed or not, the soldiers themselves were often active agents in the fate of their bodies and that many of their clearest recollections of their time in the military were physical. Agency does not simply mean resistance of course, and as stated above it seems as if many were content to go along with the instructions given, the food provided and the rules outlined in keeping themselves fit and healthy. But active service also allowed men scope for non-compliance and non-conformity. Men often had the opportunity to retake elements of control over their bodies from the army. They protested over food that was low in quality and quantity and found ways around efforts to control their sexual activities. Their drunkenness enabled them to escape the physical rigours of their lives and surroundings, and to cheer themselves up but it could also inflame them to violence and even suicide. The body was central to the experience of troops as they prepared for combat or recovered from it. The next chapter explores the experience of these bodies on the front line itself.

4

Bodies under fire: The front line

At some point during the First World War an unknown soldier painted a lurid picture of his daily experience, describing the morning routine of gunfire and shelling as a cacophony of sound, emotion and anger. 'Dirt is flung into the faces and foul language seethes through everyone's lips – the bastard. ... it's no bloody use his starting anything. Jerry responds, likewise, for it is the morning hate.'[1] While the author of this account is lost to history, his words succinctly captured the vivid horror of war on the front lines. Frequently, combat on the front lines was filled with dirt, swearing, anger, urgency and violence as men on all sides galvanized their bodies to fight. Front-line life was very different to active service behind the lines considered in the previous chapter. On the front lines, men found their bodies subjected to an entirely more gruelling physical ordeal as they adapted to an existence permanently under the threat of physical injury. Their living situation also put strain on their bodies as the meagre physical luxuries they had experienced behind the lines such as hygiene and a diverse diet evaporated. Without respite at the front, the military authorities sought to keep the bodies of troops prepared for conflict through stimulation and control. As a result of ever-impending combat and the adrenaline of battle, men's bodies were constantly subjected to immense physical and psychological pressures as they were exposed to mortal danger.

Men's bodies also lived under the constant threat of damage, death and destruction. However, during the war attitudes towards physical damage began to change. Rather than fearing or even avoiding a wound, soldiers differentiated on the impact of wounds creating an unofficial hierarchy of injury. Rather than aiming to end their service unscathed, some men began to internally negotiate the limits to which they would accept physical damage in order to retain their lives or simply to escape the trenches. During instances of front-line service, British soldiers did not simply inhabit their bodies but spent time imagining their future ones and evaluating the pros and cons of allowing certain amounts of damage to them. At the same time military authorities also regarded the bodies of the troops in multiple and complex ways. Significant effort was put into the practice of repairing wounded bodies and reiterating the indoctrinated notions of physical masculinity and duty established in training to encourage men to return to the front as fast as possible. Yet, again men's bodies also took the brunt of authoritarian control as they faced physical corporal punishment and execution for misdemeanours. This chapter considers these physical aspects of life in service in the

First World War to illustrate how the body and its experiences of life on the front line were driven by more than just the violence of fighting the enemy – but remained at the centre of the control and sacrifice endured by each man during the First World War.

Feeding under fire

Once again, to understand the lived experience of men and their bodies within the First World War, it is crucial to outline the role of food in sustaining and pleasuring the military male body on the front lines. The provision of food on the front lines was an important and contentious aspect of the soldier's experience, particularly when in close proximity to the enemy. While time at the front was limited to allow the men respite and recovery, the time that they spent closest to the enemy demanded extreme lengths to provide basic sustenance and maintain the bodies of the fighting men. Unlike the French Army, who utilized a series of mobile field kitchens which distributed cooked food on mass to their men through elected retrieval, the British Army had their meals prepared and delivered by the Army Service Corps (ASC). These men, some of which were non-combatants, were tasked with the challenge of ferrying food to the men in the trenches and front lines. Major Nicholson regarded the men in the ASC as being an essential element in the ultimate victory. He recorded in his memoirs his admiration for their dedication to duty: 'I have the highest praise for the Army Service Corps which never failed to get rations and food to us particularly when we were continually on the move in the early days before static warfare and they were sometimes under shell fire themselves.'[2]

Nicholson's allusion to the danger of the role of the ASC is not an exaggeration. As noted in Chapter 3, the ASC were commonly looked down upon for their lack of engagement with the enemy; however, Duffett points out that up until these men tended to enter the enemy sights undefended being unarmed until manpower shortages towards the end of the war pushed members of the ASC into combat duty, despite barely having wielded a rifle since basic training.[3] Private William Maltby explained in his oral history interview that the training he had received was insufficient for preparing him for combative service, having focused more on the distribution of goods and food up the lines.[4] He was to be one of the earliest causalities after he was injured early into the conflict in August 1914 by a shell while attempting to carry out distribution duties of goods and food. Private William Cowley was another such ASC soldier whose duties shifted to reflect the need for men and supplies in ever closer proximity to the enemy. After landing at Suvla Bay in 1915 he recalled how he was given a rifle to wield and was constantly warned to be wary of enemy snipers who would target him hopeful to halt the resupply of the dug in British soldiers.[5] Still, the men of the ASC did not need to be directly in front of the enemy to be injured.

Private McGuirk joined the ASC in 1916. As a driver he was frequently near the front lines moving weapons and materials, which resulted in his demobilization in 1917 after his body became badly damaged during a tractor accident behind the lines.[6] Thomas Olive joined the ASC at 17 in 1913 and was badly wounded when his lorry was hit by an enemy shell. Olive described his body being damaged and trapped within the wreck of the lorry until being rescued and returned to Britain for extensive treatment and slow physical rehabilitation.⁷ Despite comments and jokes to the contrary, the ASC was not a 'cushy' option. Their bodies were almost perpetually in danger both from enemy attack and accidental death. As the providers of rations and supplies, they were a useful target for the enemy; yet, unlike their combat counterparts the ASC steadfast ignored both the enemy and often the safety of their own bodies to support the men who relied on their diligence. Like other support services such as the RAMC, members of the ASC were an attractive target, particularly as they came with the bonus of usually not carrying a weapon with which to return fire.

There were plenty of times when it was not possible for the ASC to get through to troops on the front line and as a result men's bodies could go undernourished. Private Niblett's complaint that he had 'gone over the top on one slice of bread and jam' was not an uncommon complaint during times of ardent combat.⁸ The solution to this dilemma was the iron ration, although, as Duffett is clear to illustrate, the iron rations were barely edible and only supposed to be eaten as a last resort should an alternative not be available.⁹ This emergency measure generally consisted of hard tack biscuits wrapped in paper, a tin of stew, beans or processed meat and occasionally a small packet of flavouring such as salt, pepper or sugar. This menu had come about as the result of extensive research carried out over the course of the nineteenth century by the British Army to attempt to improve the nutritious value of the iron ration.¹⁰ Unfortunately, throughout the war the iron rations were neither particularly appetizing nor overly nutritious. Even when faced with severely limited alternatives Private Paul Whitehouse found the hard tack biscuits to be particularly inedible. He recalled that 'the bread situation was worst: if only we could have had more bread; but we had to manage on those very hard army biscuits. They told us they were full of goodness; they were damned hard.'¹¹ The promise of nutritional 'goodness' is highly questionable. Hard tack was made from flour, water and salt. Baked until rock solid the biscuits were useful as they were unlikely to spoil; eating them raw demanded a peculiar physical requirement, namely a strong set of teeth. In some cases, men decided to repurpose their makeshift meals turning the ostensible 'biscuit' into makeshift boiled pudding, a frame for a photograph, crude sculpture or, in the case of British Private Charles Shepherd in Salonika in the winter of 1915, fuel to keep warm.¹²

During the American Civil War of the previous century, hard tack biscuits of the same recipe used in the First World War were issued to the Union troops. Rumours abounded that the inedible biscuit was bulletproof.¹³ An unlikely assumption, but this says much that some men felt more confident in the biscuits' ability to save their lives as armour than a back-up source of nourishment. Despite the inventiveness of the ASC which managed to turn hard tack into pie crusts and gelatinous desserts, often by grinding them up by crushing them with the butt of their rifles, official condemnation for hard tack was extensive as early as 1903, if not before.¹⁴ In the Journal of the Royal Army Medical Corps (JRAMC) Major Cottell pointed out that in the Last South African War the army been reliant on the inedible biscuit and that a diet consisting of 'biscuits … was barely enough' to keep a soldier fit. For him it had become a 'starvation diet' that had lasting effects on the soldier's physical health so that they 'were much weakened and could only do short marches with any ease'.[15] The response was to make greater efforts to provide other elements of a meal alongside the biscuits.

This was not always a successful alternative as, has been previous noted, tinned food was susceptible to the environmental conditions of the front line. Damaged tins, poor canning processes and contamination during processing meant that the contents could become hazardous. Private Stapleton remembered taking a fellow soldier to the doctor after he became sick from eating his tinned sausages while on the front line.[16] Walter Clarke also recalled how his appetite was lost on the march to Vimy Ridge as his tin of bully beef was 'filled with maggots'. This unwelcome surprise meant that he lost his appetite for corned beef permanently.[17] Stephen Moyle was a British seaman who found himself in the trenches at Gallipoli. Moyle recalled in an oral history interview that due to his platoon's position they lived almost exclusively on rations, 'Hardtack and Bully beef'.[18] Occasionally they received some stew from behind the lines, but mostly the men made do. Moyle recalled not being particularly hungry, but thirsty a lot of the time. Both the beef and the hard tack were made with salt which may have combined with the hot conditions to encourage the men's thirst.

Relief from this drudgery came in the form of jam, which Moyle remembered as a treat and such a welcome addition that men would even sing about it. The treat could also have been the cause of sickness, though, as jam was as susceptible to contamination as the meat. However, Moyle remembers that the allure of the jam was so strong that such fears failed to stop the men from eating it. 'You know, many tins were blown, by that I mean the top of the tin, like was blown up you know? But us being short of these things really, we used to eat it of course, make use of it. But it may have been the cause of dysentery.'[19] For Moyle and his fellows, the pursuit of some variety and sweetness while at the front was seemingly worth putting their bodies at risk. Clearly the jam containers were damaged, perhaps contaminated; yet, the men considered their physical health less a priority than a sweet respite from their mundane menu.

Jam could also be lethal for other reasons. Early into the war jam tins were appropriated by innovative soldiers for the use of makeshift explosives. Tins were emptied of their sweet contents and replaced with gun cotton and nails with a safety fuse – to be then hurled at the enemy.[20] Moyle remembered how crude and dangerous they were, describing them as 'sealed up with a fuse at the top and you only had a few seconds to light the fuse and throw the bomb'.[21] 'Jam jar' grenades or 'pitcher' grenades throwers earned the nickname 'the suicide club' for a good reason as it was not uncommon for them to explode before thrown.[22] Within an anonymously written report for the Ministry of War in 1916 the importance of grenades as an offensive asset was outlined; yet, inside the pages detailing the history of thrown explosives, the issue of the improvised bomb was lambasted as lethal and dangerous concluding that 'it is hardly surprising under these circumstances, combined with the lack of training of the troops, that a very high percentage of accidents occurred'.[23] The tins that had initially been provided to protect and improve the soldier's lives at the front lines suddenly became instruments of death and destruction through the innovation inspired by desperation and necessity. This temporary measure proved lethal for both the British and enemy troops as was made clear by Private Burnett, who in his oral history explained that success and survival were not guaranteed, no matter which side of the projectile you were standing on.

> You made them – you put a hole in the center, you took the jam out first, (laughs) – it was no good covering them with jam or lick it off, now then when you open the tin and put a hole in the center, and then fill that up, there was wire we used to get of the signaler and put a hole in the lid and a hole in the side in the middle, ... put in a fuse first and the detonator, amongst your rubble, whatever you put in, put it in your catapult, release your catapult and release it and hope for the best.[24]

This hoping for the best proved to be insufficient for the some of the more enterprising men in Burnett's unit after an improved cricket ball grenade returned to sender with devastating results: 'The elastic broke and landed in the trench and there was five of them in the trench, and he threw himself on top of it and it went off and it you know wounded him pretty badly and he got awarded the VC.'[25] Private David Lauder may have earned the Victoria Cross for his personal sacrifice and bravery, yet the decision was only taken as a result of the need to protect his fellow men from the improvised unpredictable weapon that had initially been created from the food source designed to improve men's moral and bodies while they served on the front lines.

On guard

Plainly, food could both enable and disable men as they served on the front lines. Yet, this was not the only means of keeping the men physically controlled and prepared for whatever crossed the deadly chaotic chasm they guarded. Serving so close to the enemy frequently meant that men's bodies were required to be constantly alert. This was a requirement that pushed men's bodies to the limit of their endurance that no level of training could have prepared them for. Private Cook recalled in his memoirs the shock of releasing what time at the front meant would truly mean for him:

> Sgt Newsome did not only take us into his platoon he welcomed us and we took to him. His first instruction was clear and sound as he was: 'you are in the frontline, the enemy are 600 yards away at this point, which is really a long way in the part of the war, he knows you are here and you must be always alert. Whilst you are in this trench you never sleep, you never leave your rifle and you keep it loaded, but not one round in the breech remember, I don't want my head blowing off by someone who has not secured his safety catch and you never take off any equipment or clothing, nor do you wash or shave, you are on active service here and take no unnecessary chances, at any moment the enemy may strike.'[26]

Up to this point washing and grooming, the maintenance of uniforms in good condition and regular sleep had been central to strategies to control men's bodies as they were transformed from citizens to soldiers. Sergeant Newsome's speech demonstrates that in proximity to the enemy these were no longer priorities. Seemingly, at the very moment where men were to be thrown into battle, the British Army abandoned such overt efforts to discipline their bodies through managing their appearance and their health as counterproductive under the circumstances.

This abandoning of key principles of hygiene and appearance had greater consequences than the relinquishing of indoctrinated physical control. At the furthest front the conditions within which the men awaited the single to engage or defend were as treacherous as the opposing army. One of the most recurrent descriptions of the First World War is the filth in which men often lived. Public perceptions of the fighting between 1914 and 1918 invariably invoke mental images of mud, blood and rats.[27] Sergeant Ward recalled in his oral history interview that his living conditions during front-line service at the Battle of the Somme in 1916 were horrific; he recalled, 'It was terrible in the mud and the dead bodies and the stench. It is surprising, when I look back now, how we did exist. Being young, full-blooded, we just tolerated the discomfort.'[28] Private Keller also described the filth in which he and so many men existed.

> The troops wallowed in the mud and slime in the trenches on the gun pits. The horse lines became a sea of mire. Someone once wrote; 'The physical conditions in the First World War raised both fascination and disbelief. How was it that the individual soldier put up with the cold, the wet, the dirt, the frequent death of comrades, the constant dangers and the apparent inevitability sooner or later of personal extinction, perhaps by a bullet in the open, but much more often by multiple wounds caused by a shell. Often times they were left to lie and die without help. To that could be added also the danger of drowning in a sea of slime in one of the many shell holes.'[29]

Keller's account reiterates Ward's disbelief that during the height of the war the men somehow endured the constant physical and psychological strain incurred through serving on the front lines. Private Williams recalled that the mud they took shelter in was another enemy faced by both sides. He recalled in an oral testimony, 'It was a problem, the muck, it was as much a battle, an enemy, as the blooming shells, for us anyhow.'[30]

There also existed a clear causality between horrendous living conditions and sickness which was not limited to the Western Front. The Western Front trench warfare encouraged environmental sicknesses like trench foot and louse infestations, which caused fevers. In Macedonia, Palestine and Mesopotamia supply line failures and the presence of insects caused outbreaks of scurvy and malaria.[31] On the East Africa front Private Shaw of the 25th Battalion Royal Fusiliers witnessed his entire battalion succumbing to disease as over three quarters of the men in the battalion contracted malaria.

> By December, the battalion was reduced to less than 100 men (three signallers). But a draft of 400 men from England was on the way, (actually only about half the men arrived – Malaria had taken its toll). ... Onward to the Rufigi [sic] river. A few days' rest and we were issued with an extra 200 rounds of ammo in readiness

for crossing this (wider than the Thames) river. With no cover fire support, we all thought this would be the end of the Fusiliers. That very day, General Smuts arrived, took one look, and ordered a medical inspection. Now reduced to 140, only 44 were passed fit (I was getting touches of Malaria and Dysentery). Smuts order was: 'Go back immediately down to the Cape and recuperate.'[32]

Shaw noted that by the time that he had returned to Durban he had also fallen ill with malaria and had to recuperate in hospital. He reported his ability to withstand the disease proudly: 'Prior to that I had had a good run, being one of the very few to do the long trek from Moschi in May 1916 to the Rufiji and back to Morogoro by January 1917 without having to report sick.'[33]

Front-line circumstances disrupted military efforts to control those bodies so that inadequate food, poor hygiene, sleeplessness and environmental conditions all impacted upon physical discipline. Men experienced the war through their bodies as their conditions turned hostile against them. The filth disrupted military strategies to keep men clean and hygienic, but it was more of a threat still as it could kill men who were buried or drowned in it. Shells could unearth corpses that had been lost to the quagmire and return to their own trenches carrying disease and devastating blows to moral. The mud could also force men to make tactically unsound decisions, offering their bodies up for attach as they attempted to circumnavigate the mud that threated to swallow them. Private Warsop was one such man who wrote in his diary, 'I had to change my position as the side of the trench was slowly sinking being only made of mud.'[34] Between the mud, the fatigue, the limited diet and the enemy bombardments, service on the front line took a significant amount of physical toil on the fighting men. During his service as a volunteer soldier William Broadhead liked to send sketches within the letters he wrote home to his parents. On 11 April 1915, his letter home showed his physical deterioration as he sketched himself at the beginning of the war, his current status and his prediction for the end of the conflict (see Figures 8 and 9).

His drawings capture perfectly the impact of life in the front line on the bodies of British soldiers and those efforts of the military authorities to control them. Gone is the square-jawed young man in the neat uniform. Like many of the men he served besides, Broadhead had become an unshaven, emaciated veteran, with crumpled clothing and unkempt hair whose primary physical concern was to defeat the exhaustion he felt rather than fight the enemy. Broadhead literally illustrated how the basic needs of the soldier's body struggled to be met on the front lines. Dirty, exhausted and constantly under attack by the enemy, the conditions and haphazardly by their own comrades, men's bodies were continuously put through significant trials that no amount of training could have prepared them for. Yet, among all this physical debilitation and destruction, men and the military still found ways to galvanize their bodies to fight.

Fighting bodies

Of all the reasons the serving men on the front line were there, their primary purpose was to fight the enemy. Throughout the First World War the training the men underwent

Figure 8 Sketch by William Broadhead, letter dated 11 April 1915. Sheffield Archives, L.S. 1980/1-59, Private Papers of William Broadhead, letter dated 11 April 2015, p. 3.

was designed to prepare their bodies and minds for combat. Physical conditioning had instilled within the men the ability to engage in battle, while psychological indoctrination had sought to prepare the men and their bodies for the duress of battle. In his study on the behaviours of soldiers in combat, Kellett explains that fear is a common element of any military engagement and argues that fear predominately arises for soldiers in combat when they feel a lack of control over their environment.[35] Figley and Nash also consider fear as being a normal part of the military experience. They found from their research that soldiers typically claimed that death, injury and loss of

Figure 9 Sketch by William Broadhead, letter undated. Sheffield Archives, L.S. 1980/1-59, Private Papers of William Broadhead, letter undated, p. 3.

their friends were their upmost fears during combat.[36] Figley and Nash theorized that competent soldiers not only learn to control this fear but that such control is utilized by militaries as an element of control and conditioning. Demonstrating fear, failing to endure the experience and appearing weak are traits that are singled out in individuals, often publicly for humiliation.[37] This practice in training and in service creates two clear groups: the worthy and unworthy. The unworthy, as is made clear by several examples in this book, were ostracized, humiliated and punished. Failure to control one's body and emotion was an unworthy trait in a trained soldier. Noakes argues that in the early twentieth century it was widely expected that soldiers could control their responses to fear both during and after the First World War.[38] She quotes an unnamed author who wrote, 'Even the most bravest of men can feel afraid. The only difference between a brave man and a coward is the fear of one is controlled whilst the fear of the other is uncontrolled.'[39]

Of course, the control over soldier's fear had been an important aspect of training from the moment that men joined the army, as a post-war report made clear.

> Their brains accustomed during training to concentrate instantly and thoroughly, through sheer force of habit, will do the same during the mental and physical disturbance of battle. No training can be of lasting value which is performed carelessly, and which lacks the necessary mental concentration. Will, decision, and the power of concentration are among the essential characteristics of leadership. Without them, a man is mentally flabby, undecided, incapable of assimilating and imparting knowledge, and utterly useless as an instructor, or leader, however subordinate.[40]

This hardening of mind and body was a crucial element of soldiers' training as instructors used set times to encourage recruits into completing tasks under pressure as preparation for combat situations. The objective during training was to drill men and train them to be unthinking in battle to the point where their bodies reacted entirely unbidden. This appears to be the Holy Grail for the military training regimes during the war, as the individual man's body bypasses his internal agency and thought process and determined its own behaviour as determined by the needs of the military.

Control of emotions is a common theme within the accounts of soldiers from the First World War. For Sergeant Ward the fear prior to going over the top at Passchendaele was much worse than the actual fighting. He explained in his oral history testimony that once he entered the battle his fear dissipated as he focused on fighting the enemy; he claimed, 'Ahh yes, you get used to it, you had butterflies in the stomach, once you are over the top you are on your way, the worst part was getting over, when the bullets starting flying, once you were over and started walking everything was all right.'[41] Almost incredibly, Ward's fear was at its apex when he was safest and he claims, somewhat paradoxically, that 'everything was all right' once he put his body directly in the firing line. Similarly, Lieutenant Reginald Savory recalled the same feeling in his stomach, although Savoy was careful to frame it as anticipation rather than direct fear in his testimony, writing, 'Those last few minutes before Zero Hour made no deep impression on me, except possibly the familiar feeling of waiting for the pistol before a sprint with a void in the pit of one's stomach and anxiety as to the result. And, then … off you go! From that moment, I lost all control of the fighting.'[42] While serving with the 15th Battalion Durham Light Infantry at Ypres in 1917 Private Archer experienced similar feelings of anticipation and fear. Archer differs from the other men in that his fear was seemingly permeant and not limited to moments before battle. Private Archer's emotion state also differs as it was physically 'felt', manifesting as a palpitation of his heart. He demonstrated this in an oral history interview as he thumped his chest and explained his continual terror to the interviewer: '(Bangs chest), that went from the first day I went out to the last day I come away … (bangs chest again) oh bad, shocking.'[43] Archer is somewhat unique as typically accounts of the First World War tend to follow the narrative of Ward and Savory in that fear is mentioned but ultimately conquered. This is not entirely surprising as recollections of battle can glamourize or be reinterpreted to show the protagonist in the best light, often subconsciously. Fear as an emasculating emotion unbecoming of a soldier often has as much place in the recollections of the veteran as it did for the serving soldier; yet, the conquering of such emotion illustrates control over one's body and mind. This is the quintessential embodiment of the perfect masculine physical soldier.

With the notion of peak physicality and masculinity in mind in relation to the waiting soldier in the First World War, is it unsurprising that Savory compares his experience of anxiety to the starter pistol in a race? In doing so Savory implies less of a terror of injury or death and more of an adrenaline-fuelled readiness to advance. War and sport have much in common in terms of physical conditioning, teamwork and strategy, managerial and institutional control, and goal-driven indoctrination. In 1931 General Harrington reiterated the importance of sport in the winning of the war as he wrote in the preface of the army handbook *Game and Sports in the Army*,

> I am confident that leather played one of the greatest parts. Few have realised what we owe to the boxing glove and the football – the two greatest factors in restoring and upholding morale. How many times did one see a Battalion who had come out of the line in the Ypres Salient and elsewhere, battered to pieces and sad at heart having lost so many officers and men, hold up its head again and recover in a few hours by kicking a football or punching with the glove? It had a magic effect on morale.[44]

Sport both indoctrinated men and helped men to recuperate. It also allowed men to channel to reinterpret the emotions and physically produced chemicals that saturated their bodies during active service. Once the order was given and men climbed over the top or entered the fray their bodies could be transformed through a host of physical and biochemical changes as adrenaline flooded their system. Robert Sapolsky has described the effects of adrenaline as 'stress-induced analgesia', meaning that pain pathways are inhibited during times of heighted emotional stress.[45] This allows the human body to surpass its usual capabilities and demonstrate in some rare examples of almost superhuman abilities such as strength, resilience and speed. An article in *Veterans Today* demonstrates a direct link between adrenaline and combat and attributes this flooding of chemicals to creating an internal 'survival mode' which sustains soldiers during times of combat stress and claims that soldiers under periods of stress can enter a 'euphoric state'.[46]

During the First World War some soldiers interpreted this heightening of senses during battle as an excitement within their blood. After the death of Lord Kitchener at the Battle of Jutland in 1916, Lieutenant Stiven wrote to his mother and claimed that tragedies that Britain had faced would encourage the British to fight harder. He wrote, 'Pity the Bosche' as the cries of "remember Kitchener" (will) stir the men's blood to greater deeds than the "Lusitania", "Scarborough" or even Edith Cavell'.[47] Dawson shows how such language was not unusual in relation to violent events by quoting accounts of the rebellion in India in 1857 which claimed its depictions would 'set the blood of every Englishman boiling in his veins'.[48] Within soldier's diaries, memoirs and testimonies from the First World War the theme of blood pumping is common, as is the notion of bloodlust. Bourke argues that 'the characteristic act of men at war is not dying, it is killing'.[49] She quotes an unnamed army chaplain from the First World War as saying, 'The soldier's business is to kill the enemy ... he only tries to avoid *being* killed for the sake of being efficient'.[50] Niall Ferguson in *The Pity of War* argues that killing the enemy was an intoxicating opportunity for some men and claims that men considered fighting fun.[51] Private Pugh was one such soldier who fits this profile as he recounted in his oral history that he had joined the war because of his bloodlust as he was a 'professional killer' who 'killed animals for a living and humans for pleasure' and so was very keen to kill Germans.[52] On the recording the interviewer is audibly uncomfortable by this proclamation, a state that was not improved as Pugh explained that even as a quartermaster he could still kill enemy soldiers, 'was always able to do that, with a Vickers machine gun you could knock a few out'.[53] When asked if he enjoyed killing the enemy, he replied, 'I certainly did, I had a feeling that they were trying to come to England to knock us all off, so it was up to us to fight, I expect I was born a soldier see? (laughs)'.[54]

In the aftermath of the war academic interest developed around this notion of the 'born soldier'. The First World War had been unique not only in the number of participants but also in the different ways in which men were enlisted to fight. Throughout the war training processes had evolved and changed to reflect the need for men on the front lines. The result of this haphazard training and changing priorities of suitable physicality meant that a wide spectrum of British men took the field between 1914 and 1918 to varying degrees of success and widely different responses to their experiences after they returned. After the First World War the psychologist John T. MacCurdy engaged in research on such men to attempt to outline the best candidates for military service. His research determined that the ideal soldier 'must be more or less a natural butcher'.[55] To that end men like Pugh, whose temperament for killing lays at odds with social normality where the taking of a human life is an abhorrent action, appear to have been the perfect candidate for war. Pugh appears to have been the exception rather than the rule. As although men in training frequently experienced desperation to get out and do their part, the sobering reality of killing a fellow man disquieted their enthusiasm somewhat. NCO Basford recalled vividly and despondently his first experience of violence at Oppy Wood in 1917.

When we reached the German frontline were they were all in these deep dugouts and we noticed quite a few Germans retreating down the communication trench and this was really the first time I remember shooting at a German and we did, you know give them several rounds from our SMLE and then turned our attention to the deep dugouts ... and threw two mills bombs down the dugout steps, well the effect of two grenades exploding in a confined space was pretty ghastly, and I felt almost guilty at what I'd done.[56]

Clearly the killing of other men had a physically felt emotional impact on the bodies of the men who dispatched to the war. For some it was a rush of excitement, others fear or guilt. Regardless of the emotion, it is obvious that many men keenly physically felt the ramifications of their actions during combat.

Aside from allowing them to kill others or adapt to the chaos of the environment around them, battle excitement could also encourage men to ignore their own internal warnings alerting them that their bodies were at risk. In a letter to his mother in 1917 Lieutenant Renny explained being disciplined after his excitement during battle training led him to remaining mounted on his horse. He noted afterwards the foolishness of his actions and stated that this was strictly forbidden by army regulations as he would have been an easy target for the enemy.[57] This suppression of rational thought through the excitement of battle could also extend to the suppression of pain. This was the case for Private Warsop who was badly wounded during heavy shelling in 1917 as despite his injuries he was so focused on fighting that he only felt surprise at his own mortality before he lost consciousness.

There was a flash in the sky. I realized with a shock that I had been badly hit. My right arm jumped up on its own and then flopped down. It felt as if my left arm and part of my chest had been blown clear away. My first thought was 'blow me, I never thought I should get killed' a feeling of nothing but surprise. Then I thought of home, before losing consciousness.[58]

Adrenaline had a powerful effect on the bodies of fighting men. It could get them into the battle and even help to endure the agony of injury. Often this temporary protection came with a significant physical and psychological cost. Private Price had joined underage in December 1914, determined to serve his country and not be considered a coward. Price embraced soldiering and recalled at length in his oral testimony drinking, gambling, visiting brothels and being wounded several times as he served at Cambrin, Arras and Ypres. Price represents the quintessential voluntary soldier in the First World War, entering the fray eager and patriotic and leaving physically damaged, cynical but still resolute. Within his testimony Price was frank about his experiences and the impact they had on his body. In mid-1917 Price's body reached its limit as he lost control after wading through enemy corpses and getting lost in the dark and falling into a river while trying to surmise the enemy forces.

I was so bloody tired I got hold of this chair, in the middle of the road and I started crying ... I must have cried there for about half an hour you know. Sobbed my heart out ... I was just bloody exhausted or something, you know I wasn't more than a couple of 100 yards from the frontline and I was crying my bloody eyes out. Well eventually I got back [to his officer] and he says 'you alright?' I said 'yes sir', he was in a dugout and now and again we had whiskey, I'll never forget it he gave me a glass of whiskey and he said 'off you go' and I went. I was in a semi trench in a sunken road with some holes at the side and I went to sleep, had a good night's sleep.[59]

By the degree of men serving in the war by 1917, Price was considered to be a seasoned soldier, extremely capable under fire and was therefore subsequently sent out by his commanding officer for reconnaissance with the promise that if Price returned with a prisoner, he could have a month of leave or a recommendation. Price recounted that despite his exhaustion this was opportunity too tempting to turn down. Despite the promises made, after only a short distance Price and his partner elected to abandon their mission and instead dig a short trench within which they took cover for the remainder of the evening and following day as enemy shells exploded around them.[60] Unable to go back and unwilling to go forward, Price remained paralysed with only a thin layer of dirt and the prayer of good fortune to keep him alive. Price was certainly not alone in losing control of his body to unbidden emotions. After being suddenly dropped on to a beach at Suvla Bay in August 1915, Private Cowley was terrified and immobile. He recalled in his oral history the power of his terror as he took shelter in the abandoned trenches of the enemy. 'I just attached myself to somebody, I don't know who ... and there I sat all night, in my khaki drill, frighten to death. I was like that until the day where my job was picking the equipment up off the beach.'[61] In both cases the physical shift from effective soldier to incapable liability was practically instantaneous as the men's bodies failed to act according to how they were trained or directed by the men themselves.

Front-line service evidently could have a significantly detrimental effect on the ability of the men who served; this is overtly clear in the cases of Price and Cowley whose previous unwavering service was suddenly questionable as their bodies seemed unable and unwilling to continue. Corporal Glendinning also remembered that men's bodies became unsuited for purpose as the battle lay ahead of them. He recalled, 'It was a long dreary miserable night. Some chaps were crying, some praying, but most of us were optimistic. We all hoped that we would come through.'[62] Crying was something that those who witnessed it often recalled clearly as it was viewed, through the lens of a hypermasculinity, a feminine action. John Tosh argues that 'masculinity was defined by its public destiny, in a way which excluded so-called feminine qualities'.[63] This explains why Glendinning seemed so keen to distance himself from those men in his recollection by clarifying that he was one of the 'optimistic' ones.[64] Tears and sudden immobility remained at the lesser end of the spectrum for the men whose bodies suddenly imploded from the stimuli around them. At the other men's bodies reactions could be particularly extreme. British rifleman Robert Renwick, who served with 16th Battalion King's Royal Rifle Corps on Western Front between 1916 and 1918, remembered seeing some his fellow soldiers seemingly lose complete control over their own bodies as they engaged in battle: 'They seemed to lose control of themselves and shaking and we would have to go over the top of the trench, go out to em [*sic*] and sometimes had to be held down … think some people were more susceptible to it than others, something different in our bodies. If you know what I mean.'65 For Renwick, the physical failings of the men in question were entirely innate. In his view, the men were not simply physically and psychologically predisposed to the rigours of battle. Within his testimony Renwick is clear about his own role within these moments of physical crisis. He describes putting his own body at risk to rescue the stricken bodies of the affected men, plainly illustrating the difference between his physical ability to endure the shock of war and their inability.

With hindsight it is possible to recognize that Renwick is describing symptoms of 'shell shock'. The meaning of 'shellshock' changed continually during the First World War. This coverall term for the psychological breakdown of soldiers in the field has since been discussed at length by academics, theorists and social scientists as more sympathetic understanding of the impact of battle trauma has been understood over the last century. Still, for much of the war, the label was initially used to classify all a range of behaviours demonstrated by men who were unable to fight.66 Renwick was clearly describing shellshock, yet lacked the nuanced understanding of the disorder that would later develop after the war. Renwick, like many during the war, perceived the condition purely as physical, manifested through a loss of control over movements and somehow linked to the inherent nature of each body. In *Shellshock and Medical Culture in First World War Britain*, Tracey Loughran discusses a paper given to Guy's Hospital Physiological Society by a former First World War soldier, R. Hodgkinson, who had been diagnosed with the condition.67 He had experienced 'knocking heart, rapid pulse, laboured respiration, trembling muscles and limbs', sometimes so severe that 'his arms may vibrate so that he cannot light a cigarette and his knees knock together'.68 Hodgkinson experienced a significant physical response to the fear and trauma during the war, a manifestation that rendered his body completely ineffective.

Another common symptom of battle fatigue was catatonia. Within his memoirs Private Prew recalled discovering one of his friends struck dumb and catatonic in no man's land in the midst of battle at Vermelles in 1915: 'I noticed that this fellow was still lying on the ground so I went up to him and was very much surprised to find that it was my chum George, suffering from Shellshock, his nerve had evidently failed him when running across the open.'69 Others recalled similar experiences of encountering men whose bodies had become so affected by the experience of combat that they shook involuntarily. Nurse Hartley recalled such soldiers as a VAD nurse in 1917: 'All the cases were shellshocked, which meant they could not keep their hands and their heads still. I had to hold them gently behind their heads and feed them.'70 The men that Hartley describes found their bodies so affected by the trauma of war that they lost autonomy entirely. Removal from the war only displaced them from a position of remotely directed danger to one of institutional care, unlike many of the men who subsequently return wounded or demobilized. Men such as those in Hartley's care would not regain their individual autonomy as quickly, if at all.

Despite the regulations maintaining that men should not serve at the front for more than seven days, the continuing cost of the war meant that men could stay in service for much longer with significantly negative implications on the bodies of those in service. Sergeant Huggins remembered an occasion where one officer collapsed, his body refusing to endure anymore after spending five hours over the front line during the battle of the Somme, on 15 September.

> At five minutes to 12 that night the tanks went over, and at 12 o clock and we went, and we were told, the captain said, 'we went in extended over'. That's all I knew and as I said we were fully manned, officers and everything and we stumbled on and stumbled on and at round about 5 o clock breaking daylight, when I reckon, it would be about 5 o clock and er … when the officer said, 'I'm exhausted, I'm done and down he went'. I saw him fall. Well before … well in the flash like, what are you going to do and of course I was by him and I said the word halt, dig in and as I said it we were few yards ahead of him, and I did and I was to go back and ask him what to do, where we were going and what we had to all about it and I noticed this object ahead … and I saw it was Colonel Jefferies and I dropped me [sic] rifle and he walked up and he said 'Sergeant Huggins', I said 'yes', and he said 'what's the position' and I says, I told him Captain Cook is down, is exhausted and I say that can't, there isn't another officer so what I've done is stopped the halt and I've told the men to dig in and I was going back to ask the officer what to do and he went back, he was away, why like a few minutes or thing and he comes back and he says to me, he says 'get the men to fall in in two lines', and he says 'I'll take the first line and you'll take the second one and follow me in.'[71]

This officer's blackout and collapse was put down to exhaustion and the man was relieved of his command for medical treatment. This officer was lucky, as failure to perform during combat was a punishable offence. Despite the additional pressures on the men and their bodies, the British military could be particularly unsympathetic to the impact of extended combat duty. Lapses in judgement and inability to carry out orders could result in severe punishment, particularly in the initial stages of the conflict, as the army sought to reassert its control of troops by making examples of those considered to have failed. Private Cook's introductory speech from his sergeant not only told him to disregard the regulations regarding hygiene but also warned the men that they were not to sleep on sentry as they served at the front. This was an offense that could mean execution, and unsurprisingly the men in Cook's company were more than a little worried by the demand to stay awake without the possibility of rest.

> Quite a speech but what wealth of good advice from a man who knew from experience. 'Any questions' he asks. 'Sergeant' someone says 'you said we never sleep, how long are we here for? 'well son' he replies, 'when I said you never sleep I mean there are no regular hours for sleep, you drop off when you get a chance but learn to sleep with one eye open and never go to sleep on sentry no, we don't know when we will be relieved it is rumoured we are here for twenty-one days but no one knows and if they do they won't tell.'[72]

Twenty-one days were significantly over the period by which soldiers were supposed to be rotated. Still, exhaustion was not to be considered a suitable excuse for a failure to perform their duties. Regardless of the lack of relief, extended duration of watch duty or any other extenuating circumstances, being caught asleep on guard was considered a horrendous failing and could mean the death penalty. Unquestionably, it was expected that the serving men, closest to the enemy, must always retain control of their bodies. Expectations remained high that men would keep their bodies fit and fighting until relieved or fallen. To do otherwise could mean grave consequences.

Keeping the men in line – on the line

Private Herbert Chase of the 2nd Lancashire Fusiliers was executed on 12 June 1915 after being found 'dazed and exhausted' behind the lines after a gas attack. Despite the clear strain he was suffering, Chase was arrested and subsequently sentenced for desertion.[73] Putkowski and Sykes explain in *Shot at Dawn* that Chase was one of several men who were executed after being found confused and tired after lengthy engagements.[74] Lance-Sergeant William Walton of the 2nd Kings Royal Rifle Corps suffered a similar fate. During the first battle of Ypres he disappeared and was found some months later in a small village near St Omer. Under interrogation, Walton struggled to speak coherently until he claimed he had undergone a mental breakdown. Despite this, he was executed on 23 March 1915.[75] In his memoirs, Private Keller outlined the dichotomy of the non-combatant officer class standing in judgement of the men whose continual endurance on the front lines had led to a psychotic break.

> When a man lost his nerve under fire, he was sent to hospital instead of gaol, which should have been done in the first place. The only exceptions were to those who endangered the lives of the comrades by their actions. At the start of the war it was not known that most times it was not fear, but shellshock that made some men react the way they did. Often times the officers sitting on the court-martial had not been in the frontline and had no idea of the stress that the men were under when the bullets and shells were coming.[76]

Within his article *The Psychology of Killing* Edgar Jones noted the development of the view that civilians were not 'natural warriors', which means that they were more susceptible to trauma following combat than those who had been drawn to military service as a career.[77] This was built upon the work of W. H. R. Rivers who published several articles towards the end of the war which considered 'shellshock' a result of the lack of appropriate time for the individual to psychologically prepare for fear and anxiety associated with battle. In 1918 Rivers claimed that the haphazard nature of enlistment and training throughout the war had resulted in poorly indoctrinated men who were not psychologically suited for the trauma of war.

> There are few, if any, aspects of life in which repression plays so prominent and so necessary a part as in the preparation for war. The training of a soldier is designed to adapt him to act calmly and methodically in the presence of events naturally calculated to arouse disturbing emotions. His training should be such

that the energy arising out of these emotions is partly damped by familiarity, partly diverted into other channels. The most important feature of the present war in its relation to the production of neurosis is that the training in repression normal speed over years had had to be carried out in a short space of time, while those thus incompletely trained have had to face strains such as have never previously been known in the history of mankind. Small wonder that the failures of adaptation should have been so numerous and so severe.[78]

This idea of physical deficiency would remain central to much of the initial medical research and psychiatric care for those who experienced psychiatric damage during the First World War.[79] Still, much was misunderstood about the causes and manifestations of shellshock but over the course of the war the British military took pains to attempt to understand what was debilitating their soldiers. By 1917, executions such as that of Chase and Walton had ended and the RAMC had begun to identify officers with experience in treating neurosis and mental illness to join front-line facilities.[80]

The battle against shellshock was still far from over. Even as medical authorities on the front line improved their ability to recognize and 'treat' shellshock the grey area between 'treatment' and 'punishment' remained blurred and violence towards the body persisted. Encouraged to keep men on the front lines, unsympathetic doctors were often initially unwilling to remove men from the front line. To prove that the afflicted man was affected and not shirking his body could be tested through violence. Soldiers could find their bodies being physically abused to test the severity of their condition or attempt to shock them back into a coherent state. Men could be slapped, have tea poured on them and be throttled to 'treat' their condition and snap them out of their malaise.[81] While this certainly did not occur for every suspected shellshock case, it was not uncommon to find that men suffering mental trauma were treated with distain. Sergeant McKay remembered such an episode in dealing with a troubled man.

> The captain had not been gone very long when Rutherford wakened up out of his drunken sleep and wanted to go out again. Of course, I had to prevent him, and then he said he was going to hang himself. I was in a bit of quandary as Rutherford was a powerful man. Fortunately, at this time the staff-sergeant returned and enquired what the row was about. I told him Rutherford was going to hang himself because I refused to let him out. 'he's what?' I repeated Rutherford's threat, and to my surprise, the staff-sergeant said 'well, we won't stand in his way. Get a rope'. This was got, thrown over a beam and tied around Rutherford's neck. A tug was given to the rope and the victim's face went black, and he was told to go ahead and finish it, as no one would stand in his way. The result was, Rutherford went over to a corner and sat down on his bed as quiet as a lamb. This example was one of the best lessons I had learned for a long time, and one which proved invaluable to me later under trench conditions when I had to deal with cases of shellshock.[82]

While a complicated story to interpret, the threat to the body of the confused soldier illustrated an attempt to reassert control over him that had been lost in his sudden pledge to take his own life.

In other cases, violence towards the body was not dressed up as therapeutic. The military authorities continued to use a range of punishments in order to assert their control. Private Keller described the use of field punishment on a fellow soldier and recalled that it was not well received by many of the soldiers who witnessed it. 'The thing that bothered us a lot was to see British soldier tied to the gun wheels in the barracks square ... They were there as punishment for various crimes. Some of them we were told was for cowardice. This seemed to us to be inhuman and cruel.'[83] According to Strachan, after 1916, the use of field punishment during active service was revised within British Army regulations to make it 'less of a public spectacle'.[84] Still, severe forms of physical punishment retained their defenders. For example, on 31 December 1916, Sir James Macpherson, Undersecretary of State for War, asserted that physical punishment upon men's bodies was the best method of reiterating the importance maintaining their masculinity and combat readiness. 'On account of carelessness, negligence, or cowardice or other vice in the field, you have to deal with these men by the quickest and most effective method in order to encourage the others and to stimulate a sense of shame in the men themselves, and I know this punishment has had more effect than any other punishment.'[85] Lieutenant McCracken was one such officer who held the same view, as he wrote in his diary of several men who under the cover of cutting firewood had hidden from a shell barrage: 'They are to be tried by 4 officers for cowardice; I hope they are dealt with severely, that sort of thing I have no use for in the battery.'[86]

Helen McCartney has argued that officers like McCracken were not uncommon. In *Citizen Soldiers* she argues that many commanding officers displayed an enthusiasm for field punishment and notes that over the course of the war, many instances of castigation were redacted from the official record.[87] The extent to which the bodies of troops were punished as the military authorities sought to maintain and reassert control over them in the difficult conditions of battle will therefore never be known. What is clear is that the body was central to the experience of combat. Getting the blood up encouraged men to fight despite butterflies in the stomach or the pumping hearts that signalled anxiety. They could cry uncontrollably from fear or shock and collapse from exhaustion. They could revolt against the demands placed upon them so that men could no longer control them or force them into fighting. As their bodies seemed to fail them the men were put at risk both from the enemy and their own commanders who sought to use violence to dominate and control their bodies.

Despite these extreme measures to curtail and encourage the men through regulation and punishment, on the eve of battle, British military authorities continued to interfere in men's relationship between their body and their mind through the distribution of alcohol to supress the natural fear response. Private Gatley of the 7th Battalion Manchester Regiment was one of millions of men who received a drink before battle to calm his nerves. He recounted how men were each given a rum ration as they nervously awaited the whistle at Gallipoli in 1915.[88] Alcohol was regarded by many commanding officers as being a crucial tool in getting men over the top. In 1922, Lieutenant Colonel J. S. Y. Rogers, who served in the war as the medical officer to the 4th Black Watch, claimed as part of his evidence to the enquiry into Shellshock that 'had it not been for the rum ration I do not think we should have won the war.

Before the men went over the top, they had a good meal and a double ration of rum and coffee.'[89] Yet, this deadening of the senses also carried a significant risk. NCO James Davidson Pratt came precariously close to death after the liberal amount of rum consumed by his sergeant major rendered the man insensible rather than courageous as the two of them set out to organize the men for an upcoming attack.

> [The Sergeant-Major said] 'Always carry a little flask with you', and he produced a flask and I said what's that? Rum? He said 'always carry a flask of rum with you, you need it up there'. So, he said 'we better have one or two rums just now before we go, just to get up on the way.' So, we had a few rums, we got up, and put the fellows into the various trenches, and he said 'Now we have got to go and visit sergeant so and so, he's got an outpost which he's looking after.' So off we went with him, well we fell into trenches, we fell into barbed wire, we seemed to go round and round in circles, we couldn't find sergeant so and so. The old boy by this time, was getting very, bit squiffy I thought. I had a good head ... next morning I looked out and I discovered where we had been. We had been, part of the time, messing about on the German wire, instead of own wire! We were completely lost. Thank God there was no activity otherwise we'd have got shot up.[90]

When all else failed, alcohol was at hand in attempt to get the men to conform and do their duty. Naturally, this method was a temperamental, as was physical beating the psychologically afflicted. The results were not certain, and, as is visible in the case of Davidson Pratt, the introduction of alcohol could be as devastating and dangerous as the act of clambering over the top into no man's land.

Broken bodies

The physical experience of the First World War was never more keenly felt than when it resulted in damage to the bodies of the men in service. The scars, lost limbs and lost lives remain one of the most prevailing mental images of the conflict. Barely any fighting man left the front lines unscathed as their bodies were shot, frozen, blown up, scratched, stabbed, gassed, burnt, starved, dehydrated, infected or exhausted through the course of combat service. On average around four hundred soldiers died and two thousand were injured per day between 1914 and 1918.[91] Front-line duty meant that men's bodies faced two potential outcomes: either they would return bruised and potentially broken or, more likely, they would not return at all. Damage was all but certain; all that remained for the men to ascertain was to what extent their body was to be damaged during their proximity to the enemy.

Private Jones of the 4th Battalion East Surrey Regiment found his body damaged at the hands of the enemy, unsurprisingly one of the most common ways to gain an injury. In his memoirs he recalled the excruciating pain of his injuries.

> Suddenly a hefty Prussian loomed up in front of me, he seemed to be at the ready for a bayonet fight I also came to the ready. Unfortunately for me, he had a bullet

in the breach of his rifle, and he fired. I felt a terrific kick in my stomach, and I fell forward. As I did so another Londoner Frank Baylis from West Ham ran his bayonet through the Prussian. I attempted to rise but found I could not move without great pain. I then rolled into a shell hole as shrapnel bullets were flying about. My wounds started to burn and pain badly. There was about a foot of water in the crater and the pain was increasing and I was getting weaker.[92]

Wounded and enfeebled, Jones's body failed him as he tried to continue his fight. Spirit obviously willing, the flesh had endured beyond its limit and no longer recognized the commands Jones demanded of it to keep him alive. Jones was fortunate that his friend was present to protect and retrieve him. Other men were less lucky and were required to self-assess the damage their bodies had taken to determine if they could keep fighting. During the middle of battle Private Templer's thoughts as he was suddenly wounded and blinded were of his parents' need for him to come home. Stricken down, Templer thought not of the pain he was in but the fact that his handicap had made him an easy target.

I pressed the trigger and intended to check my aim, but my rifle went up and I was blinded by splinters! I could not see! Thoughts went through my head like lightning. My parents would need my help and Dais [sic] was something I would not now know, especially if I got a bayonet through my guts. I lay face down and gradually pulled myself together and groped around, found a bit of rag, carefully wiped my eyes and tried to open them and began to see again. My left hand was a mess and face felt a mess also. ... I looked at my rifle and it was now useless. The bullet had hit my back-sight protector head on and blown it away. The stock was split from the band down to the magazine. Then the officer spoke on my other side and pointed to his face where a splinter had hit him.[93]

Within his memoirs Templer makes it clear that his priority was to ensure that his body was fit enough to still engage the enemy. Before he takes stock of the total damage to his body, he attempted to make sure his rifle was still usable. Clearly his weapon, perhaps as an extension of his body in terms of self-defence, was more important than the wounds he had received.

Bullets were by no means the only hazard that men's bodies faced. Gas was a new and insidious effective weapon during the First World War. Chlorine gas filled the lungs with fluid and drowned men, while mustard gas horrifically burned skin and the lungs. Private Clarke recalled how he and his fellow soldiers' bodies reeled from a small dose of mustard gas at Petit Vimy in 1918. Clarke considered himself lucky as he only felt 'dozy', as other men around him lost control over themselves and were weeping uncontrollably as they suffered 'massive amounts of pain' from the gas attack.[94] Gas was a terrifying weapon; unpredictable and eerie, gas could creep across no man's land and fill the shell holes and trenches as it progressed. It was a devastating killer that could be far more effective than a bullet or bayonet. Private Jones endured such an attack at St Eloi in 1915 and described in his memoirs how the men stood fast at their post as their bodies deteriorated: 'We were slowly choking. There were six of us, who had to take turns at guarding the opening. The first, then the second man collapsed. By this time, I was feeling terrible and could hardly breathe.'[95]

Perhaps just as terrifying was an injury which resulted in the sudden absence of physical sensations. Private Caokes of the 10th Battalion Hampshire Regiment recalled how a surprise bullet robbed him of any mobility or sensation. He explained in his oral testimony, 'It hit me in the hip and came out in the left galling … went right through and through the bladder, yes. I had no pain because I was paralyzed.'[96] Injury often changed the purpose of the militarized body. Rendered incapacitated, the wounded body could now pose a threat to the men around them as an obstacle or stricken comrade in need of rescue. Taking stock of the injury took priority as men were forced to clinically assess to what extent their injury prevented them from continuing to fight. If they were unable to progress, the mission directive abruptly changed, with the goal being to return to home ground and seek medical attention. In this chaotic moment, the chances of survival were entirely down to the ability of the body, the level of damage it had received and the determination of the man to drag his broken and potentially useless body off the line. Private Parker's account shows that despite two bullet wounds he managed to use what was left intact of his body to get himself off the battlefield.

> It seemed as though I had been kicked by a horse, on the left knee, it gave way, and down I went, rolling down the bank. The only thing I thought of then was to get out before the only gap in the circle closed. I crawled, dragging that blasted leg, in between hundreds of our dead, towards what I hoped was the right way. I was more scared then when I was behind my gun, so helpless. Even Jerry had to give me a parting gift a bullet in the hip. I don't think he liked me![97]

Parker's determination may have been shared by many, but for some men, the impact of their injuries meant that their body was no longer capable of following simply instructions. Signalman Grindley, from the 19th Battalion Manchester Regiment in 1916, was one such man and he recounted how he would not have been able to get medical attention without the help of a fellow soldier who encouraged him to walk his shattered body to safety. 'They said it was obvious I had some fractured bones in my body. He explained to them how I had got it. I remember hearing some doctor saying, "good God, however, did you manage to walk from the frontline to us?"'[98] Grindley's account is somewhat paradoxical. He takes pride in his ability to endure his injuries and walk to gain medical attention. Yet, he also openly admits that without begging for help he would have not been able to reach the dressing station. Severe wounds often had devastating impacts on soldier's agency and masculinity as injured men like Grindley could find themselves begging other men for help. Lieutenant Anstruther adopted a bolder tone but he too had relied on the assistance of others when wounded.

> I am getting on first rate, it is only a bit of a hole through my shoulder, which will make it stiff for a bit. … Mackie was too capital when I got hit, he got me under cover, ripped my clothes off, and bandaged me up; we then set off to find the dressing-sta-tion [sic], which proved to be some way off; arrived there, they dressed me properly, and gave me some food – I lay there Monday night, with the

shells bursting all round, and wounded brought in – and on Tuesday was taken to the clearing hospital by motor lorry.[99]

Again, Anstruther demonstrates a somewhat paradoxical account. He openly admits to being tended to by another man, without whom he implies he would have not made it off the line. Yet, he also speaks of his injury with bravado and dismissiveness. Away from the front lines, measures of masculinity and soldiery were reliant not so much on the nature of the injury, but how the man presented his treatment and recovery. This brittle extension of the masculinized soldier identity is considered in detail in the next chapter.

While Grindley and Anstruther survived a 'hit', others did not. Accounts from the First World War often refer to visions of the dead and dying and echo that of Major Nicholson of the 2nd Cavalry Brigade RHA in France in 1917 who was forced to pick his way through maze of wounded and dead soldiers: 'There were dead and dying troops lying all over the place; the wounded were being taken into an improvised first aid post and any that showed any sign of life were also moved, although they could never have lived for much longer.'[100] Private Parker of the 1/8th Battalion Sherwood Foresters recounted in his memoirs witnessing first-hand the death of his captain. 'Of all the horrible deaths, that is terrible to suffer, & to see! He stood bolt upright, and his screams, even in the surrounding din, were awful to hear. Death from wounds in the abdomen are not only the most painful way of dying but the most long drawn out.'[101] In his recollection Parker illustrated not only the danger of combat but also that men began to create hierarchies that ranked preferable ways to die and types of injury. A death like the one suffered by Parker's captain was considered much worse than an instantaneous one as an abdominal wound could take hours or days to kill a man.

It is here that the issue of physical pain enters the discussion, as many men were faced with an impossible choice in recognition of the imminent damage to their bodies to exchange less pain for a quicker cleaner death rather than for endure extended agony for life. In *The Story of Pain* Joanna Bourke extensively considers the relationship between pain and physicality. She notes the complicated intersection between endurance and physical and psychological interpretation of pain for the individual, stating, 'Pain is a multifaceted sensory, cognitive, affective, motivational, and temporal phenomenon.'[102] Unquestionably, the experience of pain is typically, although not exclusively, a physical one. Within the First World War anticipation and experience of pain situated on the individual body forced men to change their typical perspective in relation to acceptable forms of physical damage. As opposed to enduring pain as a criterion for survival, instead some men hoped for quick fatal wound rather than suffer the agonizing fate of Parker's captain.

In 1915 Canadian-born John Gallishaw enlisted with First Newfoundland Regiment that joined the British Army at Malta. Gallishaw explained how many men openly wished for a 'clean' bullet over more painful ways to die in battle. 'A bullet leaves a clean wound, and a man hit by it drops out quietly. The shrapnel makes nasty, jagged, hideous wounds, the horrible recollection of which lingers for days. It is little wonder that we preferred the firing-line.'[103] For others, a balance was to be hoped for as men hoped for a debilitating wound that was as painless as possible but serious enough to remove them from the front line permanently. The infamous Dad's Army actor Arnold Ridley was relieved after being badly wounded in his hand. Against the logic of self-preservation he appreciated the pain and suffering as an alternative to continued service. He explained in an interview the complicated relationship he had with his wounded body during the war: 'It's not altogether a right thought for a young man to hope he's been maimed for life – but I did. I thought "well, if I've lost my hand I shall live. They can't send me out there again".'[104] In his view being seriously injured was preferable to death, and he admitted to hoping that his body was sufficiently damaged to require the army to release him (his hand remained virtually useless for the rest of his life). This was not an uncommon, although morbid, aspiration. George Ashurst, a former NCO who had served with the 2nd Battalion Lancashire Fusiliers on the Western Front in late 1914 claimed that blighty wounds had become culturally known quickly in Britain and commented with a laugh that 'EVERYBODY, everybody hoped to get a lightish wound!'[105]

Unlike many of his earlier enlisted comrades, Ashurst had had the opportunity to witness the physical ramifications of the war. This gave the man a much more cynical approach to his service, as he, among many other fighting men, coldly calculated to what extent he was willing to accept physical damage to save his life.

During the Battle of Arras in 1917 2nd Lieutenant Carter of 7th Battalion East Yorkshire Regiment excitedly hoped his leg wound was bad enough to allow him to go back to Britain; he noted in his journal, 'A "blighty" I thought as I put my emergency dressing on the wound.'[106] The notion of the 'blighty wound' shows that in the unusual circumstances of the First World War and combat men began to consider their bodies in new ways. Men suddenly began to assess which parts of them they would consider as expendable and to calculate the level of damage that they would be willing to endure as to allow them to escape the army with their lives and their honour. This explains Private Keller's ambivalence about his injury as he remarked, 'Fortunately, or unfortunately, depending on which way one looked at I, I wasn't too badly injured, and I was able to carry on. A slight wound meant that I stayed with the battery, a serious one would possibly mean Blighty.'[107]

However, it was not just individual men who began to quantify the seriousness of the damage to their bodies and the amount of pain they could endure. Quickly the British military medical services and officers began to designate to the extent that serving men were expected to endure physical pain and discomfort before they were deserving of care or treatment. Keller's account of seeking medical treatment makes this startlingly clear.

> When we reached our horse line, the doctor came to dress my leg. He told me that his orders were not to send any of the original expeditionary army to hospital if it could be avoided as they needed to break in the new men and to stiffen their morale. I was excused duty, but that didn't mean anything as I was up the line with our next supply of ammunition, and the wound was not reported so I didn't have the right to wear a wound stripe. When I saw men with gold wound stripes, I wondered how many of the older soldiers had suffered wounds or gas, but had no wound stripes. I have since learned that many found themselves in the same

position. I know of one man with four wound stripes and one day when the anti-aircraft guns were firing, a little blood and the next day he had five wound stripes. I have had worse cuts shaving with the straight razors that we used than he had that day.[108]

During the war the commodification and recognition of wounds and endurance of physical would become very important to individuals and the military as an institution. Continuing themes of masculinity and physical endurance Carden-Coyne explains that the awarding of a gold wound stripe was introduced by the army in 1916 to convey a heroic status to wounded man.[109] Gold stripes signified that a man had been wounded in combat, whereas silver denoted a noncombat injury. The division between the two could be very stark. Carden-Coyne quotes a soldier who complained to his girlfriend that despite having engaged in combat for years because he was invalided for enteric disease he received significantly less favourable attention than the inexperienced 'lads who were wounded on landing'.[110] This clear depiction of worth and physical endurance could have long-lasting consequences. In terms of public perception, a combat wound was linked to heroism and sacrifice while sickness was less likely to evoke sympathy or admiration. Evidently, during service different bodies had different values according to their geographical location and the time period within which they were damaged. This also created a scale of endurance that culturally implied that veterans, perhaps as 'proper soldiers', were valued for their experience and expected to put up with injuries that might have seen other less experience men sent to hospital.

In the ultimate act of consolidation of consequence and reward in relation to the fighting man's body when the war failed to provide a suitable wound to enable them to escape the front, some men turned to self-harm as means of saving their lives. Private Stone recalled how while receiving the wound that removed him from the front line temporarily, he witnessed a fellow soldier deliberately damage his body in order to remove himself from the danger.

> I got a piece of shrapnel in the finger actually, it bled quite a lot, I was very happy about it, it ran all down it, all down my arm and I went to my corporal and I said 'got a piece of shrapnel corporal and he said you better go down the dressing station …' I heard a shell coming over and I jumped into this hole and on one side of the heap and as I waited for the shelling to get easier a bit, another chap jumped in and went over the other side and there after a couple of minutes I heard a shot, a rifle shot, I saw him getting out, he had shot himself in the thigh to get back, they probably know he did because he couldn't hold his rifle far enough back, he probably made a black powder mark but he shot himself and got out.[111]

The case of the man so desperate to get out of the battle that he shot himself in the leg is not unusual. For him a damaged thigh was a price worth paying to get free of the mortal danger he was in. He ran the significant risk of being detected and if the authorities suspected that the wound was self-inflicted, he would have faced a court martial and potentially execution. Interestingly, while Stone outlined concern for the man whose self-damage may ultimately cause further physical harm in the form of punishment, he continues in his narrative to explain that he mirrored the man's actions, albeit more subtly.

> I went down the dressing station and I got a bandage on my hand it and thought I might away and he said, 'that's alright you can go back to the line now'. Up I went back to the line and the sequel to that is, after some time afterwards this thing poison it came out and a long blister like that and I let it go on and on and on and then I thought if I don't go right now I'd probably get into trouble. I kept it going hoping I'd be able to get down perhaps a week away you know into err … at one of the rest camps. I let it go there and one of the doctors said why didn't you come before and I said I didn't know it was as bad as this, and all he did was to lance it and bind it up and then back you go, back![112]

Stone's attempt to remove himself from the line was significantly less effective and less extreme, but he too played a dangerous game by deliberately allowing his body to decline as he too could have disciplined for malingering and not reporting an injury. Stone's account reiterates the price range that some men were willing to pay as they internally weighed up the cost and benefits of allowing their bodies to be damaged for a chance at respite or release. Stone may not have gone as far as to shoot himself, but he was certainly prepared to endure the discomfort of a septic finger in the hope of securing a few precious days away from danger.

Self-inflicted wounds during the First World War quickly produced an extensively negative response as men suspected of such acts were invariably labelled as cowards and treated with attitudes ranging from indifference to contempt.[113] Between 1914 and 1918 the British Army sentenced 3,080 men for cowardice.[114] Putkowski and Sykes argue in *Shot at Dawn* that the majority of the men who were executed were charged with desertion (266) with the next capital crime, aside from murder (37), being cowardice (18). They note that other crimes included 7 counts of being absent from post, 5 counts of disobedience, 5 counts of striking a superior office, 2 sleeping at their post, 2 for casting away arms, and 4 for mutiny; however, this last charge only applied to the Western Front.[115] Officially no men were executed on the basis of a self-inflicted wound; however, self-inflicted wounds were often presented as evidence of desertion and malingering in cases that resulted in the death penalty. Men who injured themselves could also be ostracized by their fellow soldiers and the public at large for their apparent lack of fortitude and commitment to duty. George Coppard recounts in his published memoirs that having been accidentally shot by a fellow British soldier he was treated with open contempt because he was suspected of being a malingerer.

> Next morning, I discovered that there was something queer about the place which filled me with misgivings. None of the nursing staff appeared friendly, and the matron looked like, and was, a positive battle-axe. I made anxious inquiries, and quickly learned that I was classed as a suspected self-inflicted wound case. Unknown to me, the letters SIW [Self-Inflicted Wound] with a query mark added had been written on the label attached to my chest.[116]

Such behaviour was perceived as unbecoming of a soldier, and as a response Coppard, under the guise of an assumed self-harmer, was not entitled to the physical care and kindness of his fellows who seemingly in the eyes of the nurses had earned their affection. During his oral history interview, territorial soldier George Ashurst, was quick to distance himself from the shameful act of malingering and make clear that no one from his battalion was ever accused of it. He categorically stated that it had never occurred in his battalion before adding, 'Well round about them, what were the rumours, oh so and so had blown his toe off you know and he been sent down the line and of course that was the last you hear about it then, don't hear nothing no more then.'[117] Ashurst's clear need to distance himself from such behaviour, even so many years after the end of the war, reiterates the unwillingness of men to be associated with such a humiliating and supposedly dishonourable act.

If the constant risk to life on the front line meant that men commodified their body parts and worked out which ones they would endanger or sacrifice in order to escape the fighting, suicide was something different altogether. Self-extinction was a very extreme response to the front line, but Joanna Bourke has argued that 'it was an important option for a minority'.[118] At time of writing, the only British suicide note known to have been written belonged to Private Robert Andrew Purvis written while serving with the Royal Scots on 29 August 1916. A survivor of the first days of the Somme, and numerous battles previous, Purvis took the decision to remove himself through suicide in order to end the pain that was his daily existence.

> I have shot myself as I cannot stand the hardship + suffering of this life any longer, and there is no chance of getting home again to see my parents whom may God bless + comfort in their trouble. Mr Clarkson + Mr Collinson are two fine officers and I hope they will come through this war safe + sound. Any of my pals can have what they wish of my things here. Goodbye and good luck to everyone.[119]

Purvis's action is one of the very few currently recorded in the history of the First World War. His note and death reiterate the fact that the destruction of body offered men a final way off the front line. Within his suicide letter, Purvis succinctly justifies his decision for taking his own life and is careful to praise his officers and even demonstrates pragmatism by asking for his kit to be distributed to his fellow soldiers. As a pioneer in the study of suicide at the end of the nineteenth century Emile Durkheim theorized that cases such as the death of Purvis could be classified as 'fatalistic suicide'. He argued that men like Purvis killed themselves because of an excess of 'social regulation'.[120] Essentially, Purvis's lack of agency, combined with the ordeal of his experience, allowed him to conclude his existence was hopeless, escape was impossible and that his suicide at least gave him the agency to end his suffering on his own terms.

Private Jones recounted the suicide of his commanding officer in a context that suggests similarly fatalistic causes as his lieutenant chose to retain control over his physical body rather than allow it to be captured by the surrounding enemy.

> Thirty minutes the enemy with reinforcements attacked again. They showed us no mercy, they were also at our rear. They drove us out of the Sangars and down

the valley, where they swept us with machine gun fire, I suddenly felt a blow on my left arm, then my right leg. Corporal Tait, Lance Corporal Lane and myself threw ourselves into a ditch. We never had a round of ammunition between us. Nearby lay Private Woodbine, suddenly a bomb came over, luckily it missed, but the blast hit Woodbine in the eyes and he cried out 'Jonesy I cants see' we quickly threw butts of our rifles away to make them useless to the enemy. Our dead were scattered everywhere, Lieutenant Nicholson then shot himself in the head.[121]

Jones does not criticize the officer who abandoned his men during the battle combat. Instead, he presents the lieutenant's death plainly without judgement as another element of the battle. Despite evidence of its occurrence, and the role that it could play in releasing men from the physical hardships and extensively controlled conditions in which they lived, very little has been written about the history of British Army suicide.

In her consideration of nineteenth-century suicide Padiak explains that, prior to the twentieth century, British soldiers statistically showed a higher risk of suicide than their civilian peers. This clashed with perception that soldiers represented the physical peak of masculinity and that their training and experience had made them physically superior as 'healthy warriors'.[122] During the First World War soldiers chose to take their own life for a multitude of reasons which impacted on them and their families, as well as those around them. Rothberg and Lande explain in their investigation into military suicide within the US Armed Forces that historically suicide was overlooked, particularly during wartime as the low number of losses could be regarded as insignificant in comparison to battle fatalities. Additionally, suicide was commonly regarded, even in the nineteenth century, as a psychological issue. Responses to the act remained outside the purview of the traditional command structure. Suicide was an individualist rather than a collective problem and therefore difficult to combat within the military.[123] Essentially, in the nineteenth and twentieth centuries, suicide cases within the armed forces were difficult for commanding officers to comprehend, explain and attempt to prevent, as well as being a relatively low priority in relation to the losses of war.

Understanding motivations for suicide in the First World War is difficult as rarely were notes left behind or evidence recorded. Even in cases outside of this period Holmes and Holmes argue that notes are left behind in only 15 percent of one hundred suicide cases.[124] Still it is possible to draw understanding of these desperate acts through individual stories from those within proximity to the act of suicide. These accounts can offer a great deal of information to help understand what could drive an individual to undertake such an extreme act of violence against his own body. As an NCO serving with Essex Regt on Western Front in 1918, John Charles Hart witnessed his sergeant get up and walk into no man's land.

We had one chap, a sergeant, I brought the post up in the trenches, he opened it, read it, he took his hat off, cause tin home ones were on loan, put his rifle on the side of the trench, opened his collar, tore the letter in four pieces, put it in his hat and deliberately walked out into the open, twenty feet away he was dead, he'd been shot. And we got his body back, whilst laying on our stomach, one after the other, one had the head of his body and one had feet … it was the wickedest thing out, a dear john letter, how a woman could write a letter telling her husband that she was living with another man and didn't want him back, could you understand it and that's what happened, not once but several times in the war … it gave us the feeling that our dear ones at home didn't understand our sorrow in France.[125]

Clearly, factors far away from the front line could influence these desperate acts. Hart's recollection of his superior's death also notes how deliberate actions of destruction could put other soldiers at risk as they attempted to retrieve the man's body from no-man's land. Despite this, Hart did not judge the sergeant for his actions as he and the other men appeared sympathetic to his misfortune. Private Burnett recalled being less sympathetic after a provost sergeant had jumped overboard during the journey to Greece and refused to grab hold of a life vest. Burnett claimed that the sergeant had been 'a devil' to his men and had taken his own life to avoid punishment.[126] Unlike Hart, Burnett was not sympathetic but again noted how the men attempted to recover the sergeant's body implying that even despite the man's reputation and suspected behaviour, his body was still worthy of the customary military burial. While these four cases suggest different motives and contexts, they point to a common feature. Each man became capable of the ultimate act of violence against his own body in order to escape his existence. In one of the only extensive reviews of suicide during the First World War, Walker argues that service and veteran suicides in the First World War were exceptionally complicated and not entirely always connected with the war. The First World War allowed for new opportunities of suicide and provided men with motives and the tools with which to take their own lives.[127] Suicide for some men offered an alternative to the desperate situation within which they lived and could see no other way out.

Conclusion

Of course, the body was at the centre of the combat experience for soldiers in the First World War. After all, the battlefield was a place designed to damage and disable them and to encourage them to attack and maim the enemy. What this chapter has shown is that the body was in the midst of multiple complex forces while in that hostile environment. The first of these were the military authorities. They had worked hard to prepare men to use their bodies unthinkingly in combat through training and drill. There was a complex system of punishment in place designed to encourage men to continue to resist fear and exhaustion in order to control their bodies in the most dangerous of contexts. Up to the moment that men launched themselves into battle officers sought to meddle in the bodies of their men by dosing them with alcohol. The enemy were also keen to shape the bodies of British troops. A wide array of weapons was deployed not simply to kill and injure men but also to terrify them. From the accounts of men on the front line, it is clear that men could overcome fear and anxiety.[128] Their bodies emboldened them for the fight as adrenaline flowed and blood raced to muscles, heart rate increased, and pupils dilated. They dragged themselves from battlefields and made their way to find medical help despite horrific injuries. But death and wounding could happen at great distances from the enemy from shelling, shrapnel or gas or from being close to them, in hand-to-hand encounters or from front-line snipers. But death and wounding could also come from within the body itself, as fear and anxiety at the constant danger caused shellshock, or exhaustion caused collapse or confusion that could be punished as desertion. It forced men to look at their own bodies in new ways, to think about which deaths they would prefer and what value the different parts of their body had should they need to damage themselves in order to escape the conflict with their lives. Utter despair drove men to resist the control of the military over their bodies through self-inflicted wounds and even suicide to allow them to escape the front line.

Yet the issue of suicide is a reminder that even on the battlefield men could exercise agency over their bodies illustrating that they were not simply driven by the interventions of the military and their own physical impulses under duress. The man who decided to walk into enemy fire because his wife has left him and the example from the previous chapter of the sergeant who did the same as he had an advanced case of venereal disease are important for this very reason. It shows that even on the front line men could make decisions that were driven by personal concerns and individual motivations. Both men decided to die of their own volition not because of the pressure of war, or because they were driven by their training, their beliefs or the biochemical coursing through. They killed themselves because of the feelings they had for people far away from the front line. Combat stripped away much of the preparation and preconceptions men had acquired prior to setting foot on the front lines. With the enemy metres away, men's bodies faced the reality of warfare as they sought to find ways to survive, battle and escape their environment. Damaged, pressured and attacked from all sides, bodies on the front lines dealt with continual onslaughts until respite came. Faced with little sleep, meagre sustenance and the ever-present chance of agony and death, it is unsurprising that some men's bodies began to dismantle physically and psychologically. As men began to trade away parts of themselves for a chance of survival, and their bodies wasted away from exhaustion, it is impossible to claim that front-line experiences were anything other than a primarily physical experience that exacted incredible costs on the bodies of the men who fought.

5

Soldiers no more: Death, debilitation and demobilization

The life of a serving British soldier in the First World War was a chaotic and physically traumatic experience. Throughout their tenure in the army their bodies had been trained, transformed and targeted. Separated from the normality of civilian life, these men found their bodies open to numerous opportunities for improvement and destruction. Medicated, intoxicated or indoctrinated, these former civilians had lived an entirely different life in khaki, until it ended. For some the end was sudden; for others it was painfully withdrawn. Many returned, some stayed – buried in the uniform that had defined their entire existence during their military service. This is the focus for this chapter. While the rest of this book has discussed the ways in which bodies transformed and became suited for conflict during the First World War, this chapter considers the reverse. All things must come to an end, and the future which awaited the men who served between 1914 and 1918 essentially fell to three exits: debilitation, demobilization or death. Sometimes several, and occasionally all, these exit avenues meant that men's status as soldiers changed, as did state and public perceptions and considerations of their bodies. Divided into these three routes of exit, this chapter begins with the men who left part of themselves on the battlefields. If wounded or sick, men's role in the conflict immediately changed from fighter to dependant. Their bodies no longer capable of the task assigned to them, their new status as patient and convalescent introduced a new set of rules for men and their bodies. Exchanging the front for hospitals, officers for medical staff, billets for wards and khaki for hospital gowns, much changed yet stayed the same as their body autonomy shifted from combat command to medical recovery. This process provided another battleground of sorts. One between the wounded and the military over the demand to quickly return men to the front while the war continued.

For those who survived with life and limb intact, or at least enough to keep them in service until the armistice, the end is a different story. Even though the fighting was officially over, and the victory bells had been rung, many soldiers remained in uniform as the logistical problems of demobilizations mounted. This interim period, when men remained soldiers despite the imminence of a return to civilian life, caused many men to question their place and their future – sometimes with contention aimed at the military that had controlled them for many years. While transferring out of khaki and the grip of the military the men experienced another physical examination remarkedly like the one that they had received upon enlistment. Once again, their bodies were catalogued and assessed, forms given and clothing exchanged, their final experience of the military seemingly like their first as again their worth was assessed physically to determine their value. Those who died mostly never left the country in which they died. Interred in their uniforms, often near the corpse of their foes, these men exited service to take up a permeant perceptual stasis encapsulated in the role they had assumed for war. Publicly, honoured, remembered and glorified, the reality of death in service was that treatment of the dead bodies was a practical problem as corpses quickly became a source of disease for the living. The ways in which those bodies were dealt with also addressed questions about how morale could be maintained among remaining troops. Soldiers to the end, many lost their individuality interred in mass graves, their bodies disposed of, separated from their names returned home in sympathetic telegrams. While the figures continue to be contested, it is likely that over nine hundred thousand British men died during the First World War – their personalized epitaphless graves standing guard over the bodies that had been sacrificed for King and country.[1]

Dead bodies

During the First World War over nine million uniformed men died around the world.[2] Dealing with the dead proved to be a complicated political, moral and medical issue. As the war progressed, the trenches established and the losses mounted, official approaches to how to deal with the bodies of the dead changed and varied. The dead had to be removed for sanitary purposes; otherwise, their corpses would infect and disturb the living. They also needed to be recovered, respectfully interred and, increasingly as civilian soldiers entered the fray, remembered. As life was extinguished, the body, kit and possessions of the former soldier remained. This was significant transition that turned a useful body into a liability that could threaten victory particularly as the dead had an extremely negative impact on the living. The British Army had long recognized the need to quickly remove corpses from the vicinity of the living as they endangered the hygiene of the surviving men and destabilized morale.[3] Wilson explains that at the start of the war the burial of the dead was considered to be the responsibility of the serving soldiers. He notes, 'The British Expeditionary Force was expected to bury the bodies of their comrades with due care and reverence where they died or within the local French and Belgian village or municipal cemeteries.'[4] As a mark of the significant physical loses that the British suffered in the first year of the First World War, the responsibility of burial and organization was increasingly spearheaded by Major General Sir Fabian Ware, the founder of the Imperial War Graves Commission. Initially tasked with organizing the logistics of transporting of casualties off the battlefield with the Red Cross, Ware increasingly recognized the need to record where fallen men had been buried. This was a sensitive and forward-thinking decision, previously overlooked by the British Army, as families would later be able to retrace the final resting place of their loved ones. Such was the significance of his work that he was later transferred to the army to establish the New Graves Registration Commission in 1915.[5]

Historically, the rank-and-file dead were buried in mass graves without individual epitaphs. Geurst explains that only the higher ranks could expect to be interred individually or transported back to the UK for burial.[6] As opposed to the conflicts that proceeded it, during the First World War the body of the British soldier was more valuable or sacred than that of professional troops who had served and died before 1914. Crane argues that a monumental shift in terms of respect for the fallen and subsequent organized interment echoed the unprecedented expanse of the First World War, demanding commemoration 'in kind' for the men's physical sacrifice. In agreement, Wittman argues that the First World War was the first equalitarian interring of combatants, as both officers and rankers received much the same treatment in death.[7] No longer was the marking of the graves of the fallen limited to the ranking officers. All nations involved in the war had publicly promised their soldiers a proper burial for their sacrifice and significant care was taken both during and after the armistice to ensure this promise was met.

As a result of this cultural awareness of the treatment of soldier's bodies in death painstaking notice was taken of where they were buried. By September 1916 public recognition of the war dead and the refusal to return them to Britain for burial caused *The Times* to publish the regulations established for the registration of the graves of the dead British soldiers. Again, in a move unique to the chaos of the war, the regulations also offered a free photograph of the grave if requested. The process of identifying and assigning burial plots to soldiers was not a simple task. The article reiterated this to the public by concluding, 'The proper registration and marking of graves will necessarily be a lengthy and difficult problem.'[8] In reality, identification and location of every war dead would be proven to be impossible. To manage the expectations of bereaved families the article also featured a series of provisos relating to the complications of identifying individuals who died on the battlefield while also clarifying that the exhumation of bodies was forbidden. The guidelines included statements such as: 'Some time may elapse after burial before the grave has been properly registered and marked and the position accurately recorded. As soon as this is done a notification will be sent to the next-of-kin. This notification may be taken as final verification or correction information received from other sources.'[9] Post war, the French government embarked on a complicated and costly campaign of 'demobilising the dead' and returning soldier's corpses back to their home villages. This respect for the fallen allowed families and communities to retrieve their lost men and inter them at home. After deliberation the British government refused to follow suit. Instead, almost all the British men who had fallen abroad remained there. Some bodies were exhumed from temporary and impromptu graves from the former front line to assigned cemeteries near where they had fallen, but for the most part almost all remained, officer or otherwise, in the War Graves plots that had initially been designated for them.[10] In practice, of course, this orderly process of burying the nation's fallen heroes in ways by which each individual contribution would be recognized often fell short of aspirations.

It is important to note that in this period burial was primarily the only option for removing the bodies of dead soldiers. Cremation was not a popular alternative in the early twentieth century, as burial had been the norm in Britain for centuries.[11] In 1916, concerns regarding the compiling and disposal of bodies however did lead to debate over cremation as an alternative for sanitation purposes. These enquires were immediately shut down by the Secretary of State for War who replied, 'It is not proposed to take any action about cremation. I may mention that this question was fully considered by the French authorities, who decided against cremation.'[12] Burial in France had already been a complicated affair with the French government becoming concerned about the responsibility of so many dead foreign soldiers buried in their land. Cremation was not an acceptable alternative to the French.

However, there were, albeit briefly and under the most special circumstances, cremations in Britain. In 1915, in accordance with the requirements of the Antyesti, an open-air cremation of Indian soldiers was carried out in Britain. This allowance of Indian burial culture was short-lived as was explained by Austen Chamberlain, the Secretary of State for India, in May 1916 in parliament as he clarified how it was impossible to cremate all the dead Indian soldiers due to the demands of the war. Chamberlain explained how the army had released responsibility for the custom as the burial rites had been left in the care of men from the same caste to ensure that respectful practice was followed.

> Under the conditions of warfare, it is not generally possible to arrange for the cremation of the bodies of Hindu soldiers killed in action or otherwise dying at the front, nor is it required by religious precept. As far as circumstances have permitted, interments have been reverently carried out by fellow caste men with appropriate rites, frequently in special plots in the local cemeteries.[13]

The brief use of cremation indicates a sensitivity to the Indian soldiers who served during the First World War and a relenting of the British government and the military of their blanket control over the bodies of the fallen. However, Chamberlain's assertion that it was not the responsibility of the government to provide an alternative to burial indicates the limit to which the British were willing to go to respect the individual preferences of the deceased. This was complicated by the relationship between India and Britain in this period with the former having spent over half a century under the rule of the latter. Mills and Sen argue that the British had habitually regulated the Indian body as a key aspect of colonial dominance.[14] As a result the ranking of the Indian military body below his British counterpart was maintained in life and death. A 2004 British War Graves Commission report highlighted that Indian burial sites were created in France, Italy and India with cremation memorials in Delhi and Myanmar. It reiterated the principles founded in 1920 that 'the dead should be commemorated individually by name either on a headstone over the grave or by an inscription on a memorial if the grave was unidentified … with no distinction made on account of military or civil rank, race or creed'.[15] However, Barringer argues that this was not the case.[16] Not only were Indian funeral practices typically denied, even in memory the Indian body maintained the uniform anonymity forced upon it, very much like the British rankers of old. As evidence Barringer explains that the very limited sporadic attempts to honour Indian sacrifice through monuments usually omitted the names of the dead.[17] As the practice of remembrance spread in 1919 with cities, towns, villages, institutions and businesses constructing personalized memorials of their dead, the practice of re-individualizing the uniformed fallen began; this was a honour that had limited extension outside of India to the sixty thousand Indian soldiers who died during the conflict.

In stark contrast to the treatment of the Indian dead, during the early stages of the war it was not unheard of for British dead to be returned for burial, although this again illustrated a divide over the importance of the fallen bodies as this was an honour typically reserved for the higher classes with means to facilitate retrieval. In April 1915, the body of Lieutenant William Gladstone, grandson of former prime minister William Ewart Gladstone, was returned to his family estate after he was killed three weeks after his arrival in France. Gladstone was returned home after correspondence between the King, the prime minister and the War Office permitted his exhumation from his military grave in Leventie. His funeral at Hawarden was a local event as people travelled for hundreds of miles to pay their respects.[18] Gladstone's funeral was the last burial in Britain of any British soldier who died on foreign soil during the First World War as the return of officers incited fury from grieving families of rankers who could not afford to return their own sons, brothers, husbands and fathers.[19]

The practice of returning corpses was prohibitively expensive and required significant dispensations and permissions which made the practice exclusive to the officers of wealthy families. Julie-Marie Strange notes that the impact of men never returning was significant as the absence of a body often compounded the grief of soldier's families as they had nothing to project their grief upon.[20] Richard van Emden argues that the practice was also abandoned as the return of dead soldiers reiterated publicly the losses that the British were experiencing over the course of the war, as well as went against conventions of the honoured military dead being interred together as a mark of their sacrifice.[21] As purported in the Commonwealth War Graves Commission report mentioned above military bodies were eventually to be treated as classless in death in the First World War but this took time to be implemented and was brought about potentially more by the sheer volume of British dead rather than a concerted effort to diminish class divides.

British troops who were buried across the UK are most commonly there because they died in the country. Controversies about the cost of dealing with them reveal much about attitudes towards their bodies. In November 1914 a question was raised in the House of Commons regarding the need for free transport for the corpses of the soldiers back to their families who died in training as currently it was the families who bore the financial brunt of the return of their bodies.[22] No response was ever officially issued in parliament to this enquiry implying an initial reticence of the military and the government to maintain control and responsibilities for men's bodies once they were no longer useful. Four months later the Undersecretary for War claimed that men who died at home were allotted a undisclosed sum based upon 'the merits of each case'.[23] This was in response to the case in January 1915 where a deceased Royal Scots Fusilier who had been invalided home with enteric fever had only been able to be buried thanks to the 'generosity of the citizens of Linlithgow' who paid for his funeral as the army refused to take any further responsibility for his body after he died in Britain.[24] In October 1915 Sir William Pearce demanded to know why suffering families were being further aggrieved by local authorities, adding insult to injury by charging families double to bury deceased soldiers as they were not parishioners.[25] This occurred again in January 1918 when the family of a young officer was required to pay £48 for his funeral to which the Undersecretary of State was forced to respond in defence of military practice, stating, 'The general rule as regards officers is that, beyond providing the gun-carriage, the State makes no contribution to the cost of officers' funerals at home unless special cause is shown.'[26] Given the extreme conditions created by the First World War and the means by which men were enlisted into service it is surprising that these conversations over responsibility for the dead continued for duration of the conflict. These cases show that if efforts were made to standardize the treatment of the dead while at the front, there was far less done for those who died while back in Britain, even where their deaths were linked to combat. This paints the progressive undertakings on behalf of the fallen abroad in a less benevolent light by illustrating an underlying reticence to continue to care for the bodies for soldiers beyond service. Evidently, the state, whether the national government or local authorities, was not keen to bear the financial burden of returning the dead to places from which they had been plucked to serve the nation. The soldier's body immediately ceased to be a cost to the state upon death and it seems that the quickest way for a soldier to once again become a civilian was to die back in Britain. As the following sections will show this was an attitude that would continue to have detrimental impact on the lives and bodies of those who survived and returned.

While burial was a complicated political, social and increasingly militarized process during the war, another significant issue was the collection of the dead as this was a particularly dangerous undertaking. In 1915, Private Wright of the 1/7th Battalion Middlesex Regiment and Machine Gun Corps joined a burial and retrieval party after the battle of Neve Chappelle. In his oral interview, he recounted how he and his colleagues put their bodies in danger as they crept around no man's land at night to retrieve the dead without joining them: 'We were sent at night-time as a burial party … in with a mile of the line, no talking, single file … it was a matter of collecting up the wounded and the dead and tidying up the place and clearing up before daylight.'[27] To get the men to collect the dead, retrieval parties could be given additional rations of alcohol. As a stretcher-bearer before being wounded out of the war Private Parker was often part of such parties and explained in his diary how extra spoonfuls of rum were distributed to help them bare the strain of body collection from a battlefield that was still being contested.[28] Indeed, it was not only soldiers and the medical services who braved no man's land to retrieve the dead. Chaplains such as Reverend Winnifrith and Reverend Watkins were renowned among their regiments for setting aside their own safety by trawling the battlefield in the dim hours of twilight to recover the bodies of dead soldiers.[29] These men belonged to a brave collection of military chaplains who frequently went beyond their mandate to support the men around them. Of course, not all bodies were retrievable, despite the best efforts of the men above. Often corpses could remain in the middle of no man's land because it was simply too dangerous to collect them. During the battle at Ypres, Medical Officer Travis Hampson MC wrote in his diary that the corpses of both sides lay out of reach and would have to remain there because neither side would allow their collection. He wrote, 'None of the dead are buried; they can't or won't trust each other to go out to do it.'[30] The burial process itself was also not without risk. Both chaplains recalled similar under-fire burials during the battle of the Marne. In his published memoirs, Winnifred recalled how the danger of his task did not deter him. He wrote, 'Bullets whistled about us; but I went on with the prayers.'[31] At another graveside at Ypres, Watkins remembered conducting a burial under the warning that an enemy sniper was trying to pick them off in the dark.[32]

Often there were no bodies to collect as modern weaponry meant that some bodies were beyond recovery. Private Parker recalled how a shell explosion could obliterate a body, denying the fallen men the dignity of assigned burial or even identification.

> The awful deaths of some of them, and the total obliteration of others, because make no mistake, although new high explosives have been invented in recent years, a man, or even a whole company, could be wiped out with those big shells. Not a shred of any man would be left![33]

Even the ground beneath the men's feet could act against them. The mud and squalor of the trenches remains a lasting mental image of the First World War and these conditions often meant the dead were swallowed up before recovery. As troop movements and shells disturbed the ground again it was not unusual for corpses to resurface as a grotesque reminder of a potential fate. Lieutenant Godfrey recounted in letter home in July 1916 coming face to face with a former British soldier who had been lost to the mud.

> We chose the two most unsavoury spots to dig in (putting in dug-outs). One had been an old refuse heap previously; and stank with a stink that would have knocked a pole-cat out: we had to work with gas helmets on very nearly! In the other spot, we unearthed the year-old corpse of a poor British Tommy; that was of course merely nauseating. We buried it again in a shell-hole nearby, and stuck up a cross, inscribed in pencil with 'TO AN UNKNOWN SOLDIER'. I added 'Requiescat in Pace' to the mystification of the Sappers. It is a sad world, and that is a sight I shall never forget; Those poor remains, laid on a bit of corrugated iron, buried in a shell hole, of some poor humble unknown who had 'done his bit'.[34]

Godfrey's actions were respectful and practical, showing that even when unable to identify the individual the uniform on the body accorded it a value. With the pressure on to create a defensive position there was no time to transport a rotten corpse behind the lines for official burial. They did what they could to mark the man's grave in a suitable way. Jay Winter reiterates the importance of burial for post-war memorial and respectful reasons while also noting the issue of lost bodies and their wider impact on British society. Within *Sites of Memory* he explains that as a rule if a body could not be found or identified then that man was assumed dead with his passing communicated on to his family as 'missing, presumed dead'.[35] Winter notes the impact of the lack of a physical body could then have on those connected to the individual, as the lack of evidence of death could deny families and friends of the certainty within which to grieve. Winter designates this as a presumptive 'gap of conjecture' which put many families in an 'excruciatingly difficult position'.[36] Therefore, the kindness of Godfrey, who was unable to do anything other than to respect the unknown fallen comrade through reburial, has a darker implication in that through relocation and reburial the family of the fallen soldier would likely be denied certainty of what had occurred. Winter's argument reiterates the importance of the body, not simply as marker or obstacle but a vessel of connection back to Britain, without knowledge of which could incur long-lasting psychological trauma beyond the chaos of the battlefield.

Given the important of recording and clarifying the identity of the dead, it is unsurprising that the practice of burial was a complicated affair despite most being given only a very brief ceremony. In a letter to Lieutenant Albert Stiven's father after his death from a shell on 26 January 1917, his commanding officer (CO) described the small congregation around the burial. 'The men of his platoon and other – men & officers – including myself were present at the simple but impressive service when he was buried by the Presbyterian padre. War is awful.'[37] The reason for this brevity was often the number of bodies who required interment. Faced with overwhelming numbers individual attention and the level of care taken in civilian life to each body was limited. During the Battle of Passchendaele between July and November 1917 photographic evidence depicts the typical preparation of dead bodies for burial, particularly during the interment of large numbers of the dead.[38] This image shows a line of dead soldiers, many of whom with their faces covered and most with their hands on their stomachs. Newlands claims that in the Second World War soldier's bodies became 'homogenized' as they were buried in identical graves, adorned with similar markers and prepared for burial in the same fashion.[39] Much of this process was perfected during the First World War as thousands of men were quickly prepared for interment. The most attention paid to the dead actually preceded their interment as part of a final medical assessment to ensure they were deceased. Stretcher-bearer Collins explained that all men needed to be assessed and certified as dead by a medical officer and that often corpses waited days for burial until this process could be carried out.

> No man was ever carried out for burial unless the medical officers said he was dead. There were always two medical officers there … They used to pull back the lids of the eyes. They used to check the pulses, I mean if there was no pulse, there was no pulse … but I wouldn't like to certify that man was dead. I think it takes a doctor to do that … You see in any case; the man wasn't buried immediately. He was probably out there for a day before we could bury him.[40]

Typical of the bodily experiences of British soldiers during the war, even in death men's bodies failed to escape the intense attention, bureaucracy and physical assessment demanded by the British military. This final review by a medical officer preceded the stripping of the dead body's boots and pockets. Significantly, nearly all the British dead would remain in their uniform in their grave, eternally enlisted and clothed in the designator of their service.

Assisting with the recognition and recording of the dead, chaplains and stretcher-bearers would frequently take identification discs and any ephemera from the men's corpses as a means of identification and a way to send something back to men's relatives. Despite the essential nature of the task stretcher-bearers developed the reputation for robbery of the wounded and corpses. A recurrent joke during the First World War was that RAMC stood for 'Rob All My Comrades'.[41] William John Collins had been a stretcher-bearer and refuted this notion on the basis that 'nobody would carry valuables, or anything worth carrying on the line'; he continued to protest the innocent of his fellows and claimed, 'I never heard of a man carrying anything valuable. They never had it. How would they do it on a shilling a day?'[42] Meyer explains that this epitaph was one of several that often served to diminish the role of the RAMC in the First World War as their lack of weaponry and inclusion of pacifists led to questions and jokes about their masculinity and bravery within the climate of the war.[43]

While accounts of robbery of the dead were certainly exaggerated it was not unknown for some men to profit from the pockets of the dead. NCO Tom Bracey explained in his oral history testimony how the practice of stripping the dead did occur but was considered poorly within the ranks. Bracey notes the fate of a fellow who he believed earned a karmic severe wounding after months of robbing the dead.

> He was the one that had both legs off and it seemed to me as if it was punishment. I was afraid afterwards to do with my conscience, I never went down a dead man's pockets. I never … I used a body in a shell hole, to get some cover, so if there were bits blowing, I would pull a body across like that. But other than that, I never touched a body. I know that they cut the fingers off to get rings, but I wouldn't touch one.[44]

Clearly uncomfortable with pilfering the valuables from a corpse, Bracey paradoxically saw no issue in using the body of a fallen comrade as a physical shield during an attempt. He explains this matter without concern while condemning the man who had dug in the 'dead man's pockets'. While officially encouraged to perceive the bodies of the dead as fallen comrades to be treated with respect, evidently this relationship was subject to change when circumstances demanded it. Seemingly the bodies of the dead when the need applied could become practical resources. For him they were a useful source of cover, for others a chance to increase their own material gains.

The reputation of the RAMC and the stretcher-bearers also suffered from perceptions of their laziness in relation to the fighting soldier. The arising of a 'Slackers in Khaki' mentality is hardly unsurprising argues Meyer as male military caregivers in the later nineteenth century were renowned for drunken and brutishness. Additionally, due the rise in Christian masculinity developed by the early twentieth century the heroic fighting man ideal increasingly reiterated the emasculated caregiver within public perception, especially when combined with the disastrous medical practices during the Second Boer War a decade previous.[45] Sutphen argues that this was also particularly visible in the way that the non-combatant doctors within the RAMC struggled to attain the respect of their rank and were almost always referred to as 'Doctor' rather than 'Captain' as designated by the stripes they wore.[46] Still, this lack of respect for the men in the medical service did not mean that all in service could be without fault or remiss in their actions. While behind the lines, Private McKay recounted being roped in to help the RAMC transfer the dead to a central site for burial. In an action particularly unbecoming of men respecting their fallen brethren, a debate broke out over if to unceremoniously dump the corpse to save their exhausted bodies.

> The morning was wet, and we got an extra tot of rum before we started. We had not gone very far down the trench until Williamson wanted to dispose of the body in the swamp in our right. Neill was shocked, as Foreman also wanted to dump it. Neill would say 'persevere, Jack, persevere.' 'ah, persevere my B.S.!' William would answer. However, we got the body down as far as paisley dump, and Williamson and I said we would take it on by wheeled stretcher. When we arrived at Authuille, no one there would have anything to do with the body: 'stand him up against the wall' said Williamson, 'and let us return'. We propped the corpse up against the wall and went back to our dug-out.[47]

There is much to unpick from this account, not least from the visible burden that the dead placed upon the bodies of the living. Mayhew explains that a bearer could always be identified by his hands as most often the wooden handles of the stretchers split through constant exposure to water leading the men to wrap metal wire around them.[48] Gloves were also often wore as despite the agony of the cut flesh the gloves made it difficult to hold the stretcher. As a result most stretcher-bearers ended the war bearing significant scaring on their hands, a memento of their bravery and physical sacrifice that was often not appreciated.[49] In McKay's account even the additional rum ration could not offset the physical strain of carrying a fallen man's body leading to the question of respect for the dead over the comfort of the living. Interestingly, in death the corpse in McKay's account retains the same level of uniformity as he had experienced in life as a serving soldier. His individuality is never mentioned, he is not named and when McKay arrives to deliver the body it is first rejected before being abandoned. The bodies' lack of animation separates them from the living men but joins the ranks of the faceless fallen. For the men in McKay's account, and despite the best efforts of men such as Sir Fabien Ware, the corpse was no longer a person, soldier or man; it was a body to be disposed of like so many others.

Recovering living bodies

In 1918, the British Army numbered 4,796,088 men including all ranks and forces having risen from 212,355 in 1913.[50] Including soldiers who served from within the dominions, the number of total causalities was estimated in 1931 as 11,096,338. As always with the First World War, the sheer size of the numbers and the chaotic way in which units were combined and records were kept, even this number is a coverall estimate which counted occurrences not individuals. However, in terms of wounds, it is estimated that at least two million British men had to be treated for wounds.[51] As the previous chapter explained, this journey from battle to medical care could be for many men the most trying of their experiences so far, as they were dragged, or dragged themselves, away from the fighting. Private Warsop was one such man who had no other choice rather than lie down and die, then to force his broken body to crawl off the line:

> I came too lying flat on my back in a nearby pillbox used as a first aid post. A doctor was just finishing bandaging me up and he said, 'get a stretcher for this man as soon as you can.' I had been hit by a shrapnel shell full of steel balls the size of marbles that stretched from a height of twenty-five yards or so, one ball had blown an inch of bone out of my upper arm. One had taken a clean bit out of my jawbone without breaking it and one had gone deep into the left of my chest, breaking the collarbone on the way in. I found this out later at the time I remembered I had always made up my mind to walk out if I possibly could. There was a bombardment going on outside and I couldn't imagine any chance of four men carrying me down on a stretcher, they needed every man on first aid. I persuaded a first aid man to put his hand in the middle of my back and hoist me to my feet, I tottered out determined to get down to the Menin Road or die in the attempt – on this occasion no idle phrase.[52]

This desperate attempt to save his life, despite the destruction of his body, was not an experience unique to Warsop as many men dragged themselves and each other back to safety. Still, despite crawling when they were unable to walk, many men were forced to find someone to carry them: this was a task that usually fell to the Royal Army Medical Corps stretcher-bearers (see Figure 10).

As noted, retrieving the wounded from the front was not a straightforward task and was often left to the same men who collected the dead. As the combat in the trenches intensified and weapons increased in devastation, it became more dangerous to withdraw the wounded from the front lines. Unquestionably stretcher-bearing was a difficult and often underappreciated role. As well as the gruelling and physically tortuous aspect of the role, bearing a red cross symbolizing medic or a blood red 'SB' on their arm was no guarantee of protection from the enemy. Stretcher-bearer Thirtle explained that that the risks to his body and those of his fellow bearers were very real as they sought to save others.

> In one case, we had a stretcher case being carried down when the squad was incapacitated through one or more of its members being hit. It is half gruesome and half humorous to relate the result of enquires when the whole ones reported for reinforcements to replace their losses.[53]

Stretcher-bearers faced the same perils as the fighting men they sought to recover, except they usually did not carry any weapons with which to defend themselves. Wearing gas masks, these were the men who walked into the gas in order to recover the bodies of their comrades at risk to their own bodies (see Figure 11). As the image below illustrates, these men dressed in military clothing were almost indistinguishable from their fighting brethren, particularly from a distance. If indeed the enemy intended to show quarter in respect of the role of the bearer amidst the chaos of war it is possible to assume that identification of such men was difficult.

Figure 10 Unknown, *World War One: Two Stretcher Bearers Removing a Wounded Man under Fire*. Wash painting, c.1916. Wellcome Collection.

Once retrieved, many men entered a gauntlet of assessments, questionings and invasive actions upon their bodies as they transferred from the front line to convalescent care through a series of medical checkpoints. First, they faced a regimental aid post supplemented by stretcher-bearers which would issue immediate medical care. Those capable of returning to the line were sent back, whereas the more seriously injured were transferred to a casualty clearing station. These medical outposts, stationed slightly further back off the line, were designed to stabilize and assess the condition of the wounded soldier before he was dispatched again back to the front line or shipped out of the battlefield completely for treatment in a hospital or to be transported back to Britain.[54] Once clear of the battlefield the wounded were medically assessed at first aid posts and casualty clearing stations. Those who could not be returned to duty were transferred back down the line to local army hospitals or could be returned home for extensive care. At least for the time being, men's physical experience of soldiering ended as they transferred from combatant to patient.

Hospitals were different to any other aspect of military custodianship – particularly as they were often not entirely military, but a combination of civilian and military

Figure 11 A scene in the trenches showing stretcher-bearers wearing gas masks as they Carry in a man who has been gassed. Unknown, *World War One: Stretcher Bearers Wearing Gas Masks*. Wellcome Library London (1916). Wellcome Collection.

establishments repurposed to care for wounded and sick soldiers. These recovery facilities were increasingly organized to aid recovery in ways that extended beyond the medical care provided to return men promptly to the front during the war. In a lecture published in the Journal of the Royal Army Medical Corps (JRAMC) in 1916, Major Grey Turner praised and emphasized the importance of the hospital in helping men to physically and psychologically recover:

> The influence of mind over body is an important factor which is well recognised by all who have to deal with the sick, and it is especially so in our military work. Here we are dealing with men who are frequently a very long way from home

and friends, who have suffered the fatigues of war and have often for the first time been introduced to many of the horrors that follow in its wake. These men are not normal in mind, there is often a temporary loss of balance, and it is a wonderful commentary on the amount of backbone possessed by our nation that the wounded are so constantly cheerful and bright in spite of their great trials. But it is most important that you should recognise this aspect of the matter, and it says much for the wisdom of the authorities that as far as possible they arrange for wounded men to be sent home to England as soon as they are fit to travel. To be once again in their home-country and within reach of friends does much to help recovery in bad cases. Similarly, the bright surroundings of our hospitals are valuable therapeutic agents and they ought to be aided by a cheery optimism which I think it will not be difficult for any of you to cultivate. Always remember that one of the most valuable and cheapest remedies we possess is HOPE.[55]

Carden-Coyne argues that often such an approach was successful and that many men claimed to have enjoyed their experiences in hospital. As wounded men left hospitals like Bishop's Knoll in Bristol, for example, they remarked on it being like 'leaving one's home', rather than being discharged from a medical facility.[56] Many men found their medicalized incarceration in hospital to be immeasurably preferable to their experience as front-line soldiers. One such man was Private Copson, who, despite entering the war relatively late as conscripted soldier in 1917, had seen plenty of action during his time at Ypres and Béthune before being gassed and shelled off the line. In his diary he celebrated the simple comforts of being in hospital back in Britain:

> What a relief! Some people hate hospitals, but I call it a haven of rest. I slept for nearly a day here, and oh the joys of a real bed! I wondered where I was when I woke a nice nurse came and washed me and brought me some breakfast. For dinner, I had some jelly and custard as a favour. I was in bed for a few days.[57]

For Copson his hospital bed was a sanctuary, completely different to the mud, blood and bullets existence of the average ranker in 1917. Joyfully Copson described being clean, comfortable, well rested and adequately fed. Being hospitalized could also mean relative safety and was regarded by some as better than the alternatives of death or continued service. This mindset could lead to odd perceptions of being wounded within the chaotic sphere of the First World War. This is evident in the letters exchanged between Lady Anstruther from Fife and her sister during the war, within one of which they oddly celebrate the hospitalizing of a mutual friend whom she describes as 'safely wounded' and 'out of danger'.[58] The reference to the man being 'safely wounded' seems oxymoronic, but, as the previous chapter identified, many came to view their bodies, and those of friends and relatives, in new ways during the war. Survival was key over physical injury. During the war, as the death toll mounted, safety from death seemed worth the price of the long-term damage and the horrific pain of an injury.

Being in a hospital also meant an entire regime change. As soldiers became patients their bodies were forced to adjust to a new environment where the priority was not combat but recovery. Upon leaving the front men found their uniforms replaced with hospital blues. This was a uniform-type garment that Carden-Coyne argues signified that men were no longer soldiers but 'disciplined invalids' under medical care and control of medical staff.[59] The experience of 2nd Lieutenant Carter of 7th Battalion East Yorkshire Regiment after he was wounded testifies the truth of this as he was separated from his uniform and kit:

> I was taken by ambulance to 22nd General Hospital at Camieres. Almost immediately I was operated on and the piece of shrapnel removed. It had not damaged the bone. It was taken out on the opposite side of the left from which it had entered on the theory that if there was a hole right through it could heal from the middle. The nurses enjoyed squirting disinfectant through! After nine days, another ambulance train took me to Boulogne and a hospital ship to Dover where several trains were waiting. It was pure chance where one was carried off to. I landed at Leicester and enjoyed eight weeks in the North Evington War Hospital. I had left all my kit and uniform in France and only possessed one set of underclothes and a blue hospital suit except that a few letters and my diary had been rescued.[60]

Unlike demobilized men, the removal of the uniform for the convalescing men did not mean a return of agency over their body, as the control transferred to those in charge of the medical care. Carter's injury meant that in the course of saving his life he had no control over the physical disfigurement that was caused by the emergency treatment he received. Nor did he have control over the garments he adorned his broken body, as his khakis were exchanged for the identifiable blue of a military patient.

Initially the blue uniform was designed to project the heroic value of the soldier having paid a significant price in the course of doing their duty. However, the hospital blue instead was interpreted negatively, as is argued by Carden-Coyne, as men suffered the psychological impact of their loss of status through the removal of their weapon, uniform and equipment – rendering them neither soldier nor civilian.[61] This was just as true for those men suffering sickness as being wounded. After enlisting as an eager volunteer in 1914, Private Parker had served with the 1/8th Battalion Sherwood Foresters at Ypres until he became violently ill with diphtheria. His return to Britain, as he recalled in his diary, proved to be a haze of medical procedures and almost complete loss of autonomy.

> Our destination turned out to be Stockport, Cheshire, not far from Manchester. The Isolation Hospital, part of what had been the infirmary, now the General Hospital. We three were put in observation wards, glass on three sides, no one but the Doctor's nurses were allowed near us. I had a silver tube down my throat, which was taken out and cleaned very often. Life was a series of throat swabbing, partial choking, bed rest etc. I must have been too ill to know much, weeks went by, which I do not even remember. I was told, afterward that it was touch and go for myself and the others.[62]

During his subsequent recovery from diphtheria Parker was forced to hand over control of his body to medical staff as he relied on the medical staff to heal and direct his weakened physique.

During this time of extreme reliance, it was the medical staff who took control of the soldier's body in place of a CO. Doctors and nurses often take a predominant role in the narratives of soldiers who have been hospitalized, but they can be presented in very different ways. Doctors are often presented in a similar regard to a high-ranking officer who remained aloof and separate from the individuals under their charge. Nurses and orderlies however seem to be presented more like non-commissioned officers. Again, in charge of the debilitated body, but having more an interpersonal relationship with the recovering man. Private Prew makes this distinction clear in his memories as he noted that the doctor in a field hospital in France ignored him almost entirely and it was the ward sister who finally told him he was to undergo emergency surgery.[63] This relationship between doctors, patients and nurses was repeated throughout many of the military hospital facilities with the doctor acting as distant authority figure in contrast with the quasi-maternal role nurses often undertook for recovering men.[64] This was certainly the case for Private Jones who recounted in his memoirs how a nurse fed him 'like a child' and gave him a drink of milk.[65] This infantilization and continued lack of physical autonomy was particularly unique to the British military hospitals over the course of the war; yet, the controls were not entirely dissimilar to restrictions of agency men had experienced while in service.

Like life in service despite the controls imposed upon them men still found ways to reassert control over their own bodies. Lieutenant Carter was one such man whose time in hospital, and the control he endured by the medical staff, meant turning to rebellious behaviour.

> It was now July 2nd (1917) and the end of eight weeks at Leicester. Now followed fourteen days' convalescence at Uppingham, Rutlandshire. The grounds of the hospital were magnificent – the lives of the patients were miserable! The matron, a severe woman with a passion for discipline, treated us like children. But for the nurses, we should have gone hungry but they played the game and we usually got two platefuls of dinner by putting the first plateful under the table and waiting for the second. We had to be in by 6.30, every evening, or spend two days in bed which was bad enough but the last straw was a message on the notice board saying 'no patient must accept an invitation to tea in the village without first obtaining matrons sanction.' We struck back. Everyone agreed to stay out until 10 pm. The next night we rushed the gate. The notice was removed.[66]

His actions suggest that often the convalescing men did not appreciate being treated like children while recovering from combat or being confined to the hospital however agreeable it might be. They took their healing and the conditions under which they lived into their own hands and acted to assert control over their bodies. This dissent towards the conditions in which they were kept in was not exclusive to being treated like children. For the sake of the maintaining national morale, some men were hidden from the public gaze as their returning conditions painted a horrific image of life at the front. After being shot in the foot by a German sniper, Private Hurst was returned to Britain for medical care in 1916. Hurst recounted in his oral history that during his six months in hospital on 'no-duty' his medical care was particularly poor, which led to increased infection. An oversight he attributed to an attitude of ignorance and secrecy by officials to keep the wounded out of sight. He recounted, 'There was a number of us … sitting out on the canal side, out on the canal side, because we weren't allowed for anyone to see us … terrible, there we were spending the day on the canal side to keep out of sight.'[67]

This concealing of the wounded was not uncommon during the war. Extensively disfigured men were often relegated to remote areas of hospitals to ensure that they were keep out of public view.[68] After the war, the *Sunday Herald* described these men as being the 'loneliest of all the Tommies' because of the way they tended to retreat from society.[69] This was an unsurprising viewpoint considering the steps taken to keep the worst wounded from public view. Wounded men were frequently shielded from the eyes of the public even before they arrived into hospitals. Mayhew notes in *Wounded* how Nurse Morgan made curtains for her carriage on the No. 3 Ambulance train to prevent the wounded men being stared at by inquisitive civilians.[70] However, in Morgan's case the shielding of the men from the public gaze was more for the soldiers' benefit than the public or the military, as historically ambulance trains lacked privacy features such as screens and curtains.

Hospitalization was certainly a change of pace for the serving men; yet, this did not always mean the end of a soldier's career. Lieutenant Lindsay described being surrounded by convalescing men as he recovered from typhoid in hospital in Alexandria. He noted that once fit again they would be redistributed for service.[71] For men like Lindsay, their stay in the medical facilities was to be a temporary one with the singular aim to re-establish their physical fitness and capability in order to return to the front line. For much of the war, this reconstruction of men's bodies was the primary purpose of the medical services as the need for men on the front lines was an ever-present challenge. Private Stinton implied within his memoirs that the current state of the conflict was a determining factor in the flexibility of the level of recuperation that was deemed acceptable before returning men to the front. Within his account he also notes how yet again soldier's bodies were awarded classifications based upon their physical presentation and capabilities.

> About this time in the war, we had suffered some reverse in the fighting with the loss of a good number of men. Any man thought fit enough was sent from the hospitals to re-join their regiments. There were quite a number of men who left our hospital this way: most of them being those that had been convalescing. Every month, a board sat at the hospital to decide who was fit enough to return to their regiments. If a man was to attend, then the letters PB [Permanent Base] were written in blue chalk across the record board at the head of the patient's bed.[72]

When describing the 'reverse fighting' and losses, Stinton was likely referring to the ongoing battle of Passchendaele during which both sides lost accumulatively over six hundred thousand men between July and November 1917. This costly battle resulted in little tactical gain for the British but meant, when combined with the losses at the Somme in 1916, that reinforcements were desperately needed. This desperation left many men in the unique situation of defending their physical inability to return to the fight. Interestingly, this interaction between the British soldier and the military over the suitability of his body shares much in common with the process of enlistment in the earliest stages of the war. The difference for the convalescing man was the diminished enthusiasm to jump into the fray as instead men began to accentuate the aspects of their physicality, which exempted them from front-line service.

Private Lewis of the 2/5th Battalion Gloucestershire Regiment had served for almost the majority of the conflict and had been wounded twice: first in October 1916 at the Somme and then again through the chest during the battle of Ypres in December 1917.[73] His injuries ultimately meant that he could not return to the front lines and instead spent the remainder of the war working as a clerk for the Royal Engineers at Sandwich in Kent until his demobilization in January of 1919. Despite his protest that he was physically incapable to fight, he was regularly submitted to assessment at the request of officers who questioned his legitimacy for not returning to the front. In August 1918 a new CO again demanded that he be reassessed by the selection committee and undergo another medical exam to determine his suitability for active service.

> The day after arrival at Ripon I was before the Board and immediately selected by the Defence Corps Officer. I thought, 'here we go again' and told him I had been retained in the army for clerical duties only. He told me there was no such arrangement and I should have to do anything right up to the limit of capacity. Having Russia in mind, I then said that I did not think I could carry a rifle and equipment because of the wound and he handed me a rifle to try. I had to admit that I could hold it for a short time but would not be able to do so as a regular duty. He then ordered me to an adjoining room where there was a doctor and said: 'God help you if he passes fit'. My luck was in; the doctor was an elderly and a very kindly man and, after examining me said 'No son, you shan't go again' and marked me BIII which was a very low category. On returning to the Selection Board I had to be careful not to show my elation and was quietly accepted by the Royal Engineers officer as a clerk in the Inland Waterways and Docks Section.[74]

Facing the pressuring need for men at the front, mirroring the relaxation of recruit physical suitability standards enacted in later stages of the war, it is perhaps unsurprising that the Defence Corps officer was determined to revise all previous decisions about disability. It is a mark of the uncertainty of the time that despite his obvious injury and previous rules Private Lewis was not at all keen to test the selection boards' ambivalence. Once again acting as a gatekeeper, it was the medical officer who cemented Lewis's safety by ruling his wounds invalidated him from front-line service leaving the Royal Engineers to locate duties away from the fighting to suit his capabilities.

Again in a repeat of the enlistment processes at the beginning of the war, some men worked hard to return to their duties and the danger of front-line service, despite being judged more suited to support functions. Such was the case for Captain Syer who had been seconded off the front lines but fought to return later after the drastic losses in the first days of the Somme. Syer paid for this gallantry with his life as he died after being hit by a sniper two months later.[75] Another such case of refusal to be removed from front-line service is the case of Lieutenant Gerald Brice Ferguson Smyth, CO of the 6th Scottish Borders. Ferguson Smyth was wounded five times in the course service which began with the loss of an arm in 1914 and later included a shot through the neck at the Somme and a bullet in his remaining arm during the German Spring Offensive in March 1918.[76] Of course, both Syer and Ferguson Smyth were officers, with the latter taking on several CO roles during the war. Given their status as upper-class men and officers they would have had more power over the utilization of their bodies for the war effort. Cohen explains that of the 2,272,998 of the British wounded, 64 per cent were returned to duty with only 8 per cent being invalided out.[77] It therefore makes logical sense that as the military was desperate to return men to the front that said men were not always fully ready physically to return. Van Bergen summed this up best as he noted contrast in the way that officers and rankers were treated during medical care. Officers could cite their rank and immediately be directed to better medical care, such as the case of B. Latham whose rank meant a sergeant immediately saluted and dispatched him to the Duchess of Westminster hospital rather than the first aid post at the battle of the Somme. Van Bergen argued, 'It can be summed up as follows: the men were to be returned to the front and officers must be made to be comfortable and content.'[78]

Not all rankers were content to be returned into the fray having found a way, albeit temporarily out of danger. Some sought to ensure that they would not be returned by damaging their own bodies in an extension of the front-line malingering considered in Chapter 4. Commonly this was achieved by neglecting treatment and stopping their bodies from healing. Private Stinton recalled a fellow convalescent who refused to carry out the exercises that the medical staff had instructed him to perform for the very reason of making sure he would not be returned.

> When my wounds were healed, I was advised to try and use my arm. The exercise, though painful, would help towards getting it better. Up until then, I had had my arm in a sling but after getting the advice I left it off. This other chap got the same advice but disregarded it. Confidentially, he told me that he didn't want it better whilst he was in the army. He said: 'I have had enough of the trenches. If my arm gets well, I will be sent out again. Let them give my discharge and then I don't mind getting the arm better!' He had been at the hospital longer than I had, and by persisting in not trying to use his arm and keeping it in one position, it was gradually getting withered.[79]

In allowing his body to decline the soldier not only risked punitive action for malingering but also permanent damage. In a return to the arguments of personal commodification of the body made in Chapter 4, yet again it is clear that men were forced to clinical surmise how much of their body they were willing to lose, and indeed how much pain they would endure, in order to retain their lives.

Recovery was a complicated process, undercut by the desires of the men, the medical staff and the British military. As such the continual physical assessment that serving men had endured since the moment of their enlistment continued with the difference now being less about fortitude or stamina but recovery. Simply put in training men's bodies were judged on their ability to improve, in service on their capability to endure and in combat on their capacity to fight. Under medical care duty and honour demanded a quick recovery in order to continue the fight; in support of this goal men's bodies continued to be assessed for their military potential as each aspect of their improvement was documented like a countdown to return to the front. Still, this is not to argue that the recuperating men were without any agency; out of uniform some men were not content to be passive participants in the clinical restoration of their physical usefulness. The response to which was the deliberate damaging of their bodies in order to protect them from any future front-line service.

Revelling bodies

Over the course of the war thousands of British men returned from the front lines having earned their freedom through the damage enacted upon their bodies. However, when the war officially ended on 11 November 1918, it was no longer just the badly wounded who faced the prospect of returning home for good, but the majority of the men who had been enlisted for the duration of the war who now saw an opportunity to relinquish their obligation to the military. In the earliest stages the end of the war was a moment of celebration and relief for many. In his handwritten journal, Trooper Wells from the 2nd Troop, 'C' Squadron, 9th Queen's Royal Lancers, joyfully noted that the war had ended, and with it, as demonstrated by a sudden dereliction of duty in favour of celebration, control over the bodies and behaviours of the British soldiers began to crumble.

> At Eleven o clock on the 11th November 1918, everyone had to stand to arms where, when & no one was to advance on the penalty of death our boys were not sorry it was all over so made the best of billets & enjoyed themselves for a week. The idea was to give Jerry time to get back into his own country & stay there after a week, 2 divisions of the 2nd army who were nearest the German Frontier advanced unto [sic] Germany.[80]

Like a bolt of lightning surging throughout the uniformed men the sudden end of fighting brought for an abrupt end to their patience with the army's control over them and their bodies.[81] This was as true at home as it was abroad. At the same time as Wells and his fellows began their celebrations, similar demonstrations erupted around Britain. NCO Johnston, having just returned from France to transfer to RFC, was caught up in the throng around London and recalled in his diary that military control completely collapsed, albeit temporarily. As disregard for the rules and regulations that had governed so many lives for the duration of the war was extremely apparent.

> About thirty of us held up an empty A.S.C motor lorry passing through Uxbridge. The tramcars swarmed with soldiers, inside and out, singing and shouting. The safety valve was fully open and, for one day at least, all the past years of misery

were forgotten. We could not get beyond Chiswick. All the trains trams, taxis, and buses had double their normal loads, crammed with people who had no desire to go anywhere in particular but who had to have some outlet for their feelings. Night fell and no one bothered to return to camp at the proper time. Men were trickling past the Guard Room at all hours of the night and early morning without a word being said. The following day, discipline was gradually restored, and things became matter of fact once more.[82]

At Marlborough College fires were started in classrooms and windows smashed in celebration, while at Lancing College the students stole the school fire engine and set off all the hoses, an act of civil disobedience that under any other circumstances would have assuredly not gone unpunished.[83] In Leeds hundreds of young women marched into the infirmary and saluted the wounded men before marching through the city, and across the country from Sunderland to Aberdeen to Birmingham, women dressed in male attire such as khaki and navy uniforms.[84] Edgar Verrall was a British gunner with the Royal Field Artillery when he celebrated the end of the war with his fellows in Rawalpindi. In his oral history interview he remembered how the camp descended into jovial anarchy.

We were in the canteen and someone comes in and says the Armistice's signed. Of course we went wild. We drunk and drunk, and the funny part of it was the Black Watch was stationed there. Everybody went in the canteen, joined in the crowd and was playing, the big drummer, he was right behind in the crowd, nowhere near the band. So we went round the sergeant's smiths, got some more beer, and some chap said 'we had busted into the canteen and got some more beer over the way' so we joined them. I always remember the corporal in the morning said, 'you was in a tidy state matey', and I said 'why?'. And he said, 'you come in there, laughing your head off, a water jug in your pigging hand, full of beer'. Dear me, oh we didn't have it straight up! We had a couple of days off, got sobered up … and then we settled down.[85]

Weeks later Verrall and the rest of his battalion were dispatched north again and faced the influenza epidemic as their concerns turned to returning home.[86] However, in the calm before the storm that would pre-empt the chaos of the return of millions of uniformed men around the world back to their homes, families and personal freedom, millions like Verrall threw rank, responsibility and caution to the wind for a well-earned burst of celebration.

Of course, not all men experience the armistice as a period of uproarious celebration. Private Barrow claimed in an interview that 'there wasn't much fuss about it' when the news came into his unit as he served on the Western Front with the 210 Brigade Royal Field Artillery.[87] Barrow's unit was told to stop making a fuss by a CO as the regimental band were silence mid celebration because 'they said, it wasn't peace. It was just an Armistice.'[88] This was not an uncommon view on the front lines. Officer George Jameson's 72nd Royal Field Artillery unit refused to believe the news as it was distributed on 11 November.

When the war actually ended, we didn't even know about it. We knew that things were getting pretty critical, we knew that we were doing well and nobody wanted to cop out on one when the war might be ending tomorrow, sort of thing. It was the wrong time to get wounded or hit or anything, you see! So we were pretty careful. But we were moving forward with the idea of taking another position when one of the drivers shouted up to somebody, 'There's a sign on that', it was an entrance to some house. He said, 'There's a sign on that thing marking somebody's headquarters and it says the wars over.' Don't believe it. Nobody would believe it. The war couldn't be over; it had been on for years; nobody would believe it could finish![89]

Even at the eleventh hour a combination of bad luck and poor communication meant that fighting briefly continued. Such was the case for Durham Light Infantry soldier Jim Fox who had witnessed his sergeant die just minutes before the armistice was made known to them, making the man one of the very last to die during the combat period of the First World War.

Of course, when the armistice was to be signed at 11 o'clock on the 11th of November, as from 6 o'clock that morning there was only the occasional shell that was sent either by us over the German lines or the German over at our lines. Maybe there was one an hour. And then, about 10am, one came down and killed a sergeant of ours who'd been out since 1915. He was killed with shrapnel, you know. Thought that was very unlucky. To think he'd served since 1915, three years until 1918, nearly four years and then to be killed within an hour of armistice.[90]

Johnston also recalled how quickly thoughts turned to the end of military life, 'The burning question now was, when would we be released from service and allowed to return home?'[91] In reality, the release of so many men was an immediate logistical nightmare leading many men's service to dragged on well beyond the armistice. Still many men were hopeful and eager to return to their lives. Johnston noted this desperation in his diary when he wrote in 1918, 'By the end of the month demobilisation papers were being filled in and, on my return before Christmas from the 12-day's leave granted to all ranks, I found the first batches leaving for the depot to be returned to civilian life.'[92]

With the war officially over, demobilization failed to echo even the sentiment of fast 'efficiency' visible at the beginning of the conflict to get the men into uniform. Getting them out of it was seemingly much more complicated. Granted, the majority of the men still in uniform had been amassed over the course of four years; still, the process began imperceptibly slowly and impatience quickly grew as many men failed to recognize why their presence was still required and why their body remained subject to military control. On 1 August 1919, the War Office announced that 106,294 officers and 2,625,811 other ranks had been processed for demobilization.[93] Over a million further men awaited their release but would only be allowed to leave the military in small numbers until 1922.[94] This was a slow and aggravating process that continued to upset many civilian soldiers who no longer saw the need for their bodies to remain outside of their own control. At Addington rest camp in late 1918, soldiers decided to take matters into their own hands and telegraphed the King with the promise to burn down Buckingham palace unless they were released from service. Among their grievousness, there was reports that they had had no leave for two years, barely any pay for nine months and atrocious hygiene facilities while in Mesopotamia.[95] An extreme reaction, which did not culminate in early release despite the hopes of the protestors. With the war concluded, the process of returning men to civilian life was immensely complicated. In February 1919 Winston Churchill, acting as the Secretary of State for War, reiterated in parliament that length of service was an important factor in identifying suitability for demobilization.[96] Churchill fell almost immediately under fire for the chaos of the demobilization process. The debate in parliament, during which he was forced to reiterate the guidelines for demobilization, forced him onto the defensive as Churchill attempted to justify the cost, fairness and logistics of cancelling an entire regiment only recently issued with travel passes and military uniforms and set to embark for the front lines. The release of these "almost fighters" ahead of battle weary veterans is typical of the complaints and concerns that Churchill faced within the role.[97] Taking the reins for the demobilization process was not a popular move for the later hero of the Second World War. In the summer of 1919, Private Jamieson recounted how during an official visit, Churchill was mocked by a troop of soldiers unhappy to still be in uniform. He recalled, 'There was a lot of dissatisfaction … Churchill was suddenly introduced and was greeted with loud booing because he had a great deal to do with drawing up the arrangements for demobilisation.'[98]

Much of this dissatisfaction came over the sudden questioning of the lack of rights men had over their own bodies, such as what to feed them, how to clothe them and where they could take them. Faced with a disorganized farcical process ahead of them that meant the controls they had resided under as soldiers would continue some men took the initiative to get out of the army as soon as they could by their own means. Several men on leave regarded their duty to be completed and refrained to return themselves to their regiments. Almost inconceivable, orders were subsequently issued that any men who were on leave after 12 January 1919 must return to their units, even if this meant returning from Britain to abroad. In defence of this absurd policy, Churchill claimed, 'This is an invariable rule for all ranks on leave from France.'[99] The logic behind this was lost on many men who sought to find their own escape route. Sergeant Robinson recounted how a fellow soldier who was in charge of general administration, who had only recently joined the army, innovatively filed his own demobilization papers within the first pile of men who were to be returned from service.[100] In keeping with the rules outlined in parliament, the man in question should have been one of the last to be released rather than first; yet, opportunity and cunning combined to give him an unfair advantage over his comrades and led to return of control over his body faster than should have been possible.

Part of the reason for the impatience of many was that life in the military continued to be hazardous to their health and their bodies. Private Barrow was one such soldier who recalled accidents occurring despite the end of the fighting. He recounted in oral history that careless stacking of shells had led to an explosion which had left 'one or two men [being] badly injured'.[101] Before being demobilized in December 1919 NCO

Wainwright also recalled an accident happening while he served in Duren with the 8th Battalion Tank Corps.

> We were just sitting pretty with nothing to do … well you kept the tanks in order and so forth and it was there that one of the tanks going down the main street as it was of this village there, something had happened and one of the battalion had gotten in front of the tank and he was flattened by the tank, there was this accident that happened he was killed. I remember that very well indeed.[102]

Amid the revelry and the period of uncertainty beyond the armistice accidents continued as even after the fighting had stopped, men's bodies remained in danger from military service. A volunteer in the Friends Ambulance Unit recalled that his last patient was an unlucky British soldier who fell afoul of the drunken antics.

> News of the armistice came into the town and there were lots of horns blowing and all that sort of thing. I had to deal with the last of my army cases during the war. An unfortunate young soldier was hit in the face by a star shell fired by some drunken Americans, who were going round the streets of Courtrai firing off their Verey pistols. And one of these things came down and hit this unfortunate man and killed him on the spot. And that was the last war casualty and the last stretcher I had to clean up.[103]

Accidents were not the only way in which men continued to die after the armistice. On 24 March 1919, Winston Churchill, still settling into his new role as Secretary of State, was forced to publicly respond to a series of soldiers' deaths from sickness, overcrowding and lack of hygiene facilities during transit back to Britain. Churchill attempted to downplay the government and the militaries responsibility in these deaths, arguing, 'I would also point out that persons travelling from one climate to another are, under any circumstances, more susceptible to illness. I very much regret the death of the four soldiers mentioned.'[104] These deaths were ultimately attributed to 'Spanish flu' of which the British Expeditionary Forces (BEF) listed 313,000 cases in 1918 as it spread to become a global epidemic.[105] Van Bergen notes in *Before My Helpless Sight* that while there is a connection between Spanish flu and the end of the war, this correlation was essentially limited to the relocation of the men which resulted in epidemiological contact to spread the disease rather than the disease arising from a physical susceptibility caused by the men's diminished bodies.[106] Spanish flu aside, transportation, relocation and, in some cases, boredom meant that even after the shells stopped falling the physical safety of the serving men was not guaranteed with more men losing their health, and in some cases lives, as attempts were made to release them from service.

Trials and tribulations

One of the primary issues associated with the process of demobilization was separation of the military from the body. In an inverse of the enlistment and training process, men had to return their kit, uniforms and weapons in exchange for civilian clothes, and the means to return home. Just as they had experienced their bodies at the centre of the process on entry, the process was the very much the same, although enacted in reverse. Once advised that they were to be officially demobilized, the first stage was a detailed physical examination. As each man had to relinquish his body for a medical assessment his attributes, scars, wounds and physical impact of the conflict were recorded and, for many, monetized. Mirroring the lines of men eager to get in during the early stages of the war, the 1918 Ministry of Information film *From Soldier to Civilian* showed demobilizing men cheerfully entering a large room and undressing for a medical officer who listened to their chest in front of a seated official who took notes.[107] The film presented the assessment process as being an orderly and well-organized experience for soldiers as they were clinically and painstakingly reviewed. While the film may have exaggerated the care and attention each man received it certainly illustrates that the final moments of a man's service in the British military were spent with their body being subjugated to significant examination. Once again, under the gaze of a military assessor, men's physical attributes such as height, weight and physical illnesses were diligently measured. Men had their hearts listened to and their chest expansion checked. Their physical ability and presentation were yet again quantified as their entire physicality, and therefore their worth to society and cost to the state, was reduced to a few columns of numbers. Part of the reason for this is that where the body had been damaged it now had to be valued, and the financial responsibility for the damage caused in service of the military had to be determined for the post-service pension.

Prior to the First World War pensions for ex-servicemen or soldier's widows were granted haphazardly; still, financial remuneration for service was not uncommon. In 1593 wounded English soldiers were awarded a benefit paid from local taxes. From 1680, medical care for former soldiers was established as the Chelsea and Greenwich hospitals were created to emulate Louis XIV's Hôtel des Invalides as a way to circumvent the need for financial dependence on the state. This system was almost immediately overwhelmed and poorly organized resulting in payments continuing to be awarded to men based on their length of service, severity of injury and service record.[108] This scheme stumbled along until the turn of the nineteenth century where a series of measures were implemented between 1806 and 1914 to introduce a rudimentary benefit distribution scale from the state based upon the capacity to work. This scale ranged from one-quarter inability to complete inability.[109] As support for the military grew in the militarized Victorian period, from 1854 the Royal Patriotic Fund (RPF), mostly funded by the state but not entirely, undertook responsibility for the pensions of former soldiers and military widows and orphans. The RPF continued until 1957, although the organization quickly gained a reputation for financial reluctance as many went without recompense due to the parsimonious judgement of the Fund officials.[110] The First World War presented to British government and the military a situation which had never occurred on the same scale before. Due to the methods of recruiting civilian men for the purpose of combat, the British state became more responsible for the lasting physical results of military service than ever before. A burden that the state went to significant measures to distance itself from in order to lessen the financial burden as the war receded into memory.

Between 1914 and 1919 there had been over forty-one thousand amputations in the army. About 69 per cent were legs, 28 per cent were arms and for the very unlucky 3 per cent there was a loss of both legs and arms.[111] Over the next two decades, the physical ramifications of the war continued to be made clear. Over four thousand veterans were diagnosed with mental illness, often classified as epilepsy, over forty-two thousand suffered from tuberculous, as well as 36 per cent of all disability pensions in the 1930s being awarded for war neuroses.[112] The government's response to these sacrifices for King and country reads like a macabre shopping list, where each missing body part or wound held a particular monetary value in the form of a veteran's pension. This commodification of the human body was made ever more complex and clinically calculating by the changes of the price index according to social status. Officers and rankers presented almost astonishing discrepancies between how the state financially valued their bodies. This meant that total paralysis, blindness, facial disfigurement or the contraction of an incurable disease could yield for a private just two shillings more (27s. 6d.) than the loss of the right arm below the elbow for an officer (25s. 6d.).[113] Yet again the body of the lower classes was deemed politically, socially and economically of lesser value than that of the higher British classes. This mirrored parallel of both British society and the military hierarchy from which the veterans, the majority of which having served as rank and file, were now trying to detach from reiterates the hypocrisy of the early war recruitment messages which had glorified the common man as a hero of the empire. It had been foot soldiers who had been desperately needed to man the battlefields and trenches; yet, with the war now over, their reward for being closer to the enemy, than their commanders, was significantly less than that of those that the class system defined as 'betters'.[114]

To clarify the financial elements for demobilization in 1918, the British government published the booklet, *Ministry of Pensions. Royal Warrant for the Pensions of Soldiers Disabled, and of the Families and Dependants of Soldiers Deceased, in Consequence of the Present War*, within which the financial remuneration for injury was minutely detailed by cost and rank for damaged body parts. At the upper range losing two limbs, an eye and a limb, total sight, being facially disfigured or becoming bedridden meant men were categorized as 100 per cent disfigurement which paid 42s. 6d. for the highest warrant officer class (Class I) and 27s. 6d. for a private. At the bottom of the scale a 20 per cent disability, which covered the loss of a thumb, four fingers of the left hand, three fingers of the right hand or the loss of two fingers of either hand, meant a warrant officer (Class I) would receive 8s. 6d. and a private just 5s. 6d.[115] This process was focused on the extent to which the debility of the man prevented him from being self-sustainable. Newlands refers to this process as a 'commodification of wounds' in her review of the pension process after the Second World War which quantified men by percentage of disability and rank.[116] A veteran of the First World War, when Private Sumpter was finally demobbed out of the army in 1921, he was classified as disabled due to a wound sustained in combat.

> I was demobbed from there at Chichester on January 26th 1921, as no longer, er ... disabled for military service, no longer able, I had a medical board and I was graded 30% disabled ... My arm was useless, for years after this the thing wouldn't

dry up ... at the medical board I got 30% disabled, got a disabled pension, which they gave me. Which was taken away from me in 1922 because the army, I was disabled according to the army, but according to the civilians I wasn't, according to the civilians I had full use because I could use it.[117]

Sumpter is a direct example of the discontinuity between the transition from soldier back to civilian. While the rhetoric of the time had been about care for the heroes of the war, the civilian reality beyond the first couple of years after the war was starkly different. Due to his wound Sumpter had been retained in the army and tasked with the care of his officer's horse. During the war, and indeed beyond it, Sumpter had still played a small but vital role for his country.[118] In due course, the British Army had acknowledged his sacrifice and granted him a non-combatant status before demobilizing him with a disability pension. Yet, like many disabled men, release from the army meant not only a return of individual agency but also the end of direct care of these men and their damaged bodies, as the onus was passed, sometimes disastrously, from the military to the state. As one of the leading historians on the history of disability after the First World War Julie Anderson argues within *War, Disability and Rehabilitation in Britain: 'Soul of a Nation'* that rehabilitation schemes placed a significant focus on ensuring that disabled men re-entered the employment market quickly as to alleviate dependence on the state.[119] While Anderson is clear to demonstrate that the First World War meant a significant increase to the attention of the disabled, this certainly did not mean that all of the returning wounded men were fully cared for by the state. Walter Burdon was another who suffered during this change of responsibility. Burdon served for most of the war as Navy Seaman but in 1915 he and many of his fellows were drafted into khaki at Gallipoli to dig trenches and engage the enemy. Wounded in the head and side, Burdon was pensioned out in 1916 as a disabled serviceman. In his oral history he explains that in 1919, as the focus on pensions increased, he was reassessed and lost his pension as a result of the prejudice of the doctors who assessed him.

> They had a resurvey as they called it, of all pensioners ... I went to St Marys place ... I was examined by two doctors. One says, 'what are you complaining about', so I told him 'I get pains in the head, and loss of memory, and sometimes I just don't know where I am.' He says 'Well, what was your profession, your trade?' I says, 'I was a Pattern Maker', so he says to the other fellow 'what is this man mean, I've never heard the term before?' [lengthy explanation follows] ... he says, 'there is no skill in that!' I said, 'I beg your pardon sir. I was to say that all you need is a box of pills and bottle of coloured water you wouldn't like it!' Them turfed us out. I lost my pension.[120]

There were also some men who chose to forsake their recompense for their physical sacrifice in order to secure their release and regain autonomy over themselves and their bodies. Such was the impatience of many that they rushed through demobilization procedures to the detriment of their financial future. Private Denison was such a man, who had volunteered early into the war and had been diagnosed subsequently as suffering from disorder action of the heart (DAH). This was a significant physical defect that later in life prevented him from obtaining an insurance policy. Denison was given the choice to self-certify himself as completely fit and suffering no ill effects of his time in service to gain his freedom despite evidence to the contrary. He recalled in an oral interview, 'I only mention this to show that I must have been in poor shape when I was demobbed – you had to sign yourself A1 before you could get yourself discharged so that then you had no claim for a disability pension.'[121] Denison's need for freedom seemingly overrode his concerns for the future. He reiterates this desire by refusing to consider any option to remain in the military. For Denison, the war was over and it was time to go home: 'They made all sorts of tempting offers to me to stay on. All I wanted was my freedom. My papers read "Transferred to the Reserve pending demobilisation." I came home with a month's leave; it was great to be free again.'[122]

After the First World War men's financial dependence on the state was entirely dependent on the physical damage they had sustained during service and the social class to which they belonged. The level of pension was dependant on the personal losses experience by the individual former soldier and extended to cover in many cases an artificial limb, if necessary.

Nevertheless, even the provision of limbs was often controversial and encouraged questioning of the British government and the military over their generosity in return for military service (see Figure 12). In April 1915, over six months after the signing of the armistice, debate raged in parliament over the poor treatment of pensioned veterans. Sir George Jones, a Conservative MP, vehemently raised his concern that men who had made the ultimate sacrifice for their country were being overlooked.

> I have had two complaints brought to my notice. I do not know the facts myself, but they are complaints of men who have lost limbs, and each tell me the same story. One wanted an artificial leg and the other an artificial arm, and each wanted one particular make of limb, because it was so much more suitable than other makes. In each case they were refused the make of limb they wanted because it was too expensive. I have a letter from one of the men, who was frankly told by the major or some other commanding officer, 'You cannot have that limb, although I frankly admit it would be the best limb for you. It is too expensive.' I do not know whether this statement is true, but if true it is a scandal. It is our duty to see that disabled men have the very best mechanical appliance that money can buy in order to make good to them what they have suffered during the War.[123]

This was an issue that was not limited to the provision of artificial limbs. By 1921, 1.1 million veterans were receiving a disability pension. By 1929 this figure had risen to 2.4 million.[124] Cohen in *The War Come Home* explains that the disabled soldier returning to society found an increasing reticence by the government to support him as a decline in his war pension soon meant the need for additional support from voluntary organizations. Charities such as the Red Cross and the Soldiers Sailors' Families Association increasingly took on crucial roles in supplementing meagre fair

CARVING OUT ARTIFICIAL HAND.

Figure 12 The manufacture of artificial limbs for the Princess Louise Scottish Hospital for limbless sailors and soldiers. Wellcome Collection, *Carving out Artificial Hand* (Scotstoun: Yarrow, 1917). Preface on the folio from which this picture was collected stated, 'The following photographs indicate the various stages in the manufacture of artificial limbs, including photographs of the Limb Fitting Workshops at the Hospital, where a number of fitters are exclusively employed in the fitting and adjustment of the limbs to the patients.' Wellcome Collection.

from the state and provided additional financial support for men who struggled to find suitable work after 1918.[125] Beckett, Bowman and Connelly explain that after the war the mishandling of the pension process encouraged many veterans to consider themselves 'the neglected living'.[126] Post-war politicians, reporters, even novelists like John Galsworthy emulated the attitude of the post-war British society and soon lost interest in the broken bodies of the returning veterans.[127] With a mind on the future and setting horrors of the war behind it, the British state and the public by and large began to overlook and neglect former soldiers despite the extent of their physical sacrifice, in much the same way it had prior to 1914.[128]

This was not the case for all men injured and in receipt of a war pension. Albert Walker came from an anti-war family and only joined the war through conscription in

1916. His brief stint on the Western Front with the 4th Bn Northumberland Fusiliers resulted in a medical discharge in 1917 as an explosion had rendered his arm useless and moved his heart to one side. The result was an extended recovery in hospital in Britain and a war pension that would last the rest of his life. Laughing with his interviewer in 1991, Walker explained how he had been more fortunate than most.

> No don't smile, I've had a 40% war disablement pension for seventy-four years. That's not on there is it? ... The point about it was that in 1917 my pension was 16s a week, at the present time it is four pence short of forty pounds ... I've had nothing to do with the army from that point of view ... this was so severe that they thought I wouldn't pull out of it. I've never had anything to do with the army from a pension point of view since 1917.[129]

Walker's mirth at receiving his pension for so long illustrates the rarity of his situation as many of his colleagues were not as fortunate. Walker himself admits that his award is something of an anomaly as he was not expected to have survived. This laughter is bittersweet, as Walker concludes that he regrets joining the army, as he has been unable to look after himself properly for seventy-four years.[130]

Beyond the financially driven medical assessment, men still found their bodies under assessment. They were directed to dispersal centres where they were given a Z18 form (certificate of employment) which outlined the skills and abilities that men had developed during active service. These forms once again reduced men to quantifiable numerical values of their physical effectiveness and usefulness. The certificate of employment was designed to allow men to demonstrate that some of these skills and abilities could enable them to secure employment. For some men, training and active service had encouraged them to develop useful abilities such as driving or technical knowledge. This demonstrates that although many soldiers returned home with physical, psychological and financial loses, some men, such as Private Floyd who returned having received a certificate in education and engineering expertise, managed to return to new opportunities, indicating a relatively rare positive impact from military service during the First World War.[131] As a result of his remaining military service in 1919 Private Joseph Biglin was able to take advantage of the army Education Scheme and pass the Special Certificate of Education. This ultimately led to him being able to acquire a grant following demobilization to achieve a first-class honours degree in civil engineering at Sheffield University.[132] This was not the case for all men as the interruption of the war had lifelong consequences for some. Like the account of Private Walker previously presented, Private Snailham was another whose service irreparably changed his future. Snailham had at first enjoyed his experiences in the army and the war because of the opportunity to play and develop his football skills. He ultimately came to resent his service in the war as his time in service had damaged his body beyond repair, something he claimed ruined his future footballing career.[133]

Once the state of their bodies was assessed soldiers were also often given a Z44 form (a plain clothes form) as part of the demobilizing process. This was an important moment captured in the film *Demobilisation* produced by the British government in

1918.[134] This depicted men being issued with civilian dress which was an important visual statement delineating the end of their service. In the film there is a direct correlation with the images of the smiling eager soldiers that were centre stage in the recruitment propaganda at the beginning of the war. In both cases, the men are presented as smiling, physical fit, patient and eager. The reality could be significantly different. Havardi argues that military films such as *From Soldier to Civilian* and *Demobilisation* should be considered carefully before accepting their presentation as reality because they were created primarily to please public audiences.[135] In *British Propaganda and the First World War*, Messinger explains that, by 1914, the cinema was growing in popularity, and that the British government had already begun to experiment with using film to alter public perception and mood during the Last South African War.[136] Films such as *Demobilisation* painted a glorious picture of men on their way home, proud of their achievements and noticeably uninjured, healthy and constantly cheerful as they moved forward into their new lives. But this message was orientated more to maintaining a calm during the process of demobilization, alerting the waiting men and their families to the fact that soon they would also be released from service. This, however, does not mean that the key aspects of the process depicted in the film were entirely inaccurate, just that any analysis must be severally questioned for validity.

The clothing of the body was the final clear evidence of the transformation into civilian life. Just as so many had been excited to put on the uniform and receive the public adulation it attracted in the early stages of the war, returning the uniform and the role it represented for many was a formative and important moment. Many began to fixate on the obtaining of civilian clothes and the shedding of their uniform as a visual representation of their end of service. In December 1919, Lieutenant Wade received a postcard from his friend Geo. D. Roche with an old soldier's hymn on the back that glorified the end of service with the words: 'This kruil war is hover, ... appy will I be, I puts my civvy clothes on, ... ore sodgerin' fer me (Ancient Army Hymn).'[137] Private Johnston was another who seized this opportunity to exchange his uniform for civilian clothes, something he poetically lamented sacrificing four years previously in his diary.

> I left Andover on April the 3rd 1919 and, proceeding to York, spent the night there before going to Ripon for demobilisation. A month's furlough was granted and the end of that time I was free. I had served 4 years and 8 months in His Majesty's Forces. In May month, I took up once more the threads of civilian life so hastily thrown down in the dark days of 1914.[138]

As part of the demobilization process, men were given the option to accept civilian clothes or to initially retain their uniform and be given a clothing allowance of 52s and sixpence but many chose to accept the civilian attire.[139] Most men received, along with their new clothes, a small amount of money and a Z50 form which required them to exchange their greatcoat for £1 at a local railway station. Many men like Private Benwell opted for the 'civy street' attire and were seemed content with what was on offer.

They gave us a suit, two pair of socks and some underclothes, a flat cap and it being summer they gave us a mac you see, it was rain proof and £27 … so err I had a bit of time off they paid us though I think it was a month to settle down.[140]

Reassessed, redressed and released, thousands of men left the military over the following five years after the signing of the armistice in 1918, in a parody of the process that had originally signed them up. Between the forms, the considerations and the controls, men's bodies remained a central focus for the military up to, and in the case of pensions beyond, the demobilization process. Once valued for service, men's bodies were now appraised for lasting detriment as their life and limbs were costed according to status and sacrifice.

Conclusion

The body remained central to the experience of the military for those who served in the First World War even at the end of that experience. Wounded men swapped one commander for another as they lived under the rule of medical staff complete with uniforms, curfews and bodily restrictions. Though damaged, their bodies remained under scrutiny as the authorities sought to reclaim them and return them to combat. Even in these circumstances, men could assert themselves and take control of what was happening, either through open resistance to hospital regimes or through covert strategies such as leaving an injury to deteriorate in the hope of avoiding a return to the front. Demobilization was sought by most men who were impatient to escape the hazards presented by military life even in peacetime and keen to regain control of their bodies and their lives. Even as they left military life their bodies were poked, assessed, classified and valued by the authorities. Injuries could mean pensions, although some were happy to forego these in the rush to escape the clutches of the army. Damaged bodies were valued carefully, and payments increased according to rank as well as severity of disability. Yet this did not cover all and support everyone. The case of Harry Green in 1917, who lay down on a railway track because his wounds meant he struggled to get work, indicates that the measures put in place by the government were ill-equipped to deal with the sheer amount of physical destruction.[141] Hundreds of thousands did not survive to enjoy a life after the conflict. Dealing with their dead bodies was a complicated and emotive issues during the First World War as morale, sanitation, grief and expense combined within debates on how best to honour the dead. The decision to stop mass burial and instead record the grave of each man meant that by the end of the war a sophisticated catalogue system had developed to inform families of that last resting place of their loved one. This was by no means perfect and over a century later bodies continue to be found that had originally been lost in the quagmire of no man's land.[142] Even in death, soldier lacked control over their bodies as the army decided where they were interred and the clothes they rested in. Those families that sought to resist this, and to take back control over the bodies of their relatives, found that they enjoyed little support from the state.

The end of the war did not mean release from service. The uniforms that the men had taken up in the time of crisis stayed with many of them beyond death. Many men returned irrevocably changed and dependant on the institution to which their association had supposed to have been temporary. In the decades to follow the signing of the armistice, many former British soldiers' bodies remained permanently impacted by and related to military and the state. Pensions, graves and memories, bound men and their bodies to the chaos of the First World War and their identity as soldiers for the remainder of the twentieth century.

Conclusion: Bodies of war

History is not neat. While this book has attempted to frame the narrative from the perspective of the physical experience of the First World War, it is difficult to maintain that thematic approach when faced with literally thousands of bodies who experienced the war in similar but unique ways. Yet, this is the point of the bottom-up experience-centric approach. The war between 1914 and 1918 was a chaotic time for much of the world. The legacy of that conflict would continue to be felt beyond a century. It is likely that Lieutenant Godfrey would have considered twentieth-century reflection on the war just as much a 'different experience altogether' as he found the reality of the conflict in 1917. Skirmishes today have shifted to the colours of remembrance poppies and liberal re-interpretive digital recreations of trench experience, rather than aiming for different colour uniforms; still, the need to commemorate, and therefore understand the 'Great War', remains. The body when examined within the context of the First World War explains much about the first global conflict of the twentieth century. Through it the transformations, endurances and societal perceptions paint a vivid image of an almost unimaginable experience.

As this book has demonstrated, from the outbreak of war in 1914, the male body in Britain became an immediate site for social and political attention. Faced with an already amassed enemy priority for the British military was to field as many able men as possible. This necessity for men to occupy battle zones around the world ultimately meant that from enlistment to release these men placed their bodies between the enemy and victory. Unquestionably, the body and institutional control of it within the British Army were an integral aspect of the British war effort. Through analysis of those bodies it is possible to view each soldier as a complicated individual caught in the middle of a chaotic existence whose actions and body were not always under their own command. The events, assessments, controls and regulations that occurred over the course of the war minutely illustrate how British men's bodies were subjected to constant evaluation, domination, augmentation and destruction between 1914 and 1918 in the name of the crisis instigated by war. While the First World War demanded a closer examination of physical health and fitness, an obsessive consideration of male physicality predated the conflict. The crisis of August in 1914 only hastened concerns that had been evident since the Last South African War regarding the physical health of the British people. The malnourished working class finally proved to be cause for societal concern when proved to hinder the ability of the British to field a fighting force at the turn of the century.[1] This fixation coincided with the Haldane reforms of the beginning of the century which worked to transform the British Expeditionary Force into the elite force that set off for France in 1914.[2] Additionally, an ailing lower class being unable to satisfactorily contribute to society through military service clashed with the cultural perception of the military body which had developed as the military had risen in public popularity. Much of the early propaganda for enlistment in Britain in 1914 utilized the heroic masculine military protagonist, in the vein of Victorian imperial champions, to draw in eager recruits with the desire to replicate their heroes. This internalized perception of the 'soldier' proved to be a fundamental element in the self-construction of the soldier identity and existence.[3]

From the outset of war men's bodies were under considerable attention from both society and the military. It is upon this subject that this book has focused and continued the analysis to illustrate how men improved, transformed and came to differently perceive their bodies in line with militarized requirements as many toiled to meet or refute the military ideal. This fixation led Private Shaw to purchase 'dumb-bells' in an attempt to realign his body to meet the chest requirements needed to enlist in 1914.[4] Shaw was certainly not alone in his concern over his own physic as the societal gaze on men's bodies during the First World War increasingly evaluated them on the basis of their potential contribution to the war. Worth for many men between 1914 and 1918 was increasingly defined by physical ability and aptitude for military service. A significant part of defining this process was the reduction of men's bodies to a useful criterion and statistics during enlistment. Here men's physical attributes were recorded and measured towards constantly changing sets of standards in order to provide men for service. Bourke explains how a complicated system of assessment developed and evolved over the course of the war as men were organized for service.[5]

As demonstrated, this system was far from perfect and almost immediately it faced challenges in the form of the vast numbers, incompetence and corruption as well as having to incorporate the fluctuating guidelines that arose as the need for men overrode concerns over physical ability. Far from a clear indication of physicality and suitability, the physical assessment was repeatedly open to negotiation between assessor and the assessed.[6] Numerous men recounted how they manoeuvred their way through the enlistment process, often because their own ambitions aligned with the goals of the men who assessed them. Those desperate to gain entry, later to be determined as a physical cost, often sought to allude the selection criteria. Men who fell short of the requirements often hoped for the situation in which Private Butler in 1914 found himself in after his assessor dismissed his inability to meet the height requirement, commenting, 'You're young, probably you'll grow the other half inch. Anyway, we'll take you on.'[7] Butler was certainly not alone in subverting the system. Private Mullis was another who gained entry despite his diminished stature. His physical failings were explained away with the promise that his training would help him become a soldier. According to the Mullis's assessor training would 'either kill you or make a man out of you'.[8] As the need for men overruled the requirements of stringent physical classifications the regulations safeguarding the recruitment of men's bodies became an increasing malleable concept over the course of the war. The need for men for the British armed forces, at least in the early years of the war, had encouraged a projected ideal of physicality that was then ostensibly tested during enlistment. Bodies were important; yet, the state in which said body would be accepted was a fluid criterion that had more to do with the desperation for men over the determination to field the most able fighting force. Still there was always training to bring the men up to shape.

Once their bodies had been assessed by the military, many men witnessed their relationship with their own bodies immediately change as they lost basic freedoms and controls over them including clothing, diet, destination and respite opportunities. From enlistment to the end of service the British Army sought to improve and tailor men's bodies and their abilities for the singular purpose of war. Training was a significant part of the process of crafting new soldier with the fundamental elements of indoctrination and acclimatization remaining unchanged from before the beginning of the war.[9] Despite the various versions of trainings that followed soldier's bodies were invariably produced through a range of arduous and regimented training processes. This transformation process between 1914 and 1918 was intrinsically a physical process which often created conflict between men and the military over the control of the body in training.[10] As recruits' bodies came under army control, men experienced the physical hardship associated with basic training that was often relatively dissimilar to any previous personal experience. Each man underwent a standard routine of drill, marching and parade as well weapon and bayonet practice. The impact of this training was varied and gruelling; still, many men recognized that their bodies significantly improved under the control of the army training process. Private Williams recalled his training positively and claimed, 'Easter came in 1915, I was in wonderful health. I was never so well in my life, I'd overcome various little defects, colds and such.'[11] This was echoed in the memoirs of Private Barraclough who felt that he was 'harder both in body and soul' as a result of his intensive army training.[12] Arduous without question, many felt the physical effects of their ordeal as necessary and beneficial to their transformation from civilian to soldier. Not all soldiers were however as positive about their experience. Private Warsop unusually gave up his newly earned command stripe because he struggled to meet the physical requirement of the drilling.[13] Yet, it is hard to argue with success, as the majority of men left training significantly fitter and stronger than they had entered service as their bodies, minds and behavioural responses were singularly adapted for the rigours of combat.

As the traditional military transformation of men's bodies was not sufficient by standards of conflict within the First World War, this focus on improving bodies was forced to quickly adapt by including the adoption of games from the United States and new tactical approaches including grenade and gas warfare. As the war progressed, training was forced to match the increasing innovation at the front, leading to new recruits adding new elements of preparation to the curriculum. This focus on experimentation and innovation meant both military staff and enlistees were required to prepare their bodies in a variety of ways to anticipate the rigours of twentieth-century combat. Sport was a popular solution to this problem as it allowed men to practice military tactics and condition their body for active service, while also having the added advantage of tiring men out and preventing casual insurrection. In his private papers Private Watson claimed that football was an essential combination of relaxation and fitness away from the lines.[14] Still, sport could also be debilitating and therefore counterproductive. Private Fox noted this after he was hospitalized during the war due to an overly excited hockey match.[15] Training was not however all fun and games. Even as their bodies improved many men rebelled over the deteriorating conditions under which they trained. From the immediate rush of men to get into uniform at the beginning of the conflict which had meant for emergency measures for billeting and uniforms through to transition to get men to the front as fast as possible as a consequence of the increasing desperation for men after 1915, the British military struggled constantly to control over the men they recruited to serve. Resistance over food, lodgings, constraints and military control continued throughout and during the war. This defiance to military control ranged from grumbling through to outright insurrection, often placing the military in an impossible position between the necessity to ensure men's readiness for battle and physically punishing the very same bodies that they were improving.

Punishment was almost always directly enacted upon the body; however, its application was made more complicated by the presence of civilian soldiers within the army. The First World War witnessed a shift in the control of soldiers as no longer could their behaviour be regulated by extensive physical punishment.[16] The men who joined during the war could not be perceived as mindless bodies to be shaped and controlled at will; instead, men had to be encouraged to act as soldiers. Still, punishment was important, and the incarceration and the strapping of a man to a gun wheel for several hours a day was a common and effective deterrent for defiance. Much more common was the interplay between verbal haranguing and positive verbal reinforcement. Indeed, men's bodies were controlled, and on occasion their bodies paid the price for misdemeanour. Yet, considering the evolution of the First World War and the various ways that men had been sourced for service, the application of punishment as a primarily physical form of coercion needed to change to accommodate the indoctrination of new civilian soldiers. Even the most severe crimes could be mediated against the need for men and recognition of the way men joined up. Punishment for shirking and deserting was directly enacted upon the body as was in keeping with military protocol; yet, over the course of the war only 362 men were imprisoned and executed for similar crimes and dereliction of duty.[17] Putkowski and Sykes explain while military rule was certainly not lax and that even falling asleep at posts could earn men the death penalty, this was the exception rather than the rule. Unquestionably, the momentary lapse of control over their own exhausted bodies could have serious repercussions such as imprisonment or physical discomfort, but these were not always fatal.[18]

During training it is evident that the body was not only central to the process of transformation into soldiers but also of the resistance to it. The initial steps into service and the indoctrination that followed remained clear in the accounts of countless men who underwent the experience and all of them invariably described these formative experiences with reference to the impact they had on their individual bodies. Of course, many of the accounts that focus on how men's bodies experienced the transition into soldiers are centred on the controls, restrictions and regulations that curtailed them. Michel Foucault argues that in the creation of an armed force, autonomy must be replaced by compliance and reliance on others through standardized practice.[19] During the First World War soldiers in the British Army consistently had their bodies directed, assessed and punished in order to retain control over them. As they served men were clothed, groomed, fed and rested according to the direction of the British Army. A crucial part of the process was adapting to the rules and regulation of military life and clothing. To enforce this the military regulated haircuts and shaving as well as controlled diet and recreational activities.[20] Food was a particularly effective way to control men's bodies throughout their career as soldiers since during training and active service the army had the primary responsibility of feeding men. Men who disobeyed army rules often found their food privileges rescinded. Private Peyton recalled how a food fight resulted in seven days of 'half rations' which encouraged him and his fellow punished soldiers to relish unappetizing additions to their diet: 'Cakes (I remember them now, hard lumps of royally overcooked flour and little else – but we scoffed them as if they were really delicious).'[21] Food was, and continued to be, an effective way of exerting control over the men in service. Limiting their intake in training and the front often ensured compliance and was a simple way of maintaining discipline over directly damaging the bodies that the military had toiled over to prepare for battle.

Control over soldier's bodies however was not always maintained effectively as men often successfully resisted army rules. As soldiers, men were directed, fed and often wholly reliant on their superiors to guide their daily existence; yet, they were also able to subvert this control to shirk their duties, get drunk, have sex and resist military regulations. Private Roberts recalled taking part in a soldier's mutiny because the bread was mouldy.[22] Private Templer witnessed a similar uprising because a drunken soldier had been splayed to a wheel as punishment.[23] Even officers were not exempt from misdemeanours as evident in the case of Lieutenant Creek who was punished for sneaking out to meet a local woman.[24] Food, alcohol and sex could be powerful motivators for men to subvert the control that the military had over their bodies. Yet, the meeting of such physical needs could mean that punishment was enacted upon the body in an attempt by the army to reassert control and demonstrate dominance over the bodies of its soldiers. As the war ended in November 1918, the army's control over men's bodies became more complicated as many civilian soldiers no longer regarded their service necessary and demanded vociferously to return home. Even as soon as the ceasefire was called aspects of military discipline diminished as soldiers celebrated victory by ignoring curfew, going AWOL and getting drunk.[25] Yet, many men's good humour turned sour as they found themselves still under military control for beyond a year after the end of war, which led to a group of frustrated soldiers at Addington rest camp in 1919 telegraphing the king and threatening to burn down Buckingham Palace if they were not immediately released from service.[26] Control over men's bodies was a core aspect of the British soldier's existence during the First World War; however, this suspension of willing autonomy was only ever temporary as frequently civilian soldiers reasserted their agency if they felt particularly aggrieved at their treatment.

During the First World War, the most destructive element on the bodies of men was undoubtedly combat. New weaponry such as gas, grenades and weaponized vehicles presented new dangers for men's bodies, alongside the more typical dangers of enemy fire, treacherous conditions and shell fire. Countless First World War historians have described the devastation inflicted upon soldier's bodies during combat and active service, including Dennis Winter, Joanna Bourke, Richard van Emden, Gary

Sheffield, Peter Simkins, Hew Strachan, Helen MacDonald and Emily Mayhew.[27] These reviews range from the sterile statistical investigations of losses and gains offered by Simkins and Strachan through to the more nuanced individual experiences explored by Mayhew, Macdonald and Bourke. Except for the latter, often the individual body is lost within the narrative, its experience diminished by the sheer numbers of casualties. Mayhew, Macdonald and Bourke have separately explored the impact on individual men and their bodies, and it is with these studies in mind that this book has focused more directly with the relationship between men's bodies and combat. Combat had lasting and often devastating impact upon men's bodies. Damage to each serving body was very likely and is repeatedly evident within the thousands of individual accounts of combat during the war. These accounts range from the seemingly trivial to the unimaginable, such as in the case of Private Parker's vivid description of his stricken screaming captain in no man's land whose cries were audible over the cacophony of battle.[28] Yet, wounds also offered men an opportunity to retake control of their bodies and their destiny as some men traded parts of their body in exchange for safety, either by managing to get a 'blighty wound' or by carrying out a self-inflicted wound which could, as a result, see them ostracized and court martialled for malingering.[29] These attempts to regain control also led some men to self-extinction which Bourke maintains remained a final but rare option for the very desperate.[30] While not common, suicide was undertaken by a number of men both on and behind the lines for a variety of reasons which were not always related to war itself. This destruction of the very bodies that the British military had worked so hard to control, regulate and direct stands as final reminder that while agency under military service was limited, it was not absolute.

The life of the serving soldier was fraught with dangers to their bodies, not all of which directly related to the weapons of the enemy. Disease presented a significant danger to the bodies of British soldiers. The expansive nature of the war brought about a myriad of diseases that impacted on soldier's bodies as they served.[31] From their first arrival on the front line, living conditions began to take their toll on men's bodies. Despite the improvements made by the Royal Army Medical Corps sanitation and disease prevention was a difficult and never-ending task. Over the course of the war men still contracted typhoid, malaria, typhus and dysentery as well as having their bodies plagued by environmental factors such as lice and rats, and developed trench fever and trench foot as a result of constantly unsanitary conditions. Inoculation was a particularly effective method at protecting soldier's bodies from diseases over the course of the First World War.[32] Still, inoculations for typhoid could actually render men's bodies incapable, albeit temporarily, and there are accounts of men being forced to accept the vaccine against their will.[33] As men developed and served as soldiers their bodies also experienced exhaustion, trauma, unsanitary conditions, injury and disease. In sketches within his letters home, Private Broadhead depicted his body visibly deteriorating after an intensive game of rugby.[34] His illustration of fatigue can also be applied to active service and combat as soldiers faced physical exhaustion along with fear on an almost permeant basis. Terror, exhaustion and excitement enacted radically different effects on men's bodies as they fought on the front line. Private A. Surfleet summed up his experiences as a soldier in the First World War as 'awfully tiring and often very monotonous, despite periods of terror and much anxiety'.[35] This constant state of tension could be very detrimental to men's bodies as some men were no longer able to deal with the strain of their existence. This was the case for the officer of Sergeant Huggins who collapsed from exhaustion seconds before the whistle blew to climb over the top for battle.[36] Fear could render men immobile and vulnerable to attack, excitement could lead soldiers to endanger their bodies through rash actions and total exhaustion could even result in being labelled as a malingerer.[37] Men's bodies were also at risk from sustained psychological traumas that manifested physical symptoms before, during and after combat. Lack of understanding of the complexities of shellshock also led men to being tried by a military tribunal and often 'treated' with violence to return them to reality.[38]

Risks to the body continued at the hands of the men themselves as often in hopes of reliving the tension of war hedonist soldiers turned to alcohol and sex. These regular acts are constantly present in the accounts of serving men and over 153,531 men were officially treated for venereal disease.[39] Venereal disease meant removal from the line and a reduction in tactical strength of the fighting force. This debilitation of men ultimately encouraged the British Army to restrict brothel usage after 1917 as the perceived benefits of relieving sexual proclivities were outweighed by concerns of a diminishing fighting force. Sex, as is typical in history, opened a Pandora's box of potential physical dangers during the First World War. For heterosexual men there was the risk of venereal disease, encouragement to break the rules in pursuit of negotiable affection and friction with the contrasting views of other men around them. Homosexual men, as was the case in British society at large, ran an even greater risk in the pursuit of sexual gratification. Such men could be arrested and incarcerated, not to mention ostracized by their fellow soldiers if their actions were uncovered. As was the case for 292 officers and rankers combined between 1914 and 1922.[40] This could also lead to a case of self-protection at the sacrifice of another – an action that went against the comradery and uniformity that had been instilled in each man during training. Sex, and the pursuit of sexual gratification, could be extremely hazardous for men's bodies; however, regardless of the punitive, physical and financial implications of engaging in sexual activities, thousands of men continued to damage their bodies for the sake of satisfying their libido. Much the same can be said for the drinking of alcohol. While the 'Demon Drink' was frequently condemned for damaging men's bodies and corrupting their morals, alcohol was very part of the soldering experience.[41] Much to the dismay of many chaplains, commanding officers (COs), temperance followers and often men who did not have the opportunity or means to partake, drinking was social pursuit, a medical requirement and ostensibly an asset crucial for getting men into battle. Private Stapleton maintained that he could not have served without his rum ration.[42] Yet, Private Ching later lamented his partaking after his invigorating multiple 'tots of rum' made him vomit on his CO.[43] This was a sentiment shared by Private Tubbs, whose predilection for drink was overridden by his dedication to duty and subsequently turned to temporary temperance to maintain a clear head during the war.[44] Alcohol was considered essential by many, including the British military command. Conversely, it also incapacitated soldier's bodies, leaving them vulnerable to attack from the enemy or even punishment from their own side.

Evidently, military service was hard on men's bodies during the First World War. Wounds and disease damaged men's bodies and forced them to be revaluated and repaired in order to return them to efficiency. Simply serving was also inherently dangerous and physically damaging. The sheer exhaustion and stress as well as the acts of pleasing and appeasing men's bodies constantly opened soldiers to debilitation. As a result of these destructive forces against the bodies of serving men focus increased on the recovery and repair of the body. Harrison, Whitehead, Meyer and Mayhew have done much to clarify the crucial role played by the medical services throughout the First World War. Most recently, Meyer has made it clear that the legacy of the RAMC during the First World War was a change in the systematic approach to treating and caring for service men which continues to permeate the modern British military.[45] Harrison explains how despite being in its infancy, the RAMC was the most prepared and well-equipped unit of its kind across the world at the start of the First World War.[46] Whitehead concedes that the RAMC initially struggled to meet the demands of such a large conflict; however, he also illustrates that technological progress and adaption to the new climate of war meant that the RAMC's reputation was on the rise by the end of the war.[47] Harrison and Whiteheads considerations are cornerstones of the medical military historiography; yet, their focus remains principally on the medical professions and the top-down consideration of the application of treatment and prevention. Experiences of the individual body are much more evident in Mayhew's *Wounded* which uses the individual experience of the protagonist expertly to illustrate soldier's perceptions from battle to bed rest.[48] It is here that this book has picked up, inspired by the research cited above, and continued the assessment further onto the focus on the body under the military medical gaze as it was recovered, repaired and reassessed for suitable service. Once damaged men's bodies needed to be recovered; men such as Private Warsop, who 'tottered' his bleeding shattered body off in search of medical attention post battle, tested the limits of their bodies as they dragged themselves and others to find medical attention.[49] Even recovery could be physically damaging as retrieval teams of stretcher-bearers, volunteers and chaplains came into enemy cross hairs and carried bodies through treacherous conditions.[50] Once in medical care, focus lay exclusively on their bodies as decisions were made about which parts of them would be saved, where they would be treated and even if they would actually survive. Anna Carden-Coyne argues that once out of the lines and out of uniform, wounded men ceased to be soldiers and transformed into 'disciplined invalids' under medical care.[51] While men were stripped of uniform and purpose they still remained under the command of medical staff. Lieutenant Carter recalled how he was 'treated like a child' as he recovered in hospital in Britain after being hit by a piece shrapnel.[52] Carter was not alone as many soldier's accounts illustrate that even as men transitioned from soldiers to patients their bodies were controlled and directed in new ways including being clothed to reflect their transition from soldier to patient. Here men like Carter found new opportunities to retake control over the experiences of their own bodies. Curfews, controlled diets and bedtimes could be met with defiance while for others like Private Copson, hospitals and existence in recovery offered much-needed rest, comfort and safety. Men could even malinger while in medical care and retook direct control over their bodies by refusing, usually by subterfuge, to allow their bodies to heal.

Plainly, initial medical reconstruction of soldiers' bodies during the First World War has not entirely been overlooked scholarly; however, the gaze has often omitted the bodies of soldiers themselves and has failed to fully explore how central men's bodies and their experiences were to the process of recovery and repair during the First World War. Therefore, this book has examined this closely by recognizing the body as a site of conflict during recovery as soldiers still lacked agency over care of their bodies. Yet, through their own actions and changing of the guard, many men found the attention on their wounded bodies meant they could regain further aspects of self-control. Still, even some of the most serious wounds could be viewed as fortunate when compared to remaining at the front indefinitely. This was the fate of over nine million uniformed men who died during the conflict as many were buried less than a mile from where they fell.[53] Often the dead remained in their uniforms, save for being stripped of valuables, identification tags and boots. Within the accounts of many men, there are numerous descriptions of corpses as part of the landscape.[54] However, the dead were not irreverently discarded but frequently shown significant respect as their graves were catalogued and ceasefires were recurrently organized to allow for the collection of the dead. Both sides would even occasionally bury the dead of their enemy as respect for the body of the soldier transcended battlefield antagonism. Indeed, much of the care for the dead arose from sanitary necessity. Still, the setting up of the war graves commission and the role of chaplains throughout the front in laying the bodies to rest illustrates how the mass dumping of bodies was no longer acceptable as the war progressed. Unlike the wars that had proceeded the twentieth century, a new respect for the bodies that fell illustrated a wider political and societal recognition of the importance of those who had sacrificed for their countries. Initially, men were haphazardly buried but by the end of the war grand cemeteries, memorials and the 'tomb of the unknown soldier' all focused on the preservation of soldiers' bodies, signifying a shift in official policy as the British government took responsibility for the bodies left behind.

Finally, it clear that men's release from their military duties was also significantly focused on their bodies. Dennis Winter has explained how demobilization struggled with the sheer numbers of men keen for release from their duties.[55] While Beckett, Bowman and Connelly have illustrated that the reintegration of the wounded meant a chaotic and complicated pension system which quickly became overwhelmed and served as a bone of contention in the decades that followed.[56] The link between release and life after service has been explored by Emma Newlands in the Second World War as she explained how soldiers' bodies were commodified as part of the demobilization assessment at the end of the conflict.[57] This book has explored how during the First World War this process was no different, as men's release from service was predicated on a physical review of their bodies. These assessments reduced each man's body again to a series of statistics which were repurposed away from a focus on potential battle efficiency towards their potential financial burden on the state because of their physical sacrifice. Many men like Private Sumpter found that between enlistment and demobilization they had exchanged a healthy body for a damaged one that experienced demobilization with an accompanying physical or psychological trauma.[58] Conversely, some men also left the army with new skill sets such as in the case of Private Floyd who left with a certificate in education and engineering skills that he could use in civilian life.[59] Even the limbo that existed between the calling of the armistice and men's eventual release allowed some men to challenge the control that their bodies had lived under throughout military service in the war as demands to be returned to civilian life transitioned in demonstrations against the army. Ultimately, release from the military service demanded extensive scrutiny of the bodies of the men who had served. As their bodies readjusted to civilian dress and men retook agency over rudimentary aspects of their lives such as grooming, eating and sleeping, bodies were catalogued once more, and those results would continue to define many men's existence outside of their military existence financially.

In closing, this book returns to Lieutenant Godfrey's words to his mother in the letter in 1917 which claimed that the First World War was an entirely different reality to anything he had experienced before. Godfrey, like thousands of other British men, had found his body constantly under the gaze of the military from the moment he had enlisted until beyond his demobilization. Men like Godfrey found their bodies assessed by 'experts' on entry before being clothed with ill-fitting uniforms of either khaki or blue and introduced to training regiments designed to craft their bodies towards filling out their uniform and station, both literally and metaphorically. This central aspect of creating the soldier from a civilian often collided almost immediately with the will and desires of the new recruits as men regularly also pursued their own aims, seeking to retain control over aspects of their own bodies, finding comfort in food and alcohol and engaging in often dangerous acts with women and each other. Within their 'different existence' soldier's 'war bodies' were constantly tested, challenged, damaged and served as a site of conflict between the agency of the individual and the demands of the British Army. On entry men's bodies were assessed and tailored for service. During service the gaze shifted to maintaining control over these bodies and ensuring that they were able to meet the enemy effectively. In battle, men's bodies were subject to all the chaos that surrounded them such as bombs, bullets and their own physical limits tested their physical and psychological ability to serve to the extreme. Post battle, these bodies would be subject to recovery, be they reclaimed for repair, revitalized in preparation for a return to combat or simply recovered for interment. Post war, those who survived often exchanged their uniforms and kit for civilian dress and a banknote during a reversal of the physical assessment process they had experienced on the way in. Many also found that by the end of the war they were forced to exchange the relatively healthy body with which they had entered the army and had been so carefully crafted through military training for a defective one complete with a promise of a potentially meagre pension commodified by their physical loss and attained rank. Starkly, no man returned without a physical reminder of their endurance and sacrifice between 1914 and 1918.

The conclusion to take away from these overlapping arguments is that within this complicated process of creation and deconstruction of the transition between civilian and soldier during the First World War it was the body upon which all these changes and experiences were enacted. Considerations of the experience of the war through analysis of the body allows for a deeper understanding of the trials and tribulations that men experienced as they served. This is not to say that men were simply marionettes at the behest of the military. Godfrey may have expressed to his mother that the war was a different experience, but he said nothing of relinquishing complete autonomous control to the army. Between the regulations over hair, bedtimes, sex, drink and inoculations resistance occurred. Lack of bodily sustenance resulted in sporadic insurrections and ill-deserved punishment elicited riots. Traditional demands for personal grooming fell away in the face of a larger body of serving men and a greater enemy than upsetting the old guard. Indeed, men's bodies were at the centre of their transition from civilian to soldier, and of course back again, but that does not mean that they were passive during the experience. Here, finally, this book reiterates its relevance by repeating that while the crafting of civilian men into solders during the First World War was certainly focused on the control of their bodies, it was not an all-encompassing, agency-stripping process, despite the best efforts of the British Army. Men improved and fought, but they also rebelled and damaged their own bodies. Essentially, soldiers or not, authoritarian control or not, during the First World War, in battle, behind the lines, in hospitals, barracks, brothels and bars, men still lived; and they did so in a different existence altogether tending their 'war bodies' until they were finally released from their service.

Notes

Introduction: 'A different existence'

1 Imperial War Museum (hereby known as IWM) 14991, Private Papers of 2nd Lieutenant J. T. Godfrey, Memoir extract, no page numbers. Letter to his mother, 25 May 2017.
2 Ibid.
3 Ibid.
4 Ibid., diary entry dated 'probably June 16th'.
5 Ibid.
6 Ibid.
7 Ibid.
8 The term 'masculinity' is used throughout this book. In the nineteenth century notions of 'manliness' developed as part of the increasing focus on physicality. Sinha argues that notions of 'manliness' were particularly distinctive within public school environments. Potentially the terms 'manliness' and 'masculinity' could be used interchangeably to identify the perceptions of ideal maleness in the later nineteenth and early twentieth centuries. However, given the association with public schooling and for the purposes of clarity, the term masculinity will be primarily used throughout the continuing analysis. M. Sinha, *Colonial Masculinity: The 'Manly Englishman' and the 'Effeminate Bengali' in the Late Nineteenth Century* (Manchester: Manchester University Press, 1995), p. 9.
9 J. Keegan, *The Face of Battle Kindle Edition* (London: Bodley Head, 2014), loc. 3013.
10 H. Cunningham, *The Volunteer Force – A Social and Political History* (London: Croom Helm, 1975), p. 155.
11 C. Brown, *'The Scum of the Earth': What Happened to the Real British Heroes of Waterloo?* (Stroud: History Press, 2015), p. 10.
12 M. Brown, '"Like a Devoted Army": Medicine, Heroic Masculinity, and the Military Paradigm in Victorian Britain', *Journal of British Studies*, vol. 49, no. 3 (2010), p. 595.
13 Keegan, *Face of Battle Kindle Edition*, loc. 3444.
14 E. Spiers, *The Late Victorian Army* (Manchester: Manchester University Press, 1992), p. 147.
15 J. Bourne, 'The British Working Man', in Huge Cecil and Peter Liddle (eds), *Facing Armageddon, the First World War Experience Kindle Edition* (London: Pen and Sword, 2003), loc. 8037; and S. Miller, 'In Support of the Imperial Mission – Volunteering for the South African War, 1899–1902', *Journal of Military History*, vol. 69, no. 3 (2005), pp. 709–10.
16 S. Barnard, *To Prove I'm Not Forgot: Living and Dying in a Victorian City* (Manchester: Manchester University Press, 1990), p. 121.
17 Ibid.
18 Bourne, 'British Working Man', loc. 7955.

19　G. Dawson, *Soldier Heroes, British Adventure, Empire and the Imaging of Masculinities* (New York: Routledge, 2005), p. 148.
20　J. Peck, *The Army Abroad: Fictions of India and the Indian Mutiny* (London: Palgrave Macmillan, 1998), p. 71.
21　J. M. MacKenzie, 'Introduction', in J. M. MacKenzie (ed.), *Popular Imperialism and the Military: 1850–1950* (Manchester: Manchester University Press, 1992), p. 12.
22　A. Summers, 'Essay: Militarism in Britain before the Great War', *History Workshop*, no. 2 (1976), p. 106.
23　Brown, 'Like a Devoted Army', p. 596.
24　A. Penn, *Targeting Schools: Drill, Militarism and Imperialism* (London: Routledge, 1999), pp. 23–4.
25　P. Deslandes, *Oxbridge Men: British Masculinity and the Undergraduate Experience, 1850–1920* (Bloomington: Indiana University Press, 2005), p. 167.
26　Ibid.
27　Dawson, *Soldier Heroes*, p. 1.
28　A. Warwick, 'Exercising the Student Body, Mathematics and Athleticism in Victorian Cambridge', in C. Lawerence and S. Shapin (eds), *Science Incarnate, Historical Embodiments of Natural Knowledge* (London: University of Chicago Press, 1998), p. 299.
29　Penn, *Targeting Schools*, p. 78.
30　G. R. Searle, *The Quest for National Efficiency* (London: University of California Press, 1971), p. 65.
31　R. Duncan, *Pubs and Patriots: The Drink Crisis in Britain during World War One* (Liverpool: Liverpool University Press, 2013), p. 21.
32　I. Zweiniger-Bargielowska, *Managing the Body, Beauty, Health, and Fitness in Britain, 1800–1939* (Oxford: Oxford University Press, 2010), pp. 193, 64.
33　Searle, *Quest for National Efficiency*, p. 65.
34　J. Vernon, *Hunger: A Modern History* (Cambridge, MA: Harvard University Press, 2007), p. 164; and R. Titmuss, *Problems of Social Policy* (London: HMSO, 1950), p. 510.
35　R. Titmuss, *Essays on the Welfare State* (Boston, MA: Beacon Press, 1969), p. 78.
36　D. Silbey, 'Bodies and Cultures Collide: Enlistment, The Medical Exam and the British Working Class 1914–1916', *Social History of Medicine*, vol 17, no. 1 (2004), pp. 61–76.
37　E. Newlands, *Civilians into Soldiers: War, the Body and British Army Recruits, 1939–45* (Manchester: Manchester University Press, 2014), p. 46.
38　Dawson, *Soldier Heroes*, p. 1.
39　J. Bourke, *Dismembering the Male, Men's Bodies, Britain and the Great War* (London: Reaktion Books, 1999), pp. 128–9.
40　Ibid.
41　M. Paris, *Warrior Nation: Images of War in British Popular Culture 1850–2000* (London: Reaktion Books, 2000), p. 126.
42　N. Gullace, *The Blood of Our Sons: Men, Women, and the Renegotiation of British Citizenship during the Great War* (New York: Palgrave Macmillan, 2002).
43　Ibid., 82.
44　A. Woollacott, '"Khaki Fever" and Its Control: Gender, Class, Age and Sexual Morality on the British Home front in the First World War', *Journal of Contemporary History*, vol. 29 (1994), pp. 326–8.
45　It is worth noting that at the outbreak of war over a quarter of the BEF was based in India. Indian troops quickly joined their British counterparts on the front line;

however, historians such as Terraine, Omissi and Erickson have argued that the Indian troops were poorly trained and badly equipped with outdated weaponry and as such their contribution to the immediate war effort is questionable. This is made clear by Morton-Jack in G. Morton-Jack, *The Indian Army on the Western Front South Asia Edition* (Cambridge: Cambridge University Press, 2014), p. 13.

46 A. Mallinson, *The Making of the British Army, from the English Civil War to the War on Terror* (London: Transworld, 2009), p. 361.
47 Ibid.
48 I. Beckett, T. Bowman and M. Connelly, *The British Army and the First World War* (St Ives: Cambridge University Press, 2017), p. 207.
49 P. Simkins, *Kitchener's Army: The Raising of the New Armies 1914–1916*, Kindle edition (Manchester: Manchester University Press, 2007), loc. 1518.
50 I. Beckett, *Britain's Part Time Soldiers, the Amateur Military Tradition 1558–1945* (Barnsley: Manchester University Press, 2011), p. 226.
51 Ibid.
52 Ibid, pp. 227–8.
53 P. Simkins, 'The Four Armies', in D. G. Chandler and I. Beckett (eds), *The Oxford History of the British Army* (Oxford: Oxford University Press, 1994), p. 240. Note: Pal's Battalions arose out of the surge of patriotic fever which marked the beginning of the First World War in Britain. As the effectiveness of harnessing local ties to encourage large numbers of men to enlist became apparent, Lord Derby dubbed the eager men 'Pal's Battalions'. For more information, see Simkins *Kitchener's Army* and Chapter 3 of this book.
54 Ibid.
55 C. Hughes, 'The New Armies', in I. Beckett and K. Simpson (eds), *A Nation in Arms* (Barnsley: Pen and Sword, 2004), pp. 101–3.
56 K. Robert, ' "All That Is Best of the Modern Woman"?: Representations of Female Military Auxiliaries in British Popular Culture, 1914–1919', in J. Meyer (ed.), *British Popular Culture and the First World Wars* (London: Brill, 2008), p. 101.
57 K. W. Mitchinson, *Gentlemen and Officers: The Impact and Experience of War on a Territorial Regiment 1914–1918* (London: Naval and Military Press, 2012), p. 140
58 I. R. Bet-El, *Conscripts, Lost Legions of the Great War* (Stroud: Sutton, 1999), p. 2.
59 Ibid., pp. 2–4.
60 G. Sheffield, 'Officer-Man Relations, Discipline and Morale in the Great War', in Huge Cecil and Peter Liddle (eds), *Facing Armageddon, The First World War Experience Kindle Edition* (London: Pen and Sword, 2003), loc. 9792.
61 Ibid.
62 Beckett, Bowman and Connelly, *British Army and the First World War*, p. 150.
63 R. Duffett, *Stomach for Fighting: Food and Soldiers of the Great War* (Manchester: Manchester University Press, 2012); A. Clayton, *Battlefield Rations: The Food Given to The British Soldier for Marching and Fighting 1900–2011* (Solihull: Helion, 2013); and A. Robertshaw, *Feeding Tommy: Battlefield Recipes from the First World War* (London: History Press, 2013).
64 J. D. Campbell, *The Army Isn't All Work: Physical Culture and the Evolution of the British Army, 1860–1920* (Oxon: Routledge, 2016), pp. 140–1.
65 Duffett, *Stomach for Fighting*, p. 21.
66 Clayton, *Battlefield Rations*, p. 20.
67 R. Porter, *Disease, Medicine and Society in England, 1550–1860* (Cambridge: Cambridge University Press, 1993), pp. 53–5.

68 G. Williams, *Angel of Death, the Story of Smallpox* (New York: Palgrave Macmillan, 2010); and D. Brunton, *The Politics of Vaccination: Practice and Policy in England, Wales, Ireland, and Scotland 1800–1874* (Suffolk: University of Rochester Press, 2008).
69 M. Harrison, 'Public Health and Medicine in British India: An Assessment of the British Contribution', *Bulletin of the Liverpool Medical History Society*, vol. 10 (1998), p. 45.
70 S. Walker, 'The Greater Good: Agency and Inoculation in the British Army, 1914–1918', *Canadian Bulletin of Medical History*, vol. 36 (2019), pp. 131–2.
71 M. Harrison, *The Medical War: British Military Medicine in the First World War* (Oxford: Oxford University Press, 2010), pp. 125–6.
72 Ibid., p. 24.
73 J. Meyer, *An Equal Burden: The Men of the Royal Army Medical Corps in the First World War* (Oxford: Oxford University Press, 2019), p. 196.
74 J. Bourke, 'Wartime', in R. Cooter and J. Pickstone (eds), *Companion to Medicine in the Twentieth Century* (New York: Routledge, 2000), p. 591.
75 Ibid.
76 Ibid.
77 J. Lane, *A Social History of Medicine: Health, Healing and Disease in England, 1750–1950* (Oxon: Routledge, 2001), p. 180.
78 M. Harrison, 'Medicine and the Management of Modern Warfare: An Introduction', in R. Cooter, M. Harrison and S. Sturdy (eds), *Medicine and Modern Warfare* (Amsterdam: Clio Medica, 1999), pp. 18–19.
79 R. Cooter, 'War and Modern Medicine', in W. F. Bynum and R. Porter (eds), *Companion Encyclopaedia of the History of Medicine* (London: Routledge, 1993), p. 1544.
80 J. Pickstone, *Medicine and Industrial Society: A History of Hospital Development in Manchester and its Region, 1752–1946* (Manchester: Manchester University Press, 1985), p. 208.
81 Ibid.
82 D. A. Simpson and D. J. David, 'World War I: The Genesis of Cranimaxillofcial Surgery', *ANZ Journal of Surgery*, vol. 74 (2004), pp. 71–7.
83 M. Foucault, *Discipline and Punish: The Birth of the Prison* (New York: Vintage, 2012), p. 138.
84 Ibid., p. 136.
85 C. Shilling, *The Body and Social Theory* (London: Sage, 1993), p. 81.
86 Ibid., p. 80.
87 Ibid.
88 M. Weber, 'The Nation', in J. Hutchinson and A. D. Smith (eds), *Nationalism* (Oxford: Oxford University Press, 1994), pp. 25–7; and K. Marx and F. Engels, *The Communist Manifesto: Penguin Classics Deluxe Edition* (London: Penguin Random House, 2011).
89 A. Rabinbach, *Human Motor: Energy, Fatigue and the Origins of Modernity* (Berkeley: University of California Press, 1990), pp. 238–40.
90 Searle, *Quest for National Efficiency*, p. 65; and S. Kreis, 'The Diffusion of Scientific Management: The Bedaux Company in America and Britain, 1926–1945', in D. Nelson (ed.), *A Mental Revolution: Scientific Management since Taylor* (Columbus: Ohio State University Press, 1992), p. 169.
91 F. Taylor, *The Scientific Management: The Early Sociology of Management and Organizations Reprint* (New York: Routledge, 2006).

Notes

92   P. Miller and N. Rose, 'Governing Economic Life', *Economy and Society*, vol. 19 (1990), p. 20.
93   Ibid., pp. 20–1.
94   Rabinbach, *Human Motor*, pp. 274–5.
95   S. Kreis, 'Early Experiments in British Scientific Management: The Health of Munitions Workers Committee, 1915–1920', *Journal of Management History*, vol. 1 (1995), p. 67.
96   Ibid.
97   V. Long, The *Rise and Fall of the Healthy Factory: The Politic of Industrial Health in Britain, 1914–1960* (New York: Palgrave Macmillan, 2011), pp. 16–48; and A. J. McIvor, *A History of Work in Britain, 1880–1950* (New York: Palgrave, 2001), p. 147.
98   P. Bourdieu, *Distinction: A Social Critique of the Judgment of Taste* (London: Routledge, 2010), p. 190.
99   A. Howson, *The Body in Society: An Introduction* (Cambridge: Polity, 2011), p. 21.
100 E. Goffman, *Behaviour in Public Places* (New York: Free Press, 1966), pp. 30–1.
101 P. Simkins, 'Voluntary Recruiting in Britain, 1914–1915', The British Library, (29 January 2014), accessible at https://www.bl.uk/world-war-one/articles/voluntary-recruiting (accessed 1 July 2017).
102 Newlands, *Civilians into Soldiers*, p. 14.
103 P. Hart, *Voices from the Front: An Oral History of the Great War* (New York: Oxford University Press, 2016), p. 5.
104 Bourke, *Dismembering the Male*, p. 77.
105 S. Morillo, *What Is Military History?* (Cambridge: Polity, 2006), p. 105.
106 Ibid.
107 A. Brundage, *Going to the Sources: A Guide to Historical Research and Writing*, 6th edn (London: John Wiley, 2017), p. 17.
108 Ibid., p. 20.
109 R. van Emden, *Tommy's Ark: Soldiers and Their Animals in the Great War* (London: Bloomsbury, 2010), p. 10.
110 The term 'ranker' is a common term used colloquially in this period and previously to describe men of the rank and file. This is used extensively throughout the primary histography into military history and is solely used throughout this book to identify those men who were neither NCOs nor officers.
111 E. R. Mayhew, *Wounded: From Battlefield to Blighty, 1914–1918*, Kindle edition (Leicester: Thorpe, 2014), loc. 141.
112 Ibid.
113 D. Leder, *The Absent Body* (Chicago: Chicago University Press, 1990), p. 1.
114 J. Bourke, *The Story of Pain: From Prayer to Painkillers* (Oxford: Oxford University Press, 2014), p. 14.
115 Zweiniger-Bargielowska, *Managing the Body*, pp. 192–3.
116 J. Winter, *The Great War and the British People* (New York: Palgrave Macmillan, 2002), p. 280.
117 R. Woodward, 'Locating Military Masculinities: Space, Place and the Formation of Gender Identity in the British Army', in P. Higate (ed.), *Military Masculinities: Identity and the State* (London: Praeger, 2003), p. 51.
118 Harrison, *Medical War*, p. 291.
119 Bourke, *Dismembering the Male*, p. 152.
120 While several of these texts have already been mentioned in the opening analysis, this book lacks the space to do justice to the seminal works that have come

before it. While the approach taken here is new, it has been inspired by many past studies on the expansive histories of the British military, masculinity, power, gender and society and culture. This includes but is certainly not limited to: R. van Emden, *The Somme: The Epic Battle in the Soldiers' Own Words and Photographs* (London: Pen and Sword, 2016); G. Sheffield, *The Somme: A New History* (London: Cassell Military, 2003); H. Strachan, *The First World War: A New History* (London: Simon and Schuster, 2001); M. Oliver and R. Partridge, *Napoleonic Army Handbook: The French Army and Her Allies* (London: Constable, 2002); S. H. Myerly, *British Military Spectacle: From the Napoleonic Wars through the Crimea* (Cambridge: Harvard University Press, 1996); T. Royal, *Crimea: The Great Crimean War* (New York: St. Martin's Press, 2014); H. Small, *The Crimean War: Queen Victoria's War with the Russian Tsars* (Stroud: Tempus, 2007); J. Grehan and M. Mace, *The Zulu War: The War Dispatches Series* (Barnsley: Pen and Sword, 2013); I. Knight, *Companion to the Anglo-Zulu War* (Barnsley: Pen and Sword, 2008); T. Pakenham, *The Boer War* (London: Abacus, 1979); B. Farwell, *The Great Anglo-Boer War* (New York: W. W. Norton, 1990); and D. Reitz, *God Does Not Forget: The Story of a Boer War Commando* (London: Fireship Press, 2010).

1 A fine body of men: Recruitment and enlisting for war 1914–18

1 J. B. Ingle, *A Fine Body of Men*, monographic (Chicago: Delmar Music, 1919) [Notated Music]. Retrieved from the Library of Congress, https://www.loc.gov/item/2009371440/ (accessed 1 July 2017).
2 H. Strachan, *The First World War: A New History* (London: Simon and Schuster, 2001), p. 21.
3 J. Grehan and M. Mace, *The Boer War 1899–1902: Ladysmith, Megerforntein, Spion Kop, Kimberley and Mafeking* (Barnsley: Pen and Sword, 2014), p. vii.
4 The War Office, *Statistical Abstract of Information Regarding the British Armies at Home and Abroad 1914–1920* (London: HMSO, 1920), p. 363.
5 P. Simkins, *Kitchener's Army: The Raising of the New Armies 1914–1916* (Manchester: Manchester University Press, 2007), loc. 205.
6 Great Britain War Office, *Statistics of the Military Effort of the British Empire during the Great War, 1914–1920* (London: HMSO, 1922), p. 364. This is also displayed in I. Beckett and K. Simpson (eds), *A Nation in Arms: A Social Study of the British Army in the First World War* (Manchester: Manchester University Press, 1985), p. 364. However, Beckett also adds in the existing strength of the British Army, territorials and reserve to bring the total figure of serving men up to 5,704,416.
7 Beckett, *Nation in Arms*, p. 364.
8 C. Barnett, *Britain and Her Army, 1509–1970: A Military, Political and Social Survey* (London: Allen Lane, 1970), p. 371.
9 Ibid., p. 372.
10 In 1918, this was raised to 51 and throughout men widowed with children, serving in the Royal Navy, a minister of religion or working in one of a number of reserved occupations could be exempt from service.
11 D. Gilmore, *Manhood in the Making: Cultural Concepts of Masculinity* (New York: Yale University, 1990), p. 3.

12 G. Dawson, *Soldier Heroes, British Adventure, Empire and the Imaging of Masculinities* (New York: Routledge, 2005), p. 148.
13 Gilmore specifically refers to penis size and height. For more information on the rise of masculinity as a socialized construct within this period, see Christina Jarvis on the Second World War in C. S. Jarvis, *The Male Body at War: America Masculinity during World War II* (New York: Northern Illinois University Press, 2004); J. M. MacKenzie on the late Victorian period and first half of the twentieth century in J. M. MacKenzie, *Propaganda and Empire: The Manipulation of British Public Opinion, 1880-1960* (Manchester: Manchester University Press, 1984); and particularly Meg Albrinck for the First World War in M. Albrinck, 'Humanitarians and He-Men: Recruitment Posters and the Masculine Ideal', in Pearl James (ed.), *Picture This: World War I Posters and Visual Culture*(Lincoln: University of Nebraska Press, 2009).
14 P. Simkins, *Kitchener's Army: The Raising of the New Armies 1914–1916*, Kindle edition (Manchester: Manchester University Press, 2007), loc. 204.
15 P. Simkins, 'Voluntary Recruiting in Britain, 1914–1915', The British Library (29 January 2014), accessible at https://www.bl.uk/world-war-one/articles/voluntary-recruiting (accessed 1 July 2017).
16 A. G. V. Simmonds, *Britain and World War One* (New York: Routledge, 2012), p. 47; and M. L. Sanders and P. M. Taylor, *British Propaganda during the First World War, 1914–1918* (London: Macmillan, 1982), p. 103.
17 M. Albrinck, 'Humanitarians and He-Men', pp. 277–87.
18 IWM PST 4903, 'To the Young Women of London', Recruitment poster (1915).
19 J. Tynan *British Army Uniform and the First World War: Men in Khaki* (London: Palgrave Macmillan, 2013), p. 19.
20 Dawson, *Soldier Heroes*, p. 81; J. Q. Adams and Philip Poirer, *The Conscription Controversy in Great Britain* (London: Palgrave Macmillan, 1987); and M. Brown, '"Like a Devoted Army": Medicine, Heroic Masculinity, and the Military', *Journal of British Studies*, vol. 49, no. 3 (2010), pp. 592–622.
21 IWM, 7275, Private Papers of Lieutenant K. Palmer, p. 10.
22 Ibid. Source is presented exactly as is written within the Private Papers of Lieutenant K. Palmer.
23 IWM, 7104, Private Papers of E. Buffey, pp. 4–5.
24 Ibid.
25 A. Woollacott, '"Khaki Fever" and Its Control: Gender, Class, Age and Sexual Morality on the British Homefront in the First World War', *Journal of Contemporary History*, 29, no. 2 (1994), p. 333.
26 C. Acton, 'Best Boys and Aching Hearts: The Rhetoric of Romance as Social Control in Wartime Magazines for Young Women', in J. Meyer (ed.), *British Popular Culture and the First World War* (London: Brill, 2008), p. 175.
27 V. Cree, '"Khaki Fever" during the First World War: A Historical Case Study of Social Work's Approach towards Young Women, Sex and Moral Danger', *British Journal of Social Work* (2016), pp. 1839–54.
28 IWM, 4872, Private Papers of T. A. Bickerton, pp. 3–4. Source is presented exactly as is written within the Private Papers of T. A. Bickerton.
29 IWM, 7715, Private Papers of T. A. Silver, p. 4.
30 Ibid., p. 5.
31 J. Meyer, 'Introduction', in J. Meyer (ed.), *British Popular Culture and the First World Wars* (London: Brill, 2008), p. 5.
32 IWM, 17024, Private Papers of J. Brady, p. 40.

33 A. Kramer, *Conscientious Objectors of the First World War: A Determined Resistance* (Barnsley: Pen and Sword, 2013), pp. 74–7.
34 IWM, 14, Private Papers of F. J. Murfin, pp. 3–4.
35 Tynan, *British Army Uniform and the First World War*, p. 3.
36 IWM, 1693, Private Papers of G. Ewan, p. 3.
37 Ibid, p. 6.
38 L. Bibbings, *Telling Tales about Men: Conceptions of Conscientious Objectors to Military Service during the First World War* (Manchester: Manchester University Press, 2009), p. 54.
39 M. H. Manser, *The Facts on File Dictionary of Proverbs* (New York: Infobase, 2007).
40 R. Duffett, *The Stomach for Fighting, Food and Soldiers of the Great War* (Manchester: Manchester University Press, 2012), p. 77.
41 I. Zweiniger-Bargielowska, *Managing the Body, Beauty, Health, and Fitness in Britain, 1800–1939* (Oxford: Oxford University Press, 2010); and J. Winter, *The Great War and the British People* (New York: Palgrave Macmillan, 2002), p. 280.
42 T. P. Dooley, *Irishmen or English Soldier: The Times and World of a South Catholic* (Liverpool: Liverpool University Press, 1995), p. 101.
43 R. Roberts, *The Classic Slum* (Manchester: Penguin, 1971), p. 189.
44 Duffett, *Stomach for Fighting*, p. 76.
45 J. Winter, 'Military Fitness and Civilian Health in Britain during the First World War', *Journal of Contemporary History*, vol. 15 (1980), pp. 211–44.
46 J. Bourke, *Dismembering the Male, Men's Bodies, Britain and the Great War* (London: Reaktion Books, 1999), p. 172.
47 Bourke, *Dismembering the Male*, pp. 173–5.
48 Ibid., p. 175.
49 D. Silbey, 'Bodies and Cultures Collide: Enlistment, the Medical Exam and the British Working Class 1914–1916', *Social History of Medicine*, vol. 17, no. 1 (2004), pp. 67–8.
50 S. T. Beggs, *Selection of the Recruit* (London: Baillière, Tindall & Cox, 1915), p. 14. This is also mentioned by Silbey, 'Bodies and Cultures Collide', p. 64.
51 G. F. Shee, 'The Deterioration in the National Physique', *Nineteenth Century and After: A Monthly Review*, vol. 49 (May 1903), pp. 734–8.
52 The National Archives (hereby known as TNA), W0364 4405, Enlistment form for Arthur James Walkden (17 August 1914).
53 IWM, 14729, Private Papers of Lieutenant G. Cotton, p. 2. This is exactly how the source is presented within the Private Papers of Lieutenant G. Cotton.
54 IWM, 14729, Private Papers of Lieutenant G. Cotton, p. 2. This is exactly how the source is presented within the Private Papers of Lieutenant G. Cotton.
55 Great Britain War Office, *Regulations for Army Medical Services* (London: HMSO, 1890), p. 132.
56 Winter, 'Military Fitness', p. 215.
57 I. Beckett, T. Bowman and M. Connelly, *The British Army and the First World War* (St Ives: Cambridge University Press, 2017), pp. 121–2.
58 Silbey, 'Bodies and Cultures Collide', p. 75.
59 HC Debate, 2 March 1916, vol. 80 cc1182-3.
60 Ibid.
61 A. Marwick, *The Deluge: British Society and the First World War* (London: Little Brown, 1966), p. 41.
62 P. Simkins, '"Each One a Pocket Hercules": The Bantam Experiment and the Case of the Thirty-Fifth Division', in S. Marble (ed.), *Scraping the Barrel: The Military Use of*

Sub-Standard Manpower: The Military 1860–1960 (New York: Fordham University Press, 2012), pp. 80–1.
63 Ibid.
64 Ibid., pp. 91–2.
65 IWM, 17024, Private Papers of J. Brady, p. 40. Source is presented exactly as is written within the Private Papers of J. Brady.
66 Ibid.
67 Ibid, pp. 40–1.
68 IWM, 17426, Private Papers of C. Shaw, p. 1.
69 Zweiniger-Bargielowska, *Managing the Body*, pp. 88–92.
70 Dawson, *Soldier Heroes*, p. 57.
71 Zweiniger-Bargielowska, *Managing the Body*, p. 89.
72 IWM, 17426, Private Papers of C. Shaw, p. 2.
73 R. van Emden, *Boy Soldiers of the Great War*, Kindle edition (London: Headline, 2005).
74 Z. Marriage, 'Worst Forms of Child Labour', in H. D. Hindman (ed.), *The World of Child Labor: An Historical and Regional Survey* (New York: Routledge, 2015), p. 102.
75 IWM, 8013, Private Papers of F. Mulliss, p. 1.
76 IWM, 17024, Private Papers of J. Brady, p. 40. Source is presented exactly as is written within the Private Papers of J. Brady.
77 IWM, 6659, Private Papers of D. Starrett, p. 1.
78 Silbey, 'Bodies and Cultures Collide', pp. 61–76.
79 IWM, 12369, Private Papers of G. Calverley, p. 3.
80 IWM, 11417, Private Papers of Private E. S. Styles, p. 1 Note: Clarification of what the doctor actually meant is not within with the account; however, it is likely this was in reference to eyesight or the overall condition of Styles in the mind of the assessor.
81 Winter, 'Military Fitness', p. 215.
82 IWM, 1878, Private Papers of S. E. Butler, p. 31.
83 IWM, 8013, Private Papers of F. Mulliss, p.1.
84 Bourke, *Dismembering the Male*, p. 174.
85 IWM, 7104, Private Papers of E. Buffey, p. 5.
86 Simkins, *Kitchener's Army*, loc. 2051.
87 D. Silbey, *The British Working Class and Enthusiasm for War, 1914–1916* (New York: Taylor & Francis, 2004), p. 32.
88 van Emden, *Boy Soldiers*, p. 43.
89 IWM, 7275, Private Papers of Lieutenant K. Palmer, p. 10.
90 IWM, 22065, Private Papers of R. McKay, p. 1.
91 A. Robertshaw, *Feeding Tommy: Battlefield Recipes from the First World War* (London: History Press, 2013).
92 P. C. Kochhar, *History of the Army Dental Corps and Military Dentistry* (New Delhi: Lancer, 2000), p. 36.
93 Ibid.
94 HC Debate, 26 August 1914, vol. 66 cc38-9 39.
95 IWM, 1467, Private Papers of Lieutenant P. Creek, p. 27.
96 Ibid.
97 IWM, 11804, Private Papers of C. W. Williams, p. 1.
98 IWM, 1876, Private Papers of A. C. Warsop, p. 1.
99 IWM, 7104, Private Papers of E. Buffey, p. 5.

2 Forging bodies: Training and creating soldiers

1. Brigadier E. A. James, *British Regiments 1914–1918 Digital Edition* (East Sussex: Naval and Military Press, 2012), Appendix II to Part II.
2. P. Simkins, *Kitchener's Army: The Raising of the New Armies 1914–1916*, Electronic edition (Barnsley: Manchester University Press, 2007), loc. 8180.
3. I. R. Bet-El, *Conscripts, Lost Legions of the Great War* (Stroud: Sutton, 1999), p. 41.
4. Special and Supplementary Tables for Physical Training, 1916, located within A. Curling, *Fighting Fit, 1914* (Stroud: Amberley, 2014), p. 68.
5. P. Simkins, 'The Four Armies 1914–1918', in D. Chandler and I. Beckett (eds), *The Oxford History of the British Army* (Oxford: Oxford University Press, 1994), p. 236.
6. IWM, 20761, Private Papers of H. Milner, pp. 4–6.
7. IWM, 14165, Private Papers of T. Parks, Letter to Wife and Children (13 June 2017). Source is presented exactly as is written within the Private Papers of T. Parks.
8. IWM, 17631, Private Papers of Lieutenant B. A. Minnitt MC, p. 4.
9. IWM, 2797, Private Papers of C. G. Rickett, p. 5.
10. IWM, 14938, Private Papers of C. E. Jones, p. 14.
11. IWM, 14729, Private Papers of Lieutenant G. Cotton, p. 4.
12. IWM, 16692, Private Papers of Lieutenant H. L. North, p. 6.
13. IWM, 1700, Private Papers of H. G. Smith, p. 1.
14. J. Tynan, 'Tailoring in the Trenches: The Making of the First World War British Army Uniform', in J. Meyer (ed.), *British Popular Culture and the First World War* (London: Brill, 2008), p. 72.
15. R. van Emden, *Boy Soldiers of the Great War*, Kindle edition (London: Headline, 2005), pp. 59–60.
16. HMSO, *The King's Regulations and Orders for the Army 1912: Official Copy: Re-Printed with Amendments Published in Army Orders up to 1st August 1914* (London: HMSO, 1914), p. 325.
17. IWM, 22065, Private Papers of R. McKay, p. 11.
18. On the front line short hair was also essential for sanitary purposes such as restricting the spread of lice; see Chapter 3 for more details on the hygiene-related reasons for shaving and haircuts.
19. IWM, 7104, Private Papers of E. Buffey, p. 6. From this quote, Buffey seems to imply that it was possible to bribe the hairdresser by paying him 'Twopence'.
20. IWM, 2614, Private Papers of P. G. Copson, Diary Entry, 8 March 1917.
21. Tynan, 'Tailoring', p. 73.
22. J. Tynan, *Men in Khaki, British Army Uniform and the First World War* (London: Palgrave Macmillan, 2013); see also G. Dawson, *Soldier Heroes, British Adventure, Empire and the Imaging of Masculinities* (New York: Routledge, 2005).
23. IWM, 7988, Private Papers of 2nd Lieutenant C. Carter, *Army Life as It Really Was 1914–1919*, unpublished memoirs, p. 2.
24. Ibid.
25. IWM, 11876, Private Papers of C. R. Keller, pp. 8–9.
26. IWM, 20761, Private Papers of H. Milner, p. 4.
27. IWM SA, 577, W. E. Clarke, reel 2.
28. IWM, 3453, Private Papers of E. C. Barraclough, p. 7. The puttee was a long strip of bandage which was useful for keeping out water to the lower legs but was notoriously difficult to put on, particularly the first time.

29 IWM, 7104, Private Papers of E. Buffey, p. 6.
30 R. van Emden and S. Humphries, *All Quiet on the Home Front* (Barnsley: Pen and Sword, 2002), p. 79.
31 IWM SA, 25548, D. Murray, reel 2.
32 IWM, 12383, Private Papers of J. A. Johnston, p. 4.
33 Simkins, *Kitchener's Army*, p. 263
34 IWM, 1700, Private Papers of H. G. Smith, p. 1; and IWM, 13108, Private Papers of P. Whitehouse, p. 4.
35 R. Duffett, *Stomach for Fighting, Food and Soldiers of the Great War* (Manchester: Manchester University Press, 2012); A. Clayton, *Battlefield Rations: The Food Given to the British Soldier for Marching and Fighting 1900–2011* (Solihull: Helion, 2013); and A. Robertshaw, *Feeding Tommy: Battlefield Recipes from the First World War* (London: History Press, 2013).
36 Duffett, *Stomach for Fighting*, p. 21.
37 R. Duffett, 'A War Unimagined: Food and the Rank and File Soldier of the First World War', in J. Meyer (ed.), *British Popular Culture and the First World War* (London: Brill, 2008), p. 50.
38 Anon, 'Third Report of the Committee on Physiological Effects of Food, Training, and Clothing on The Soldier', *JRAMC*, vol. 13 (1909), pp. 669–81.
39 Ibid., p. 669.
40 Ibid., p. 672.
41 Ibid.
42 Ibid.
43 This average applied to both training and active combat. By comparison, the modern equivalent is not entirely dissimilar within the British Army, with the estimated requirements for male soldiers in the 2016 ranging from an average 3,600 calories in active service to 4,600 during training. Anon, 'SACN Statement on Military Dietary Reference Values for Energy', *Scientific Advisory Committee on Nutrition*, vol. 2 (2016), p. 8.
44 Duffett, *Stomach for Fighting*, p. 77.
45 Great Britain War Office, *Manual of Military Cooking and Dietary, Mobilisation, 1915* (London, HMSO, 1915), pp. 4–37.
46 Ibid.
47 B. Williams, *Raising and Training the New Armies – Reprinted* (London: Forgotten Books, 2012), pp. 50–1.
48 Ibid.
49 IWM, 17631, Private Papers of Lieutenant B. A. Minnitt MC, p. 3. Source is presented exactly as is written within the Private Papers of B. A. Minnitt – the underlining of 'rolled' appears this way in the original source.
50 IWM, 2617, Private Papers of C. G. Templer, pp. 2–3.
51 Ibid.
52 IWM, 7863, Private Papers of E. H. Lenfestey, p. 3.
53 J. Boff, 'Training to be Soldier', The British Library, https://www.bl.uk/world-war-one/articles/training-to-be-a-soldier (accessed 5 August 2017).
54 J. D. Campbell, *The Army Isn't All Work: Physical Culture and the Evolution of the British Army, 1860–1920* (Oxon: Routledge, 2016), pp. 140–1.
55 HC Debate, 3 August 1916, vol. 85, cols 522–3W.
56 IWM, 17248, Private Papers of S. Roberts, pp. 11–12.
57 Duffett, *Stomach for Fighting*, pp. 84–5.

58 IWM, 17248, Private Papers of S. Roberts, p. 2.
59 IWM, 15268, Private Papers of E. Grindley, no page numbers.
60 IWM, 20504, Private Papers of Lieutenant W. B. St. Leger, p. 7. Lieutenant Leger's reference to the Salt River Railway workers refers to a unit made up of men who were mainly from Cape Town, South Africa.
61 IWM, 17248, Private Papers of S. Roberts, pp. 11–12.
62 D. Winter, *Death's Men: Soldiers of the Great War* (London: Penguin, 1985), p. 38.
63 Ibid., pp. 38–9.
64 IWM, 17674, Private Papers of E. Drage, Diary entry, 16 August. Source is presented exactly as is written within the Private Papers of E. Drage.
65 E. Lycette, *Being an Account by Ernest Lycette of His Life as a Young Man and Soldier in the Years between 1911 and 1921, Army of Occupation – Rhineland, Auxiliary Corps – Ireland* (Levin: R. R. Lycette, 2007), p. 13.
66 Quoted in Winter, *Death's Men*, p. 39.
67 IWM, 3453, Private Papers of E. C. Barraclough, pp. 1–2.
68 IWM, 20761, Private Papers of H. Milner, pp. 3–4.
69 IWM, 11804, Private Papers of C. W. Williams, p. 2.
70 IWM, 13108, Private Papers of P. Whitehouse, p. 4.
71 IWM, 7976, Private Papers of F. B. Wade, p. 26.
72 Dawson, *Soldier Heroes*, p. 148.
73 M. Brown, '"Like a Devoted Army": Medicine, Heroic Masculinity, and the Military Paradigm in Victorian Britain', *Journal of British Studies*, 49, no. 3 (2010): 592–622.
74 D. Russell, '"We Carved Our Way to Glory": The British Soldier in Music Hall Song and Sketch, c.1880–1914', in J. M. Mackenzie (ed.), *Popular Imperialism and the Military: 1850–1950* (Manchester: Manchester University Press, 1984), p. 77.
75 D. Silbey, *The British Working Class and Enthusiasm for War, 1914–1916* (New York: Taylor & Francis, 2004), p. 32.
76 IWM, 14165, Private Papers of T. Parks, Letter to his Daughters (13 July 2016), p. 5.
77 IWM, 8408, Private Papers of C. A. Niblett, p. 3.
78 Ibid., pp. 2–4.
79 IWM SA, 12252, J. P. Murray, reel 1.
80 IWM SA, 11582, A. Hurst, reel 2.
81 Ibid., reel 1 and 2.
82 IWM SA, 16058, R. Davidson, reel 1.
83 Great Britain War Office, *Field Service Manual, Infantry Battalion* (London: HMSO, 1914), p. 13.
84 Curling, *Fighting Fit*, 1914, p. 86.
85 N. Clark, *Unwanted Warriors: The Rejected Warriors of the Canadian Expeditionary Force* (Vancouver: UBC Press, 2016), pp. 88–9. Note: In 2020, the British Army actively support the inclusion of left-handed recruits; however, this still presents an issue for training and equipment particularly as the current SA80, the rifle used by all British soldiers, is designed to be fired from the right shoulder as the cartridge is ejected to the right.
86 Ibid., p. 89.
87 C. McManus, *Right Hand, Left Hand* (London: Weidenfeld and Nicolson, 2002), p. 219.
88 Great Britain War Office, *Games for Use with Physical Training Tables and Training in Bombing* (London: HMSO, 1916), p. 2.

89 D. French, *Military Identities: The Regimental System, the British Army and the British People, c.1870–2000* (Oxford: Oxford University Press, 2005), pp. 115–21.
90 T. Mason and E. Riedi, *Sport and the Military: The British Armed Forces 1880–1960* (Cambridge: Cambridge University Press, 2010), p. 89.
91 Ibid.
92 Great Britain War Office, *Hints on Assault, Physical and Recreational Training* (France: Army Printing and Stationery Services, 1916), p. 15.
93 Mason and Riedi, *Sport and the Military*, p. 67.
94 'Sport at the Front: British Officers with a "Bag" of Partridge and Hare', *Illustrated War News*, 10 December 1914 (Part Two), p. 45.
95 Instructions found in 'Games for Use with Physical Training Tables and Raining in Bombing, 1916', collected in S. Bull (ed.), *An Officer's Manual of the Western Front 1914–1918* (London: Conway, 2008), pp. 108–11.
96 J. Mannell, 'The Service Football Program of World War I: Its Impact on the Popularity of the Game', *Journal of Sport History*, vol. 16, no. 3 (Winter 1989), p. 253.
97 IWM SA, 9954, J. Snailham, reel 1.
98 Lycette, *Being an Account by Ernest Lycette*, p. 15.
99 Parks, letter dated 13 June 2017.
100 IWM, 15015, Private Papers of W. H. Fox, p. 1.
101 Ibid.
102 Ibid., p. 10.
103 IWM, 2624, Private Papers of J. M. Cordy, p. 5.
104 D. Englander, 'Mutinies and Military Morale', in H. Strachan (ed.), *The Oxford Illustrated History of the First World War* (Oxford: Oxford University Press, 2014), pp. 191–2.
105 IWM, 1698, Private Papers of H. Calvert, p. 2.
106 J. Brophy and E. Partridge, *The Long Trail Songs and Slang of the British Soldier: 1911–18* (London: E. Partridge, 1930), p. 82.
107 IWM SA, 9433, A. J. Smith, reel 3.
108 IWM SA, 10917, B. Smedley, reel 3.
109 IWM SA, 9831, J. Goodson, reel 5. Note: By 'over leave' Goodson is referring to be returning late to the barracks.
110 Lycette, *Being an Account by Ernest Lycette*, p. 13. Lycette unfortunately does not explain who Mrs Grocott is, or what her relevance is to the situation.
111 Ibid.
112 Ibid.
113 J. Fairley and W. Allison, *The Monocled Mutineer: The First World War's Best Kept Secret: The Etaples Mutiny* (London: Quartet Books, 1978), p. 49.
114 HC Debate, 8 August 1916, vol. 85 cc841-2.
115 Great Britain War Office, *Kings Regulations and Orders for the Army* (London: HMSO, 1914), p. 112, paragraph 493, iiia.
116 Ibid., p. 114, paragraph 496a.
117 Ibid.
118 HC Debate, 31 December 1916, vol. 88 cc1738-63.
119 Englander, 'Mutinies and Military Morale', p. 193.
120 A. Kilday and D. S. Nash, *Shame and Modernity in Britain: 1890 to the Present* (London: Palgrave Macmillan, 2017), p. 37.
121 K. Jeffery, 'The Post War Army', in I. Beckett and K. Simpson (eds), *A Nation in Arms* (Barnsley: Pen and Sword, 2004), p. 231.

122 Ibid.; and C. R. M. F. Cruttwell, *A History of the Great War: 1914–1918* (Oxford: Clarendon Press, 1936), p. 531.
123 IWM, 2617, Private Papers of C. G. Templer, p. 6.
124 D. Gill and G. Dallas, *The Unknown Army* (London: Verso, 1985), p. 44.
125 Ibid.
126 Winter, *Death's Men*, pp. 38–9.
127 Davidson, reel 1.
128 Ibid.
129 M. Foucault. *Discipline and Punish: The Birth of the Prison* (New York: Vintage, 2012), p. 135.
130 Duffett, *Stomach for Fighting*, p. 204.

3 Lives on the line: Active service

1 IWM, 17248, Private Papers of S. Roberts, p. 158.
2 Ibid.
3 R. Holmes, *Tommy: The British Soldier on the Western Front, 1914–1918*, Kindle edition (London: HarperCollins, 2004), loc. 613.
4 Ibid., loc. 4805.
5 P. Cornish, 'The Daily Life of Soldiers' World War One', The British Library, https://www.bl.uk/world-war-one/articles/the-daily-life-of-soldiers#authorBlock1 (accessed 31 August 2017).
6 D. Eaton, *At the Going Down of the Sun: The Men from Clayton Who Died in the Two World Wars* (Durham: Roundtuit, 2007), pp. 42–3.
7 IWM SA, 27424, G. L. P. Hollis, reel 1.
8 IWM SA, 26877, C. A. Swales, reel 2.
9 IWM SA, 24550, W. Ward, reel 2.
10 R. Gervais, *The Silent Sixtieth 100 Years On* (Victoria: Friesen Press, 2014), p. 159.
11 IWM, 11905, Private Papers of F. Philipson.
12 Ibid., pp. 9–12.
13 IWM, 20211, Private Papers of F. Hubard, Letter to Mr and Mrs Underhill, dated 7 September 2015.
14 IWM, 11625, Private Papers of W. Fowler (Hicken), p. 8.
15 Anecdotal evidence from members of the armed forces today attest that can often still be the case, as this attendance at sick parade can be ordered but often times needs to be self-determined as necessary first.
16 Great Britain War Office, *Manual of Military Cooking and Dietary, Mobilisation, 1915* (London, HMSO, 1915), pp. 48–50.
17 Ibid., p. 60.
18 IWM, 7715, Private Papers of T. A. Silver, pp. 4–7. In this account, 'Medicine and Duty' potentially refers to the patient being given activities such as massage or to clean his feet instead of being removed completely from the line. Robert Atenstaedt makes the point that in 1915 training was introduced to encourage men to massage their feet back to help, rather than pull them completely off the line. R. Atenstaedt, *The Medical Response to the Trench Diseases in World War One* (Newcastle: Cambridge Scholars, 2011), p. 171.
19 Ibid.

20 M. Harrison, *The Medical War: British Military Medicine in the First World War* (Oxford: Oxford University Press, 2010), p. 129.
21 Great Britain War Office, *Royal Army Medical Corps Training Manual* (London: HMSO, 1911), pp. 64–5.
22 Atenstaedt, *Medical Response to the Trench Diseases*, p. 199.
23 Ibid., pp. 198–9.
24 Great Britain War Office, *Royal Army Medical Corps Training Manual*, pp. 22–3.
25 Ibid., p. 23.
26 IWM, 11876, Private Papers of C. R. Keller, pp. 26–7. In relation to the difference between British and French hygiene, it has already been noted that the French soldiers were famed and nicknamed for their commonly more rugged appearance. Additionally, Zdatny argues in an article on historic French hygiene that France was slower to adopt to twentieth-century hygiene practices than Britain or Germany. Bathing had been a slow cultural adoption in the nineteenth century, and sanitary reform developed across France as a by-product of rebuilding post-war and the spread of American brands linked to a rise in consumerism. With these aspects in mind, it is understandable why the British soldiers may have seemed overly obsessed with hygiene. S. Zdatny, 'The French Hygiene Offensive of the 1950s: A Critical Moment in the History of Manners', *Journal of Modern History*, vol. 84, no. 4 (December 2012), pp. 897–932.
27 IWM SA, 11040, J. W. Watson, reel 3.
28 I. Rosenberg, *Selected Poems and Letters Reprint* (London: Enitharmon Press, 2003), p. 99.
29 Ibid.
30 Holmes, *Tommy*, loc. 10142.
31 J. Evans and A. Withey, 'Introduction', in J. Evans and A. Withey (eds), *New Perspectives on the History of Facial Hair: Framing the Face* (London: Palgrave Macmillan, 2018), p. 5.
32 A. Clayton, *Paths of Glory, the French Army 1914–18* (London: Cassel, 2005), p. 73.
33 C. Oldstone-Moore, *Of Beards and Men: The Revealing History of Facial Hair* (Chicago: University of Chicago Press, 2015), p. 215.
34 C. Oldstone-Moore, 'The Beard Movement in Victorian Britain', *Victorian Studies*, vol. 48, no. 1 (2005), p. 13, pp. 7–34.
35 HC Debate, 31 October 1934, vol. 293, cc201-71.
36 General Sir N. Macready, *Annals of an Active Life* (London: Hutchinso,1924), pp. 258–9.
37 The author of this book feels that it is only fair to ask for recognition of his incredible self-restraint by not including at any point in this section of the analysis a pun relating to how this repeal constituted a 'close shave' in relation to power dynamics between the soldier and the British military.
38 Harrison, *Medical War*, pp. 141–4; Anne Hardy, '"Straight Back to Barbarism": Antityphoid Inoculation and the Great War, 1914', *Bulletin of the History of Medicine*, vol. 74, no. 2 (2000), pp. 265–90.
39 'Research in War', *The Times* (8 February 1919), p. 5.
40 Harrison, *Medical War*, p. 144.
41 Hardy, 'Straight Back to Barbarism', p. 265.
42 IWM, 17248, Private Papers of S. Roberts, p. 159.
43 IWM SA, 8764, L. J. Stagg, reel 1.
44 IWM SA, 315, T. Mitchell-Fox, reel 3.

45 For more information, see D. Brunton, *The Politics of Vaccination: Practice and Policy in England, Wales, Ireland and Scotland* (Suffolk: University of Rochester Press, 2008), pp. 91–105; N. Durbach, *Bodily Matters: The Anti-Vaccination Movement in England* (Durham, NC: Duke University Press, 2005), p. 159, pp. 238–43.
46 HC Debate, 17 November 1914, vol. 68, cols 318–19. Note: Prior to the First World War, the term 'conscientious objector' commonly referred to those who refused vaccination on moral or religious grounds.
47 Harrison, *Medical War*, pp. 148–9.
48 G. Sims Woodhead, 'Preventative Inoculation', *Journal of the Royal Sanitary Institute*, vol. 36 (1915), p. 23.
49 Ibid.
50 HC Debate, 7 January 1915, vol. 18, cols 341–6.
51 HC Debate, 4 February 1915, vol. 69, cols 139–40.
52 HC Debate, 7 January 1915, vol. 18, cols 341–6. The use of the phrase 'conscientious objector' here relates to its original meaning, referring to those who legally refused smallpox vaccination after the enactment of the 1898 Smallpox Act.
53 Ibid.
54 IWM SA, 4609, J. B. Masefield, reel 1.
55 IWM, 17138, Private Papers of F. Watson, Letter to his mother dated 1915.
56 IWM SA, 577, W. E. Clarke, reel 1.
57 Woodhead, 'Preventative Inoculation', p. 23.
58 HC Debate, 2 November 1916, vol. 86, cols 1854W.
59 Ibid.
60 S. Walker, 'The Greater Good: Agency and Inoculation in the British Army, 1914–1918', *Canadian Bulletin of Medical History*, vol. 36 (2019), pp. 131–57.
61 F. Reid, *Medicine in First World War Europe: Soldiers, Medics, Pacifists* (London: Bloomsbury, 2017), p. 44.
62 Major T. J. Mitchell and G. M. Smith, *Medical Services: Casualties and Medical Statistics of the Great War* (London: H. M. Stationery Office, 1931), p. 144.
63 J. R. Novak et al., 'Associations between Masculine Norms and Health-Care Utilization in Highly Religious, Heterosexual Men', *American Journal of Men's Health*, vol. 13, no. 3 (2019), p. 8.
64 Ibid.
65 IWM SA, 4440, O. Croft, reel 2.
66 IWM SA, 9263, E. Booth, reel 3.
67 IWM, 14937, Private Papers of Lieutenant P. Erskine, p. 71.
68 IWM, 11625, Private Papers of W. Fowler (Hicken), p. 11.
69 IWM, 863, Private Papers of R. G. Prew, p. 9.
70 IWM SA, 11440, W. Hare, reel 7.
71 IWM, 17236, Private Papers of T. C. Reynolds, p. 4.
72 It is difficult to ascertain why the emergency ration that was only supposed to be eaten on the command of the ranking officer was referred to as the 'Iron Ration'; common assumption is that this originated from the metal tins that the rations were kept in. A 1921 dictionary claimed, 'Iron Ration is adapted from Ger. Eiserne portion used of a reserve ration enclosed in a metal case.' E. Weekley, *An Etymological Dictionary of Modern English, Volume 1* (London: John Murray, 1921), p. 771.
73 R. Duffett, *The Stomach for Fighting: Food and Soldiers of the Great War* (Manchester: Manchester University Press, 2012), pp. 110–11.
74 IWM, 11545, Private Papers of H. N. Peyton, p. 2.

75 O. Creighton, *Letters of Oswin Creighton, C. F., 1883-1918*, Electronic edition (London: Hard Press, 1923), loc. 3639.
76 Ibid.
77 IWM, 13108, Private Papers of P. Whitehouse, p. 6.
78 IWM, 8408, Private Papers of C. A. Niblett, p. 4. 'Crown and Anchor' was a simple gambling dice game that was originally popular with British sailors. See W. M. Mark, *Everyday Probability and Statistics: Health, Elections, Gambling and War*, 2nd ed. (London: Imperial College Press, 2012), p. 53.
79 'With "Spit" Held by Rifles, a Spade, and a Couple of Sticks: Cooking the Christmas Geese at the Front', *Illustrated War News*, 10 December 1914 (Part 2), p. 45.
80 Duffett, *Stomach for Fighting*, p. 204.
81 IWM, 11876, Private Papers of C. R. Keller, pp. 32-3.
82 Ibid., p.33.
83 IWM, 11765, Second Lieutenant W. Lindsay, Letter dated 15 July 2015.
84 Duffett, *Stomach for Fighting*, p. 197.
85 University of St Andrews Archive/Special Collections, MSDEP121/8/3/6/1/3 1917, Letters and collection of Lt. Col. Philip George Anstruther.
86 IWM, 1878, Private Papers of S. E. Butler, p. 44.
87 IWM, 13108, Private Papers of P. Whitehouse, p. 6.
88 I. Beckett, T. Bowman and M. Connelly, *The British Army and the First World War* (St Ives: Cambridge University Press, 2017), p. 150.
89 Anon, *British Pharmaceutical Codex Pub Pharmaceutical Society* (London: The Pharmaceutical Society, 1907), p. 69.
90 Great Britain War Office, *Field Service Manual, Infantry Battalion* (London: HMSO, 1914), p. 54.
91 A. Weeks, *Tea, Rum and Fags, Sustaining Tommy 1914-1918* (Stroud: History Press, 2009), p. 21.
92 R. Phillips, *Alcohol: A History* (Chapel Hill: University of North Carolina Press, 2014), p. 242.
93 IWM, 16428, Private Papers of E. Stapleton, p. 21.
94 IWM, 22065, Private Papers of R. McKay, p. 51.
95 IWM SA, 10115, E. Bigwood, reel 1.
96 IWM SA, 12236, A. West, reel 4.
97 IWM SA, 15435 F. Ching, reel 4.
98 IWM SA, 8865, C. B. Tubbs, reel 3.
99 IWM SA, 12231, J. Yarwood, reel 2.
100 J. Supitup, 'The Drink Habit - Advert', *Wipers Times* (10 April 1917), p. 2.
101 E. Jones, 'Alcohol Use and Misuse Within the Military: A Review', *International Review of Psychiatry*, vol. 23 (April 2011), pp. 166-7.
102 Ibid.
103 IWM, 7244, Private Papers of H. G. Perry, Diary entry, 12 August 2016.
104 IWM SA, 8270, P. V. Harris, reel 1.
105 IWM, 16435, Private Papers of G. Thorley, p. 34.
106 IWM SA, 15435 F. Ching, reel 4.
107 University of St Andrews Archive/Special Collections, MS38961/2, Letters of Lieutenant Stiven, Letter to his parents, dated 31 October 1915, pp. 3-4. Source is presented exactly as is written within the records of Lieutenant Stiven.
108 G. R. Iriam, *In the Trenches 1914-1918* (Indiana: ebookit.com, 2011), p. 155.
109 IWM SA, 9552, B. Farrer, reels 8-9.

110 Ibid.
111 IWM SA, 33034, F. T. J. Lancaster, reel 1. The British were not the only soldiers who could be incapacitated by alcohol. On 20 October 1918, the *New York Times* reported that drunken German troops were taken unawares by Belgian forces advancing into the area. Anon, 'Left Soldiers behind to Destroy Ostend but Unofficered Men Got Drunk and Failed to Set Off Mines before the Belgians Arrived', *New York Times* (20 October 1918), p. 5.
112 IWM, 11617, Private Papers of 2nd Lieutenant A. M. McCracken, p. 13.
113 J. Putkowski and J. Sykes, *Shot at Dawn: Executions in World War One by Authority of the British Army Act*, Kindle edition (Barnsley: Pen and Sword, 2007), loc. 471.
114 Ibid., loc. 1083.
115 J. Bourke, *Dismembering the Male, Men's Bodies, Britain and the Great War* (London: Reaktion Books, 1999), pp. 156–60; and B. Cherry, *They Didn't Want to Die Virgins: Sex and Morale in the British Army on the Western Front 1914–1918* (Wolverhampton: Helion, 2016).
116 J. Weeks and K. Porter, *Between the Acts: Lives of Homosexual Men 1885–1967* (London: Rivers Oram, 1998), p. 6.
117 G. Robb, *British Culture and the First World War* (London: Palgrave, 2015), p. 83.
118 A. D. Harvey, 'Homosexuality and the British Army during the First World War', *Journal of the Society for Army Historical Research*, vol. 79, no. 320 (Winter 2001), pp. 313–14.
119 Ibid., p. 316.
120 Ibid., p. 318.
121 Ibid., p. 319.
122 R. Norton (ed.), *My Dear Boy: Gay Love Letters through the Centuries* (San Francisco, CA: Leyland, 1998), pp. 210, 235.
123 P. Fussell, *The Great War and Modern Memory* (Oxford: Oxford University Press, 1975), p. 273.
124 IWM SA, 9339, W. Holbrook, reel 2.
125 Ibid., reel 6.
126 E. Goffman, *Behaviour in Public Places* (New York: Free Press, 1966), p. 30.
127 Weeks and Porter, *Between the Acts*, p. 6.
128 Ibid., p. 7.
129 Ibid., p. 16.
130 J. Ward, *Not Gay: Sex between Straight White Men* (New York: New York University Press, 2015).
131 Ibid., p. 164.
132 Ibid., p. 168.
133 A. Belkin, *Bring Me Men: Military Masculinity and the Benign Facade of American Empire, 1898–2001* (London: C. Hurst, 2012), p. 80.
134 Holmes, *Tommy*, p. 11.
135 Ward, *Not Gay*, p. 163.
136 C. Makepeace, 'Male Heterosexuality and Prostitution during the Great War', *Cultural and Social History*, vol. 9, no. 1 (2012), p. 71.
137 Ibid., p. 73.
138 Anon, '"The Control of Veneral Diseases"', *BMJ*, vol. 1 (1916), p. 597.
139 Thomas Barlow, Hubert M. Scuthwark, and M. R. C. S. Daddy, 'The Report of the Royal Commission on Venereal Diseases', *British Medical Journal*, vol. 2, no. 2907 (1916), p. 408.

140 Ibid., p. 70.
141 IWM, 3453, Private Papers of E. C. Barraclough, pp. 1–2.
142 IWM SA, 9875, G. Ashurst, reel 8.
143 Ibid.
144 IWM, 1467, Private Papers of Lieutenant P. Creek, pp. 59–60.
145 IWM SA, 10768, J. Grainger, reel 3.
146 IWM SA, 9339, W. Holbrook, reel 2.
147 IWM SA, 9364, R. E. Bethell, reel 5.
148 P. Levine, *Prostitution, Race, and Politics: Policing Venereal Disease in the British Empire* (New York: Routledge, 2003), p. 145.
149 IWM, 22369, Private Papers of A. Surfleet, Preface.
150 Anon, 'The Control of Veneral Diseases', *BMJ*, vol. 1 (1916), p. 597.
151 P. Simkins, 'Soldiers and Civilians: Billeting in Britain and France', in I. Beckett and K. Simpson (eds), *A Nation in Arms: A Social Study of the British Army in the First World War* (Barnsley: Pen and Sword, 1985), pp. 187–8.
152 Harrison, *Medical War*, p. 157.
153 M. Arthur, *Forgotten Voices of the Great War* (St Ives: Random House, 2011), p. 94.
154 Ibid.
155 IWM SA, 9894, J. A. Payne, reel 5.
156 Ibid., reel 6.
157 Ibid.
158 IWM SA, 24540, R. Trafford, reel 1.
159 Ibid.
160 M. Harrison, 'The British Army and Venereal Disease during the First World War', *Medical History*, vol. 39 (1995), p. 141.
161 L. Hall, 'War Brings It On', in R. Cooter, M. Harrison and S. Sturdy (eds), *Medicine and Modern Warfare* (Amsterdam: Clio Medica, 1999), p. 212.

4   Bodies under fire: The front line

1 Anon, 'A Day in the Trenches', in G. Cooke (ed.), *Poetry and Writing of the First World War* (London: Lulu.com, 2015), p. 34. This account is presented exactly as quoted in Cooke.
2 IWM, 6827, Private Papers of Major W. J. Nicholson, p. 17.
3 R. Duffett. *The Stomach for Fighting: Food and the Soldiers of the Great War* (Manchester: Manchester University Press, 2012), p. 111.
4 IWM SA, 12258, W. Maltby, reel 1.
5 IWM SA, 8866, W. T. Cowley, reel 2.
6 IWM SA, 10418, A. D. McGuirk, reel 2.
7 IWM SA, 9177, T. A. Olive, reel 1.
8 IWM, 8408, Private Papers of C. A. Niblett, p. 4.
9 Duffett, *Stomach for Fighting*, p. 35.
10 Ibid., pp. 34–7.
11 IWM, 13108, Private Papers of P. Whitehouse, p. 32.
12 IWM, 4222, C. Shepherd, reel 1.
13 S. M. Gillon and C. D. Matson, *The American Experiment: A History of the United States Volume 1: To 1877* (Boston, MA: Wadsworth, 2013), p. 434.

14 IWM, EPH 1513, Picture Frame, Army Biscuit.
15 Major R. J. C. Cottell, 'The Medical Services in the First Line', *Journal of the Royal Army Medical Corps*, vol. 1 (1903), p. 303.
16 IWM, 16428, Private Papers of E. Stapleton, p. 11.
17 IWM SA, 577, W. E. Clarke, reel 2.
18 IWM SA, 8257, S. J. Moyle, reel 3.
19 Ibid.
20 G. L. Rottman, *The Hand Grenade* (Oxford: Osprey, 2015), p. 67.
21 IWM SA, 8257, S. J. Moyle, reel 4.
22 TNA, Experiments of new trench weapons – WO 142/272, p. 41.
23 Ibid.
24 IWM SA, 8342, A. Burnet, reel 5.
25 Ibid.
26 IWM, 12149, Private Papers of W. Cook, p. 24.
27 P. Simkins, *From the Somme to Victory: The British Army's Experience on the Western Front 1916–1918* (London: Pen and Sword, 2014).
28 IWM SA, 24550, W. Ward, reel 2.
29 IWM, 11876, Private Papers of C. R. Keller, pp. 52–3.
30 IWM SA, 9993, A. C. Williams, reel 2.
31 Ibid.
32 IWM, 17426, Private Papers of C. Shaw, pp. 6–7.
33 Ibid., p. 7.
34 IWM, 1878, Private Papers of A. C. Warsop, p. 16.
35 A. Kellett, *Combat Motivation: The Behaviour of Soldiers in Battle* (New York: Springer, 1982), p. 305.
36 C. R. Figley and W. P. Nash, *Combat Stress Injury: Theory, Research, and Management* (New York:: Routledge, 2015), p. 25.
37 Ibid.
38 L. Noakes, '"War on the Web": The BBC "People's War" Website and Memories of Fear in Wartime in 21st Century Britain', in L. Noakes and J. Pattinson (eds), *British Cultural Memory and the Second World War* (London: Bloomsbury Academic, 2013), p. 57.
39 Ibid.
40 Anon, *Report of the War Committee of Enquiry into 'Shell-Shock'* (London: HMSO, 1922), p. 203.
41 IWM SA, 24550, W. Ward, reel 2.
42 Quoted in P. Hart, *Gallipoli*, Kindle edition (London, Profile Books, 2011), p. 242.
43 IWM SA, 8949, G. T. Archer, reel 2.
44 Anon, *Games and Sports in the Army Handbook*, (London: HMSO, 1931), Preface.
45 R. M. Sapolsky, *Why Zebra's Don't Get Ulcers: The Updated Guide to Stress, Stress Related Disease and Coping* (New York: W. H. Freeman, 1998), p.194.
46 E. Mattson, 'Adrenaline and Post Traumatic Stress Disorder (PTSD)', *Veterans Today* (2011), https://www.veteranstodayarchives.com/2011/06/20/adrenaline-and-post-traumatic-stress-disorder-ptsd/ (assessed 1 March 2017).
47 University of St. Andrews Archive/Special Collections, MS38961/2 Private letters of David Sime Stiven, p. 2 – Stiven is talking about the sinking of the *Lusitania*, an American ship that was sank in 1915 by the German Navy, the attack on Scarborough by the German Navy in December 1914 and the execution of the Nurse Edith Cavell by German firing squad on 12October 1915 after being found guilty by court martial

of aiding British and French soldiers. All of these events had an international outcry and were used to galvanize propaganda against the Germans and goad men into joining up.
48   G. Dawson, *Soldier Heroes, British Adventure, Empire and the Imaging of Masculinities* (New York: Routledge, 2005), p. 92.
49   J. Bourke, *An Intimate History of Killing: Face to Face Killing in Twentieth-Century Warfare* (London: Granta Books, 1999), p. 1.
50   Ibid., p. 2.
51   N. Ferguson, *The Pity of War* (London: Penguin Press, 1998), p. 447.
52   IWM SA, 9928, R. Pugh, reel 1.
53   Ibid.
54   Ibid.
55   Quoted in Bourke, *History of Killing*, p. 113.
56   IWM SA, 9987, H. Bashford, reel 3.
57   IWM, 1374, Private Papers of Lieutenant G. M. Renny, letter dated April 1917.
58   IWM, 1876, Private Papers of A. C. Warsop, pp. 16–17.
59   IWM SA, 10168, D. Price, reel 10.
60   Ibid.
61   IWM SA, 8866, W. T. Cowley, reel 2.
62   IWM SA, 1963, Corporal E. W. Glendinning, reel 1.
63   J. Tosh, *A Man's Place: Masculinity and the Middle-Class Home in Victorian England* (London: Yale University Press, 2007), p. 184.
64   IWM SA, 1963, Corporal E. W. Glendinning, reel 1.
65   IWM SA, 12679, R. Renwick, reel 4.
66   B. Shephard, *A War of Nerves: Soldiers and Psychiatrists 1914–1994* (London: Pimlico, 2002), p. 3.
67   T. Loughran, *Shellshock and Medical Culture in First World War Britain* (Cambridge: Cambridge University Press, 2016), p. 182.
68   Account of R. Hodgkinson speech to Guy's Hospital Physiological Society, 'Fear – the Major Emotion in War' (28 February 1919), as quoted by Loughran, *Shell-Shock and Medical Culture*, p. 182.
69   IWM, 863, Private Papers of R. G. Prew, p. 12.
70   Quoted in M. Arthur, *Forgotten Voices of the Great War* (St Ives: Random House, 2011), p. 197.
71   IWM SA, 11943, E. Huggins, reel 4.
72   IWM, 12149, Private Papers of W. Cook, p. 24.
73   J. Putkowski and J. Sykes, *Shot at Dawn: Executions in World War One by Authority of the British Army Act* (Barnsley: Pen and Sword, 2007), p. 44.
74   Ibid.
75   Ibid., p.37.
76   IWM, 11876, Private Papers of C. R. Keller, p. 27.
77   E. Jones, 'The Psychology of Killing: The Combat Experience of British Soldiers during the First World War', *Journal of Contemporary History*, vol. 41, no. 2 (2006), p. 231.
78   W. H. Rivers, 'The Repression of War Experience', *Proceedings of the Royal Society of Medicine*, vol. 11 (1918), p. 2 (pp. 1–20).
79   For more information on the history of shell shock, see Shephard, *War of Nerves*, chapters 1–12; Jones, 'Psychology of Killing'; and Loughran, *Shell-Shock and Medical Culture*.

80 F. Reid, *Broken Men: Shellshock, Treatment and Recovery in Britain 1914–30* (London: Bloomsbury, 2012), p. 67.
81 Ibid., pp. 65–6.
82 IWM, 22065, Private Papers of R. McKay, p. 11.
83 IWM, 11876, Private Papers of C. R. Keller, p. 27. Source quoted exactly as printed within the Private Papers of Keller.
84 H. Strachan, *The Oxford Illustrated History of the First World War* (Oxford: Oxford University Press, 1998), p. 192.
85 HC Debate, 31 December 1916, vol. 88, col. 1738–63.
86 IWM, 11617, Private Papers of 2nd Lieutenant A. M. McCracken, p. 71.
87 H. McCartney, *Citizen Soldiers: The Liverpool Territorials in the First World War* (New York: Cambridge University Press, 2005), p. 166.
88 IWM, 15727, Private Papers of J. S. Gatley, p. 30.
89 E. Jones and N. Fear, 'Alcohol Use and Misuse within the Military: A Review', *International Review of Psychiatry*, vol. 23 (2011), p. 167.
90 IWM SA, 495, J. D. Pratt, reel 6. Source is presented exactly as spoken in his interview by J. D. Pratt.
91 Putkowski and Sykes, *Shot at Dawn*, Kindle edition, loc. 4672.
92 IWM, 14938, Private Papers of C. E. Jones, p. 4.
93 IWM, 2617, Private Papers of C. G. Templer, pp. 25–6.
94 IWM SA, 577, W. Clarke, reel 3.
95 IWM, 14938, Private Papers of C. E. Jones, p. 4.
96 IWM SA, 8287, F. Caokes, reel 1.
97 IWM, 11787, Private Papers of G. K. Parker, p. 31.
98 IWM, 15268, Private Papers of E. Grindley, no page number.
99 University of St Andrews Archive/Special Collections, msdep121/8/2/11/1/4, Letter from Robert Anstruther to his mother dated 20 September 2014.
100 IWM, 6827, Private Papers of Major W. J. Nicholson, p. 7.
101 IWM 11787, Private Papers of G. K. Parker, p. 26.
102 J. Bourke, *The Story of Pain: From Prayer to Painkillers* (Oxford: Oxford University Press, 2014), pp. 12–13.
103 J. A Gallishaw, 'Gallipoli', in F. Reynolds and A. L. Churchill (eds), *World's War Events, Recorded by Statesmen, Commanders, Historians and by Men Who Fought or Saw the Great Campaigns* (New York: P. F. Collier, 1919), p. 231.
104 Quoted in a BBC article, Bethan Bell, 'The Real-Life Wars Of *Dad's Army* Actor Arnold Ridley', *BBC News*, vol. 5 (2016), https://www.bbc.co.uk/news/uk-england-35491036#:~:text=He%20appeared%20in%20numerous%20shows,and%20had%20one%20child%2C%20Nicolas (accessed 13 December 2016).
105 IWM SA, 9875, G. Ashurst, reel 5. Emphasis added to highlight the tone in the oral history interview.
106 IWM, 7988, Private Papers of 2nd Lieutenant C. Carter, p. 20.
107 IWM, 11876, Private Papers of C. R. Keller, p. 41.
108 Ibid., p. 42.
109 A. Carden-Coyne, *The Politics of Wounds: Military Patients and Medical Power in the First World War* (Oxford: Oxford University Press, 2014), p. 8.
110 Ibid.
111 IWM SA, 24883, H. V. Stone, reel 1.
112 Ibid.

113 A. Carden-Coyne, *Gender and Conflict since 1914: Historical and Interdisciplinary Perspectives* (New York: Palgrave Macmillan, 2012), p. 49.
114 N. Barber, *World War I: The Western Front* (Lewis: White Thompson, 2003), p. 52.
115 Putkowski and Sykes, *Shot at Dawn*, p.18.
116 G. Coppard, *With a Machine Gun to Cambrai: The Tale of a Young Tommy in Kitchener's Army 1914–1918* (Great Britain: Cassell, 1999), p. 100.
117 IWM SA, 9875, G. Ashurst, reel 5.
118 J. Bourke, *Dismembering the Male, Men's Bodies, Britain and the Great War* (London: Reaktion Books, 1999), p. 77.
119 National Records of Scotland, SC70/8/418/2, Will of 4397 Private Purves or Robert Andrew Purves, 9th Bn., Royal Scots (Lothian Regiment), 1916. Note: Within Purves's letter, he uses '+' as an alternative to 'and'.
120 N. Thompson and G. Cox, *Handbook of the Sociology of Death, Grief and Bereavement: A Guide to Theory and Practice* (New York: Routledge, 2017), p. 23.
121 IWM, 14938, Private Papers of C. E. Jones, p. 17.
122 J. Padiak, 'Death by Suicide in the British Army, 1830–1900', in J. C. Weaver and D. Wright (eds), *Histories of Suicide, International Perspectives on Self-Destruction in the Modern World* (Toronto: University of Toronto, 2009), pp. 119–20.
123 C. P. McDowell, J. M. Rothberg and R. G. Lande, 'Homicide and Suicide in the Military', in F. D. Jones (ed.), *Military Psychiatry: Preparing in Peace for War* (Washington, DC: Office of the Surgeon General at TMM Publications, 2000), p. 102.
124 R. Holmes and S. Holmes, *Suicide: Theory, Practice and Investigation* (London: Sage, 2005), p. 81.
125 IWM SA, 32171, J. C. (Jonas) Hart, reel 3.
126 IWM SA, 8342, A. Burnett, reel 2.
127 S. H. Walker, '"Silent Voices": British Soldier Suicides in the First World War', in H. Da Silva, P. Teodoro De Matos and J. M. Sardica (eds), *War Hecatomb: International Effects on Public Health, Demography and Mentalities in the 20th Century* (Lisbon: Peter Lang, 2019), p. 58.
128 J. Bourke, *Fear: A Cultural History* (London: Virago, 2005), pp. 199–200.

5 Soldiers no more: Death, debilitation and demobilization

1 J. Winter, 'Army and Society: The Demographic Context', in I. Beckett and K. Simpson (eds), *A Nation in Arms: A Social Study of the British Army in the First World War* (Manchester: Manchester University Press, 1985), p. 201.
2 E. Kuhlman, *Of Little Comfort: War Widows, Fallen Soldiers, and the Remaking of Nation* (New York: New York University Press, 2012), p. 3.
3 M. Harrison, *The Medical War: British Military Medicine in the First World War* (Oxford: Oxford University Press, 2012), pp. 130–1.
4 R. Wilson, 'The Burial of the Dead: The British Army on the Western Front, 1914–18', *War & Society*, vol. 31, no. 1 (2012), p. 28.
5 Ibid.
6 J. Geurst, *Cemeteries of the Great War by Sir Edwin Lutyens* (Rotterdam: 010 Publishers, 2010), p. 13.

7 L. Wittman, *The Tomb of the Unknown Soldier, Modern Mourning and the Reinvention of the Mystical Body* (Toronto: University of Toronto Press, 2011), p. 54.
8 Anon, 'Soldiers' Graves', *The Times*, 18 September 1916, p. 5.
9 Ibid.
10 J. Winter, *Sites of Memory, Sites of Mourning: The Great War in European Cultural History* (Cambridge: Cambridge University Press, 1995), p. 23.
11 D. Davies, *The Theology of Death* (London: T&T Clark, 2008), p. 128.
12 HC Deb, 14 November 1916, vol. 87, cc567-8.
13 HC Deb 9 May 1916, vol. 82, cc448-9.
14 J. H. Mills and S. Sen, 'Introduction', in J. H. Mills and S. Sen (eds), *Confronting the Body: The Politics of Physicality in Colonial and Post-Colonial India* (London: Wimbledon, 2004), p. 4. The relationship between Indian and Britain in relation to the First World War is complicated and demands more attention that is possible within this review. Many seminal works have considered this in detail including: K. Coates-Ulrichsen, 'Learning the Hard Way: The Indian Army in Mesopotamia 1914–1918', in R. Johnson (ed.), *The British Indian Army: Virtue and Necessity* (Newcastle Upon Tyne: Cambridge Scholars, 2014), pp. 51–64; G. Morton-Jack, *The Indian Army on the Western Front*, South Asia edition (Cambridge: Cambridge University Press, 2014); K. Roy, *Indian Army and the First World War: 1914–18* (Oxford: Oxford University Press, 2018); I. Cardozo, *The Indian Army in World War I, 1914–1918* (New York: Routledge, 2019); S. N. Saxena, *Role of Indian Army in the First World War* (Delhi: Bhrava Prakashan, 1987); and R. Long and I. Talbot (eds), *India and World War I: A Centennial Assessment* (New York: Routledge, 2018).
15 Anon, 'Report: India and the Commonwealth War Graves Commission', in *Commonwealth War Graves Commission* (London: HMSO, 2007), pp. 1–3.
16 T. Barringer, 'An Architecture of Imperial Ambivalence: The Patcham Chattri', in M. J. K. Walsh and A. Varnava (eds), *The Great War and the British Empire Culture and Society* (Oxon: Routledge, 2017), p. 248.
17 Ibid., p. 248.
18 Image referenced from H. J. Gladstone, *William G. C. Gladstone: A Memoir* (London: Nisbet, 1918), p. 121.
19 J. Strange, *Death, Grief and Poverty in Britain 1870–1914* (New York: Cambridge University Press, 2005), p. 267.
20 Ibid.
21 R. van Emden and S. Humphries, *The Quick and the Dead* (London: Bloomsbury, 2012), pp. 132–3.
22 HC Deb, 18 November 1914, vol. 68, c435W.
23 HC Deb, 4 February 1915, vol. 69, cc140-1.
24 Ibid.
25 HC Deb, 19 October 1915, vol. 74, cc1629-30W.
26 HC Deb, 31 January 1918, vol. 101, cc1773-4W.
27 IWM SA, 33696, A. H. Wright (Alec), reel 1.
28 IWM, 11787, Private Papers of G. K. Parker, p. 28.
29 S. H. Walker, 'Saving Bodies and Souls: Army Chaplains and Medical Care in the First World War', *Postgraduate Journal of Medical Humanities*, vol. 3 (2016), p. 36.
30 T. Hampson MC and T. P. Davies. (eds), *A Medical Officer's Diary and Narrative of the First World War*, http://www.ciaofamiglia.com/jcsproule/WWI_PDFS/Travis-Hampson-Diary/A-Medical-Officers-Diary-Travis-Hampson.pdf (accessed 1 September 2017).

31 D. P. Winnifrith, *The Church in the Fighting Line with General Smith-Dorrien at the Front: Being the Experiences of a Chaplain*, Electronic edition (London: Kessinger, 1915), loc. 1407.
32 Ibid.
33 Parker, p. 20.
34 IWM, 14991, Private Papers of 2nd Lieutenant J. T. Godfrey, letter dated 10 July 1916.
35 Winter, *Sites of Memory*, p. 36.
36 Ibid.
37 University of St Andrews Archive/Special Collections, MS38426/55. David Stiven Collection, Letter to David Stiven from Captain P. Skeil, 27 January 1917, pp. 2–3. Extract cited exactly as printed within the records of David Stiven.
38 IWM, Q7815, Dead soldiers of one of the Highlanders regiments awaiting burial, August 1917, Photograph taken by Lieutenant J. W. Brooke (3 August 1917).
39 E. Newlands, *Civilians into Soldiers: War, the Body and British Army Recruits, 1939–45* (Manchester: Manchester University Press, 2014), p. 161.
40 IWM SA, 9434, W. J. Collins, reel 10.
41 J. Brophy and E. Partridge, *The Long Trail Songs and Slang of the British Soldier: 1914–18* (London: E. Partridge, 1930), p. 136.
42 IWM SA, 9434, W. J. Collins, reel 10.
43 Meyer also explains that the inverse to this dismissal of their ability and character occurred towards the end of the First World War as recognition of the hardships and sacrifice of these men also gave them the nickname 'Knights of the Red Cross', which Meyer succinctly describes as 'the non-combatant version of the apotheosis of heroic wartime masculinity achieved by combatants through death'. J. Meyer, *An Equal Burden: The Men of the Royal Army Medical Corps in the First World War* (Oxford: Oxford University Press, 2019), p. 179.
44 IWM SA, 9419, T. Bracey, reel 8.
45 Meyer, *Burden*, p. 157.
46 Molly Sutphen, 'Striving to be Separate', in R. Cooter et al. (eds), *War, Medicine and Modernity* (Thrupp: Sutton, 1998), pp. 48–9.
47 IWM, 22065, Private Papers of R. McKay, p. 19.
48 E. R. Mayhew, *Wounded: From Battlefield to Blighty, 1914–1918*, Kindle edition (Leicester: Thorpe, 2014), loc. 420.
49 Ibid.
50 T. J. Mitchell and G. M. Smith, *Medical Services: Casualties and Medical Statistics of the Great War* (London: HMSO, 1931), p. 7.
51 Ibid., p. 12.
52 IWM, 1876, Private Papers of A. C. Warsop, pp. 16–17.
53 IWM, 16647, Private Papers of T. O. Thirtle, p. 15.
54 I. Gordon, *Lifeline: A British Casualty Clearing Station on the Western Front, 1918* (Stroud: History Press, 2013), p. 31.
55 G. Grey Turner, 'The Importance of General Principles in Military Surgery', *Journal of Royal Army Med Corps*, vol. 26 (1916, p. 577. Emphasis is given in the original source.
56 A. Carden-Coyne, *The Politics of Wounds: Military Patients and Medical Power in the First World War* (Oxford: Oxford University Press, 2014), p. 192.
57 IWM, 2614, Private Papers of P. G. Copson, p. 12.
58 University of St Andrews Archive/Special Collections, MSDEP121/8/2/10/1/5, Letter from 'Rosie to Lady Anstruther', undated. Emphasis given in the letter.
59 Carden-Coyne, *Politics of Wounds*, p. 215.

60 IWM, 7988, Private Papers of 2nd Lieutenant C. Carter, p. 20.
61 J. Reznick, *Healing the Nation: Soldiers and the Culture of Caregiving in Britain during the Great War* (Manchester: Manchester University Press, 2004), p. 111; and Carden-Coyne, *Politics of Wounds*, p. 215.
62 Parker, p. 16.
63 IWM, 863, Private Papers of R. G. Prew, p. 27.
64 A. Fell, 'Afterword: Remembering the First World War Nurse and Britain and France', in A. Fell and C. Hallett (eds), *First World War Nursing: New Perspectives* (New York: Routledge, 2013), p. 173.
65 IWM, 14938, Private Papers of C. E. Jones, p. 5.
66 IWM, 7988, Private Papers of 2nd Lieutenant C. Carter, p. 20.
67 IWM SA, 11582, A. Hurst, reel 9.
68 F. Reid, 'Losing Face: Trauma and Maxillofacial Injury in the First World War', in J. Crouthamel and P. Leese (eds), *Psychological Trauma and the Legacies of the First World War* (Switzerland: Palgrave Macmillan, 2017), pp. 30–1.
69 Ibid., p. 31.
70 Mayhew, *Wounded*, loc. 2666.
71 IWM, 11765, Private Papers of Second Lieutenant W. Lindsay, letter dated 30 August 1915.
72 H. Stinton and V. Mayo (eds), *Harry's War: A British Tommy's Experience in the Trenches in World War One* (London: Bloomsbury, 2002), pp. 217–18. Note: 'Permanent Base' meant that men were deemed no longer suitable for active service and restricted to base duties only.
73 IWM 16506, Private Papers of F. C. Lewis, p. 86.
74 Ibid., pp. 86–7. Extract is presented exactly as printed in Private Papers of F. C. Lewis.
75 M. Lloyd, *The London Scottish in the Great War* (London: Pen and Sword, 2000), p. 179.
76 P. E. Hodgkinson, *British Infantry Commanders in the First World War* (Surrey: Ashgate, 2015), p. 197.
77 S. Cohen, *Medical Services in the First World War* (Oxford: Shire, 2014), p. 101.
78 L. van Bergen, *Before My Helpless Sight: Suffering, Dying and Military Medicine on the Western Front, 1914–1918* (Surrey: Ashgate, 2009), p. 320.
79 Stinton and Mayo, *Harry's War*, p. 217.
80 IWM, 18542, Private Papers of A. Wells, no page numbers.
81 A. R. Seipp, *The Ordeal of Peace: Demobilisation and the Urban Experience in Britain and Germany, 1917–1921* (Farnham: Ashgate, 2010).
82 IWM, 12383, Private Papers of J. A. Johnston, pp. 149–50.
83 G. Cuthbertson, *Peace at Last: A Portrait of Armistice Day, 11 November 1918* (Cornwall: Yale University Press, 2019), p. 139.
84 Ibid, p. 140.
85 IWM SA, 9763, E. Verrall, reel 3.
86 Ibid.
87 IWM SA, 8327, H. Barrow, reel 7.
88 Ibid.
89 IWM SA, 7363, G. B. Jameson, reel 17.
90 IWM SA, 9546, J. Fox, reel 6.
91 IWM, 12383, Private Papers of J. A. Johnston, p. 150.
92 Ibid.
93 D. Winter, *Death's Men: Soldiers of the Great War* (London: Penguin, 1985), p. 109.

94 Ibid.
95 Ibid, p. 240.
96 HC Deb, 13 February 1919, vol. 112, cc306-7W.
97 HC Deb, 13 February 1919, vol. 112, c306W.
98 Account of Private Alexander Jamieson, 11th Battalion Royal Scots, 27th Brigade, 9th Division, quoted in P. Heart, *A Very British Victory*, Kindle edition (London: Hachette UK, 2010), loc. 8980.
99 HC Deb, 3 March 1919, vol. 113, cc51-2W.
100 IWM SA, 11461, H. Pettit, reel 6.
101 IWM SA, 8327, H. Barrow, reel 7.
102 IWM SA, 10600, J. Wainwright, reel 14.
103 IWM, SA, 10173, L. Fox, reel 4.
104 HC Debate, 24 March 1919, vol. 114, cols 59-61W.
105 P. Weaver and L. van Bergen, 'Death from 1918 Pandemic Influenza during the First World War: A Perspective from Personal and Anecdotal Evidence', *Influenza Other Respiratory Viruses*, vol. 5 (2014), p. 538.
106 van Bergen, *My Helpless Sight*, pp. 164–5.
107 IWM, 457, Still from *Soldier to Civilian*, British Government Film, 1918, reel 1, 03:37.
108 J. Hampton, *Disability and the Welfare State in Britain: Changes in Perception and Policy 1948–79* (Bristol: Polity Press, 2016), p. 37.
109 Ibid., p. 38.
110 A. Skelley, *The Victorian Army at Home: The Recruitment and Terms and Conditions of the British Regular 1859–1899* (London: Croom Helm, 1977), p. 217.
111 I. Beckett, T. Bowman and M. Connelly, *The British Army and the First World War* (St Ives, Cambridge University press, 2017), p. 168.
112 Ibid., pp. 168–9.
113 Ministry of Pensions, *Royal Warrant for the Pensions of Soldiers Disabled and of the Families and Dependents of Soldiers Deceased in Consequence of the Great War* (1918), p. 771.
114 Ibid.
115 Ibid.
116 Newlands, *Civilians into Soldiers*, p. 171.
117 IWM SA, 9520, F. E. Sumpter, reel 8.
118 Ibid., reel 7–8.
119 J. Anderson, *War, Disability and Rehabilitation in Britain: 'Soul of a Nation'* (Manchester: Manchester University Press, 2011), pp. 7–8.
120 IWM SA, 11041, W. Burdon, reel 3.
121 IWM, 12168, Private Papers of D. G. Denison, pp. 19–20.
122 Ibid.
123 HC Deb, 15 April 1919, vol. 114, cc2819-63.
124 Beckett, Bowman and Connelly, *British Army and the First World War*, p. 169.
125 D. Cohen, *The War Come Home: Disabled Veterans in Britain and Germany 1914–1939* (Berkeley: University of California Press, 2001), pp. 35–8.
126 Beckett, Bowman and Connelly, *British Army and the First World War*, p. 170.
127 J. Reznick, 'History at the Intersection of Disability and Public Health: The Case of John Galsworthy and Disabled Soldiers of the First World War', *Disability and Health Journal*, vol. 4 (2011), p. 26.
128 Cohen, *War Come Home*, pp. 17–19.

129 IWM SA, 12415, A. Walker, reel 4.
130 IWM, 1481, Private Papers of W. Floyd, Certificate of Employment during the War, 1919.
131 Ibid.
132 IWM SA, 11342, J. Biglin, reel 8.
133 IWM SA, 1987, J. Snailham, reel 6.
134 IWM, 486, 'Demobilisation', The Ministry of Information, 1918, reel 1, 2.24.
135 J. Havardi, *Projecting Britain at War: The National Character in British World War II Films* (Jefferson: McFarland, 2014), p. 68.
136 G. S. Messinger, *British Propaganda and the State in the First World War* (Manchester: Manchester University Press, 1992), p. 42.
137 IWM, 7976, Private Papers of F. B Wade, Postcard from Geo D. Roche, December 1919.
138 IWM, 12383, Private Papers of J. A. Johnston, p. 153.
139 T. Lynch, *Great War Britain Sheffield: Remembering 1914–18*, Kindle edition (Stroud: History Press, 2014), loc. 1553.
140 IWM SA, 6838, H. M. Benwell, reel 1.
141 'Soldier Suicide', *Birmingham Daily Gazette*, 30 November 1917, p. 3.
142 Anon, 'WWI Soldier Whose Remains Were Found 100 Years after His Death Is Laid to Rest with Full Military Honours', *The Telegraph*, 27 July 2016 (accessed 1 November 2017).

Conclusion: Bodies of war

1 I. Zweiniger-Bargielowska, *Managing the Body: Beauty, Health, and Fitness in Britain, 1800–1939* (Oxford: Oxford University Press, 2010), p. 64.
2 C. Barnett, *Britain and Her Army, 1509–1970: A Military, Political and Social Survey* (London: Allen Lane, 1970), p. 371.
3 G. Dawson, *Soldier Heroes, British Adventure, Empire and the Imaging of Masculinities* (New York: Routledge, 2005), p. 81; K. Roberts, '"All that is Best of the Modern Woman"?: Representations of Female Military Auxiliaries in British Popular Culture 1914–1919', in J. Meyer (ed.), *British Popular Culture and the First World War* (London: Brill, 2008), p. 101; and M. Albrinck, 'Humanitarians and He-Men: Recruitment Posters and the Masculine Ideal', in Pearl James (ed.), *Picture This: World War 1 Posters and Visual Culture* (London: University of Nebraska Press, 2009), pp. 277–87.
4 IWM, 17426, Private Papers of C. Shaw, p. 1.
5 J. Bourke, *Dismembering the Male: Men's Bodies, Britain and the Great War* (London: Reaktion Books, 1999), p. 172.
6 D. Silbey, 'Bodies and Cultures Collide: Enlistment, the Medical Exam and the British Working Class 1914–1916', *Social History of Medicine*, vol. 17, no. 1 (2004), p. 75.
7 IWM, 1878, Private Papers of S. E. Butler, p. 31.
8 IWM, 8013, Private Papers of F. Mulliss, p. 1.
9 D. Winter, *Death's Men: Soldiers of the Great War* (London: Penguin, 1985), p. 38.
10 R. Woodward, 'Locating Military Masculinities: Space, Place and the Formation of Gender Identity in the British Army', in P. Higate (ed.), *Military Masculinities: Identity and the State* (London: Praeger, 2003), p. 51.

11 IWM, 11804, Private Papers of C. W. Williams, p. 2.
12 IWM, 3453, Private Papers of E. C. Barraclough, pp. 1–2.
13 IWM, 1876, Private Papers of A. C. Warsop, p. 2.
14 IWM SA, 17311, R. Watson, reel 2.
15 IWM, 15015, Private Papers of W. H. Fox, p. 1.
16 D. Englander, 'Mutinies and Military Morale', in H. Strachan (ed.), *The Oxford Illustrated History of the First World War* (Oxford: Oxford University Press, 2014), p. 192.
17 J. Putkowski and J. Sykes, *Shot at Dawn: Executions in World War One by Authority of the British Army Act*, Kindle edition (Barnsley: Pen and Sword, 2007).
18 Ibid., loc. 837.
19 M. Foucault, *Discipline and Punish: The Birth of the Prison* (New York: Vintage, 2012), p. vi.
20 Meyer, *British Popular Culture*, p. 101; and R. Duffett, *The Stomach for Fighting: Food and the Soldiers of the Great War* (Manchester: Manchester University Press, 2012), p. 21.
21 IWM, 11545, Private Papers of H. N. Peyton, p. 2.
22 IWM, 17248, Private Papers of S. Roberts, pp. 11–12.
23 IWM, 2617, Private Papers of C. G. Templer, p. 6.
24 IWM, 1467, Private Papers of Lieutenant P. Creek, pp. 59–60.
25 IWM, 18542. Private Papers of A. Wells, no page numbers.
26 Winter, *Death's Men*, p. 109.
27 Bourke, *Dismembering the Male*; Meyer, *British Popular Culture*; Winter, *Death's Men*; R. van Emden, *Boy Soldiers of the Great War*, Kindle edition (London: Headline, 2005); G. Sheffield, *The Somme: A New History* (London: Cassell Military, 2003); P. Simkins, *Kitchener's Army: The Raising of the New Armies 1914–1916* (Manchester: Manchester University Press, 2007); H. Strachan, *The First World War: A New History* (London: Simon and Schuster, 2001); L. Macdonald, *Roses of No Man's Land* (London: Penguin Books, 1993); and E. R. Mayhew, *Wounded: From Battlefield to Blighty, 1914–1918*, Kindle edition (Leicester: Thorpe, 2014).
28 IWM 11787, Private Papers of G. K. Parker, p. 26.
29 G. Coppard, *With a Machine Gun to Cambrai: The Tale of a Young Tommy in Kitchener's Army 1914–1918* (London: Cassell, 1999), p. 100.
30 Bourke, *Dismembering the Male*, p. 77.
31 M. Harrison, *The Medical War: British Military Medicine in the First World War* (Oxford: Oxford University Press, 2012), p. 291.
32 Ibid., p. 144.
33 'Research in War', *The Times* (8 February 1919), p. 5.
34 Sheffield Archives, L.D. 1980/54/1 and 980/54/2, Private Papers of W. Broadhead.
35 IWM, 22369, Private Papers of A. Surfleet, Preface.
36 IWM SA, 11943, E. Huggins, reel 4.
37 Putkowski and Sykes, *Shot at Dawn*, p. 10.
38 Ibid., pp. 65–6.
39 P. Simkins, 'Soldiers and Civilians: Billeting in Britain and France', in I. Beckett and K. Simpson (eds), *A Nation in Arms: A Social Study of the British Army in the First World War* (Barnsley: Pen and Sword, 1985), p. 185.
40 G. Robb, *British Culture and the First World War* (London: Palgrave, 2015), p. 83.
41 V. Berridge, 'The Art of Medicine Drugs, Alcohol, and the First World War', *Lancet*, vol. 384 (2014), pp. 1840–1.

42 IWM, 16428, Private Papers of E. Stapleton, p. 21.
43 IWM SA, 15435 F. Ching, reel 4.
44 IWM SA, 8865, C. B. Tubbs, reel 3.
45 J. Meyer, *An Equal Burden: The Men of the Royal Army Medical Corps in the First World War* (Oxford: Oxford University Press, 2019), p. 179.
46 M. Harrison, 'Public Health and Medicine in British India: An Assessment of the British Contribution', *Bulletin of the Liverpool Medical History Society*, vol. 10 (1998), p. 45.
47 I. Whitehead, *Doctors in the Great War* (Barnsley: Pen and Sword, 1999), pp. 269–72.
48 Mayhew, *Wounded*.
49 IWM, 1876, Private Papers of A. C. Warsop, pp. 16–17.
50 IWM, 16647, Private Papers of T. O. Thirtle, p. 15.
51 A. Carden-Coyne, *The Politics of Wounds: Military Patients and Medical Power in the First World War* (Oxford: Oxford University Press, 2014), p. 215.
52 IWM, 7988, Private Papers of 2nd Lieutenant C. Carter, p. 20.
53 E. Kulman, *Of Little Comfort: War Widows, Fallen Soldiers, and the Remaking of Nation* (New York: New York University Press, 2012), p. 3.
54 IWM, 2880, Private Papers of G. S. Smith, no page numbers.
55 Winter, *Death's Men*, p. 109.
56 I. Beckett, T. Bowman and M. Connelly, *The British Army and the First World War* (St Ives: Cambridge University press, 2017), p. 169.
57 E. Newlands, *Civilians into Soldiers: War, the Body and British Army Recruits, 1939–45* (Manchester: Manchester University Press, 2014), p. 171.
58 IWM SA, 9520, F. E. Sumpter, reel 8.
59 IWM, 1481, Private Papers of W. Floyd, Certificate of Employment during the War, 1919.

Bibliography

Primary source materials

Archive material

Imperial War Museums (IWM)

Department of Documents
IWM, 10640, Sir Arthur Pinero's Recruitment Message (1914).
IWM, 11417, Private Papers of E. S. Styles.
IWM, 11425, Private Papers of H. G. Taylor.
IWM, 11545, Private Papers of H. N. Peyton.
IWM, 11617, Private Papers of Second Lieutenant A. M. McCracken.
IWM, 11625, Private Papers of W. Fowler (Hicken).
IWM, 11765, Private Papers of Second Lieutenant W. Lindsay.
IWM, 11787, Private Papers of G. K. Parker
IWM, 11804, Private Papers of C. W. Williams.
IWM, 11876, Private Papers of C. R. Keller.
IWM, 11905, Private Papers of F. Philipson.
IWM, 12149, Private Papers of W. Cook.
IWM, 12168, Private Papers of D. G. Denison.
IWM, 12369, Private Papers of G. Calverley.
IWM, 12383, Private Papers of J. A. Johnston.
IWM, 13108, Private Papers of P. Whitehouse.
IWM, 1374, Private Papers of Lieutenant G. M. Renny.
IWM, 14, Private Papers of F. J. Murfin.
IWM, 14165, Private Papers of T. Parks.
IWM, 1467, Private Papers of Lieutenant P. Creek.
IWM, 14729, Private Papers of Lieutenant G. Cotton.
IWM, 1481, Private Papers of W. Floyd.
IWM, 14937, Private Papers of Lieutenant P. Erskine.
IWM, 14938, Private papers of C. E. Jones.
IWM, 14991, Private Papers of Second Lieutenant J. T. Godfrey.
IWM, 15015, Private papers of W. H. Fox.
IWM, 15087, Private Papers of W. J. Sensecall.
IWM, 15268, Private Papers of E. Grindley.
IWM, 15333, Private Papers of Captain J. D. Mackie CBE.
IWM, 15727, Private Papers of J. S. Gatley.
IWM, 16428, Private Papers of E. Stapleton.
IWM, 16435, Private Papers of G. Thorley.
IWM, 16506, Private Papers of F. C. Lewis.
IWM, 16647, Private Papers of T. O. Thirtle.

IWM, 16692, Private Papers of Lieutenant H. L. North.
IWM, 16892, Private Papers of G. Crew.
IWM, 1693, Private Papers of G. Ewan.
IWM, 1698, Private Papers of H. Calvert.
IWM, 1700, Private Papers of H. G. Smith.
IWM, 17024, Private Papers of J. Brady.
IWM, 17138, Private Papers of F. Watson.
IWM, 17158, Private Papers of E. F. Flynn.
IWM, 17236, Private Papers of T. C. Reynolds.
IWM, 17248, Private Papers of S. Roberts.
IWM, 1742, Private Papers of C. Shaw.
IWM, 17631, Private Papers of Lieutenant B. A. Minnitt MC.
IWM, 17674, Private papers of E. Drage.
IWM, 18542, Private Papers of A. Wells.
IWM, 1876, Private Papers of A. C. Warsop.
IWM, 1878, Private Papers of S. E. Butler.
IWM, 20211, Private Papers of F. Hubard.
IWM, 20504, Private Papers of Lieutenant W. B. St Leger.
IWM, 20761, Private Papers of H. Milner.
IWM, 22065, Private Papers of R. McKay.
IWM, 22369, Private Papers of A. Surfleet.
IWM, 22718, Private Papers of Reverend E. V. Tanner.
IWM, 2614, Private Papers of P. G. Copson.
IWM, 2617, Private Papers of C. G. Templer.
IWM, 2624, Private Papers of J. M. Cordy.
IWM, 2797, Private Papers of C. G. Rickett.
IWM, 2880, Private Papers of G. S. Smith.
IWM, 3453, Private Papers of E. C. Barraclough.
IWM, 4872, Private Papers of T. A. Bickerton.
IWM, 6659, Private Papers of D. Starrett.
IWM, 6827, Private Papers of Major W. J. Nicholson.
IWM, 7104, Private papers of E. Buffey.
IWM, 7244, Private Papers of H. G. Perry.
IWM, 7275, Private Papers of Lieutenant K. Palmer.
IWM, 7715, Private Papers of T. A. Silver.
IWM, 7863, Private Papers of E. H. Lenfestey.
IWM, 7976, Private Papers of F. B. Wade.
IWM, 7988, Private Papers of Second Lieutenant C. Carter.
IWM, 8013, Private Papers of F. Mulliss.
IWM, 8408, Private Papers of C. A. Niblett.
IWM, 863, Private Papers of R. G. Prew.

Sound Archive (IWM SA), Oral History interviews

IWM SA, 10115, E. Bigwood.
IWM SA, 10168, D. Price.
IWM SA, 10600, J. Wainwright.
IWM SA, 10768, J. Grainger.

IWM SA, 10914, E. Rhodes.
IWM SA, 10917, B. Smedley.
IWM SA, 11040, J. W. Watson.
IWM SA, 11041, W. Burdon.
IWM, SA, 10173, L. Fox.
IWM SA, 10418, A. D. McGuirk.
IWM SA, 11440, W. Hare.
IWM SA, 11461, H. Pettit.
IWM SA, 11582, A. Hurst.
IWM SA, 11943, E. Huggins.
IWM SA, 12231, J. Yarwood.
IWM SA, 12236, A. West.
IWM SA, 12252, J. P. Murray.
IWM SA, 12258, W. Maltby.
IWM SA, 12679, R. Renwick.
IWM SA, 13709, A. Y. Robbins.
IWM SA, 11440, W. Hare.
IWM SA, 15435 F. Ching.
IWM SA, 16058, R. Davidson.
IWM SA, 17311, R. Watson.
IWM SA, 19073, T. A. Dewing.
IWM SA, 1963, Corporal E. W. Glendinning.
IWM SA, 24540, R. Trafford.
IWM SA, 24550, W. Ward.
IWM SA, 24883, H. V. Stone.
IWM SA, 24984, S. Bielby.
IWM SA, 25548, D. Murray.
IWM SA, 26877, C. A. Swales.
IWM SA, 27424, G. L. P. Hollis.
IWM SA, 315, T. Mitchell-Fox.
IWM, SA 32171, J. C. (Jonas) Hart.
IWM SA, 33034, F. T. J. Lancaster.
IWM SA, 33696, A. H. Wright (Alec).
IWM SA, 4222, C. Shepherd.
IWM SA, 4258, S. K. Westmann.
IWM SA, 4440, O. Croft.
IWM SA, 4609, J. B. Masefield.
IWM SA, 495, J. D. Pratt.
IWM SA, 569, U. B. Burke.
IWM SA, 577, W. E. Clarke.
IWM SA, 6838, H. M. Benwell.
IWM, SA, 7363, G. B. Jameson.
IWM SA, 8257, S. J. Moyle.
IWM SA, 8270, P. V. Harris.
IWM SA, 8327, H. Barrow.
IWM SA, 8287, F. Caokes.
IWM SA, 8342, A. Burnett.
IWM SA, 8764, L. J. Stagg.
IWM SA, 8865, C. B. Tubbs.

IWM SA, 8949, G. T. Archer.
IWM SA, 9263, E. Booth.
IWM SA, 9339, W. Holbrook.
IWM SA, 9364, R. E. Bethell.
IWM SA, 9419, T. Bracey.
IWM SA, 9433, A. J. Smith.
IWM SA, 9434, F. Collins.
IWM SA, 9434, W. J. Collins.
IWM SA, 9520, F. E. Sumpter.
IWM, SA, 9546, J. Fox.
IWM SA, 9552, B. Farrer.
IWM SA, 9763, E. Verrall.
IWM SA, 9875, G. Ashurst.
IWM SA, 9894, J. A. Payne.
IWM SA, 9928, R. Pugh.
IWM SA, 9954, J. Snailham.
IWM SA, 9987, H. Bashford.
IWM SA, 9993, A. C. Williams.

Images/films (IWM)

IWM, 457, *From Soldier to Civilian*, British Government Film (1918).
IWM, 486, 'Demobilisation', The Ministry of Information (1918).
IWM, Art. IWM PST 0318, Printed by David Allen and Sons, Parliamentary Recruiting Committee Poster No. 104. W.2846 (1915).
IWM, Art. IWM PST 2712, 'Are You in This?' Recruitment poster by Baden Powell, published by the Parliamentary Recruiting Committee, printed by Johnson, Riddle and Co, Parliamentary Recruiting Committee Poster No. 112 (1915).
IWM, Art. IWM PST 4903, 'To the Young Women of London', Recruitment Poster (1915).
IWM, EPH 1513, Picture Frame, Army Biscuit (1918).
IWM, PST 7803, Printed by Hazell Watson and Viney Ltd, London (1914).
IWM, Q7815, Dead soldiers of one of the Highlanders regiments awaiting burial, August 1917, Photograph taken by Lieutenant J. W. Brooke (1917).

National Records of Scotland

SC70/8/418/2, Will of 4397 Private Purves or Robert Andrew Purves, 9th Bn., Royal Scots (Lothian Regiment), 1916.

The National Archives, Kew (TNA)

W0364 4405, Record for Arthur James Walkden.
WO 142/272, Experiments of new trench weapons.

Wellcome Archives, London

'Specimens of Men in Each of the Four Grades, Report by the Ministry of National Service 1920', Wellcome Library, London (1920), https://wellcomecollection.org/articles/war-and-body/?image=1 (accessed 4 April 2017).

Sheffield City Archives and Local Studies Library

L.D. 1980/54/1, Private Papers of W. Broadhead.
L.D. 980/54/2, Private Papers of W. Broadhead.

University of St Andrews Archive/Special Collections

MS38426/55, Daily Mail Battle Picture Postcard – 1916, Series III, No. 23.
MS38961/2, Private letters of David Sime Stiven.
MSDEP121/8/2/10/1/5, Letter from Rosie to Lady Anstruthers, undated.
MSDEP121/8/2/11/1/4, Letter from Robert Anstruther to his mother, dated 20 September 2014.
MSDEP121/8/3/6/1/4 1917, Letters and collection of Lt Col Philip George Anstruther.

Ministry of Government and Consumer Services Archive

Ministry of Government and Consumer Services Archive, C233-2-0-1-299, Unknown Creator, 'Here's Your Chance – It's Men We Want', Canadian Recruitment Poster (1914–18).

Official papers

Parliamentary papers

Cd. 8485, *The Drafts of a Royal Warrant and of an Order of Council for the Pensions of Soldiers and Sailors Disabled and of the Families and Dependents of Soldiers Deceased in Consequence of the Present War* (1917).
Cd. 8750, *Report of the War Pensions and Statutory Committee for the Year 1916* (1917).
Cd. 9040, *Royal Warrant for the Pensions of Soldiers Disabled and of the Families and Dependents of Soldiers Deceased in Consequence of the Great War* (1918).
Cd. 9165, *A Royal Warrant for the Pensions of Soldiers and Sailors Disabled in Consequence of Former Wars* (1918).

Hansard parliamentary debates

HC Debate, 2 March 1916, vol. 80, cc1182-3.
HC Debate, 2 November 1916, vol. 86, cc1854W.
HC Debate, 3 August 1916, vol. 85, cc522-3W.
HC Debate, 4 February 1915, vol. 69, cc139-40.
HC Debate, 4 February 1915, vol. 69, cc140-1.
HC Debate, 7 January 1915, vol. 18, cc341-6.
HC Debate, 8 August 1916, vol. 85, cc841-2.
HC Debate, 9 May 1916, vol. 82, cc448-9.
HC Debate, 10 September 1914, vol. 66, cc663-76.
HC Debate, 14 November 1916, vol. 87, cc567-8.
HC Debate, 15 April 1919, vol. 114, cc2819-63.
HC Debate, 17 November 1914, vol. 68, cc318-9.
HC Debate, 18 November 1914, vol. 68, c435W.

HC Debate, 19 October 1915, vol. 74, cc1629-30W.
HC Debate, 24 March 1919, vol. 114, cc59-61W.
HC Debate, 26 August 1914, vol. 66, cc38-939.
HC Debate, 31 December 1916, vol. 88, cc1738-63.
HC Debate, 31 December 1916, vol. 88, cc1738-63.
HC Debate, 31 January 1918, vol. 101, cc1773-4W.

Newspapers and contemporary journals

Birmingham Daily Gazette
Black and White
Brain
British Medical Journal
Journal of the Royal Army Medical Corps
Lancet
Manchester Courier and Lancashire General Advertiser
Manchester Guardian
Morning Post
New York Times
The London Gazette
The Nursing Record and Hospital World
The Times
The Wipers Times
Yorkshire Post

Contemporary works

Published memoirs

Beggs, S. T., *Selection of the Recruit* (London: Bailliere, Tindall & Cox, 1915).
Coppard, G., *With a Machine Gun to Cambrai: The Tale of a Young Tommy in Kitchener's Army 1914–1918* (London: Cassell, 1999).
Creighton, O., *Letters of Oswin Creighton, C. F., 1883–1918*, Electronic edition (London: Hard Press, 1923).
Elder, G. R., *Geordie Land to No Man's Land* (Bloomington: AuthorHouse, 2011).
Lycette, E., *Being an Account by Ernest Lycette of His Life as a Young Man and Soldier in the Years between 1911 and 1921, Army of Occupation – Rhineland, Auxiliary Corps – Ireland* (Levin: R. R. Lycette, 2007).
Plater, C. *Catholic Soldiers* (London: Longmans, 1919).
Macready, N., *Annals of an Active Life* (London: Hutchinson,1924).
Ross, P. T., *A Yeoman's Letters*, Kindle edition (London: Kent, 1901).
Stinton, H., and V. Mayo (ed.), *Harry's War: A British Tommy's Experience in the Trenches in World War One* (London: Bloomsbury, 2002).
Titmuss, R., *Problems of Social Policy* (London: HMSO, 1950).
Watkins, O. S., *With French and Flanders Being the Experience of a Chaplain Attached to a Field Ambulance*, Electronic edition (London: Kelly, 1915).
Winnifrith, D. P., *The Church in the Fighting Line with General Smith-Dorrien at the Front: Being the Experiences of a Chaplain*, Electronic edition (London: Kessinger, 1915).

Published reports

Anon, *British Army Field Service Manual, 1914* (London: HMSO, 1914).
Anon, *British Pharmaceutical Codex Pub Pharmaceutical Society* (London: Pharmaceutical society, 1907).
Anon, *Games and Sports in the Army Handbook* (London: HMSO, 1931).
Anon, *Report: India and the Commonwealth War Graves Commission*, Commonwealth War Graves Commission (London: HMSO, 2007).
Anon, *Report of the War Committee of Enquiry into 'Shellshock'* (London: HMSO, 1922).
Great Britain, War Office, *Regulations for Army Medical Services* (London: HMSO, 1890).
Great Britain, War Office, *The King's Regulations and Orders for the Army. 1912; Reprinted with Amendments Published in Army Orders up to 1st August, 1914* (London: HMSO, 1914).
Great Britain, War Office, *Field Service Manual, Infantry Battalion* (London: HMSO, 1914).
Great Britain, War Office, *Games for Use with Physical Training Tables and Training in Bombing* (London: HMSO, 1916).
Great Britain, War Office, *Hints on Assault, Physical and Recreational Training* (France: Army Printing and Stationery Services, 1916).
Great Britain, War Office, *Kings Regulations and Orders for the Army* (London: HMSO, 1910).
Great Britain, War Office, *Kings Regulations and Orders for the Army* (London: HMSO, 1914).
Great Britain, War Office, *Manual of Military Cooking and Dietary, Mobilisation, 1915* (London: HMSO, 1915).
Great Britain, War Office, *Royal Army Medical Corps Training Manual* (London: HMSO, 1911).
Great Britain, War Office, *Statistics of the Military Effort of the British Empire during the Great War, 1914-1920* (London: HMSO, 1922).
HMSO, *The King's Regulations and Orders for the Army 1912: Official Copy: Re-printed with Amendments Published in Army Orders up to 1st August, 1914* (London: HMSO, 1914).
Mitchell Major T. J., and G. M. Smith, *Medical Services: Casualties and Medical Statistics of the Great War* (London: HMSO, 1931).
Rivers, W. H., 'The Repression of War Experience', *Proceedings of the Royal Society of Medicine*, vol. 11 (1918), pp. 1-20.
The War Office, *Statistical Abstract of Information Regarding the British Armies at Home and Abroad 1914-1920* (London: HMSO, 1920).
Woodhead, G. Sims, 'Preventative Inoculation', *Journal of the Royal Sanitary Institute*, vol. 36 (1915), pp. 1.23.

Publications

Ashton, H. A., *One Clear Call: An Explanation and a Reminder* (London: Voluntary Recruiting League, 1914).
Gladstone, H. J., *William G. C. Gladstone: A Memoir* (London: Nisbet, 1918).
Rosenberg, I., *Selected Poems and Letters*, reprint (London: Enitharmon Press, 2003).
Weekley, E., *An Etymological Dictionary of Modern English, Volume 1* (London: John Murray, 1921).

Williams, B., *Raising and Training the New Armies*, reprint (London: Forgotten Books, 2012).

Secondary source material

Publications

Acton, C, 'The Rhetoric of Romance as Social Control in Wartime Magazines for Young Women', in J. Meyer (ed.), *British Popular Culture and the First World War* (London: Brill, 2008), pp. 173-94.
Adams, J. Q., and P. Poirer, *The Conscription Controversy in Great Britain* (London: Palgrave Macmillan, 1987).
Albrinck, M., 'Humanitarians and He-Men: Recruitment Posters and the Masculine Ideal', in Pearl James (ed.), *Picture This, World War 1 Posters and Visual Culture* (London: University of Nebraska Press, 2009), pp. 276-303.
Alenstaedt, R., *The Medical Response to the Trench Diseases in World War One* (Newcastle: Cambridge Scholars, 2011).
Anderson, J., *War, Disability and Rehabilitation in Britain: 'Soul of a Nation'* (Manchester: Manchester University Press, 2011).
Anon, 'SACN Statement on Military Dietary Reference Values for Energy', Scientific Advisory Committee on Nutrition (2016).
Arthur, M., *Forgotten Voices of the Great War* (St Ives: Random House, 2011).
Barber, N., *World War I: The Western Front* (Lewis: White Thompson, 2003).
Barham, P., *Forgotten Lunatics of the Great War* (Bury: St Edmundsbury Press, 2004).
Barnard, S., *To Prove I'm Not Forgot: Living and Dying in a Victorian City* (Manchester: Manchester University Press, 1990).
Barnett, C., *Britain and Her Army, 1509-1970: A Military, Political and Social Survey* (London: Allen Lane, 1970).
Barringer, T., 'An Architecture of Imperial Ambivalence: The Patcham Chattri', in M. J. K. Walsh and A. Varnava (eds), *The Great War and the British Empire Culture and Society* (Oxon: Routledge, 2017), pp. 215-49.
Beckett, I., *A Nation in Arms: A Social Study of the British Army in the First World War* (Manchester: Manchester University Press, 1985).
Beckett, I., *Britain's Part Time Soldiers: The Amateur Military Tradition 1558-1945* (Barnsley: Manchester University Press, 2011).
Beckett, I., T. Bowman and M. Connelly, *The British Army and the First World War* (St Ives: Cambridge University press, 2017).
Belkin, A., *Bring Me Men: Military Masculinity and the Benign Facade of American Empire, 1898-2001* (London: C. Hurst, 2012).
Berridge, V., 'The Art of Medicine Drugs, Alcohol, and the First World War', *TheLancet*, vol. 384 (2014), pp. 1840-1.
Bet-El, I. R., *Conscripts: Lost Legions of the Great War* (Stroud: Sutton, 1999).
Bibbings, L., *Telling Tales about Men: Conceptions of Conscientious Objectors to Military Service during the First World War* (Manchester: Manchester University Press, 2009).
Bourdieu, P., *Distinction: A Social Critique of the Judgment of Taste* (London: Routledge, 2010).
Bourke, J., *Dismembering the Male, Men's Bodies, Britain and the Great War* (London: Reaktion Books, 1996).

Bourke, J., *An Intimate History of Killing: Face to Face Killing in Twentieth-Century Warfare* (London: Granta Books, 1999).
Bourke, J., *Fear: A Cultural History* (London: Virago, 2005).
Bourke, J., 'The British Working Man', in Huge Cecil and Peter Liddle (eds), *Facing Armageddon: The First World War Experience*, Kindle edition (London: Pen and Sword, 2003), pp. 336–52.
Bourke, J., *The Story of Pain: From Prayer to Painkillers* (Oxford: Oxford University Press, 2014).
Bourke, J., 'Wartime', in R. Cooter and J. Pickstone (eds), *Companion to Medicine in the Twentieth Century* (New York: Routledge, 2000), pp. 589–600.
Boyd, K., *Manliness and the Boys' Story Paper in Britain: A Cultural History, 1855–1940* (Basingstoke: Palgrave Macmillan, 2002).
Brophy, J., and E. Partridge, *The Long Trail Songs and Slang of the British Soldier: 1914–18* (London: E. Partridge, 1930).
Brown, C., *'The Scum of the Earth': What Happened to the Real British Heroes of Waterloo?* (Stroud: History Press, 2015).
Brown, M., '"Like a Devoted Army": Medicine, Heroic Masculinity, and the Military', *Journal of British Studies*, vol. 49 (2010), pp. 592–622.
Brundage, A., *Going to the Sources: A Guide to Historical Research and Writing*, 6th edition (London: John Wiley and Sons, 2017).
Brunton, D., *The Politics of Vaccination: Practice and Policy in England, Wales, Ireland, and Scotland 1800–1874* (Suffolk: University of Rochester Press, 2008).
Bryder, L., 'The First World War: Healthy or Hungry?', *History Workshop Journal*, vol. 24 (1987), pp. 141–57.
Bull, S. (ed.), *An Officer's Manual of the Western Front 1914–1918* (London: Conway, 2008).
Burnham, K., *The Courage of Cowards: The Untold Stories of the First World War Conscientious Objectors* (Barnsley: Pen and Sword, 2014).
Campbell, J. D., *The Army Isn't All Work: Physical Culture and the Evolution of the British Army, 1860–1920* (Oxon: Routledge, 2016).
Carden-Coyne, A., *The Politics of Wounds: Military Patients and Medical Power in the First World War* (Oxford: Oxford University Press, 2014).
Cardozo, I., *The Indian Army in World War I, 1914–1918* (New York: Routledge, 2019).
Cherry, B., *They Didn't Want to Die Virgins: Sex and Morale in the British Army on the Western Front 1914–1918* (Wolverhampton: Helion, 2016).
Clark, N., *Unwanted Warriors: The Rejected Warriors of the Canadian Expeditionary Force* (Vancouver: UBC Press, 2016).
Clayton, A., *Battlefield Rations: The Food Given to the British Soldier for Marching and Fighting 1900–2011* (Solihull: Helion, 2013).
Clayton, A., *Paths of Glory: The French Army 1914–18* (London: Cassel, 2005).
Coates-Ulrichsen, K., 'Learning the Hard Way: The Indian Army In Mesopotamia 1914–1918', in Rob Johnson (ed.), *The British Indian Army: Virtue and Necessity* (Newcastle Upon Tyne: Cambridge Scholars, 2014), pp. 51–64.
Cohen, D., *The War Come Home: Disabled Veterans in Britain and Germany 1914–1939* (Berkeley: University of California Press, 2001).
Cooke, G., *Poetry and Writing of the First World War* (London: Lulu.com, 2015).
Cooter, R., 'War and Modern Medicine', in W. F. Bynum and R. Porter (eds), *Companion Encyclopaedia of the History of Medicine* (London: Routledge, 1993), pp. 1536–73.
Cooter, R., *War, Medicine and Modernity* (London: Sutton, 1998).

Cooter, R., M. Harrison and S. Sturdy (eds), *Medicine and Modern Warfare* (Amsterdam: Clio Medica, 1999).
Corns, C., and J. Hughes-Wilson, *Blindfold and Alone: British Military Executions in the Great War* (London: Cassell, 2001).
Corrigan, G., *Mud, Blood and Poppycock* (London: Hachette UK, 2003).
Cree, V., ' "Khaki Fever" during the First World War: A Historical Case Study of Social Work's Approach towards Young Women, Sex and Moral Danger', *British Journal of Social Work*, vol. 46 (2016), pp. 1839–54.
Cruttwell, C. R. M. F., *A History of the Great War: 1914–1918* (Oxford: Clarendon Press, 1936).
Cunningham, H., *The Volunteer Force – A Social and Political History* (London: Croom Helm, 1975).
Curling, A., *Fighting Fit, 1914* (Stroud: Amberley, 2014).
Cuthbertson, G., *Peace at Last: A Portrait of Armistice Day, 11 November 1918* (Cornwall: Yale University Press, 2019).
Davies, D., *The Theology of Death* (London: T&T Clark, 2008).
Dawson, G., *Soldier Heroes, British Adventure, Empire and the Imaging of Masculinities* (New York: Routledge, 2005).
Deslandes, P., *Oxbridge Men: British Masculinity and the Undergraduate Experience, 1850-1920* (Bloomington: Indiana University Press, 2005).
Dooley, T. P., *Irishmen or English Soldier: The Times and World of a South Catholic* (Liverpool: Liverpool University Press, 1995).
Doyle, P., and C. Foster, *Remembering Tommy: The British Soldier in the First World War* (Gloucestershire: Spellmount, 2013).
Duffett, R., *The Stomach for Fighting: Food and Soldiers of the Great War* (Manchester: Manchester University Press, 2012).
Duffett, R., 'A War Unimagined: Food and the Rank and File Soldier of the First World War', in J. Meyer (ed.), *British Popular Culture and the First World War* (London: Brill, 2008), pp. 47–70.
Duncan, R., *Pubs and Patriots: The Drink Crisis in Britain during World War One* (Liverpool: Liverpool University Press, 2013).
Eaton, D., *At the Going Down of the Sun: The Men from Clayton Who Died in the Two World Wars* (Durham: Roundtuit, 2007), pp. 42–3.
Englander, D., 'Mutinies and Military Morale', in H. Strachan (ed.), *The Oxford Illustrated History of the First World War* (Oxford: Oxford University Press, 2014), pp. 192–3.
Evans, B., 'The National Kitchen in Britain in 1917–1919', *Journal of War & Culture Studies*, vol. 10 (2016), pp. 115–29.
Evans, J., and A. Withey, 'Introduction', in J. Evans and A. Withey (eds), *New Perspectives on the History of Facial Hair: Framing the Face* (London: Palgrave Macmillan, 2018).
Fairley, J., and W. Allison, *The Monocled Mutineer: The First World War's Best Kept Secret: The Etaples Mutiny* (London: Quartet Books, 1978).
Farwell, B., *The Great Anglo-Boer War* (New York: W.W. Norton, 1990).
Fell, A., 'Afterword: Remembering the First World War Nurse and Britain and France', in A. Fell and C. Hallett (eds), *First World War Nursing: New Perspectives* (New York: Routledge, 2013), pp. 173–92.
Ferguson, N., *The Pity of War* (London: Penguin Press, 1998).
Figley, C. R., and W. P. Nash, *Combat Stress Injury: Theory, Research, and Management* (New York: Routledge, 2015).
Foucault, M., *Discipline and Punish: The Birth of the Prison* (New York: Vintage, 2012).

French, D. *Military Identities: The Regimental System, the British Army and the British People, c.1870–2000* (Oxford: Oxford University Press, 2005).
Fussell, P., *The Great War and Modern Memory* (Oxford: Oxford University Press, 1975).
Gervais, R., *The Silent Sixtieth 100 Years On* (Victoria: FriesenPress, 2014).
Geurst, J., *Cemeteries of the Great War by Sir Edwin Lutyens* (Rotterdam: 010 Publishers, 2010).
Gill, D., and G. Dallas, *The Unknown Army* (London: Verso, 1985).
Gillon, S. M., and C. D. Matson, *The American Experiment: A History of the United States Volume 1: To 1877* (Boston, MA: Wadsworth, 2013).
Gilmore, D., *Manhood in the Making: Cultural Concepts of Masculinity* (New York: Yale University Press, 1990).
Goffman, E., *Behaviour in Public Places* (New York: Free Press, 1966).
Gordon, I., *Lifeline: A British Casualty Clearing Station on the Western Front, 1918* (Stroud: History Press, 2013).
Grayzel, S. R., *Women and the First World War* (New York: Routledge, 2013).
Grehan, J., and M. Mace, *The Zulu War: The War Despatches Series* (Barnsley: Pen and Sword, 2013).
Grehan, J., and M. Mace, *The Boer War 1899–1902: Ladysmith, Megerforntein, Spion Kop, Kimberley and Mafeking* (Barnsley: Pen and Sword, 2014).
Grieves, K., *The Politics of Manpower 1914–18* (Manchester: Manchester University Press, 1988).
Gullace, N., *The Blood of Our Sons: Men, Women, and the Renegotiation of British Citizenship during the Great War* (New York: Palgrave Macmillan, 2002).
Hall, L., 'War Brings It On', in R. Cooter, M. Harrison and S. Sturdy (eds), *Medicine and Modern Warfare* (Amsterdam: Clio Medica, 1999), p. 212.
Hallett, C. E., *Containing Trauma: Nursing Work in the First World War* (Manchester: Manchester University Press, 2009).
Hallett, C. E., *Nurse Writers of the Great War* (Manchester: Manchester University Press, 2016).
Hallett, C. E., *Veiled Warriors: Allied Nurses of the First World War* (Oxford: Oxford University Press, 2014).
Hampton, J., *Disability and the Welfare State in Britain: Changes in Perception and Policy 1948–79* (Bristol: Polity Press, 2016).
Hardy, A., *Health and Medicine in Britain since 1860* (New York: Macmillan Education UK, 2001).
Hardy, A., '"Straight Back to Barbarism": Antityphoid Inoculation and the Great War, 1914', *Bulletin of the History of Medicine*, vol. 74, no. 2 (2000), pp. 265–90.
Harris, K., '"All for the Boys": The Nurse-Patient Relationship of Australian Army Nurses in the First World War', in A. S. Fell and C. Hallett (eds), *First World War Nursing: New Perspectives* (New York: Routledge, 2013), pp. 71–6.
Harrison, M., *The Medical War: British Military Medicine in the First World War* (Oxford: Oxford University Press, 2012).
Harrison, M., 'Medicine and the Management of Modern Warfare: An Introduction', in R. Cooter, 'Public Health and Medicine In British India: An Assessment of the British Contribution', *Bulletin of the Liverpool Medical History Society*, vol. 10 (1998), pp. 32–48.
Harrison, M., 'The British Army and Venereal Disease during the First World War', *Medical History*, vol. 39 (1995), pp. 133–58.
Hart, P., *Gallipoli*, Kindle edition (London: Profile Books, 2011).

Hart, P., *Voices from the Front: An Oral History of the Great War* (New York: Oxford University Press, 2016).
Harvey, A. D., 'Homosexuality and the British Army during the First World War', *Journal of the Society for Army Historical Research*, vol. 79, no. 320 (Winter 2001), pp. 313-19.
Havardi, J., *Projecting Britain at War: The National Character in British World War II Films* (Jefferson: McFarland, 2014).
Heart, P., *A Very British Victory*, Kindle edition (London: Hachette UK, 2010).
Hockey, J., 'No More Heroes: Masculinity in the Infantry', in Paul R. Higate (ed.), *Military Masculinities: Identity and the State* (Westport: Praeger, 2003), pp. 15-25.
Hodgkinson, P. E., *British Infantry Commanders in the First World War* (Surrey: Ashgate, 2015).
Holmes, R., *Tommy: The British Soldier on the Western Front, 1914-1918*, (London: HarperCollins, 2004).
Holmes, R., *Tommy: The British Soldier on the Western Front, 1914-1918*, Kindle edition (London: HarperCollins, 2004).
Holmes, R., and S. Holmes, *Suicide: Theory, Practice and Investigation* (London: Sage, 2005).
Horne, J. (ed.), *The Diaries and Memoirs of the Rev. Charles Edmund Doudney, M, A., C.F. (1871-1915)* (London: Jonathan Horne, 1995).
Howson, A., *The Body in Society: An Introduction* (Cambridge: Polity, 2011).
Hughes, C. 'The New Armies', in I. Beckett and K. Simpson (eds), *A Nation in Arms* (Barnsley: Pen and Sword, 2004), pp. 99-127.
Iriam, G. R., *In the Trenches 1914-1918* (Bloomington, IN: ebookit.com, 2011).
James, Brigadier E. A., *British Regiments 1914-1918*, Digital edition (East Sussex: Naval and Military Press, 2012).
Jarvis, C. S., *The Male Body at War: America Masculinity during World War II* (New York: Northern Illinois University Press, 2004).
Jeffery, K., 'The Post War Army', in I. Beckett (ed.), *A Nation in Arms* (Barnsley: Pen and Sword, 2004), pp. 211-34.
Jones, E., 'The Psychology of Killing - the Combat Experience of British Soldiers during the First World War', *Journal of Contemporary History*, vol. 4 (2006), pp. 229-46.
Jones, E., and N. Fear, 'Alcohol Use and Misuse within the Military: A Review', *International Review of Psychiatry*, vol. 23 (2011), pp. 166-72.
Keegan, J., *The Face of Battle*, Kindle edition (London: Bodley Head, 2014).
Kellett, A., *Combat Motivation: The Behaviour of Soldiers in Battle* (Boston, MA: Springer, 1982).
Kilday, A., and D. S. Nash, *Shame and Modernity in Britain: 1890 to the Present* (London: Palgrave Macmillan, 2017).
Knapik, J., and K. Reynolds, 'Load Carriage in Military Operations: A Review of Historical Physiological, Biomechanical and Medical Aspects, in K. Friedl, W. R. Santee and the Borden Institute (eds), *Military Quantitative Physiology: Problems and Concepts in Military Operational Medicine* (Fort Detrick: Office of the Surgeon General, 2012), pp. 45-56.
Knight, I., *Companion to the Anglo-Zulu War* (Barnsley: Pen and Sword, 2008).
Kochhar, P. C., *History of the Army Dental Corps and Military Dentistry* (New Delhi: Lancer, 2000).
Kramer, A., *Conscientious Objectors of the First World War: A Determined Resistance* (Barnsley: Pen and Sword, 2013).

Kreis, S., 'Early Experiments in British Scientific Management: The Health of Munitions Workers Committee, 1915-1920', *Journal of Management History*, vol. 1 (1995), pp. 65-78.

Kreis, S., 'The Diffusion of Scientific Management: The Bedaux Company in America and Britain, 1926-1945', in D. Nelson (ed.), *A Mental Revolution: Scientific Management since Taylor* (Columbus: Ohio State University Press, 1992), pp. 156-74.

Kuhlman, E., *Of Little Comfort: War Widows, Fallen Soldiers, and the Remaking of Nation* (New York: New York University Press, 2012).

Lane, J., *A Social History of Medicine: Health, Healing and Disease in England, 1750-1950* (Oxon: Routledge, 2001).

Leder, D., *The Absent Body* (Chicago, IL: Chicago University Press, 1990).

Levine, P., *Prostitution, Race, and Politics: Policing Venereal Disease in the British Empire* (New York: Routledge, 2003).

Lloyd, M., *The London Scottish in the Great War* (London: Pen and Sword, 2000).

Long, R., and I. Talbot (eds), *India and World War I: A Centennial Assessment* (New York: Routledge, 2018).

Long, V., *The Rise and Fall of the Healthy Factory: The Politic of Industrial Health in Britain, 1914-1960* (New York: Palgrave Macmillan, 2011).

Loughran, T., *Shellshock and Medical Culture in First World War Britain* (Cambridge: Cambridge University Press, 2016).

Lynch, T., *Great War Britain Sheffield: Remembering 1914-18*, Kindle edition (Stroud: History Press, 2014).

Macdonald, L., *Roses of No Man's Land* (London: Penguin Books, 1993).

MacKenzie, J. M., *Propaganda and Empire: The Manipulation of British Public Opinion, 1880-1960* (Manchester: Manchester University Press, 1984).

MacKenzie, J. M., 'Introduction', in J. M. McKenzie (ed.), *Popular Imperialism and the Military: 1850-1950* (Manchester: Manchester University Press, 1992), pp. 1-24.

Makepeace, C., 'Male Heterosexuality and Prostitution during the Great War', *Cultural and Social History*, vol. 9, no. 1 (2012), pp. 65-83.

Mallinson, A., *The Making of the British Army: From the English Civil War to the War on Terror* (London: Transworld, 2009).

Mannell, J., 'The Service Football Program of World War I: Its Impact on the Popularity of the Game', *Journal of Sport History*, vol. 16, no. 3 (Winter 1989), pp. 248-60.

Manser, M. H., *The Facts on File Dictionary of Proverbs* (New York: Infobase, 2007).

Mark, W. M., *Everyday Probability and Statistics: Health, Elections, Gambling and War*, 2nd edition (London: Imperial College Press, 2012).

Marwick, A., *The Deluge: British Society and the First World War* (London: Little Brown, 1966).

Marx, K., and F. Engels, *The Communist Manifesto: Penguin Classics Deluxe Edition* (London: Penguin Random House, 2011).

Mason, T., and E. Riedi, *Sport and the Military: The British Armed Forces 1880-1960* (Cambridge: Cambridge University Press, 2010).

Mayhew, E. R., *Wounded: From Battlefield to Blighty, 1914-1918*, Kindle edition (Leicester: Thorpe, 2014).

McCartney, H., *Citizen Soldiers: The Liverpool Territorials in the First World War* (New York: Cambridge University Press, 2005).

McDowell, C. P., J. M. Rothberg, and R. G. Lande, 'Homicide and Suicide in the Military', in F. D. Jones (ed.), *Military Psychiatry: Preparing in Peace for War* (Washington: Office of the Surgeon General at TMM Publications, 2000), pp. 91-113.

McIvor, A. J., *A History of Work in Britain, 1880–1950* (New York: Palgrave, 2001).
McManus, C. *Right Hand, Left Hand* (London: Weidenfeld and Nicolson, 2002).
Messinger, G. S., *British Propaganda and the State in the First World War* (Manchester: Manchester University Press, 1992).
Meyer, J., *British Popular Culture and the First World Wars* (London: Brill, 2008).
Meyer, J., *Men of War: Masculinity and First World War in Britain* (Hampshire: Palgrave Macmillan, 2008).
Meyer, J., *An Equal Burden: The Men of the Royal Army Medical Corps in the First World War* (Oxford: Oxford University Press, 2019).
Miller, P., and N. Rose, 'Governing Economic Life', *Economy and Society*, vol. 19 (1990), pp. 1–31.
Miller, S., 'In Support of the Imperial Mission – Volunteering for the South African War, 1899–1902', *Journal of Military History*, vol. 69, no. 3 (2005), pp. 691–711.
Mills, J. H., and S. Sen, 'Introduction', in J. Mills and S. Sen (eds), *Confronting the Body: The Politics of Physicality in Colonial and Post-Colonial India* (London: Wimbledon, 2004), pp. 1–15.
Mitchinson, K. W., *Gentlemen and Officers: The Impact and Experience of War on a Territorial Regiment 1914–1918* (London: Naval and Military Press, 2012).
Morillo, S., *What Is Military History?* (Cambridge: Polity, 2006).
Morton-Jack, G., *The Indian Army on the Western Front*, South Asia edition (Cambridge: Cambridge University Press, 2014).
Myerly, S. H., *British Military Spectacle: From the Napoleonic Wars through the Crimea* (Cambridge: Harvard University Press, 1996).
Newlands, E., *Civilians into Soldiers: War, the Body and British Army Recruits, 1939–45* (Manchester: Manchester University Press, 2014).
Noakes, L., '"War on the Web": The BBC "People's War" Website and Memories of Fear in Wartime in 21st Century Britain', in L. Noakes and J. Pattinson (eds), *British Cultural Memory and the Second World War* (London: Bloomsbury Academic, 2013), pp. 47–66.
Norton, R. (ed.), *My Dear Boy: Gay Love Letters through the Centuries* (San Francisco, CA: Leyland, 1998).
Novak, Josh R., et al., 'Associations between Masculine Norms and Health-Care Utilization in Highly Religious, Heterosexual Men', *American Journal of Men's Health*, vol. 13, no. 3 (2019), pp. 1–11.
Oldstone-Moore, C., *Of Beards and Men: The Revealing History of Facial Hair* (Chicago, IL: University of Chicago Press, 2015).
Oldstone-Moore, C., 'The Beard Movement in Victorian Britain', *Victorian Studies*, vol. 48, no. 1 (2005), pp. 7–34.
Oliver, M., and R. Partridge, *Napoleonic Army Handbook: The French Army and Her Allies* (London: Constable, 2002).
Padiak, J., 'Death by Suicide in the British Army, 1830–1900', in J. C. Weaver and D. Wright (eds), *Histories of Suicide, International Perspectives on Self- Destruction in the Modern World* (Toronto: University of Toronto, 2009), pp. 119–34.
Pakenham, T., *The Boer War* (London: Abacus, 1979).
Paris, M., *Warrior Nation: Images of War in British Popular Culture 1850–2000* (London: Reaktion Books, 2000).
Peck, J., *The Army Abroad: Fictions of India and the Indian Mutiny* (London: Palgrave Macmillan UK, 1998).
Penn, A., *Targeting Schools: Drill, Militarism and Imperialism* (London: Routledge, 1999).
Phillips, R., *Alcohol: A History* (Chapel Hill: University of North Carolina Press, 2014).

Pickstone, J., *Medicine and Industrial Society: A History of Hospital Development in Manchester and Its Region, 1752-1946* (Manchester: Manchester University Press, 1985).
Porter, R., *Disease, Medicine and Society in England, 1550-1860* (Cambridge: Cambridge University Press, 1993).
Porter, R., *The Greatest Benefit to Mankind: A Medical History of Humanity from Antiquity to the Present* (London: W.W. Norton, 1999).
Putkowski, J., and J. Sykes, *Shot at Dawn: Executions in World War One by Authority of the British Army Act*, Kindle edition (Barnsley: Pen and Sword, 2007).
Putkowski, J., and J. Sykes, *Shot at Dawn: Executions in World War One by Authority of the British Army Act* (Barnsley: Pen and Sword, 2007).
Rabinbach, A., *Human Motor: Energy, Fatigue and the Origins of Modernity* (Berkeley: University of California Press, 1990).
Reid, F., *Broken Men: Shellshock, Treatment and Recovery in Britain 1914-30* (London: Bloomsbury, 2012).
Reid, F., 'Losing Face: Trauma and Maxillofacial Injury in the First World War', in J. Crouthamel and P. Leese (eds), *Psychological Trauma and the Legacies of the First World War* (Switzerland: Palgrave Macmillan, 2017), pp. 25-47.
Reid, F., *Medicine in First World War Europe: Soldiers, Medics, Pacifists* (London: Bloomsbury, 2017).
Reitz, D., *God Does Not Forget: The Story of a Boer War Commando* (London: Fireship Press, 2010).
Reznick, J., 'History at the Intersection of Disability and Public Health: The Case of John Glasworthy and Disabled soldiers of the First World War', *Disability and Health Journal*, vol. 4 (2011), pp. 24-7.
Robb, G., *British Culture and the First World War* (London: Palgrave, 2015).
Robert, K. '"All that is Best of the Modern Woman"?: Representations of Female Military Auxiliaries in British Popular Culture 1914-1919', in J. Meyer (ed.), *British Popular Culture and the First World Wars* (London: Brill, 2008), pp. 97-122.
Roberts, R., *The Classic Slum* (Manchester: Penguin, 1971).
Robertshaw, A., *Feeding Tommy: Battlefield Recipes from the First World War* (London: History Press, 2013).
Roper, M., *The Secret Battle: Emotional Survival in the Great War* (Manchester: Manchester University Press, 2009).
Roy, K., *Indian Army and the First World War: 1914-18* (Oxford: Oxford University Press, 2018).
Royal, T., *Crimea: The Great Crimean War* (New York: St Martin's Press, 2014).
Russell, D., '"We Carved Our Way to Glory". The British Soldier in Music Hall Song and Sketch, c.1880-1914', in J. M. Mackenzie (ed.), *Popular Imperialism and the Military: 1850-1950* (Manchester: Manchester University Press, 1992), pp. 50-79.
Sanders, A. G. V., and P. M. Taylor, *British Propaganda during the First World War, 1914-1918* (London: Macmillan, 1982).
Sapolsky, R. M., *Why Zebra's Don't Get Ulcers: The Updated Guide to Stress, Stress Related Disease and Coping* (New York: W. H. Freeman, 1998).
Sauerteig, L. D. H., 'Sex, Medicine and Morality', in R. Cooter, M. Harrison and S. Sturdy (eds), *War, Medicine and Modernity* (Thrupp: Sutton, 1998), pp. 167-88.
Saxena, S. N., *Role of Indian Army in the First World War* (Delhi: Bhrava Prakashan, 1987).
Searle, G. R., *The Quest for National Efficiency* (London: University of California Press, 1971).

Seipp, A. R., *The Ordeal of Peace: Demobilisation and the Urban Experience in Britain and Germany, 1917–1921* (Farnham: Ashgate, 2010).

Shee, G. F., '"The Deterioration in the National Physique": The Nineteenth Century and After', *A Monthly Review*, vol. 49 (May 1903), pp. 734–8.

Sheffield, G., *The Somme: A New History* (London: Cassell Military, 2003).

Sheffield, G., 'Officer Man Relations, Discipline and Morale in the Great War', in Huge Cecil and Peter Liddle (eds), *Facing Armageddon: The First World War Experience*, Kindle edition (London: Pen and Sword, 2003), pp. 135–64.

Shephard, B., *A War of Nerves: Soldiers and Psychiatrists 1914–1994* (London: Pimlico, 2002).

Shilling, C. *The Body and Social Theory* (London: Sage, 1993).

Silbey, D., *The British Working Class and Enthusiasm for War, 1914–1916* (New York: Taylor & Francis, 2004).

Silbey, D., 'Bodies and Cultures Collide: Enlistment, the Medical Exam and the British Working Class 1914–1916', *Social History of Medicine*, vol. 17, no. 1 (2004), pp. 61–76.

Simkins, P., *From the Somme to Victory: The British Army's Experience on the Western Front 1916–1918* (London: Pen and Sword, 2014).

Simkins, P., '"Each One a Pocket Hercules": The Bantam Experiment and the Case of the Thirty-Fifth Division', in S. Marble (ed.), *Scraping the Barrel: The Military Use of Sub-Standard Manpower: The Military 1860–1960* (New York: Fordham University Press, 2012), pp. 70–104.

Simkins, P., *Kitchener's Army: The Raising of the New Armies 1914–1916* (Manchester: Manchester University Press, 2007).

Simkins, P., 'Soldiers and Civilians: Billeting in Britain and France', in I. Beckett and K. Simpson (eds), *A Nation in Arms: A Social Study of the British Army in the First World War* (Barnsley: Pen and Sword, 1985), pp. 178–86.

Simkins, P., 'The Four Armies 1914–1918', in D. Chandler and I. Beckett (eds), *The Oxford History of the British Army* (Oxford: Oxford University Press, 1994), pp. 241–62.

Simmonds, A. G. V., *Britain and World War One* (New York: Routledge, 2012).

Simpson, D. A., and D. J. David, 'World War I: The Genesis of Craniomaxillofacial Surgery', *ANZ Journal of Surgery*, vol. 74 (2004), pp. 71–7.

Sinha, M., *Colonial Masculinity: The 'Manly Englishman' and the 'Effeminate Bengali' in the Late Nineteenth Century* (Manchester: Manchester University Press, 1995).

Skelley, A., *The Victorian Army at Home: The Recruitment and Terms and Conditions of the British Regular 1859–1899* (London: Croom Helm, 1977).

Small, H., *The Crimean War: Queen Victoria's War with the Russian Tsars* (Stroud: Tempus, 2007).

Spiers, E., *The Late Victorian Army* (Manchester: Manchester University Press, 1992).

Strachan, H., *The First World War: A New History* (London: Simon and Schuster, 2001).

Strachan, H., *The Oxford Illustrated History of the First World War* (Oxford: Oxford University Press, 1998).

Strange, J., *Death, Grief and Poverty in Britain 1870–1914* (New York: Cambridge University Press, 2005).

Summers, A., 'Essay: Militarism in Britain before the Great War', *History Workshop*, vol. 2 (1976), pp. 104–23.

Sutphen, M., 'Striving to Be Separate', in R. Cooter et al. (eds), *War, Medicine and Modernity* (Thrupp: Sutton, 1998), pp. 48–64.

Taylor, F., *The Scientific Management: The Early Sociology of Management and Organizations*, reprint (New York: Routledge, 2006).

Thompson, N., and G. Cox, *Handbook of the Sociology of Death, Grief and Bereavement: A Guide to Theory and Practice* (New York: Routledge, 2017).
Titmuss, R., *Essays on the Welfare State* (Boston, MA: Beacon Press, 1969).
Todman, D., *The Great War: Myth and Memory* (London: Bloomsbury, 2011).
Tosh, J., *A Man's Place: Masculinity and the Middle-Class Home in Victorian England* (London: Yale University Press, 2007).
Tynan, J., *British Army Uniform and the First World War: Men in Khaki* (London: Palgrave Macmillan, 2013).
Tynan, J., 'Tailoring in the Trenches: The Making of the First World War British Army Uniform', in J. Meyer (ed.), *British Popular Culture and the First World War* (London: Brill, 2008).
Van Bergen, L., *Before My Helpless Sight: Suffering, Dying and Military Medicine on the Western Front, 1914–1918* (Surrey: Ashgate, 2009).
van Emden, R., and S. Humphries, *All Quiet on the Home Front* (Barnsley: Pen and Sword, 2002).
van Emden, R., and S. Humphries, *Boy Soldiers of the Great War*, Kindle edition (London: Headline, 2005).
van Emden, R., and S. Humphries, *The Quick and the Dead* (London: Bloomsbury, 2012).
van Emden, R., and S. Humphries, *The Somme: The Epic Battle in the Soldiers' Own Words and Photographs* (London: Pen and Sword, 2016).
van Emden, R., and S. Humphries, *Tommy's Ark: Soldiers and Their Animals in the Great War* (London: Bloomsbury, 2010).
Vernon, J., *Hunger: A Modern History* (Cambridge, MA: Harvard University Press, 2007).
Walker, S. H., 'Saving Bodies and Souls: Army Chaplains and Medical Care in the First World War', *Postgraduate Journal of Medical Humanities*, vol. 3 (2016), pp. 24–38.
Walker, S. H., 'The Greater Good: Agency and Inoculation in the British Army, 1914–1918', *Canadian Bulletin of Medical History*, vol. 36 (2019), pp. 131–57.
Walker, S. H., '"Silent Voices": British Soldier Suicides in the First World War', in H. Da Silva, P. Teodoro De Matos and J. M. Sardica (eds), *War Hecatomb: International Effects on Public Health, Demography and Mentalities in the 20th Century* (Lisbon: Peter Lang, 2019), pp. 25–55.
Ward, J., *Not Gay: Sex between Straight White Men* (New York: New York University Press, 2015).
Warwick, A., 'Exercising the Student Body, Mathematics and Athleticism in Victorian Cambridge', in C. Lawrence and S. Shapin (eds), *Science Incarnate, Historical Embodiments of Natural Knowledge* (London: University of Chicago Press, 1998), pp. 288–326.
Watson, A., *Enduring the Great War: Combat, Morale and Collapse in the German and British Trench* (Cambridge: Cambridge University Press, 2008).
Weaver, P., and L. Van Bergen, 'Death from 1918 Pandemic Influenza during the First World War: A Perspective from Personal and Anecdotal Evidence', *Influenza Other Respiratory Viruses*, vol. 5 (2014), pp. 538–46.
Weber, M., 'The Nation', in J. Hutchinson and A. D. Smith (eds), *Nationalism* (Oxford: Oxford University Press, 1994), pp. 25–6.
Weeks, A., *Tea, Rum and Fags, Sustaining Tommy 1914–1918* (Stroud: History Press, 2009).
Weeks, J., *Sex, Politics and Society* (London: Wikinson-Lanthan, 1981).
Weeks, J., and K. Porter, *Between the Acts: Lives of Homosexual Men 1885–1967* (London: Rivers Oram, 1998).

Whitehead, I., *Doctors in the Great War* (Barnsley: Pen and Sword, 1999).
Williams, G., *Angel of Death: The Story of Smallpox* (New York: Palgrave Macmillan, 2010).
Wilson, R., 'The Burial of the Dead: the British Army on the Western Front, 1914–18', *War & Society*, vol. 31, no. 1 (2012), pp. 22–41.
Winter, D., *Death's Men: Soldiers of the Great War* (London: Penguin, 1985).
Winter, J., 'Army and Society: The Demographic Context', in I. Beckett and K. Simpson (eds), *A Nation in Arms: A Social Study of the British Army in the First World War* (Manchester: Manchester University Press, 1985), pp. 193–209.
Winter, J., 'Military Fitness and Civilian Health in Britain during the First World War', *Journal of Contemporary History*, vol. 15 (1980), pp. 211–44.
Winter, J., *The Great War and the British People* (New York: Palgrave Macmillan, 2002).
Wittman, L., *The Tomb of the Unknown Soldier, Modern Mourning and the Reinvention of the Mystical Body* (Toronto: University of Toronto Press, 2011).
Woodward, R., 'Locating Military Masculinities: Space, Place and the Formation of Gender Identity in the British Army', in P. Higate (ed.), *Military Masculinities: Identity and the State* (London: Praeger, 2003), pp. 43–56.
Woollacott, A., ' "Khaki Fever" and Its Control: Gender, Class, Age and Sexual Morality on the British Home Front in the First World War', *Journal of Contemporary History*, vol. 29 (1994), pp. 325–47.
Yeomans, H., *Alcohol and Moral Regulation: Public Attitudes, Spirited Measures, and Victorian Hangovers* (Bristol: Policy Press, 2014).
Zdatny, S., 'The French Hygiene Offensive of the 1950s: A Critical Moment in the History of Manners', *Journal of Modern History*, vol. 84, no. 4 (December 2012), pp. 897–932.
Zweiniger-Bargielowska, I., *Managing the Body, Beauty, Health, and Fitness in Britain, 1800–1939* (Oxford: Oxford University Press, 2010).

Internet sources

Anon, 'Who Is George Mills', 1919: Statement as to Disability, 17 February 1919, http://www.whoisgeorgemills.com/2011/03/1919-statement-as-to-disability.html (accessed March 2017).
Bell, B., 'The Real-Life Wars Of Dad's Army Actor Arnold Ridley', *BBC News*, 5 (2016), Http://Www.Bbc.Co.Uk/News/Uk-England-35491036 (accessed 13 December 2016).
Boff, J., 'Training to Be Soldier', The British Library, https://www.bl.uk/world-war-one/articles/training-to-be-a-soldier (accessed 5 August 2017).
Cornish, P., 'The Daily Life of Soldiers', World War One – The British Library, https://www.bl.uk/world-war-one/articles/the-daily-life-of-soldiers#authorBlock1 (accessed 31 August 2017).
Cullen, A., '10 Golden Rules of Fitness for First World War Soldiers', *History Extra* (2014), http://www.historyextra.com/feature/first-world-war/10-golden-rules-fitness-first-world-war-soldiers (accessed 31 July 2017).
Hampson MC, T., and T. P. Davies. (eds), 'A Medical Officer's Diary and Narrative of the First World War', http://www.ciaofamiglia.com/jcsproule/WWI_PDFS/Travis-Hampson-Diary/A-Medical-Officers-Diary-Travis-Hampson.pdf (accessed 1 September 2017).
Ibbetson, E., and J. McNeill, 'Vacancies Exist in All Branches of His Majesty's Army', Recruiting poster for British Army Ernest Ibbetson and John McNeill (Aldershot: Gale

& Polden, 1914–18), http://www.ww1propaganda.com/ww1-poster/his-majestys-army-vacancies-exist (accessed 3 April 2017).

Simkins, P., 'Voluntary Recruiting in Britain, 1914–1915', The British Library, (29 January 2014), https://www.bl.uk/world-war-one/articles/voluntary-recruiting (accessed 1 July-2017).

Spiers, E., 'Learning from Haldane', The Royal United Services Institute (2010), article posted on the RUSI website, 19 August 2010, https://rusi.org/commentary/learning-haldane (accessed 14 August 2017).

Withey, A., 'More Popular than Ever? Beards and Masculinity in History', https://dralun.wordpress.com/2014/09/22/more-popular-than-ever-beards-and-masculinity-in-history (accessed 31 August 2017).

Index

accidents 88-9, 112, 161-2
   tractor 110
adrenaline 109, 119, 121, 137
agency 14-15, 49, 54, 88, 90, 135, 153-4, 158, 177-8, 181-2
   exercise 57, 138
   individual 20-1, 49, 79, 165
   internal 118
   women's 28
alcohol 18, 21, 93, 95-8, 127-8, 137, 177, 179, 182
ambulance trains 153, 155
APC (Army Pay Corps) 48
armistice 22, 139, 141, 159-60, 162, 166, 170-1, 182
Army Biscuit 55, 91, 93, 111-12. See *hard tack*
Army Medical Services 53
Army Pay Corps (APC) 48
Army Service Corps. *See* ASC
ASC (Army Service Corps) 77, 90, 110-11
attire 29, 52, 159, 169

Bantam battalions 37
barracks 46-8, 52, 57, 60, 70, 81, 90, 97, 99-100, 104, 183
beards 83-4
beef, bully 93, 112
beer 93, 96, 159. Also *see* alcohol
BEF (British Expeditionary Force) 9, 24, 85, 140, 162, 174
billeting 47, 77, 80, 102, 139, 158, 176
bodies
   dead 114, 140, 146, 170
   wounded 109, 130, 132, 181
Boer War 5-7
bombing accident 89
bombs 75, 112, 136, 182
   improvised 112
Bourke, Joanna 8, 13, 18, 21, 33, 135, 174, 178

boxing 28, 63, 69
British Army Field Service Manual 93-4
British Propaganda 169
bullying 60, 87
burial 140-7

calories 7, 32, 53, 74
Canadian Expeditionary Force 78
canteen 77, 91, 159
casualties 88, 150, 162, 178
cemeteries 141
chaplains 91, 103, 120, 144-6, 179-81
Churchill, Winston 161-2
clothes and clothing 21, 29-30, 35, 50, 53, 57, 81, 83, 113, 140, 163, 169, 175, 177
clothing allowance 169
conscientious objectors 29-30, 44
control
   army 22, 87, 158, 177
   authoritarian 22, 84, 109, 183
   institutional 5, 119, 173
   social 28
corporal punishment 70, 109
corpses 35, 62, 78, 89, 140, 143-8, 181
cowardice 30, 72, 87, 121, 127, 134
Crimean War 5
crimes 56, 70, 72, 91, 97-8, 100, 127, 134, 176
culture 10, 15, 38, 96, 99, 103

death penalty 97, 125, 134, 176
death toll 152
defiance 55-6, 73, 176, 180
demobilization process 161, 169-70
diet 7, 11, 21, 32, 52-3, 57, 91, 109, 111, 175, 177
disability 13, 156, 164-5, 170
disability pension 164-6
discipline 14, 21, 70, 74, 107, 114, 154, 159

discomfort 19, 48, 57–8, 69–70, 114, 132, 134
disease 18, 21–2, 78–9, 85–9, 102, 105–7, 114–15, 162, 164, 178
  venereal 102, 105, 138, 179
disease prevention 13–14, 85, 178
disobedience 56, 70, 134
doctors 33, 40–2, 87–8, 105–6, 112, 130, 132, 134, 146–7, 149, 154, 156, 165
dressing station 130, 133–4
drill 21, 45, 58, 61, 70–4, 79, 118, 137, 175
drunk 47, 60, 72, 95–8, 107, 159, 177
Duffett, Rachel 11, 56, 110–11
dysentery 80, 112, 115, 178

emotions 16, 109, 118–19, 121, 125–6
employment 37, 72, 168
Englander, David 70
enlistment 2, 5–7, 10, 17, 20, 23, 26–8, 30, 32, 35–8, 40–4, 84–5, 156–7, 173–5
enthusiasm 24, 37, 120, 127
Étaples 71
execution 72, 98, 109, 124, 126, 133
exhaustion 58–9, 63, 115, 122, 124, 127, 137–8, 178
experiments 169, 175

fatigue 16, 70, 74, 77, 87, 115, 152, 178
fear 29, 32, 99–100, 116, 118–19, 121, 123, 125, 127, 137–8, 178–9
Field Ambulance 80, 95
field hospital 154
field kitchens 90, 110
field punishment 71–3, 98, 103, 127
fitness 6, 38–9, 63, 70, 74, 104, 173, 175
football 62–3, 104, 119, 175
Foucault, Michel 14–15, 19, 28, 176
French Army 82, 110
Friends Ambulance Unit 162
Fussell, Paul 99

Gallipoli 112, 127, 165
Galsworthy, John 167
games 1, 6, 57, 61–3, 99–100, 104, 175–6
gas 129, 132, 138, 149, 177
Gay 100. *See* homosexuality
Gladstone, Lieutenant William 143
Godfrey, Lieutenant 1–3, 145, 182–3, 185, 209, 215
Green, Harry 170

grenades 112, 121, 175, 177
grief 143, 170
grooming 49, 82, 84, 113, 182
gun, machine 62, 89, 136
gun wheel 71, 98, 103, 127, 176

hair 2, 49, 51, 84–5
  facial 84–5
Haldane reforms 173
hard tack 11, 42, 90, 111–12
Harrison, Mark 12, 21, 81–5, 180
height 33, 35–7, 42, 44, 114, 149, 163, 174
heroes 5, 27, 165, 174
heterosexuality 98–100, 101, 179
Hindu soldiers 142
Home Front 33, 37
homosexuality 99–101, 179
hospital 79, 81, 85, 89, 92, 97, 105–6, 132–3, 150–5, 157, 167–8, 180, 183
humiliation 35–6, 60, 72, 100, 118, 135
hunger 32, 74, 112, 154
hygiene 12, 47, 78, 82, 84–5, 107, 109, 114, 124, 140, 162

identification 35, 141, 145–6, 149
illness 105, 107, 162
improvements 21, 24, 41, 57, 69, 139
  nutritional 7
  physical 7, 45, 57–8
  sanitary 85
  societal 15
India 63, 120, 142–3
Indian burial culture 142
Indian soldiers 142–3
indoctrination xi, 3, 21–2, 55, 57, 69, 88, 104, 119, 175–6
  physical 57
  psychological 116
influenza 85, 159
injuries 69, 109, 116, 119, 121, 128, 130–4, 138, 143, 152, 156, 163–4, 170
inoculation 12, 20–1, 85–8, 106, 178
inspections 35, 57, 70
intelligence testing 35
Ireland 70
iron rations 111

jam 92, 111–13
Jarvis, Christina 191

Jones, George 166

Keegan, John 5
Keogh, Alfred 53
khaki 27, 29–30, 50–2, 139, 153, 165
Khaki Fever 8, 28
Kitchener 9, 75

Last South African War 24, 33, 42, 111, 169, 173
latrines 47, 97
Levine, Philippa 104
limbs 123, 139, 164, 166–7, 170
   artificial 166–7
   lost 33, 128, 166
living conditions 18, 47, 49, 81, 109, 114, 178
Lord Haldane 24
Lord Kitchener 9, 120

MacDonald, Helen 178
Machine Gun Corps 144
MacKenzie, John 5
malaria 114–15, 178
manhood 7, 24, 190
Marwick, Arthur 37
masculine heroes 60
masculinity 8–10, 20–4, 119, 122, 130–3
Mayhew, Emily 19, 178
McCartney, Helen 127
meat 53–4, 90, 112
medical assessment 29, 40–1, 163, 168
medical care 12–14, 81, 148, 150–1, 153–4, 157, 163
Meyer, Jessica 13, 29, 147, 180
Mobilisation 80
Monocled Mutineer, The 71
morale 22, 54, 91, 98, 102, 119, 132, 140
morality 102–3
Mutinies 56, 177

Napy twopence 49
nerves 123, 125, 127, 205, 230
neurosis 126
Neve Chappelle 144
Nicoletta Gullace 8
nurses 106, 135, 152–4
nutrition 5, 7, 53, 91–2

obedience 35, 69, 80

Officer Training Corps (OTC) 87
OTC (Officer Training Corps) 87
Owen, Wilfred 99

parcels 90, 92
patriotism 8–9, 28–30, 32, 37, 39
pensions 164, 165
physical pleasure 101, 104
physical punishments 70–2, 97, 99, 103–4, 127, 176
Post-Traumatic Stress Disorder (PTSD) 17, 25–6
prison 49
privacy 24, 46, 101
propaganda 10, 20, 23, 27, 43, 48, 104
Prostitution 101, 104
public perception 30, 114, 133, 139, 147, 169
punishment drill 70, 81, 97, 176

RAMC (Royal Army Medical Corps) 12–13, 17, 86, 89, 111, 147, 149, 151
rape 101, 104
rations 53, 55, 91, 93, 96, 110–12, 144
rats 96, 114, 178
recreation 63, 69, 78
recruiting sergeants 28, 32, 48, 51, 93
recruitment campaigns 23, 28, 74
recruitment process 23, 41
recruitment propaganda 20, 169
recuperation 78, 82, 155
Red Cross 140, 166
regulars 3, 8–9, 20, 50, 85
Rehabilitation 2, 165
rejection rates 36
relaxation 9, 156, 175
remembrance 142
reserve 78–9, 166
respite 10, 78, 96, 109–10, 134, 138
restrictions 2, 56, 154, 176
Robertshaw, Andrew 11, 42, 52
Royal Flying Corps 158
Royal Patriotic Fund (RPF) 163
rum 93, 95, 97, 128, 144, 148

sacrifice 97, 141, 148, 165, 167
sanitation 12, 83, 170
sappers 45, 145
Sassoon, Siegfried 99, 101
Scarborough 120, 204

schools 7, 159
sea pussy 101
self-care 81–2
self-control 79
self-damage 133
self-diagnosis 82, 107
self-discipline 85, 104, 107
self-extinction 135, 178
self-harm 89, 133
sex 18, 21, 28, 100–4, 177, 179
sexual gratification 101, 179
sexuality 99–101
shaving 49, 83–4, 88, 133, 177
Sheffield, Gary 11
shellshock 123, 125–7, 138, 179
sickness 21, 80, 87, 112, 114, 133, 153, 162
Silbey, David 7
Simkins, Peter 52, 178
smallpox 85
Somme 78, 84, 93, 95, 97, 114, 155–7
Spanish flu 162
sport 1, 6, 54, 61–3, 69, 119
stress 120, 125, 180
stretcher-bearers 144, 146–51, 180
suicide 55, 89, 106, 108, 135–8, 178
Summers, Anne 5

tanks 124, 162
tea 28, 54–5, 83, 126, 154
teeth 42–3, 111
territorials 8–9, 20
training 43, 46–8, 55, 59, 79, 84, 162
trench foot 81–2, 114, 178
trench newspaper 96
tuberculous 164
Tynan, Jane 48, 50

typhoid 12, 85, 88, 155, 178

uniformity 9, 47–8, 50, 148, 179
uniforms 22, 29, 50–2, 82–8, 113, 163, 170–1, 181–2
  blue 74

vaccine 86–7, 178
Vimy Ridge 112
vocabulary 62
volunteering 24

war graves commission 17, 181
Warwick, Andrew 6
Waterloo 185
wealth 16, 22, 124
weaponized vehicles 177
weapons 46, 50, 61, 88, 129, 149, 153, 175
whipping 70
whiskey 122
Whitehead, Ian 180, 214, 232
Winter, Dennis 177, 181
Winter, Jay 32, 41, 145
Wipers Times 96
wounds 19, 21, 109, 129, 131–3, 148, 156–7, 163–4, 178, 180–1

Young Men's Christian Association (YMCA) 91
Ypres 77, 93, 97, 119, 121, 125, 144–5, 152–3, 156

Zulu War 190
Zweiniger-Bargielowska, Ina 32, 38

www.ingramcontent.com/pod-product-compliance
Lightning Source LLC
Chambersburg PA
CBHW072143290426
44111CB00012B/1959